Rise of The West

By

Frank L. DeSilva

RISE OF THE WEST

A Study of Race-Culture and History

Copyright © 2003, 2011 Frank L. DeSilva

ISBN-10: 1461001501

ISBN-13: 978-1461001508

All rights reserved

Dedicated to all those who have lived and died,

Who Defend,

And

Protect the Soul of the West

CONTENTS

	Acknowledgments	i
1	Introduction	ii
2	Chapter I	2
3	Chapter II	28
4	Chapter III	76
5	Chapter IV	146
6	Chapter V	225
7	Afterword	251
8	Addendum	255
9	Appendices	265
10	Index	335

ACKNOWLEDGMENTS

It is not easily admitted as to how many persons actually inspired this work to come to fruition.

This Work was envisioned while on a long journey, and the numerous individuals who came into my life was myriad.

This work was developed over long years. It came to me in a dark and dangerous world and, was, perhaps, a Light unto myself, making the dark paths less pressing.

And to that ever-present Muse, whispering softly – thanks for being there.

INTRODUCTION

Cause and effect. Origin and Purpose. Destiny.

These are the actualizations of the consciousness. This is the *spirit* of Innerman. This is the essence of all that is, of all that has been, and all that is to be (the *becoming*, in the Nietzschean sense). In this light may one see, as if looking down a long, dark tunnel, the past, illuminated by this realization; even as we see the future, glimmering ahead, beckoning for all to follow or lead: a path that, one way or another, all must tread. This is Life, the animation of which we possess, a gift by which we can better ourselves, our families, our Race-Culture. Thus, as the light of day shines upon us, the Rise of the West begins its ascent upon the modern age; a recurring motif. *To be more specific, we see that presence, that essence of spirit, which we call Culture in our Western Civilization begin its ascent as in ages past*

The Rise of the West is a *metaphor*. It is a study, albeit in large part metaphysical, concerning the metamorphosis of Western culture. We shall cover few known and unknown dates, genealogies, Kings or Empires. This seems best left for the 'historian' proper. No, this study is the transvaluation of history - it is the science of, and hence, the study of the 'science of history' as it relates to the continuing evolution of everything Western: its organic conception, its purpose (stated or unstated), its values (religions, mores, etc.,), its past and its present; but more importantly, its future prospects based on what has gone before. This requires much study, contemplation, and spiritual guidance.

The historian ponders through enormous amounts of 'facts', facts which may or may not be such. He reads voluminous studies, statistics, personal histories, and their accounts of happenings related to known time and space. He composes treatise upon treatise, calculations immeasurable, and hypothesizes constantly about events and happenings that he regards as vital to his premise. In this regard, this author is no better or worse than they, those who have gone before. In all due respect however, this science of history is commensurate to traditional or lineal history, perhaps, even more compelling. It is important for one to understand this perception: *It is the animation of organic thought.*

The origin of all history starts with the first thought. This thought was nothing but the *spirit* of that present presence, that moment, long ago, which grew from incidental happenstance, to the total out-growth of its particular environment, its animate being, its *soul*-culture. From the daily routines of Cro-Magnon man and their complexities, to the complex Industrial age of our 'present presence', we remain, constant, fixed to a landscape, a territory; *a definable place we call our own*. A place where all our future happenings will occur, occupying a place also, in history. Unspoken, this origin draws attention to us only in the dim recesses of the primitive race-soul, disclosing yet another constant: that being, *the long extended chronology of 'souls' behind us*. Those, which gave us Life. Man, Western man, must understand this link with himself if he is to comprehend his actual presence in a world of externals [material substance] and thoughts [spirit].

This is the whole history of Western man. That of his great will-to-express his environment, his feelings, his dreams, and his inner being: *that of himself*. This has been his consuming fire. Every mark he has left, monuments, languages, writing, all have been an expression of higher-culture never fully attained; seemingly just beyond his reach. He has molded his environment like no other culture. Through his machines, he has conquered, at last, his natural elements, thereby making slaves out of ancient masters.* Nevertheless, his battles are legion, and it is his lot in life to struggle daily. His toil brings him rest.

He dreams.

His thoughts soar ever upward to the stars; he touches them. His spirit, seemingly just behind, or in front of him. He grasps it, sideways, but never from its *source*. He understands the heartbeat of his ancient spirit but, seemingly, can never master it. Himself, he cannot master. Therefore, he seeks a method, a formula, and a projection of himself: He creates. As in a Wagnerian music score, the *leitmotif* recurs, always apparent to the searching eye. The vast structures of his design parade themselves throughout the ages, telling of himself, his spirit, and his continual driving for excellence and

---

* This only is temporary, and for certain periods of duration. It is only if Nature herself stands to the side, waiting to see how the passion play finds fruition in its particular destiny. Nature is the ultimate master in all things, and seeks not the Good or the Bad of a 'thing', but will bless only those which 'overcome'. FLS

purpose. His language, the parent to most higher cultures, flows as music, lyrically denoting a science in motion. He then, finally, actualizes his inner most spirit through his science of the deed: He writes.

All these things and more belong to Western Man.

What belongs to Western Man is, externally, an obvious point if the distinctions between past and present are to be asked: For what is seen can be believed. But, what of the unseen? Of Fate? Incident? Destiny? What does this culture (as with all higher culture) owe to the intangible? To that psychic presence that, individually or collectively, affects the existence of its race-soul? Is it mere chance, coincidence, or luck that leads a tribe, a city, or nation to reach its potential unrealized by those that have come before? Are the facts of history simply to be analyzed as events [actualized] that had only tangible components by which to become? Moreover, just what are the 'forces' behind the creations of fire, or the wheel, of atomic fusion? What is tangible? Intangible? Is the 'fact' that we *see* enough? On the other hand, is there a deeper, more spiritual - yes, simpler answer? Let us discover one if we may.

Historians often quote this axiomatic verse: "Those who do not learn from history and its mistakes, are condemned to repeat them." We see, hence, we believe. Yet, these selfsame historians (and Science too!) cannot or will not, acknowledge what is not seen; the child of the Enlightenment can only understand the god of Reason. They repeat as if a mantra: "Let me touch thy scars, so that I may believe."

The existence of the intangible is a condemnation of their reality.

And so the Tangible.

Of Flesh and bone, of blood, the modern historian would, in all likelihood, answer in this fashion: "What of this? Is not history the sum of its greater parts? The numbering of facts and figures which measure the course of events the more important?" And so they repeat.

To Western culture known, and unknown, the body of flesh, blood, and bone has been its only foundation. It is the sum of its soul. This is Race-Culture in the purest sense. It is a biological fact of independent units, individuals, in which its total substance makes up each particular race-culture. Each distinct Race. This is self-evident to any but the Modern. He is blind. Yet, it is precisely this constant amalgamation, this conglomerate, which forms the literal body of each specific culture. It is this mass, like the individual, which wills its direction; it is this organic [will to express] momentum that decides its modes of conduct and attaches itself to known history; it is the link to the past, present, and future. This organism, this whole, is the race-culture of Western Man.

This embodiment of the race-culture has soul [spirit], it has body [physical extension], and it has a life-force [blood], which flows in the bodies that are Western. This life-force, both physical and spiritual compels, commands, and are harnessed only with the knowledge of each, alone; it is the positive and negative of the eternal cosmos. It is neither good nor evil: It simply is. This life-force has driven the tribe ever upwards to attain culture; it has brought it down into the depths of civilization. For in the final analysis, *Culture* is the higher value. *Civilization* on the other hand, is the stagnant principle, it is decadence. Thus, to our reality: We *cannot* believe.

Reality is waking consciousness. Therefore, the consciousness of a culture, a people, must needs be a reality also, for it animates in everything we feel and think of ourselves. So, it is that the culture, as the individual, feels needs, desires; it shares dreams and a will-to-express this consciousness. This reality, also, defines itself through the landscape that enfolds the culture: we are part of the Earth itself. There is always the one who seeks this reality, and one who has already found it. Let us be more precise for those who are not sure of their place in the world. We define the reality of 'earth' in many ways: *Plains, Mountains, Home, Family, and Mate.* The overall designation may be termed Territory - since the word Homeland* is frowned upon, being too Nationalistic for the Modern; the metaphysical implications being too

---

* Authors Note: This 'word' was written long before the modern usage of today [2004]. Those who seek its innermost spirit, have sought to manipulate its ancient implications. It is used here in its 'pure' sense, not in the Legal Romanic sense of 'Idea' versus its Racial Parent. A Homeland is a "space inhabited by a specific group, i.e. Racial component; a 'specific' People." Not the ambiguous and legally defined 'people' as in today's modern 'State'. The modern revolutionary state of Russia, as in the 'soviet republics', were based on the lie of the 'creation' of a '<u>Peoples State</u>' which comprises a great Diaspora of racial types who, by definition are disparate in thought and action and are only *contained* in the 'legal' sense, as members of a Homeland. A family, a tribe, a People is *more than Idea.* Homeland is for the creators and its children. Strangers may reside with the family or tribe, but are never measured *as* the People. This, of course, destroys the very 'concepts' of Home *and* Land. FLS

v

tenuous, dark, and foreboding to those that would hide the meaning of Kinship and racial dynamics. Nevertheless, no man, no culture, can imagine itself without space, without a connecting source bringing him closer to those around him. It is true, even today, which even nomadic/primitive peoples have a close contact with territory, and fiercely defend this unseen border/domain with their lives if necessary. Like Kabobs of Africa, lions, bullfinches, osprey, baboons, and man himself, each follows this *'territorial imperative'*. *Each in turn to occupy a unique and distinct area; a 'tangible' and 'intangible' imperative.* Each to hold and occupy this area at the expense of the other creatures wishing to occupy with them. Kind supports Kind. These unique cultures offer no right or wrong; no ethical code by which to say to the world: "Here we live, and here we stay." They offer no pretext when dealing with their specific culture and its intimate reality.

Cultures, just as those of the animal kingdom, have these feelings of primacy, territory, and *needs* inherent in each; all, in turn, following nature's perfect order and design. The primacy of each recurrent culture in history is apparent. It feels the need of its particular group, manifested in its race-culture, its cultural soul. Nevertheless, so also the culture developing beside it, which is to say, any contemporary parallel culture existing along side each other. Here, then, we have a *contest*, a nature imperative which, the Modern, has not accepted. It is held with contempt, ridicule, and distaste. However, there is an intruder-man and a territorial-man, a *duality*, which has always existed; *will* always exist. Vibrant, young, and healthy cultures do not feel repelled by this natural phenomenon, but attack it; they bask in its fraternity with this ever-revolving cycle: One dies, one survives. The Nationalist has evoked these same types of opposing antagonisms simply because the Modern has led us to believe that this very nationalism (i.e., territorial imperative) breeds dissension, mistrust, and global conflict. But does it? The fact that nature is replete with this natural contest of wills over such areas as territory is beyond the Modern; it is not part of his blood, of his presence. He is civilized. This, then, too, is the meaning of decadence: It is the *disintegration* of that particular and personal [will-to-power] presence that surrounds us.

The will-to-power, as Nietzsche put it, is that which is behind all the building momentum of a fledgling culture and its many diverse and numerous prime symbols that synthesize its external technics, which is to say, its various forms of government, art, language, religion, science and, ultimately, its method of warfare and the type of man that accompanies its fighting spirit. It will always accept its warriors.

It is said of this class:

> They call you heartless: but
>
> You have a heart, and I love
>
> You for being ashamed to
>
> Show it. You are ashamed of
>
> Your flood, while others are
>
> Afraid of their ebb.
>
> (Frederick Nietzsche)

The higher-culture, the race, is but the flicker of a morbid ego without the momentum of the warrior; it is he, truly, which acts out, and *feels* the soul of the culture. By warrior, it is not to be inferred that what we pass off in today's world armies is what we speak of. On the contrary, it is the *spirit* of the warrior of old of which we speak. It is true that soldiers of all ages were given (wages) booty, spoils taken from the enemy: this is only common sense. But underlying the spirit of the mercenary (i.e. taking the financial end out of the equation), is that of the Patriot (ic); a feeling which, as the modern sees it, must be kept to a minimum, or he will see that spirit, once unleashed and able to ask the proper questions of the day, will then see the end of the Modern, for he cares not for Patriots: He *is* the ultimate mercenary, and he must hire (not be loved by) his troops or fall from grace. No, it is not to the mediocre that our culture has to thank for those things we take for granted, nor the mercenary. Once again, No! *It is to those pure in heart who have given their blood, courage, and yes, the very spirit they possess - freely.* It is not given to the mediocre political parties [although it is demanded of them by these mercenaries]; it is for their tribe, their land, and their families. Their root and stock. Thus, they see. Thus, they believe! So, it is with all higher-cultures that have made their marks on the history of the West. It is a presence, a value, a tradition, yes, a Faustian drive ever upwards and onward which marks the West. It is the destiny mark of its People.

Today, in this mediocre civilization we call 'modern society', it is not now in vogue to speak of a healthy, vibrant past; to speak of men like Hector, Achilles, Charlemagne, Frederick the Great and Napoleon is to somehow transgress some unspoken law of [modern] civility which, the West, has now wrapped itself. It is called by some the new Illumination, the 'new world' order of Western man. However it may be called, is it the light of the Sun, which would shine on us, or is this simply the death-throes of a higher-culture? Our Culture? Has the West, like Greece and Rome, passed through the phases of Birth, Life, and Senility of all great cultures like those before them? At first glance, one might say that we have. Yet not since the likes of Napoleon, Gustav Adolphus, Alexander and Pompey, has a higher-culture gone through such a metamorphosis, as have the colonists of this Northern Continent. It is few and far between whom have considered the prospects of a Pax-Americanum, an American Imperium; and though children of the Enlightenment, our roots grow much, much deeper. To be sure, there have been occasional outbursts, a race-memory beckoning us on, and which the modern knows only too well as that 'old spirit', such as the War Between the States, or the Monroe Doctrine which defined the Epic, the larger *will-to-express* of the race-culture. Nevertheless, nothing has come of it; rather it has enhanced those forces of money and power, which has ever and anon been at war with higher-culture for their own, ends. But not all is lost. It is a rhythm, which, while hard to grasp and repeat, nevertheless continues to move, to sway with each willing partner. The Rise of the West is such a partner. It moves to the rhythm of the future, and that future is almost upon us. It is not the intentional direction of the Modern, but rather of the patriot, the warrior; it is the rhythm of the pure in heart, grown larger and stronger than before. Europe has expressed this desire for the Epic, for the grand design. It is that of Culture overcoming Civilization. It is part of the Rising West.*

---

*Since the introduction to the Rise of the West was written, many things, events, and changes worldwide have occurred. I have known, instinctively, that my premise would show itself, such as this thesis is promoting, and which was written in the early months of [Feb] 1990. I feel some gratification in knowing that my course runs true. Culture is, without a doubt, overcoming civilization.
From Iraq and the entire Middle East, to the Serbian/Albanian/Croatian conflict; from places like Whidbey Island, Ruby Ridge, and Waco, TX. there exists a source of upheaval, a realignment of values and ideas, which have lain dormant for many years. In each example above, each in their own small way, have challenged the modern, and his society. To be clear on this, let us add that it is not the race-culture of the

This 'becoming' has, however, brought about another change. It has brought about a shift in perceptions and values recognized by the [white] American race-culture and reintroduced the warrior: both in the traditional sense (i.e. the paid soldier/patriot) and in the non-traditional sense (i.e. the zealot/patriot). This reality will have far reaching implications not fully appreciated by the Modern nor, sadly, by the very people to whom I am directing this work. It will, nevertheless gestate, grow, and come to its birthing even as I have said. This is our time. Those who understand what I say will listen and act. The storm is now upon us - even more so than since the second war of Fratricide. It has been the slowest of processes. Yes, the storm is upon us, and it but waits for the helmsman to direct its power. He will respond to the Rise of the West.

We [the race-culture] will not be the only ones to respond. The machine that is behind this ostensible 'spirit of democracy' will use, has used, this as a ruse. Not only to equip themselves better in such as events have thrust upon them, and it is most precarious, but also to insure those policies here at home (now known as the anti-terrorism bill, anti-gun legislation, etc.) which will assure those of the Modern that all dissent concerning Nationalist activities as defined in this work, and promulgated by patriotic and sincere men and women the world over, will not succeed; and will assure that their social programmes, so long in the making, will survive the embryonic inroads of the organic race-culture here at home and abroad. And these the self-same people, being of the white Nordic/Celtic Aryan stock of Europe who through long years have made their home of this Northern Continent, and whom also having been dispossessed of their land, their labor, their freedom.

To those of you who recognize your dispossession, you have my heartfelt sympathy. We all have much work to do. Do not fail to set your goals high; do not fail to pick your leaders wisely. They must be men with their ideals firmly set, their vision clearly understood. No more Politicians - but Statesmen, like of old. Those who understand the Rise of the West, and who also have worked, sacrificed, and labored to that end.

West that is under attack, but only the 'technics' which have come to dominate the race specifically. These events but attack what the West has *become*. It points out the decadence of the Modern. FLS

The Rise of the West is a reality. How it now evolves is up to each one of us: The smallest part of the Race-culture is you, the individual. Do not slack while your brother next to you labors; sacrifice is rarely, or permanently shared, it must be experienced, it must be felt in every sinew of ones body and soul. Most of us feel a change; it is part of our racial memory. But *recognition* is only part of the equation. A 'doing', of necessity, follows a sense of recognition and is defined by the 'act', that presence which defines all of Western man. Each of us, in turn, is judged by what he does, not by what he 'believes'. Only the Modern has perversely accommodated the concepts of 'thought crimes'. Do not fear the enemy of freedom. This battle is for the whole of Western man. The race must be run, and not any too quickly; but it must be run to the finish. It must be experienced; it must be felt in every sinew of ones body and soul.

Through the pages of this work, I hope that you might feel a little of what I have felt, what better men than I have felt in promoting this love of ones people, ones culture, and ones nation. In 1995, the Militia Movement has hit the press in scorching controversy. I am not a Militia member; although every able bodied white-male is a member at 21 years of age. This is historical common law. It is biblical law for those of you who claim to follow that religious belief: This has always served as the standing army of any Folk. One does not need the benefit of either documents, governmental authority, or law. *All public authority stems directly from the concept of a people standing together to stave off all enemies; from this has come our laws, our values, and our freedom.* For the most part, the modern militiaman is a raceless, faceless, creation of the modern; he forgets that it was his race's creation for the preservation of his own stock, against all comers. It was never intended, nor will it ever work for the melting-pot, a specific creation of the enemies of the very freedom, which the militiaman says, he fights for. Let this, then, serve as a call to those of this movement to choose whose side they will fight on: Will it be Culture or civilization?

The causality of all history is a still small voice, ever calling its champions ahead, forward, toward the future. Sumer, Babylon, Akad, Tyre, Egypt Persia, Athens, Troy, Carthage, Greece and Rome all, each in turn, had their cycles: Primitive, Classical, and recedent phases. Each experimented with their democracies, their tyrannies, their oligarchies, their plutocracies; they followed Ahura Mazda, Mithras, Indra, Zeus, Jove, Saturn, Aphrodite, and Venus.

They were heard through public speakers, philosophers, kings, and slaves. They rose and fell according to the laws of birth, life, and senility. Nevertheless, through this rising and falling man, Western man, has progressed, he has molded his destiny. No one 'system' of civilization can prepare for this cycle. In this vein America, indeed all the Western peoples of the Northern Continent, are now coming upon the epoch of the ages, and can be seen through history and its cycles, which will draw the attention of the world. It cannot be stopped. Moreover, just who would want to take on history? Who would deny its destiny? Who can stop the Rise of the West?

The Modern wills not to accept this. The international 'cosmopolis' of the modern wants the status quo to continue as it is; one rightly thinking would expect no less. For each organism must survive. The Modern looks neither 'left nor right,' but only at himself, what he has, what he wants. The Culture, however, is following a higher calling: *It follows Destiny*. Its life is apparent to all that would see the present presence in the culture they are a part of. The great epic of European re-unification, and to a lesser extent here at home, shows that which Nietzsche called the will-to-power; it is the expression of the race-soul. Many want nothing to do with this power; they fear it. Some say it is the death of the West. Whichever it will lead - to death or life, it will be for the entire race-culture. The world has too many who would *take* what we have struggled over aeons to create, and once taken from us, will only be returned to us by force, by yet more sacrifice.

We stare over the precipice, dark and rocky it appears. The sea pounds upon the foundation of our edifice, always making sure that we are prepared, and will not be caught off guard. In the distance a trickle of light may be seen, some fling themselves off the precipice afraid that the sun brings destruction. Others respond by rejoicing and thanking those who stood watch for them, for those who gave their lives protecting their shores. It is daylight now. It is the Rise of the West.

Frank L. De Silva

February 6, 1990

North Carolina

Chapter I

The origin of Western culture is learned through the records of the past. It is History in the purest sense. If we as a People, as a culture, are to progress, we must ascertain first and foremost, what has gone before. That the Arts of Science, Literature, of the Free Institutions of our society, our forms of Religious Beliefs and Government, all have come to us by way of accumulated methods of experimentation, by long ages of development and instruction. This is a very important point, and must not be forgotten as you continue your study into the Rise of the West.

The history and origin of Western Culture is learned through the records of the past. What occurs throughout is called 'causality', and is seen as the study of those things considered *organic*, not simply a lineal progression of 'dates', and events recorded by their present day observers. Actions and interactions are stimulated by more than simple 'recorded events', and are predicated on the totality of the *spirit* of that particular age in which a culture, embryonic or decadent, is directed on its evolutionary struggle. Those which make up the culture of the West are, like all other diverse people unique, specific, and designated anthropologically. We will, for the present, use the word Aryan to denote, as did Huxley, the "Blond Long-Heads" of Europe and the British Isles. This is more than a simple 'linguistic' definition. If this makes you more comfortable, think in terms of Nordic, or Northern European. This most noble of ancient names "Arya" was established by the Indian and Persian branch of our great extended family. The designation Arya, or noble, exalted ones, *is used solely in a racial and in no other sense.*

In passing, let me say to the reader that the study of words, Philology, is a fascinating subject, and is packed full with information that will cast a brighter light, on just *who*, and *what* you are. From the word Arya, for instance, comes our word 'Aristocrat' which, in our mother tongue still means "noble, or noblest governor." This title, Arya, or 'Aryan', is found as a designation of rulers or masters, which is to run throughout the whole family of the Aryan [language], including the Egyptian, presumably because the early rulers and masters were of this race. In its aspirated form *Her, Hera, Hearra or Herr*, "lord or master" of the Goths, Scandinavians, Germans and Anglo-Saxons; the *Aire* "chieftain" of the Irish Scots and Gaels. It is the *Arios, Harios, or Harri* of the Medes, and *Arya* and *Airya* of the Ancient Persians in a similar exalted and racial sense; and it is proudly used by Darius the Great on his tomb where he calls himself "An Arya of Arya (n) descent." In addition, King Xerxes called himself a "Harri." The Amorites (i.e. of Biblical fame), the sea-going branch of the Sumerians, called themselves *Gutt* [Goth], and *Kad* [Khatti, Catti, "Hittite"], as well as Ari, which is a dialectic form of this title Aryan.

Western civilization, created by those people historically called Aryan, Nordic, or Caucasoid, primarily lived in Western Asia and later in Egypt. Some scholars of anthropology and archaeology have put the Great Sargon [cir. 4200 b.c. - 3500 b.c.] as the 'originator' of the greatest ancient civilization known to man: The Sumerian Empire. This was the beginning of our present day civilization. Migrations occurred in time that eventually brought these people into contact with the Mesopotamian Valley, India, and Egypt. The records they have left, leave no doubt as to their arrival and departure. These 'movements' are part of the cycle of *birth, life, and senility* of all cultures. The great higher-culture of the Sumerians blossomed in Mesopotamia where they founded great centers of learning, religious institutions, and codes of law that, perforce, were designed to contain the new monolith of 'modern' society. Surrounded by various competitive tribes, both of Aryan and Semitic cultures, they secured a relatively pure empire. Nevertheless, with time, as they became civilized, the surrounding peoples became aware of that loss of vitality, so common with decadent culture, and then they struck. The Falcon People, the People of the Sun, had forgotten the ways of their ancestors.

These Semitic peoples, absorbed by the ruling class, soon began a systematic attempt which, in time, succeeded in dispossessing the once established order. They learned the ways of the Sumerian [West] and completely absorbed their culture. When they struck their final blow, the force was such that the farmer/warrior caste of this proud people fell with little historical force: It was the first cycle of birth, life, and senility in recorded [that we can now verify] history of the West.

Each succeeding generation, in each particular life-cycle, from the Sumerian to the Babylonian; from the Egyptian to the Hittite; from the Medes to the Persians and Assyrians, all followed the ebb and flow of the natural cycles of birth, life, and senility of each 'pre' or 'post' culture. In modern times, like our own nation, our parent(s) were European/Nordic, sending out colonists throughout Europe and then into the *new world* - America is, or at least was, an outpost of the English speaking branch of our European ancestors. From England, to Europe, into antiquity we can trace our ancestors. The same is to be seen with the starting point of the great Sumerian Empire.

Many records of these events have been kept, including the codified laws of Hamurabi, the Vedas [Indian King Lists], the Kalavela [Finnish], and the Edda's of Western Europe. All have given us an organic view of the soul of our past. The migrations of these people of the West have pushed ever westward, culminating in the creation of the empire of the Northern American Continent. One cannot but help to see the natural rhythms of the life of the West. It rises here, it rises there; its flags and banners take on various colors, its *emblems* [prime symbols] such as the Eagle, Falcon, Lion, and Bear, *disclose a continuous actualization of the 'soul' of this race-culture.* From the 'lineal' mathematical perfection of the Egyptian hieroglyphs, to the prime symbol of 'visual perfection vs. space' [the dimension of height, width, depth] of the Greeks, to the fluid, complex signature of Da Vinci, Michael Angelo, Pousin and Rubens who used line and brush, right-angle and square-root, to develop what was both seen and unseen; all sought the same perfection in form: *the manifestation of soul and body.*

These constant cycles of development needed the momentum, on a ongoing basis, of conflict and struggle to retain their vitality. This, of course, requires tremendous energy. Over the centuries man, in his search for the Utopia of his spirit, has developed ways and means by which to relieve the pressure of his tireless struggle, which burdens the individual and his race. To increase his security and well being, he envisioned and created collective groups [cohorts to the demographer] of like blood and cultural experiences: *united by the dual code of man within and man without, he maintained his hegemony.* These 'codes' are consistent with nature, and nature's law. Without this law [man within, and man without: a constant dynamic, constituting struggle], no higher-culture would exist - and a *civilization* must have culture to exist! Inner-man, like parts of the animal kingdom, which is to say, one who is defined as part of a particular group rules, or is ruled, within his environment by mutual trust, loyalty, and cooperation. Amity is the general feeling 'within'. From the primitive beginning, the origin of *all* culture has been the prerequisite of homogeneity; and in the collective sense, the individual, the tribe, and the nation were finalized as the Race-Culture.

Once finalized, the race-culture as both mass and individual, lended stability to the now organized organism. It protected the individual as never before; he in turn now ready to protect the *extension* of himself: that of race and nation [even if confined only to geography]. This protected, also, the culture from the outsider who, for better or worse, was now seen as not being a part of the individuals instant group. This seemingly bitter attitude was/is the other side of the duality of nature - it meets the outsider with indifference, suspicion, antagonism, and preparedness for war. For in the final analysis, there is no peace in nature. Neither is there any real peace in diverse cultures. Here, as in nature, the rule is enmity. This duality is not dysfunctional, and has served well the social status and security of all higher-culture. This duality has, in any event, done what nature has ordained:

a. Maintained a segregated gene-pool that has protected the original integrity, shared mores, and unadulterated homogeneity from outside racial diversity; and this being so essential to any people's stability and long-term survival, or meaningful cultural experience. After many centuries, this will leave an indelible mark defining the past, present, and future:

b. Increases the group's total strength, and multiplies the chances and frequency for mastery and survival in its struggle with any and all enemies. This has been the origin of all races and cultures. It has been the catalyst of all we call human evolution and direction. It continuously reminds those of a particular group that they each share a specific relationship with those closely related people with whom they share their daily lives: This maintains those within. This guarantees the survival of the group.

This dual code equipped man with one of the first requirements of his moral health. The security provided by the associated numbers [members] of like-kind, that is, race-culture, created a *belonging*, which is something every man and woman is continually striving and searching for, but cannot seem to find in the modern's understanding, "except in a circumscribed group or community made up of individuals much the same as himself." This will add, with time and circumstance, a certain moral aptitude to the individual which, by extension, is the race-culture, and direct his perceptions in the ways and means by which he should act, and meet, the most vital issues of life. He would do this with no remorse; for he knew instinctively, that he was not only protecting himself, *but that of the whole of his culture as well.* By standing together, united, he [the individual] could put everything he had into the fight. The lesson he learned was that the 'welfare' of each was best ensured by one and all standing together, solid, such as a mountain of granite; and this in mutual trust and effort. This, after several hundreds of thousands of years became the *unconsciousness* of his spirit, integrated into every ounce of his physical and mental condition. It was, and is, his very soul.

Homogeneity, as stated above however, is not the 'melding' into that chasm of total conformity; rather, it is the conglomerate of persons that can be directed by a social government to become its political consciousness. This, in its simplest term, is the Nation, *a state*, founded upon the corporate race-culture. For in the final analysis, it is a *people*, which define the 'nation' and not any complex infrastructure, which passes *as* the People. In its truest sense, this is the pluralistic society spoken of by the Fathers of the Western Nations: For a People, even if of the same race-culture, will have as many varied positions concerning life, politics, and religion as there are persons occupying that State. This is true pluralism. To add *'divergent race-cultures'* is not the pluralism sought after by the progenitors of this Northern Continent. Those who say otherwise, have their own agendas; they are modern.

In the realm of political thought, the opinions offered will be varied and complex, human nature being what it is. But this is the body-politic, and is as it should be. This is not to infer that decisions will, of necessity, be confused, distorted, or thwarted [such as is presented to us in our present 'mobocracy']. In a requisite state of homogeneity, political decisions will be faced squarely by a *spirit which is consonant with a people's entire past tradition* and, also, those other parallel cultures existing with us, will more readily be able to gauge [and more effectively] and judge this Western culture. Moreover, this is due because of its inherent *stability*. If there is to be anything like a 'world peace', then it must come from this viewpoint of race, and race-culture as a "unit', be it the State, Family or Nation. It will come from each *distinct* race-culture, inhabiting their *own* place, knowing full well their potentials and weaknesses.

The value of Race-culture will be the deciding factor in all political, social, or religious endeavors, embarked upon by the ruling State. Such is a government "of the People, by the People, and for the People." The Modern, however, wills not to accept this.

Is it any wonder, then, that America, in contrast, has now degenerated from that singular higher-culture, to that amalgamated hodge-podge which is call the 'melting-pot'? What had proved so significant to the very existence of all higher-cultures, America has deemed unnecessary, worthless, and has cast aside under the guise of 'civilization'. Let America, then, serve as our immediate example:

The founders of the original [Republic] Thirteen Colonies, which developed into the Federal Union, were remarkably alike in racial origins. In fact, with few exceptions, they came mostly from the nations (i.e. race-cultures) of Northwestern Europe. In the mid 1800's however, shortly after Lincoln's assassination, the nation was continuously given over to looters who, after the War between the States, were [and are] fanatically driven in their desires for wealth, equality (which is anti-nature], and power over and above that which had been mandated a scant eighty years previously. The body-politic still shared similar [racial] origins, yet their political agenda was demonstrably different from the original intent of their predecessors, namely, that a balanced Federal system be coupled with individual State rights to protect the Union [of voluntary States] from a overwhelming tyranny of leadership concentrated on the same lines as had the European continent.

These new leaders exercised their power to import cheap labor, the exploitation of 'free-trade', and other sundry excuses to increase their stranglehold on the war-torn Republic. In the following forty-year period [after 1880], America took in over twenty-three millions of immigrants, most of which were of southeastern Europe. By 1920, this brought the American population to one hundred and five million. Since that time, America has allowed virtually every racial 'type' imaginable to come to these, our shores. Included in this influx of immigrants were persons known to be feeble-minded, along with other dysgenic disorders which, while being cognizant of their own needs, did not, strictly speaking, understand the race-culture of the West or its tremendous advances in technology. These individuals were not of the same quality.

The catchwords 'superior and inferior' are not consonant in regards to this difference in quality. The simple fact is that we [as unique specie] are different as a Western people. We are *incommensurate* with other race-cultures. The most 'gifted' of all these non-Nordic elements Jews and Mongolians, to prove a point, have never assimilated, but remain, as always, a foreign organism in the American body-politic, as well as all other Western nations. It should be stated that, in relation to what has just been said, over and beyond, is that these people, which were in fact so different racially, or mentally, should never, and I repeat, never should have been allowed to come here in the first place - even those of the same race-culture, if lacking in the highest qualities of life. It is not intended to be mean-spirited when we say that their very soul is different. Their traditions [non-Western] so vastly coloured as to create a veritable impasse of values [perceptions]; indeed, it has become the 'transvaluation' of values belonging to the traditional [American] Western values. Add to this some thirty million Negroes who, after no fault of their own, have added such a weight of alienness, that the full-blooded Western-man is virtually swamped by such a catastrophe. Consequently, he has felt the loss of his country, his culture - even now, he sees it pass from his hands. He is now dispossessed of his supremacy.

Like a victorious army, once becoming victorious, then pulling back, denies itself that 'territorial victory' allotted to the victor, and thereby forgetting and insulting the memory of those brave men before him, who sacrificed all for that very victory, and thereby relinquishing their 'right' to any accompanying political considerations in the future. In like fashion, consequently, he [Western man] has lost his country; he has lost his identity. In the alienness that surrounds him he can find no escape: the names on the television screen become increasingly alien, the names from far away places which appear on local store-fronts, or the names of University professors and National leaders increasingly overwhelm him. Escape? He can find none.

All this has its consequences. Of these, the most deadly (although not readily seen), has been the attack on the *spirit* of Western man. Not only in America (for we are but a symptom), but the 'entire' Western world. This attack is at the very root of Western man's soul. Once the sureness by which he could make his daily decisions were replaced by those 'spirits' so unlike him, that is, by those not of his own stock, he failed, and is failing to act with any *real* telling force; he is now impotent. *No longer does he look upon faces such as his own, seeing what he sees.* Can he know, for instance, that all *his* spirit feels, all *he* lives for, all that he is prepared to *die* for, all he holds *sacred*, is matched by his neighbor's? In more poetic verse, Rudyard Kipling had this to say:

> The stranger within my gate,
>
> He may be evil or good,
>
> But I cannot tell what powers
>
> Control, What reasons sway his
>
> Mood,
>
> Nor when the Gods of his far-off land
>
> May repossess his blood.
>
> The men of my own stock,
>
> Bitter bad they may be,
>
> But, at least they hear the
>
> Things I hear, and see the things I see;
>
> Whatever I think of them and their likes,
>
> They think the likes of me.

It is this view, precisely, which Western man feels *intuitively*.*

And this regardless of what those promoters of that 'great leveling' (that of 'equality'), would have him believe. This solidarity then, being lost, Western man is also lost; he can no more see himself merged, grafted as it were, with

---

* See chapter III. Also see, "end note" by Alexis Carrel on the value of intuition. See Bibliography.

those of his own stock. He can no longer feel himself as part of those, which surround him; he has lost the sense that his nation, his very birthplace, is himself, multiplied as it were, a hundred million fold. To speak of this 'type' of belonging is to see, clearly, a sense of Homeland; that illuminating, and mystical concept of *belonging* that will fight any imposture, which seeks to replace the continuity of Race. The Legions of Rome pale considerably when compared to that of Sparta.

It is not now in vogue, nor is it 'politically correct' in today's world, to invoke this reminder of our Western past; yet, Western man has *proved* himself a conqueror. (Do not balk at this comment, for behind every modern hard drinking worker, behind every homebody husband, there stands, albeit weakly, the warrior; sad it is, that most modern men rarely listen to that 'ancient', and noble calling. He is civilized today. But deep inside he hungers to be what his fathers were. All it will take is just one moment; just one passion that is able to pass through him during his daily routines that will wake him.) His records and monuments are immemorial, and display his conquests since the earliest of epochs. Even in our present day, it is obvious that our conquests have given us what we consider our 'heritage', *and our territory*. The 'concept' of conquest, however, is a dirty word, almost criminal in nature. The Modern has labeled it a 'hate crime', and is wont to remind the world of its evil designs and consequences. The Modern would have us lay our spirit on the altar of mediocrity.

The West has, indeed, left its warrior spirit behind.*

---

* Note: Recent events in the Middle East, Africa, and Europe have brought this *spirit* back in focus. But, the 'warriors' that are participating in these contests are anything but a 'cohesive unit' in the ancient sense; that is to say a 'unit' fighting for its racial/cultural survival - *as* Nation - or *as a People*. These present-day warriors, brave though they are, as are all mercenary troops, fight for a geo-political interest. The outcome, win or lose, will not be for any so-called freedom, or democracy, but simply for the interests of other race-cultures (or race/cultural *betrayers*) which are involved in their own imperatives, without thought for our Western race-culture. *The struggle for supremacy, in one sphere of influence or another, is millennial.* It will remain so, for as long as there are men who take pride in themselves and their culture. To interdict ourselves into the spheres of interest of these other race-cultures is deleterious to our best long-term interest (our first President said as much); and to deny those fledgling race-cultures the right to their 'will-to-power', their 'will-to-express' is only expressed in ignorance or based upon an agenda of *money and power* (money serves itself; and very few who control vast treasuries will ever side on the

Western man, deep inside, is ashamed of his ebb. *Western man is now ashamed of his empires, ashamed of his very mastery, ashamed of his very ancestors - and these the very reason for his existence!* Moreover, Empire, in the final analysis, was for the Nation; expansion necessary for the future of the race-culture. Only later was empire utilized by 'money', even as today, for its own end. Yet, today, what does he have to live or die for? What then is the 'great attempt' of Western man? He moans and pouts. He will not defend himself - nationally or individually. He presses not, in any direction, steadily or firmly in the direction of his survival; he apologizes not only for what he is, but also for what went before; his children know not whom their Fathers were, or the dreams they lived by. Yes, Western man is ashamed. But is he guilty? Must Western man demand and receive his untimely death/suicide? Must the West cease to exist because her sense of Destiny has made her the most *beautiful of the families of man?* Does the West accede to the demands of the masses that we become the same as they? Ask yourself, now, are our needs the same as the other race-cultures, which surround us? No! A thousand times no!!

Of all the contagious, feeble-minded lies, it is that preached today of Human Equality, which is most harmful to us! The religious leaders of today pound the pulpit, they scream their clarion calls to the mass that 'man is equal', that he shares equally the burdens of life: Of Higher-Culture. But these high priests speak of worlds other than their own. They wish for the *becoming* of space and time to *be.* They speak of the otherworld. They speak of a world of which they know absolutely nothing. *They speak, as do all moderns, from altars of guilt, from bended knees.* The Byzantine priests of yesteryear have been reborn. But what, exactly, gave these men that very power, yes that very spirit to exhort and guide these masses, their own as well as others? The answer: *Those to whom conquest allotted such power!!* There is no such thing as equality in nature; only 'man' may, at times, control his environment and 'establish law' that will

---

team which places culture above the monied interests) which will not serve our people well in the long run. In fact, most if not all of recent military incursions have been against middling countries with little or no political strength, not to mention money or support mechanisms with which our sacrifice could be justified! *No war of defense can be waged, honestly, which is not a war in defense of our past traditions and values particular to the West; or which is not done in direct consequence of alien territorial expansion on our own soil.* The deaths of our young men, even those not of Western stock, is a crime against *our* humanity, *our* sense of the right and wrong of things. It is sure sign of decadence. FLS

provide a modicum of relief to society - past, present, or future. Each man will have, of necessity, similarities in his human nature that corresponds to his fellows, but he will not be equal. The truth is that each man has his worth; but truly, *some* men are worth more. Nature speaks clearly on this issue if one is honest in their search. She raises one, and crushes another. Can we see, yet disbelieve?

i.

The Purpose of

Race Culture

In the first part of this chapter, we briefly outlined an *organic* process by which Western culture has traversed the ages in its development. It has done so vigorously, and at every opportunity; it has lasted as long as the *original intent* and *singular homogeneity* of the culture-bearing strata existed. When this ceased to be, the culture passed away into history. The words 'beginning', 'original', and the like, denote a more readily understood position, namely, some sense of *idea*, *concept*, or *scheme* of things that the individual or group (i.e. early political state) maintained for the betterment of their tribe, or nation [the race culture]. This took on many shapes, it evolved into many 'established' ways of government, and it continues to evolve today.

The original evolutionary form of high-culture was the absolute Monarchy established in the Sumerian Empire and before in Asia Minor [Cappadocia]. This evolutionary cycle followed one upon the other as oligarchy, plutocracy, democracy, and Dictatorship. At each specific point in time, in every particular 'presence of the present', *every* system was necessary at the moment it appeared. Looking at an over-all picture in time, events and circumstances lead the way for these particular creations, which either help or hinder the race-culture and its members. Causality, as a science, must be pursued here. Were not the oligarchies of Rome, the dictatorships of Greece necessary for the continuation of these very cultures at the moment they appeared?

Was not their very survival at stake?

If one is honest, was it not the Culture, which ultimately benefited by these cycles? What of those extreme personalities? One thinks of Caesar or

Alexander, men who at their moments of presence felt instinctively that they must do what was necessary [Caesar by destroying the Republic, to again rebuild it; and Alexander by following a vision given him by destiny and Aristotle], regardless of the outcome, to see the fulfillment of their race-culture's aspiration to greatness. *This was the pure will-to-power of the race*; it was seen through the heart and mind of its greatest members. It was the grandeur of their vision. It was their *vision* that made all the difference. This was simply the personification of the group, manifested in the individual. It was from the 'group' (i.e., the race-culture) that the energy required to complete the task was taken, in a spiritual sense; in the end however, it is, and will always be, a personal manifestation.

It has never been the mass, which has made the important decisions of the day. In the very beginning, at every starting point of a historic epilogue, it has been the individual who has risen to the occasion: this, the champion. Thus, the purpose of the State, tribe, or nation ultimately rests upon a single mind; and only through a 'group' of like minds can any real government or methodology of government be realized. So, it was in the beginning. So, it is now, today. It is not a matter of 'good and evil', which brings us these leaders - it has simply been the organic continuum of this distinct race-culture. It will continue time, and time again. Each a full page in the once and future West.

These various leaders, as individuals, had agendas as diverse and select as their personalities would allow. Many outside their camp have offered definitions as to their motives and greater goals, and have placed them within categories that would seek to 'explain' their positions to us. The Modern, also, has delivered his commentary. In point of fact, however, no one really knows what motivated them. How can one, for instance, know the tangible and intangible elements, which directed them? What *was* their vision? As men of the West, what were the tangible and intangible elements, which brought the triumphs of the intellect to us? That of Physics and its many related sciences - in this, certainly, the foremost thinkers were of the West. But to what end?

Curiosity, of necessity, must have played a large part; and this 'part', that element which seeks all knowledge. In fact, the West has always been criticized for the ostensible search for knowledge 'for knowledge's sake'. We are condemned for every advancement (some justifiably so) by those who have never created their own language, or built their own ships to sail the oceans of our world; by those who still practice female circumcision or sell their kinsmen into bondage. This evolutionary progression of ideas continues to mark the West.

Dr. Alexis Carrel, one of America's great visionaries, addressed this issue when be wrote, "curiosity *impels* us to discover the universe." [emph. mine.] Dr. Carrel, in his monumental work *Man the Unknown* proved, in the tradition of his fathers, that in asking the question was more than half the battle in finding out the answer. He, too, was a curious one. Mere curiosity however, was not the greater goal. The raising of man above his incumbent limitations was: his spirit could now soar. It has become that most ancient of pursuits, the ennobling of man. This has always been the noble goal of all great thinkers. This was the great 'doing' of all the great thinkers; it was their far horizon.

These far horizons, as such, are esoteric truths to most of us. Yet, they remain eternal truths to Western man. Men like Aristotle, the famous student of Plato, sought to follow this will-to-express, which his mentor had displayed. Aristotle, however, did not simply go over the ideas formulated by Plato, rather, his presence defined his environment in the mathematical and biological advances of his day; and these rhythms an organic part of the race-culture. The higher-culture of the West however, did not start with either Aristotle or al-Farabi. The Classical Science of our past lies in the work of three men: Archimedes, Erastothenes, and Aristarchus of Samos.

Archimedes, as may be remembered, helped [cir. 250 b.c.] the Greeks, during the Roman three-year siege of Syracuse, using 'engines of war' of his own design, including the somewhat fantastic application of 'thermal warfare' by utilizing the power of the Sun together with a polished curved mirror (a polished bronze perhaps), and destroyed the entire enemy fleet. Archimedes died by a Roman sword in 212 b.c. He also reduced Aristotle's concept of 'center of gravity' to a geometric precision and thereby solved the problem of the 'lever' that had so baffled Aristotle. Likewise, his contemporary, Erastothenes of Cyrene [cir. 270 b.c.], applied mathematics to Geography and scientific chronology [i.e., his crouografia, in which he endeavored to fix the dates of the chief literary and political events from the conquest of Troy]; and Aristarchus of Samos [cir. 270 b.c.] a prime originator of things 'astronomical'. In fact, this latter laying the groundwork for Copernican astronomy. He is said to have been the first to propose a heliocentric or sun-centered theory of the universe by adducing that the Sun, not the earth, was the center of the universe. These great minds were contemporaneous with one another and belonged to the same race-culture, having access to one another's work, thereby increasing the general dynamics of knowledge itself. This point should not be lost on the reader, and will make itself apparent in later chapters.

Today, the descendants of these men, you and I, see little of the intangible *belonging* to these men; and what is tangible we see only in the physical representation of the classical beauty of the Greek 'architrave', and the Roman 'vault'. It has taken many hundreds of years for the West to try and absorb the tangible and intangible elements of these sciences; this process of absorption continues today. The Renaissance and Reformation attempted to distil this information for the peers of its day; and both sought a new purpose for Western man, in which these sciences might help them learn and maintain. In today's presence, many perceive these moments in history as the birthing of a new order, a glorious new purpose in the higher-culture of Western man. It was, however, not the beginning, but a 'mid-point' in the birthing of a new West. It was but an awakening amongst so many slumbers; a waking consciousness amongst so many nights of wistful dreams. It was the 'great becoming' of Nietzsche. Thus, it is that the Middle Ages were an important prelude to the visible signs of the Rise of the West. Yet, we are [at least the modern] still looking for the antecedents of the Renaissance; he still cannot grasp the esoteric logic of freedom and all the catch phrases associated with it.

It was the Church of this period which, ironically, gave a rising impetus to this Renaissance, to this Freedom of thought. It was in the arena of Church dogma and dispute that Francesco Petrarca, better known as the 'Patriarch Petrarch', became imbued with this new order of man.

Born in 1304, his origins spring more from the perspective of Humanism, than from theology; yet, both were inextricably bound together. His was the mind of the poet, for he did not feel comfortable with the Law. His compelling instructor was the primal mountains of the Alpine, and the historical romance of his Roman past. In fact, it was his study of the great Personalities which, like Alexander, led Petrarch to his own personal conquests. His favorite discourse was that of Scipio Africanus, in his Latin Epic, *Africa*. For him, there was no schism between Rome and Galilee; between classical genius and sacred inspiration. Like a true 'dualist', he saw both the role of the Church and Humanism as necessary to the dual nature of man. Classical Genius, in his mind, was the *perfection* of man's intellect and the cultivation of his manners as would be expected by any cultured, responsible man. Sacred inspiration, on the other hand, was that balance, which maintained the welfare of man's continued existence. He spent many years of his life teaching this to the peers of his day. For he saw that it was the 'outgoing' of the old values of the church, and things [he deemed] antiquated, which held back that process, which would ineluctably bring about the birthing of a new Western culture *as it should be;* as Nature herself, directed it. Ironically, it would be the followers of Augustine, ostensibly the father of the church, who would embrace *the* 'truth', would be the staunchest of opponents by protecting the 'status quo' simply for its own sake. The 'status quo' of his day demanded conformity. He thought otherwise, and saw also that for any new order, even if only reestablishing old values, that it was imperative that certain values holding back a new West be overcome, and replaced. In large part, he achieved this by reaffirming the balance of mind and body, of that balance of tangible and intangible elements. His wellspring was that true search for knowledge and justice.

The duality of man is constantly reminding us of our own opposites.

Take Aurelius Agustinus, better known as St. Augustine, born in ancient Numidia, a African Province of Carthage, of possible Numidian/Punic blood-lines, and founder of what Francesco Petrarca would attempt to change and correct in his own fashion, was quite different. He was learned in Latin history, but more importantly, he was steeped in Mysticism. Not the mysticism of the Sages, but of Levantine mystical thought and orthodoxy. As was the custom of the age, even for Christians, he took a concubine and had a son. He gave both up, not only because he was becoming imbued with puritanical purity, but also to seek political and theological power. Tutored by the statesman/bishop of Milan, Ambrose, he attained these ends.

He became obsessed with 'overcoming the flesh', and pursued an unbalanced orthodoxy of 'spiritual' awareness. He eventually renounced both. His orthodoxy became the 'Slave of God' orthodoxy; that man is inherently sinful, and therefore a mere slave of fortune, or God's will. He was also a Neo-Platonist, which would cause him no uncertain pain when he became so adamant concerning the sinfulness of man. He became a Universalist, a truly catholic believer, for the sake of expediency. For the church was the 'all', and *all must conform.* In later years, both his Neo-Platonism and his Manicheanism, fell to the wayside, and he embraced 'empiricism'. He believed in empirical evidence, yet he purported the belief in 'original sin', as opposed by Pelagius[Σ]. All in all he, and his later followers, were happy with the way things were. There was no new horizon as Petrarch saw. Thus do we see that perfect 'duality' of inner and outer man.

Even so, this antipathy was necessary for the West to grow. Without the conflict of ideas, there can be no distillation. There can be no rising. In our millennia, this distillation may be summed up concerning the spiritual soul of man: *"If it did not possess this greatness, then it could not become God even through grace."* This from the mouth of a *truly* Western thinker, [Meister] Echehart of Hocheim. This man was not the crass bastard of Africa, but of Thuringian nobility. True, this may be conceit, but let us assume that it represents the pride of personality rather than some baser instinct, for the premise is purely Western. True Western values, and that is the essence of religion, values, and is the belief that the nobility of the self-reliant soul is the highest of all values. This in no way absolves us of the 'value' of God; rather it reinforces the

---

[Σ] See also, *Pelagianism*: A so-called Christian heretical sect that rose in the fifth century challenging St. Augustine's conceptions of grace and predestination. The doctrine was advanced by the celebrated monk and theologian Pelagius (c.355–c.425). He was probably born in Britain. After studying Roman law, rhetoric, and later theology in England and Rome, he preached in Africa and Palestine, attracting able followers, such as Celestius and Julian of Eclannum. Pelagius thought that St. Augustine was excessively pessimistic in his view that humanity is sinful by nature and must rely totally upon grace for salvation. Instead Pelagius taught that human beings have a *natural* capacity to reject evil and seek God, that Christ's admonition, "Be ye perfect," presupposes this capacity, and that grace is the natural ability given by God to seek and to serve God. Pelagius rejected the doctrine of original sin; he taught that children are born innocent of the sin of Adam. Baptism, accordingly, ceased to be interpreted as a regenerative sacrament. Pelagius challenged the very function of the church, claiming that the law as well as the gospel can lead one to heaven *and that pagans had been able to enter heaven by virtue of their moral actions before the coming of Christ.* (See, also: J. E. Chisholm, The Pseudo-Augustinian Hypomnesticon against the Pelagians and Celestians (Vol. I, 1967); J. Pelikan, The Emergence of the Catholic Tradition (1971).

interrelationship between the seen and unseen. The tangible and the intangible.

The modern claims that 'freedom' is the higher value. But this simply is Idea. It stands alone *as* Idea. But what of Honor? Is it not a 'higher' ideal? Is it not higher, because without it, there would be no freedom?! The idea of freedom is inconceivable without honour, and so likewise. The soul is capable of good in and of itself. No dalliance with the almighty will assure honour or freedom. That comes from within; it comes from the soul *marked* with Honour, and which *begets* Freedom.

The renaissance, then, was the *transvaluation* of those values inherited from that Levantine thought of Byzantium, through the last vestiges of the Roman empire (so-called 'holy'); yet, that empire had truly died with Marcus Aurelius. It had become a reassertion of Western thought. The 'stoic' philosophy of a dying Rome added just the right amount of poison to a senile 'civilization', which ultimately led to the Renaissance itself. But to what purpose? To what scheme of things?

In the 'scheme of things', to the student of causality, what is the purpose, what is the meaning of such radical change, of such transvaluation? The cause, or 'scheme of things', will ever be that sense of real *culture-purpose* which, will ever and anon, be the 'purpose', of and by itself, which *wills* itself to show the world its inner most purpose. So, it was, that this renaissance showed to the entire world that it was race, and by definition, its culture, which was to be seen [visually], and which was to rule [demonstrably].

It was into this age, this modern age of Western man that a *re-awakening* showed itself in a unique 'culture-purpose' for the world to see. Not since Alexander had such a cultural-becoming been seen: The *purpose* of culture was finally realized. *It was to the ennobling of the individual to which culture owed its very heartbeat and hence, to the body; to the Race-culture.*

Erasmus, Bacon, Cervantes to name a few, defined this process; each in turn, seeing a part of the growing consciousness. Yet, it was much more, this renaissance, than simply the *extension* of the Liberal Arts. It was, and always is the convolution of a new birth: But it was more – it was the interplay of amity and enmity. It was 'man within' and 'man without'. It was the inner feeling, that spiritual guide, which was to speak for the race-culture saying: '…all things foreign must be kept out…all things foreign existing must be cut out…' which was crying out to be heard. It was to the very survival of that *inner core of culture-bearers*, which must survive at all costs; for it is, precisely, these 'culture-bearers', like the individual, who are the healthiest, for they live only for the continuation and benefit of the whole. This growing consciousness would transmit itself time and again to future generations, sometimes clearly and sometimes with unintended dimness. In a word, the Renaissance was the 'Unconscious' expression of the race-culture; that very sense of survival, which ever and anon, seeks its own survival, at the expense of the whatever lies 'outside' itself. It is the Race Memory seeking to extend itself by reissuing the experiences of the ancestors as empirical proof of its own self worth. This feeling ultimately led to a re-ordering of their society: *The Reformation.*

It is well true, that in some cases this transvaluation, this experience, is oft times the violent reactions of a people that has resented a foreign presence as not being a *natural* part of itself; sensing a change in direction unfamiliar with sound historical reason; or changes in specific or general [public] thought processes of the race-culture. It is *reaction*. In addition, while a true 'reactionary' is limited by the emotional elixir of the moment, it is nevertheless the *impetus*, which should show the way to his more rational, yet nonetheless courageous, cousin. This process is seen clearly in the Renaissance and the Enlightenment respectively. In more benign clothing perhaps, we see another birthing, a growing sense of aspiration and purpose, although just as revolutionary in the battleground of the <u>*Arts.*</u>

Thoughts and ideas are continually at odds. Expression of these thoughts and ideas are constantly being promoted. The Modern loves the conflagration, the confusion, and the obfuscation of what 'art' has always represented: The simple display of beauty, courage, love, devotion, form, and vitality of the human spirit is downplayed, even discouraged, by the modern, for he knows that deeply ingrained in the common man and nobility alike, there is a resonance, which *truly* transcends class. Art was that medium, which was truly democratic: if every worth was equal, then the art of the day would trace that equality. Spirit *in* man may designate equality, but truly, the visual arts decree the superior and inferior. Let the Modern paint this, as he will. He will be judged by what *he* portrays on his canvass.

As the Egyptian hieroglyphs were to the ancients, in their unique balance of *line and angle* so, also, in the Western period of 1500-1700* [a.d.]; for even the Greeks and Romans had not *actualized* the becoming of its race-culture as did these, for their respective time periods. This is simply the will to express oneself. It is this constant searching to express oneself, *for* expression, which has marked the West. Was it not, after all, from the canvasses of Rubens, Pousin, Botticelli, Titian, Da Vinci, David, and Caravaggio that the essence of the West finally began to awaken? *

If one were to carefully analyze the tangible and intangible elements of each higher-culture, one would most likely see that the *manifestation of purpose* was seen in the visual and written arts of that particular culture and, more importantly, is inextricably bound with it. As stated above, the Egyptian hieroglyphs were line and angle, and beautiful no doubt when viewed by their creators. But from our point of view, this art was 'flat', and not representative

---

* Here we speak of the juxtaposition of values. The fact that we as a Western stock, today, see no 'value' artistically in the two-dimensional value of Egyptian art is not to demean it; rather, let the fact that even as the Greeks beheld the beauty of the human body, its form, the three-dimensional quality of their perception, that the advance of the Egyptian in 'becoming' more than their ancestors was mind boggling, so also the West, through the eyes of Da Vinci, and those of his generation and beyond, than their previous ancestors.

If one were to carefully analyze the tangible and intangible elements of each higher-culture, one would most likely see that the *manifestation of purpose* was seen in the visual and written arts of that particular culture Let me here anticipate the Modern. He, of course, will exclaim that this, precisely, is the ultimate beauty of our modern order; that it is the inclination of every artist to follow his or her inner most being – regardless of what that inclination may be. Hardly. Using Elephant dung, urine, or whatever putrid element deemed worthy to make a 'point' is exactly why we condemn it. It is the agenda, the thought process, which we condemn; the visual depiction speaks for itself. Yes, artists have a right to expression, even an unlimited right, but we do not have to view it; and certainly, the State must, if it chooses to buttress the one must, absolutely, buttress the other mental process: That of the romantic, the racialist, the lovers of beauty as seen by artists, which ascribe to concepts such as man and woman as partners and lovers*; in the deeper context of Nationhood as extension of Blood and Soil;* of the many realists who would paint in the Prime symbols of the past, of the shared values of our tribal existence, in short, artists who see the life around them as extensions of the past, which, if shared with their contemporaries, would promote that racial memory and vitality so necessary for the survival of the race itself. FLS

of what we see in the environment that surrounds us. Their reality was not ours. Thus the duality of consciousness.

Art, as a perspective, brings out the 'psychic' picture of each and every artist. To bring such a 'perspective' to the eye of the observer is a mystical one. It was this mysticism, regardless of the medium employed, which brought about the ennobling of the individuals or people who shared in this perspective.

Western art, deeply held that mysticism was part and parcel to the examination of the 'body and spirit', which enabled the individual to express himself in ways and means that heretofore had been seen only on the rarest of occasions. The Renaissance brought out much that was unseen, at least within the boundaries expressed by this movement, by allowing the artist to burst out, so to speak, with colours, draftsmanship (all true sciences), and a realistic 'perspective' (allowing three dimensional viewing) specifically on the 'canvasses' of the modern artists. This full colour was, and can be seen with all art, an expression of the inner mind (i.e. the individual outlook on personality, rage, courage, love, war, etc.) both from the artist himself and the viewer who is *contemplating* the specific work. In contemplating this very same art, it was possible, unlike the Grecian art of ages past; one could 'see' the *story* behind the art (in its minute form). Art had become a medium to explore the greater elements of nature and Life; of spirituality, and leadership; of manliness, and poetry.

The mysticism of Allegory, of fable, of Myth, that epoch creating motif of a people was brought to bear by such men as Rubens, Titian, David, Girodet, and Pousin told of the original mystical spirit of the West. To be sure, these artists were schooled in the 'styles' and 'traditions' of Greek classical art. But more than typical 'classicism' in art was their teacher. The 'total' history of their past, our past, included the common history of the Nordic, Roman/Celt, east European race-cultures. The total panorama of their art was of a 'family of men', the men of the West. This 'art' described the complete breaking away from the art of the past, and described in lucid and compelling pictures of the race-culture; it was the 'story of the ages' for all to see and share. It was the storytelling motif of the history of our ancestors, of its very antecedents. It broke the confines of Orthodox Church dogma.

Once the floodgates were open, there was no turning back.

Architecture, for instance, brought to bear by Archimedes, was utilized in its own artistic fashion to 'house' this very art: the Gothic cathedrals of Milan, Tours, Notre Dame, Mt. St. Michael and others (who were often targeted for destruction by the armies of the allies in the second fratricidal war in the last century) and others which were the epitome of the Western soul in actualizing, in the 'outward form', the total essence of its spirit, while the canvass art showed the deep, rich, 'inner spirit'. The tangible and intangible made manifest.

These great and beautiful cathedrals were designed on a four-square pattern; balance and symmetry being understood to best represent the balance of Heaven, Earth, body, and soul. A curiously 'pre-christian' belief. From every angle, one's eye is drawn simultaneously to its entrance as well as its 'spires' pointing, as it were, to a higher power, antennae, perhaps, to assemble those unseen frequencies in the mind of the attendant. Each doorway and façade reduces in size, bringing one's mind into sharp relief, as if concentrating on focusing the thought process.

Conversely, the spires rising straight up pierce the sky, a pathway to the greater God himself. As one enters the main entrance, a porthole to that deep, somber inner space, one is shunted down further and further into deepest consciousness. As the columned, arched ceiling stood above you, creating that 'womb-like' feeling of protection, surrounding you. Traveling deeper into this majestic cavern, it is the various forms of art, particularly that of the canvass art, which draw one, on an unbroken travel into that inner space of the psychic, of the mystical. One's eye follows each frame, is moved by each distinct contour of colour, centering one's mind on the theme of each. Each picture essentially providing the context of the very place and time of its telling; the mystical connection between the inner and outer man.

In this spiritual, mystical repose, one begins to wander, and once again the very structure of the inner sanctum compels the individual to look up into those majestically vaulted ceilings, feeling insignificant, knowing that the power of God must, indeed, be immense. The atmosphere is dark, and mystical, corners and pockets illuminated or dense, creating a feeling of aloneness, shared only by the paintings themselves. The mind is an amazing mechanism, and will fill in the vacancies, even if on a primordial level; the presence which one feels will overwhelm him, will consume him. His spirit then, will begin to *soar*. Perhaps, if he listens closely he, truly, will hear that 'still small voice' so often described by mystics and prophets. This edifice, truly, is the place made by man, that is the closest to the cathedral of Nature herself.

All of this, of course, began long before the 'modern' cathedrals of the Renaissance. To be sure, the complex structures, engineering, and 'typology' was an evolutionary one. The Chinese, even before the 13th century, was complex. In fact, the 'lineal-line' of history of the modern, even though not thoroughly mean spirited, does not even trace their 'cultural-civilization' as they would of the West. Any student of the West will, if he is honest, seek to understand the interrelatedness of all cultures: some to a lesser or greater extent. How much of Western technology relating to the physical sciences of architecture were borrowed or copied? Perhaps quite a lot. Chinese technology was considerably more developed then that of the early medieval West, and after the middle of the 13th century there was a fair amount of knowledge available concerning China It seems likely today, that the 'unity-of-mankind' Modern will overreach in the matter by overstating the influence of Chinese 'priority', which is undoubted, to Chinese causal influence as the hidden author of Western mechanics. But this is not necessarily on target. Consider this: The epoch we are discussing was supra-natural, and the five-hundred years, which we are over-seeing was but an extraordinary spark which shines the brighterfor our attention. There were no Chinese blueprints nor Chinese engineers available to *teach* the West. At most, there were scattered whisperings of this or that invention, or building, or science. It was, and is, the Faustian logic of our Western people: we were willing to try and emulate, from anyone, a good Idea. The kingdoms of the Levant, Africa, or India were not the same; yet, they had much greater influence, and were influenced by the Chinese civilization. The point here is that as a 'presence', or a state of mind, it was the West who stands out. Yes, the 'vision' of a people may be seen in many sciences, but Art defines the embryonic, and rising spirit.

The 'form' by which the West defined itself was changing in ways unthought-of in years previous to this renewal of the West. The Daedalic style [cir. 645 b.c.] existed before the founding of Athens. This style was considered as a marvel, an unknown expression of the social and technical achievement of the day, especially in the new science of 'sculpture'; yet when compared with Michael Angelo and Da Vinci, it lacked everything we see, today, as beautiful.

It lacked, in the modern sense, the poise, the grace, the symmetry known for the Renaissance period. When one thinks of Angelo's *David* and *Pieta*, when one thinks of Danatello and Raphael, one can understand, or begin to understand, the tremendous difference in both perspective and raw talent.

The very attention paid to detail and perspective was proof of a becoming in the 'inner soul' of the West. This was the birthing of that primordial 'will-to-express', that sense of 'ordering a thing', that sense of a 'universal perfection' of what man *could* become. It is true, regardless of what the modern wills-to-express, that people, the individual Races, show 'markers', those way signs which delineate the world's families of man, which mark them as different; the West still maintains, as do the many other peoples, those selfsame markers which we have always displayed. Inferior and Superior is a designation that is not commensurate with the modern taboo of discussing the racial differences of mankind. The West will, as long as she is vibrant and healthy, continue to embrace and live well with what she is.

Spirits such as Locke, Hobbs, Dederot, Smith, Quisnay, and Rousseau in our modern times were the children of the so-called enlightenment, which, in turn, was the child of the renaissance of Western culture. The distillation that these men participated and anticipated through the technics of their day included economics, 'myth' [the sense of history, and analysis, which was history in the pure sense]; of property rights and the most powerful of the modern 'idea' was that of the organized State. So many improvements and experiments, for good or bad, would be proposed by men like those listed above. It was their generation, their presence, who would become the role models for generations. It would all usher in the age of Technology [i.e. technics]. Men like Jethro Tull (steel plow, Arthur Bakewell (animal husbandry), James Watt (steam engine), and many others that found the tangible elements to express their will. From the *mind* of Western man, to the *hands* of Western man, this will-to-express had blossomed like no other age.

This would ever mark Western man as different, like no other before him.

Western man now had that which he could call his own: *His Mark*, shared by no other race-culture to the extent and panorama as the West could claim.

The ennobling of man was now within his reach. His capacities were myriad; each man was now becoming 'motive' [purpose], each man had value. His spirit, complex as ever, was soaring in ever- upward directions, which pointed him towards everything that was greater than himself; it was the 'humanities' in the purest sense. Ultimately, he valued what he could create; thus spoke Fredrich Nietzsche:

> *"...We created the world of will on this basis as a world of cause, a world of will, a world of spirit. The most ancient and enduring psychology was at work here and did not do anything else; all that happened was considered a doing, all the doing the effect of a will; the world to it became a multiplicity of doers; a doer was slipped under all that happened."* [emph. mine]

All this, *spirit*, *will*, *motive* and the *need* of a people manifested itself in many ways to those of the West. A spirit is part of an individual, who in turn is shared with the people at large; the will of a people becomes the spark, the 'spirit' of the extended family. For those who understand these concepts, these words, will see clearly the aspect of *'natural law'* in the living, breathing aspects of the 'presence' of the race-culture; any race-culture. In the modern world of today, one cannot discount that as inhabitants of this selfsame planet, every race-culture displays a 'consciousness' in which they seek to express themselves; only the modern would be so arrogant as to think that all must, because all are equal, act and think the same, purchase the same, eat the same 'mass-produced' meals, in short, think and create on an 'equal' par with his neighbor, discounting the immense differences in each and every sovereign people. As with all 'concepts' however, its abstraction is the centerpiece. All 'thoughts' are singular, and based on all the parts assembled to create the individual who, in turn, 'conceives' the idea.

The terms Home and Fatherland, for instance, is an 'idea'. It is hard to express – words do not adequately describe this individual spirituality. It is the 'inner and outer' man, which is so apparent in nature. Some, especially the Modern, may question the use of 'fatherland' for it is hard to comprehend in one's waking consciousness, let alone accept its consequence in today's world: it would accept, for instance, the inequality of man. Even though hard to comprehend, to those who do understand, Fatherland is a concept that is murky, filled with metaphysical connotations and establishes a thought process in each individual alone, in his own mind, and defies quantitative analysis, yet each knows 'what he knows' concerning these issues. It nevertheless is true and undeniable, in all its natural tendencies, in all cultures, to possess and act on these feelings. Such concepts are self-evident.

Oswald Spengler, seeking to understand and share these feelings as the 'prime symbol', or the will-to-express, carefully analyzed the causes and effects of that which has molded Western man. He states:

> "...And those specially Western creations of the soul-myth called 'will', 'force', and 'deed', must be regarded as derivatives of the prime symbol." [emph. mine]

Yes, everything that was, that will be, is the way-sign of Western man. He has risen, fallen, and risen again. He has had a will, a motive, and most importantly, has proved himself a People, that collection of imperatives, which define all groups. It shows the way-sign of destiny, and conforms to all the rules of nature. Science, as well, in spite of the modern, will be discussed in the following pages. Though dimly, we will see just where the West will rise again.

Chapter II

> The duality of a people and state is axiomatic.
>
> But the force behind the state has always been
>
> The people. The will of any government must
>
> Recognize this process.

The abiding truth in everything that has gone before in history, is that *people*, the race-culture, has been the very foundation of all higher-culture. It is not its technics, for this is simply *manifestation*, but it is ever anon blood and bone.

It is practical observation, the obvious, that makes us nod and gesture about this or that description of a particular nation and its people. The 'essence', which has been imbued into a place, a 'territory', that which has invoked a particular presence, has been, as always, that 'flesh and bone' which has inhabited and held a defined territory. It is this 'area' specifically, in which the 'collective group', the race-culture, calls their own. This is Homeland, fatherland, motherland; whatever the regional designation. A tribe of Scythian nomads, or a fertile city-state of the Attica peninsula could very well inhabit this area; it could be the empire of Charlemagne and Pippin; it could be the continent of North America. Moreover, each had, had to have, a place where the god's could protect them. A place were each body of water held some kind of picture, a mystical place perhaps, surrounded by mountains, trees, the blue canopy of heaven. A place where one could remember the closeness of family, grandparents, and siblings. Places where growing pains of childhood remain with one for one's entire life; inextricably bound with the memories of a 'place', a time, a territory. The Modern wills not to accept this. He *denies* family, tribe, and race. He defines all as an 'idea', something to be molded to his purchasing designs, his fast food, his idea of harmony and aesthetics, all based upon his science of the 'status quo'. He will not admit or recognize family, or tribe; the consequence not appealing to his varied tastes.

We know, however, that as long as the earth has sustained a human organism, such as family or tribe, people have congregated; they have held possessions in common; they have made war, they have made peace, but have done so as individual 'united' units.

Mankind has always confined himself to specific localities, with their distinctive habits and form, colour, social relations and religions. For this very reason, the collective body has always enacted some form of control over each other for the benefit of the *whole*. We have mentioned briefly, those particular bodies, which have been employed in each variation of Western man's evolution. Let us now inspect the relationship, the organic necessity, of *People vs. State*. How it affects the culture of the West. We will look into the responsibilities of both parties in relation to each other. We will search for the spirit of Western man, we will see it rise and fall; we will see a birth, life and senility of Western culture. All organisms have these relationships, and to study its past [birth] is to see clearly its life and senility. Thus the study of causality.

The West, like many other cultures, has been organic, that is to say, it has had at its very root, a *homogeneous* group of collective people, sharing similar traits, habits, mores, and certain particular 'physical' characteristics created after a millennia of race-history. Inherent in this body of persons, you have a natural system of selection from this body that dictates which shall serve and which shall lead. In most cases, this process has been through a violent process of elimination. Being cultured, then, means through long years of evolution, a higher culture has learned with experience what methodology works best to both maintain and extend its spiritual and physical form.

The oldest records of the West in our northern climes, specifically Nordic, the methodology closest to our 'modern' governments was the All Thing, that body of the collective leaders of the tribes and clans endeavoring to fulfill the needs and disputes of their people. The needs of the people were the needs of the Nation.

This most ancient of customs survives in Scandinavia, and the surrounding countries. The people [Folk] were always a part of these gatherings, their leaders/spokesmen having been chosen from amongst them; individuals that came directly from the village or county in which the legal dispute or need arose. When a solicitation arose, it was strictly speaking, a local affair. This people arrangement has been ambiguous at best. It is doubted that any 'perfect' form of government will ever exist; it is, and will always be, a continuing and evolving process. Governments will always follow on the heels of what had gone before. So, with every passing generation, a natural 'aristocracy' has risen to perform the basic function of leadership in government that would best serve the tribe or nation. This presupposes the long *continuity* of generations who have followed 'basic' rules of conduct, 'common law' in today's parlance, which was both easy to follow (i.e. no voluminous texts existed that could be 'perceived' one way or another) and understand, having come from local/national experiences shared by the common man.

In our 'american' experience, men like Thomas Jefferson and Samuel Adams, who wrote extensively to each other about this subject in the waning years of their lives, insisted that there was *"...a natural aristocracy among men. The grounds for this are virtue and talents...the natural aristocracy I consider the most precious gift of nature for the instruction, the trusts, and the government of society..."* [1] Jefferson was not, however, speaking literally of an inherited aristocracy, although one could make many valued criticisms as to the validity and valuable nature of this methodology; instead, he found that the 'natural order' of things to be studied and reasoned, to be worthy of consideration and in certain cases, emulation where possible. In considering Mr. Jefferson's reasoning, one could make the assertion that mankind has changed very little through its trial of 'consideration and emulation' over these many years; human nature has changed little, even in 'modern' society. The rugged travails of our evolution have done little to affect our 'inner' nature.

It is doubtful, therefore, whether any venture into our proposed future (for that is precisely what the Rise of the West is concerned with) can be expected to work very well that is not an *integral* part with that which has proved itself in our human past. But, of this future, of its end, its fulfillment, what shall it be? More importantly: Who shall take us?

The future of *any* People, race or nation, must needs be based on a certain quality, harmony, and experience (i.e. traditions, mores, perceptions and values that are an organic part of the 'entire' race-culture), which has proven

---

[1] [Intro, Quoted by] Simpson, William Galey – Which Way Western Man – National Alliance, 1978, pg. 206.

itself to be most essential to that body of persons in question. This is race history in the greater sense.

In this context, history has shown many ways and means by which to judge, and most rightly, that *end* most qualified for a superior culture, indeed, a superior people. Thus, that future, that end *worthy* to be the 'primary' object of any people's existence *is* "*...to produce the largest number of truly superior men – of robust health, overflowing energy, unspoiled instinct, mind powerful to both analyze and create, and – above all – of that integrated, masterful personality and elevated spirit that ever characterizes the truly noble man"*[2] *[emph. mine]*, must be present if an enduring people or state is to be expected. It is, therefore, that it is great men, from a great people, which must be molded, directed and formed by their environment to succeed at bigger and better things; that such great men, upon whom the people put their trust alone, can organize its life to make it basically satisfying, which supports soundness, and steers that particular culture past those perils that would attempt to disorganize the very life of its people.

The guarantee of 'happiness', on the other hand, is *not* a valid proposition necessarily, by which to base the life of a nation, such as we have been led to believe; for such a premise has led to such excess in areas from sexual relations to child rearing, which has such a bearing on our future. Happiness is counted only through the eye of the beholder, and individual license seen to be the 'right to happiness'. *Happiness, to be sure, must be the by-product of a sound and healthy people*. Hence, it is not to the 'pursuit of happiness', which thinking men and women should abide by, but that of personal greatness; that is, the *personal will,* which a great nation/society, *must* produce in *itself*.

This leads us to another area, which causes, unnecessarily, the assumption that it is the 'demos', the mass, which specifically carries the seed of greatness, in and of itself. It never has been the 'mass' specifically, which has idealized greatness, but most certainly contributes to it: "*When they [the mass] seize the helm [of government] and undertake to steer affairs in their own interests, all they can do, all they have ever done, ultimately, is to run the ship aground, and be forced in the end to return command to 'one' or the 'few'.*"[3] *[emph. mine]* that can rule wisely and efficiently for all concerned. The mass, on the other hand, 'democracy of the modern', or 'rule by the many, *as a type*', was something that, in particular, our

---

[2] Ibid, pg. 162
[3] Ibid, pg. 164

founding fathers were very careful to see we did not realize – at any rate, we do not have now – and stands apparent in the light of the history of our race-culture as the most fragile, corrupt, transparent, and least fruitful of all forms of government; since Pericles, this has been the same.

It should be self-evident, at least to all honestly intellectual people, that the 'equality' provided to the mass, at least in (democratic) theory, which unflinchingly gives equal status to those in the highest and lowest ranks of humanity leads, inevitably, to the lowering of all standards of the highest ranks to the lowest, so that the lowest mind may claim equality with the highest. This is the equality of the modern. The 'playing field', surely, offers the flat-line effect of the cadaver.

The 'right' of equality however, invariably means the 'denial' of opportunity to those of the superior few, and there are superior people; only an imbecile, or liar, would say otherwise. In fact, throughout history, despite the clamoring of egalitarians, the only reason we have evolved in every area of science, of the arts, of industry, is precisely because some individual of *superior* quality had overcome prejudice, narrow-mindedness, and social convention of the day, to 'overcome' mediocrity. The genius has never had an easy row to hoe. It is because of this personal sense of 'achievement', ambition, or vision, which has put us into the 'first world' of nations. The push for equality, by degree, can deny those persons who, living with us, an opportunity to achieve what others are simply unable to achieve, and that is simply because it may 'deny' others the accolades deserved by a particular few – *this* is un-democratic. It denies those rare, unique, costly, and valuable opportunities to be squandered by those who, at best, cannot reach the zenith of potential of our greatest intellects and spirits, if allowed to blossom and show their worth.

The West has balanced itself precariously between these two spheres of influence: Between the 'mass' and the 'few'.

In the final analysis, it is an organic process that defines the 'common solution': we must foster a *metamorphosis* of the entire body politic. In short, we must define the direction and, ultimately, create a solution best suited to ourselves, *as* a People. This has been true of the past, hence, our instruction. The West has achieved its greatness not by disallowing this evolution, rather, it has embraced change and its evolutionary continuum with revolution, new forms of government, and ideas which have shed even more light on its continuing cycles of birth, life, and senility.

Defining the People:

Origin, duty, and responsibilities.

Discussed above were those two (2) elements required for a people, a race-culture, to survive and grow: (1) *A homogeneous grouping* (i.e. biological nation*), designed to enhance those ideals inherent in the race-aspiration – or its 'race-soul'*; (2) *a territory, a place to call their own, a presence created by a singular environment.*

In looking at both these important considerations one, necessarily, sees that he is looking at this 'understanding' from the outside, looking in – this is the 'micro' element of the West – not of the individual, but of the individuals smallest collective unit and its function in relation to earth [soil], spirit [soul], and the embodiment of those particular secular restraints [i.e. government]: the *Family*.

As far back as Western cultural history (i.e. indo-European) can be studied and ascertained, it has been the family, proper, which has created, maintained, and fostered all values relating to its cultural heritage; in fact, it is our *oldest* institution. In the ancient past, the 'state' was an aggregate, not only of individuals, such as we see today, but *of* Families.

The Modern recoils at this memory. It would destabilize so many of his plans; for he has had much, of which he can be proud; he wants to continue it. The Modern would not want 'his' family traditions to be interrupted and changed. But change will come, has always come, for better or worse. As with all things organic, families change in constitution and form, just as did Justinian Rome yet, the family remains, as always, the *basis* for a sound and healthy society.

Let us, then, in the infinite search for truth, seek to detach ourselves for the moment: *Looked at objectively, without fear of favor, the family, proper, is our breeding institution. Through this institution, ultimately, defines and maintains that which will come after, that which will provide and lead our culture on its many paths to achieve its goals, endeavors, and destiny-will.* Without this family 'unit', its strength, we can have no higher-culture. This means, of course, that no effective government also, can exist.

So it is, through every succeeding generation, perhaps through centuries, that a family with a sense of worth and responsibility has held its seed sacred; instilled talent, virtue, honesty, and the highest 'capabilities' of an individual who, through wise 'marriages', carefully stored each minute grain of potential until, at last expectant with need, the 'family-energy' bursts open with desire and expectation, creating the superior person. *This person, the genius of his race.* At times this person, or persons, may be aloof, distant, even from the 'laws' of society, and seems to follow some ambiguous, or unseen path known only to himself, nevertheless follows that inner desire, that still small voice of instinct delivered to him of his family. This instinct, purified, tried through all that life may offer, ceaselessly carries the individual forward; this, the heavily charged 'will-to-express' of his ancestors – which is himself.

The modern may cry foul, as he is wont to do when jealous of an idea, or an individual. He certainly dislikes this attitude, that of the superior person(s). He claims to be content with 'humanity' as it comes; with the poor unfortunates bred into existence by dysgenic mating, for all are loved, for those who, by no fault of their own, are dull-witted, or worse, stupid, are given equal opportunity. This makes him compassionate. But the Rise of the West is not concerned with 'compassion' as the modern sees it, rather, it is Nobility. Nobility of character, of blood, of will.

To be Noble, which is being *greater than the whole*, to shout to the world the rightness and character of a higher culture means, of necessity, that one must *strive* to be 'worthy' of this refrain. Not simply limited to an individual basis, but collectively as well. National health, like individual health, starts with a healthy body – the organism of the smallest and largest of the units present – all start with the basic idea of Family, its health, and foundation. We should *want* this. We should want to create and maintain the highest quality of men and women, regardless of race or culture. *This and this alone, should be a truly Universal imperative.*

The Family will always build the *superior* person. It is the family, and one cannot say this enough, or too often, that is the *'life-womb'* of a continuing higher-culture. It is the wisely nurtured soil of the family – out of which the race-culture achieves its greatness through the individual genius – that finally creates its final and finest fruit. This is not 'social science', as the Modern continuously exhort us to believe. It is the observable, the traditional common place, day to day, facts that one can clearly see with one's own eye. It is the 'family' that everyone knows, the family who stands out: the Family that is beautiful, harmonious, intelligent, and numerically large, and is precisely these families, sadly, that are disappearing. The family, however, is not the only foundation upon which the life of its people rests; it is, however, the cornerstone of the race-culture (i.e. social mores, emotional stability, inner-strength, etc.) and that, which is built upon it. When one sees the dying vestiges, as one saw in Greece, Rome, as well as Sumer and beyond, even as we see in the West today, one knows that senility is upon us, for the very understanding of the root-strength of the family has passed away from us: We are 'civilized'. The Family, to be a real family, must be rooted in the earth. Its source must be recognizable to all which *spring* from it.

In Greece, after the Ionian invasion [cir. 1600 b.c.], *Homer* tells us vaguely of the modes of [Family] life that these 'Hellenes' were used to practicing after many hundreds of years of consistent, homogeneous, tribal life. They were, simply, individualists, independent, owned and possessed their own land, a *prerequisite* for all free people. They voluntarily joined into political decisions with their neighbors. They were Farmers belonging, as it were, to that ancient class of 'peasant stock' that was deeply rooted to the soil.[Ψ] They lived

---

[Ψ] In today's world, especially in the West of this Northern continent, it is not now generally grasped by the American population, especially those children of their European ancestors, that it is 'precisely' this class of person (i.e. the Farmer, Yeoman, or Rancher) who is responsible for the continuing strength of this People, this Nation. This 'class' of persons who, by the very sweat of their brows, have continued to feed a Nation, are rarely thanked, let alone discussed on a national level. And those who blindly partake of these labors without giving thanks for those who nourish them represent the ultimate in what has become 'modern'. True it is however, that those who once tilled the soil are increasingly leaving the land, and those not of our Western stock, taking their place. Skills may be learned by whomsoever *will* learn, and it is apparent that our own stock, Western stock, has begun that final descent into barbarism by forgetting the *root*s of their Fathers. In addition, it is with this final generation, if we do nothing, that this great and independent class of persons will cease to produce not only the yield of the field, but of the *womb* as well. It is a tragedy that has precedent, and all the great Western cultures have gone through it. The leaders of today's Western powers know this historical axiom, but address it as in ancient times: They fill the ranks of their own kind with cheap labor, with Treaties which trade out the hard-work ethic of our fathers, and fill that void with others which are 'land-poor' and struggle against oppressive governments which deny them

sparsely at home, giving impetus to the later 'christian' frugality of modern race-history. They built extra-ordinarily majestic temples for their gods and goddesses. The men of the day produced the food and crafts; the women, those garments, which would clothe the family, raise the children with her husband, and be ruled by the *Paterfamilias*. As a whole, however, not much of family life was entertained. The 'Spartan' life however, was more conducive to the family as a 'unit', with one purpose in mind: That of the creation of the warrior/protector, and all the family energy went into this end. This meant that the individual's highest aim was the protection of his unit, and by extension, his corporate unit, the State.[ϕ]

The Romans, on the other hand, were the first to *institutionalize the value of obedience*, in a demonstrable form, and finalize the 'concept' of family life. The Spartan, on the other hand, considered *duty*, proper, as the most important embodiment of the family. The 'duality' here is apparent. It is significant, that while one is a political directive, the other is organic (spiritual), yet one must come before the other. A child, for example, must be receptive to the obedience demanded of his parents before he will fully understand, in a mature sense, the demands of the State upon this duty

---

also, of land by which they could feed their own families, but would rather give in to, and go to where it is 'easier' for them. This is only human nature, as most people would rather go around the wall than through it. Compassion is due to these people, to all people who have suffered, for all people share these cycles in common; yet it is hoped that not only our Western people/leaders will realize the inevitable result of this compulsion (i.e. to those who would make money on cheap labor, making slaves of the guest worker) to make *more* money, or to simply fulfill some altruistic, well intended purpose, will be that of the total destruction of the Western man and woman from the soil itself. This cannot be allowed! Not by anyone. No leader, no political body, no human rights commission, no international treaties can be allowed to separate us from the land won at such great costs to our fathers and mothers. It is more than 'shameful' for their progeny to forget them, become lazy, and give up what was won through so much struggle and suffering. All of us must once again regain that imperative so necessary to our continued survival. Remember, the man or woman who does not control the land he lives on is a 'slave', and if one is a slave, how can one say he is truly free? FLS

[ϕ] Not in the sense of the 'modern' state. The modern sees the state as a means to 'control' the mass, for the few *always fear the many*, whereas the noble man sees the state as a means by which the people may then be served *by* the servants. The state is, in the final analysis, simply the *mode*, or *technic*, by which a People may extend themselves, seek and strive for peace, and comfort. FLS

This is Patriotism in the nascent stage.

From its birth, into life, the Roman family was larger that ours. It consisted of Father, Mother, unmarried daughters, sons, grandsons, as well as wives, clients and slaves. It was the Father, the man, who held paramount leadership, and loyalty: he was the *Paterfamilias* to his whole extended family and descendants. Consequently, the early Romans learned the first rule of government: Obedience to Authority.

We can hear the shrill cry of 'foul' from the Modern.

The Roman's first, however, owed their life to the skill of Agriculture, as have *all* indo-European peoples. So it was, that every Roman could run a furrow, and take care of their own stock. These Romans were a more connected people than the Greeks to the earth. They followed the examples of their ancestors for several centuries, never becoming materialistic in the modern sense, that is, not until their fall. They clung to the 'old ways' because they were good, because they worked. In the same stubborn way, they held on to their property rights. Gibbons, in his great treatise, *Rise and Fall of the Roman Empire*, goes to great lengths in discussing this agri-based family structure and disintegration. He [Gibbon] places the loss of Roman vitality, of which the empire needed to remain a world power (i.e. higher-culture), on the breakdown of the Family; other factors, to be sure, also coincided with this loss but, by far, the *breakdown* of the family was paramount. Sharing a considerable, and deleterious effect, was the rise of a 'matriarchal' dominance, instilled through a series of judicial imperatives, designed to level the playing field. This destabilizing process went right through the very heart and soul of Roman authority, since their very inception was based on the concept of paterfamilias. This shook the very fabric of Roman society, and never again (although many Caesars attempted to correct it) did they resume the direction and vision of their fathers.

In more modern times, we have seen Europe tossed by this selfsame storm.

The French Republic, from which we Americans, have taken many of our customs and legal applications, before Napoleon's rise to power, pressed for the 'rights' of women in many new legal areas. Every culture moves through these organic phases, and certain aspects of French society needed to be corrected/changed, as seen by us today. A certain validity to the legal maneuvers before Napoleon may be agreed, yet, by the time of Napoleon, the centers of France, specifically Paris, showed such a remarkable [even for this period of Europe] femininity in dress, speech, and decorum which so angered the general population that Napoleon met little opposition when he ultimately 'invalidated' the many legal maneuvers precipitated by this assertive liberalization of *woman and family*.

The Modern of today lays many untrue charges against Napoleon, yet we use much from the 'code Napoleon'* to this day in our modern [Western] legal

---

- First modern legal code of France, promulgated by Napoleon I in 1804. The work of J. J. Cambacérès and a commission of four appointed by Napoleon I in 1800 was important in making the final draft. The Code Napoléon embodied the private law of France (i.e., law regulating relations between individuals) and, as modified by amendments, it is still in force in that country. It is a *revised* form of the Roman law, i.e., the civil law, which prevailed generally on the Continent. It shows, of course, many specific French modifications, some based on the Germanic law that had been in effect in northern France. The code follows the Institutes of the Roman Corpus Juris Civilis in dividing civil law into personal status (e.g., marriage), property (e.g., easements), and the acquisition of property (e.g., wills), and it may be regarded as the first modern analogue to the Roman work. Not only was it applied by Napoleon to the territories under his control—northern Italy, the Low Countries, and some of the German states—but also it exerted a strong influence on Spain (and ultimately on the Latin American countries) and on all European countries except England. It was the forerunner, in France and elsewhere, of codifications of the other branches of law, including civil procedure, commercial law, and criminal law. The Quebec province and the state of Louisiana owe much of their law to the Code Napoléon. In addition to the Code Civil, Napoleon was responsible for four other codes: the Code of Civil Procedure (1807), Commercial Code (1808), Code of Criminal Procedure (1811), and the Penal Code (1811).
- *Corpus Juris Civilis*, the most comprehensive code of Roman law and the basic document of all modern civil law. Compiled by order of Byzantine Emperor Justinian I, the first three parts appeared between 529 a.d. and 535 a.d. and were the work of a commission of 17 jurists presided over by the eminent jurist Tribonian. The Corpus Juris was an attempt to *systematize* [traditional historic] Roman law, to reduce it to exhaustive order after over 1,000 years of development. The resulting work was more comprehensive, systematic, and thorough than any previous work of that nature, including the Theodosian Code. The four parts of the Corpus Juris are the Institutes, a general introduction to the work and a general survey of the whole field of Roman law; the Digest or Pandects, by far the most important part, intended for practitioners and judges and containing the law in concrete form plus selections from 39 noted classical jurists such as Gaius, Paulus, Ulpian, Modestinus, and Papinian; the Codex or Code, a collection of imperial legislation since the time of Hadrian; and the Novels or Novellae, compilations of later imperial legislation issued between 535 a.d. and 565 a.d. but never officially collected. Because it was published

system[s], which was some two to three-thousand years in the making, with England being an exception. He was 'hard' on the 'status' of women, to be sure, but through his 'code', as well as the relaxation of marital status, specifically, allowing a form of Polygamy to exist settling, perhaps for a time, the curse of adultery and divorce, which plagues all decadent civilizations.

Napoleon's view of *no* divorce after ten years may not be accepted in the Modern's society, but it was clear after Napoleon's code that married partners remained married not only ten years, but well beyond, keeping that stability so necessary to a society who seeks to *extend* stability and peace. His 'orientalism' must not frighten those who seek to better understand the organic process of nature; and if, as Napoleon said, "women are treated too well, and in this way have spoiled [or been spoiled] in everything," should be looked at as something that has occurred, and is occurring in the modern West. In anticipation of the modern to the use of someone like Napoleon, let me add that he also granted suffrage to Jews, and relaxed the measures against negroes, both of which, with time, proved onerous to the population.

It was not animosity towards 'woman' in particular, nor was it animosity toward any liberalizing trend or force that had caused events and circumstances to thwart this trend. Rather, it was from that *non*-organic social change, the absolute cultivation of it, which affected society from the top, down. It was the ancient *Fati Machi Parole Femine*. It was the *'reaffirmation' of deeds over words*; it was the ancient law of nature, with its organic understanding of all those who search and listen to the laws of nature. It was a reaffirmation of a balance in nature, made manifest by a single issue: *childbearing*. It was the knowledge that the first-fruit of every marriage, children, was becoming passé. In all civilizations, this is the benchmark of decadence. Of Death.

---

in numerous editions, copies of this written body of Roman law survived the collapse of the Roman Empire and avoided the fate of earlier legal texts—notably those of the great Roman jurist Gaius. With the revival of interest in Roman law (especially at Bologna) in the 11th century, the Corpus Juris was studied and commented on exhaustively by such scholars as Irnerius. Jurists and scholars trained in this Roman law played a leading role in the creation of national legal systems throughout Europe, and the Corpus Juris Civilis thus became the ultimate model and inspiration for the legal system of virtually every continental European nation. The name Corpus Juris Civilis was first applied to the collection by the 16th-century jurist Denys Godefroi.

In the Classical world, the question of life, and its myriad meanings, became paramount. They asked themselves: *"What am I to be?" "For what goal am I to be sacrificed for?" "Am I, as man or woman, not to be master of my own design?"* For millennia, such searching, and deeply held psychic/spiritual questions have been asked by men and women alike; for woman, these questions become 'symbolized' through the act of childbearing. Since 'woman' was the sole mechanism by which life was produced, she was then, in a position of authority to dictate certain terms in regards to the interactions between man and woman. In the modern world, woman has certainly reclaimed her 'right' to do what she will with her body, and this includes, in the Modern's creation, the destiny of the life within her as well. She has choices. *It is this point of deliberation, that of the 'weighing of pro and con' by women concerning childbirth, that inevitably points a higher-culture to it great turning point in history; its own very 'personal' history.*

At this point, begins the prudent limitations of Births.

Limitations soon, however, become widespread, rampant both in design and understanding. It becomes accepted as an 'individualistic imperative' held mostly by women who now recognize its limitation as their only source of power in a world run by power. It is the ultimate act of selfishness. To empower oneself, it is not requisite to force one down; but inevitably, this will occur. But to hold hostage a burgeoning life, is the ultimate 'deed' of the modern. In the Classical world, this practice was denounced by Polybius as the 'ruin of Greece", yet, even at his date, the greatest of Greek cities practiced it; in subsequent Roman times, it become profusely common in practice. As this occurrence became commonplace, so also, the changing mores of choosing a mate.

A Man's preference of 'woman', who is to be, not simply the mother of his children, like the most singular rudimentary understanding of the common folk and primitives, but his own compatriot, friend, or fellow traveler for life, then, becomes a problem of personal views: Freedom to be all one can be begins to assert itself.

This type of marriage appears, as it were, as a *contradiction*, which the Modern still expects the masses to 'accept'. This 'type' is a liberal contradiction, which stresses the spirituality and affinity between both parties. They are now both free. Free, that is, as 'units' of individual intelligence; free from the simple, organic urge of the blood, to carry on at any cost. This lack of race-consciousness enables certain men to shout to the world that unless Woman repudiates her sense of womanliness, her obligation and duty to her husband, to her very blood, her children, even to her very social environment, to the organic laws of nature, and to everyone but herself, she cannot set herself free. This concept, of course, stands apart from the natural prime symbol of woman – that of Mother; this always industrious, intelligent and consistent woman who, being a part of the whole, sees herself as part of the earth, an extension of its natural being, its rhythms and cycles, as well as her culture, in which she is, in large part, responsible. Yes, she is mother, understanding all that this title entails; she would have it no other way. The Modern, of course, cries foul. After all, woman owes 'nothing' to no one; she is *modern* as well.

What has devolved from these higher aspirations of woman and higher-culture in general, such as was held in Greece, Rome and early America, is now that strange 'der Geist der stets ver neint'. Instead of child, of duty, woman has 'conflicts of the soul'. To her, today, marriage is the 'art of war', and is to be used for the advancement of that 'mutual understanding between woman and man'; that they both belong to themselves, alone. Yes, they both belong to themselves, and they will both be barren, leaving nothing by which the future will know them. Alone, together, they will share in the ultimate selfishness. Yet, perhaps, these individuals are a solution to the very problem facing the West.

It is to the 'fruitful' that we owe the rise of higher culture. We must recognize, and I venture to say that a majority feels this way, that anything which does not facilitate the race-culture in a physical, or spiritual sense is, consequently, to the detriment, to the denial of, higher-culture. The time, the place, the race, or culture makes no difference. The Family, then, is the sole basis of all unity and strength. The spirit and organic unity, that very continuity of individual presence, manifest in both its cultural and personal progress on which a higher-culture is built. So, also, the Rise of the West. The origin and strength of a higher-culture is but a part, albeit an important one, to this discussion. It must be shown that as the biological nation grows, it will, of necessity, assume many responsibilities inherent to its rate of growth or cultural destiny.

The Modern however, rejects any concepts of this nature, not because he fears it necessarily, but because he knows, he cannot control it. Whether this system is good or harmful is not my intention to decide at the moment, of the future either, this alone depends on the situation in which this system, or any system would find itself confined. What is good for the race-culture, whatever its name, is good simply because it is a factor in continuing the race-culture in the direction that is good for its people.

It has been said that the mass is feminine in nature, and must needs be led by a manly group or individual, which the mass will follow. This simple truism is a historical fact. The few examples of Hamurabi, Alexander, Caesar, Napoleon, Louis XIV, and Frederick of Prussia all show just how justified the above truism is.

Whatever the arbitrary will of the people, this will-to-express was made manifest in the exploits of her great leaders: Joan de Arc, was a recent exception to the [military] rule, but the point is still that it always takes the great personality, that essential 'spirit' of nobility, to carry the mass to its potential. It is only when this pyramidal system becomes contrary to the collective good that revolutions have served to end a perceived or real absence of leadership and, by extension, their movement, if they no longer serve the people by which they deem to secure a future.

What, then, truly, are the responsibilities of People vs. State? Has the West, in particular, showed any lasting ability to maintain itself in this fashion? More importantly, does the West continue to maintain these responsibilities?

ii.

The People

As plant-life is related to nature in a biological sense so, also, is a distinct People [race-culture] as a *biological* nation. It is this large body of persons, which make up a known and distinct culture, this is self-evident; for we know a specific culture by the very character of its people in manners, physical looks, mental aptitudes and national outlook (i.e. how the nation as a whole looks at its role in the world, as well as its national imperative). This people/body characterizes itself by those things listed above through long years of race-culture, that ongoing evolutionary struggle with itself and with others; the land, which they inhabit also, contributes to this effect, making some nations resilient, making others soft and content. In varying degrees, the destiny-will of each culture, which provides for the 'outward' [technical] expressions of its people, will show itself. The mass, as the single largest collective force, owes no allegiance to any power other than its own 'will-to-express' which, in essence, is its will to *survive*. No law, no power, no government has the right or need to try and circumvent this imperative.

Survival is pure instinct.

Carl Jung, in his study into 'prime symbols', saw this very process at work in the conscious and unconsciousness mind, when he said: "These psychic contents might fittingly, be called subliminal, on the assumption that every psychic content must possess a certain energy value in order to become conscious at all"[4] Jung acknowledges the inherited factors of blood, yet would rather call this process 'intuition' rather than the more descriptive designation 'instinctual actualization' which presupposes instinct to be inherited by past generations, genetically, showing itself in the visible actions of each particular subject. For an example, let us discuss two subjects in particular: the Yucca Moth and Cicadas.

The Cicadas, in a non-variable seventeen-year cycle, emerge from a silent, solitary 'nymph' evolution. They emerge, at the end of this cycle, by the millions. Living only a short six-week cycle, they nevertheless reproduce, laying their eggs in the branches of trees, and dying by early July. The cycle then, begins again. August brings the eggs to fruition as nymphs, which fall to the ground, crawl into cracks in the soil, and once again start their seventeen-year cycle.

The Yucca Moth, likewise, follows this strange odyssey. This moth goes to the flowers of the Yucca, which open during night only. The moth takes pollen from each flower and kneads it into a small ball; he then seeks another flower. Slicing this kneaded ball, he lays its eggs between the ovules and packs the ball into the funnel shaped pistil of the flower. The important aspect of this subject is that this only happens once in his life. Only one fraction of his

---

[4] Jung, Carl – Instinct and the Unconscious, The Portable Jung, The Viking Press, 1971, pg. 52.

allotted time on earth, as our reckoning goes, is spent in this operation. But, this process is always carried out.

What do we call this? Is this process called intuition or instinct? What is it, which allows these small creatures the knowledge, the know-how, to do these complicated maneuvers? What allows this actualization to manifest itself, time after time, in the same unfailing fashion? Perhaps science will never agree as to which element takes precedent. Whichever the case, whether it is environment or heredity, it is apparent that the 'mass', like these creatures, share a certain instinct, proclivity, direction, call it what you will, as a mass, which are not simply learned habits of mores of social conduct. It is logical, therefore, that certain examples of human traits are passed down to us through the continuum of genetic heredity (i.e. race-memory).

All organic creatures know what they are. They instinctively know what to do: What is healthy or harmful; what is pleasant or unpleasant. Human [organic] creatures are no different. In the modern's world however, we have been cut off, the ancient memories blotted out because of bad food, propaganda, and the lack of will with which to follow our instincts.$^{\Psi}$ The governments of the modern West are afraid to allow these instincts to remain in the forefront; for it demands a certain position, which presupposes a genetic link with the past, with tradition. All species feel this inborn quality rising, and seeking release in the youth of every generation. But these instincts run 'counter' to the Modern's alliance between divergent racial stocks with which he has made compromise.

In ages past, following one's ancient history was called, simply, *Folkways*, and bespoke the simple harmony of conduct, traditions, mores and customs of a people. A sound and healthy people accepts this as a natural part of their

---

$^{\Psi}$ It is apparent that it is specifically those laws and forms of punishment in today's modern world, which are nullifying those natural and noble instincts, which makes it possible for every race-culture to survive. If those in power are concerned with money, at the expense of intellect, as some would assert, then it is genocide, at the very least, to prohibit those of like kind from associating together; giving and taking in marriage, living in 'groups' together, as communities, and voting in [racial] blocs, would more than likely be the case if a group were to 'think' as a group. If it is money which dictates the future of all races, and if we are only economic 'units' then, as organism, as a living breathing creature, we are certainly dying, if not dead already. Certainly, we are not free to achieve those dictates of our own consciousness. Once again, free-will belongs to a free people. FLS

race-culture. They accept it because it has endured. They accept it is as something that expresses themselves, above all others, as a unique and satisfying experience, which must, at all costs, be extended.

In a biological nation, one which presupposes close racial affinity, it is self-evident that anthropological *inequality* is the norm; so, in this same sense, is societal value, that is, in the physical sense. That all men [i.e. of the same race] should be equal or alike in every sense is contrary to all the facts of nature and conditions of human life. Of necessity, we must have a balance between categories and subdivisions of equality; in any event, this is what we have. Thus does nature speak, and man is part of nature. Yet, man is not totally subject to nature. But he *is* subject. This has been Western man's struggle throughout the ages.

Man, outside of nature, is in 'control' – he is the only animal to do this. "Only through laws and perceptions of equality can [he] we provide each other with a common structure of government; a structure that will always lift the one up, never bringing the other down."[5] The paradox however, is that man is never truly apart from nature. Even his laws, his mechanism of control over the elements, must be consonant with 'nature's' law. If his laws are contrary to nature, in the end, he will fall short of his goals. His actualization running contrary to his elements.

The 'system', which promotes these laws and perceptions, is that government or state which has *de jure* right to lead. This government or state will 'lead' the people, in essence, if both share the same traditions and mores, but can never truly 'rule' them, except through force. Without both parties sharing these same perceptions and laws, these same laws will, of necessity, become self-serving to whichever class has gained power – and that inevitably becomes the State: It is the duty and responsibility of the people, in relation to their State (i.e. chosen form of government), to *maintain* that which is healthy for them, their specific race-culture. This is simply a matter of survival. If they do not attempt this, then, their survival is dependent upon factors unrelated to their survival, and they will die, slowly, to be sure, but they will die.

Power is survival. Traditionally, power was held by strong houses made up of Families, chieftains, or some other autocratic body, which was usually a direct

---

[5] One Nation – 1987, NPAP Press.

product of the masses. It was not a collective army that owed specific allegiance to Agamemnon when he decided to attack the city of Troy. Rather, it was to the local family 'princes', and houses that voluntarily [some will admit coercion] came to the call of the King. In any event, it was a 'mass' response, by those who felt the same stinging insult heaped upon them by the theft of Helen. The Greek City 'states', unlike today ruled, and was ruled by dictators, and authority for authority's sake; yet this pyramidal system [i.e. rule from the top down], as the Modern would hide from us, was totally consonant with its people, with their aspirations, and did not alienate the people from their leaders. As stated before, only when the shepherd(s) became enamored of power for powers sake, did any telling revolt take place.

While the modern may well find the conquering of a people over a possible willing 'femme fatale' distasteful, it is incumbent on one to understand the spiritual condition here: One was slighted, *all* reacted.

Power, while being *a priori* to survival, is also a constant changing force in any higher culture. Since power by 'the people' cannot be gauged effectively until generally mobilized, it is to those State controlled arms of 'delegated' authority by which a National culture is determined. It is axiomatic that power is directed or controlled by the Ruling class. Those belonging to this class of persons who rule their fellows are, of necessity, of the same race-culture, at least in the beginning. In modern times however, this has changed, and is constantly changing in a dysfunctional manner. This modern age, not unlike those in ancient times, has provided a new class of leaders, which defies the intention of the so-called democracies. It is no longer the 'mass', that embryonic reserve of the 'superior person', which define the leader's of the modern; this reserve is now drawn from the Industrialist and Money lender of the Machine Age. It is now the merchant.

This designation then becomes, as before, a perception of values, for one cannot exclude these groups from any gain rightly or honestly made. A State, however, guided and controlled by these fiscal powers, as they seem to always serve interests that may or may not be in accord with the organic continuum of the host race-culture; for the primary duty and responsibility of the State has always been:

"...To protect the tribe, or closely related group of persons that do, and have sought, mutual protection and sustenance from one another, with the hope that, in sharing these prescribed responsibilities, the group would grow, gain more control of territory, thereby increasing their area of strength, while also guaranteeing the future of their children, and defining a territory [nationhood] for that people."[6]

This, and only this, is the primary duty and responsibility of any government in relationship with its people. All other considerations must be in accord with the destiny-will, or the will-to-express of this same people. The actualizations of the present presence must be from their very soul.

These conditions, of course, change with time, precisely through the process of birth, life, and senility of every higher-culture. It is only through careful introspective analysis that one may observe and, thereby, prepare for these eventualities of change. This will assure the higher-culture of maintaining its direction and healthful vigor. If, then, these observations and careful analysis are made, if the sum is agreed upon, and the eyes that see, see the present presence which surround them, and admit that these responsibilities are not being met with vigor and constant appraisal then, what of it? Has not the balance between People and State gone to the last of all organic phases, senility? Do the promises yet remain unfulfilled?

The West has maintained these 'organic precepts' as well as any other. The Chinese, as well, have maintained one of the single most powerful higher-cultures in history, sharing antiquity with that of the West. Unlike the West however, this race-culture seeks that greater personal introspective spirituality which seeks to be at one with the cosmos; while the West, in finding its own spirituality, seeks ever to express itself upwards, and beyond, through the doing of the 'act'. This 'act' shows itself in the 'Finis Coronat opus'; it is 'the end' which crowns the work. This is Western man's mark. It marks him forever different. Truly, it is his never-ending struggle, his striving for achievement, which will crown the works of his millennia. It is certainly as true, that this work can only be achieved through that system of government inherently a part of his Culture. It will protect the individual, the tribe, and the

---

[6] [see] Political Position Paper – National Pan-Aryanist Party, pg. 7, 1989, NPAP Press.

soul. It will seek to ennoble the very essence of 'self'. This is the practical, truthful, and proper explanation of the State.

iii.

The Will [force] and Direction of Government

Government is the *technics* of the mass.

Government is the outward manifestation of its Race-Culture. It shares, or one could say, 'should share', the mores, traditions (e.g. common-law, precedents, customs), and combined historical outlook of the entire body of persons making up the Nation. As experience teaches us however, technics will always take on a life of its own in the systematic evolution of all organisms through birth, life, and senility. It may be that these changes in technics will be considered good or bad by those which stand to lose or gain power over their particular agendas; to protect these investments, sometimes literally, a monolith of control, that is to say, a government large enough to control whatever may chance to arise and disrupt it, had to be created. Hence, the concept 'bigger is better' was justified.

The literal growth of individuals, nationally, becomes the Race-Culture with the passing of time, so also, its technics. Western culture has always evolved within this cycle of change, and has created various 'forms' of government to deal with the ongoing role of 'people vs. state'. In this age however, technics, as a tool 'of and for the People', has become synonymous with overt control, manipulation of the press, and behavior modification on a mass scale for the purpose of directing the life of the 'the people' to the aims and goals of persons who are, for the most part, out of step with the 'host race-culture' of the West.

These persons who control the technics of our age, through an ongoing process, have convinced the people that bigger armies, buildings, and 'bigger and better' government are essential to a free world; yet the bigger the government then, conversely, means that its [government] will or force of will becomes, as rudimentary probability will show, as BIG as the technics of government have become. In other words, the force of a government is matched simply by its very size. This has always been seen as the natural outcome of any civilization, which, seeks to extend itself for as long as possible. It is simply the birth, life, and senility of every organism.

The largest organic manifestation of the modern Western technic has been the ascendancy of that ever-encroaching 'mechanism', *over* man. Bigger and faster machines seemed the panacea of capitalism, for absolute production was the art of the Modern; but in doing so, he ensured that ever 'brutal and microscopic man, his capacity ever smaller, to fulfill the spiritual and esoteric truths of his 'inner soul'. Ever 'less' was his sense of aspiration and manly self-discipline, which is, ultimately, his mark of nobility, and which lies at the very root of his 'genius' – true Aristocratic Nobility – which will lead, ultimately, to that very disintegration of that 'noble character' under that unpleasant reality of the 'mob', that dearest of maneuvers, so loved of the Modern who, having no direction, other than its own 'direction', its own needs, devolves to the level, that inevitable level, of the mediocre and selfish 'mass man'. This, of course, levels all to the lowest 'value' of the one mind, the ethos' of the smallest and meanest; this, the continuing experiment of the modern 'equalitarian'.

It is, then, in consequence, that this 'value of the mechanism', this value given to 'production', is the *true* value, the true *sense* of 'god', in which the Modern has placed his values. It is part of his present and future presence. But has this method, this 'value' proven itself through the ages?

It has not.

This force/value, this 'technic of the mechanism', has not come to fruition in Western man's perception of himself as a Noble man, as a character, which holds to the spirit, as well as the body, in harmonious union. He, the Modern, happily seeks the bigger and faster machine, while remaining microscopic in outlook, as well as meaner, or low born, in his daily intercourse with his fellows. His laws increase proportionately, and his spirit grows meaner in order to overcome his opponents. He shows not that care and compassion so readily needed for a social organism to survive. Swept away by the daily demands upon his time by unrelenting machines and their owners, his pace is unnatural, artificially keeping pace with something that is, inherently, non-human. His natural needs and duties are now subsumed by the need and duties of the 'mechanism'. The technics of this age however, were to bring 'all mankind' that equity, that equality of labor and production so sought after by the [French] Revolutionists. It was to bring Democracy.

Democracy, or at least a 'form' of democracy, has been brought to bear upon every established Western, and even non-Western countries, not by simple ballot, but through the force of arms, revolution, assassination, kidnapping, fiscal maneuvers and the like, to prove that democracy works; that is, which 'speaks' for the mass.* The Modern is used to 'coercion', in the name of 'democratic' ideals – hence the 'proof' that it works. Coercion, especially under the colour of 'law', at whatever level, has been the driving force behind 'all' forms of government, including the Modern's vision of 'democracy' since the 15th century.

In his writings on the German philosopher Goethe, G.H. Lewes gives us a view of the precepts and form of democracy demanded of by the [democratic] revolutionaries of France [of which the hungry American revolutionaries suckled from], which numbered three principle characteristics promulgated by these revolutionaries which, to Goethe, were the ultimate in absurdities:

---

* The simple examples of Haiti, Somalia, South Africa, Bosnia, and places relatively obscure to many, should show any knowledgeable person what is meant here; to the student of history, it is only verification of what is meant here. It is not for any 'democratic policy', which has brought such force of arms and propaganda to bear in these many and diverse places. It is to the 'hegemony of power' alone, which has brought the Modern to call for *'democratic supremacy'*. As the 'Whiskey Rebellion' and 'War between the States' will show, the Modern has displayed his devout need to control the 'masses', the diverse children of 'his' grand experiment, and form them in his own image, has been the way-sign of *his* idea of democracy. It remains the same today. The most telling has been the Modern's inroads into the European theatre, and not in the dessert of the Middle East, as many would suppose. Danger is always brought to the masses as if looking through a glass darkly. National *retrogression* has been the logical step in relation to this trend. The feeling of antipathy by the populace for the governmental technics of today is to be expected, adding, also, the weight of 'such diverse ethnic imperatives, which cry out to be heard, has forced the hand of the Modern by destroying and murdering those who would declare themselves independent of this control. The escalation of this attitude is also obvious given the rate of disease and crime brought on by the ridiculous attitude of 'open immigration' and the *de*-Nationalization of this continent. It all comes down to 'who' will control the destiny of the mass, and the nation as a whole. Each man must decide his own fate, and discover which fate is best for both himself, and his fellows. FLS

> The first was the doctrine of equality; not simply in the eyes of the law (this was accepted), but of 'absolute equality'...the second revolutionary principle was the doctrine of government by the people...the mob became the tyrant...the third revolutionary principle was, that political freedom is necessary to man...[emph. added][7]

Over the past five-hundred years, Western man has come to believe these tenets with the utmost veracity, so as to cringe at any criticism whatsoever regarding his monopoly of power based, as it were, on anything but the democratic process.

To accept democracy however, one must believe that every 'man's opinion has its worth equal to that of the next man's'. This, of course, is the accepted appearance of the democracy of the West. But to the waking eye, it is obvious that something is wrong with the machine, with the process by which we have put so much faith in; as Lawrence Brown points out however, democracy *"...in operation is not concerned with everyone's opinion – that is merely its technical form – but only with the organized opinion of those whose opinion's can be made politically 'effective'."*[8] *[emph. added]* All these points must be addressed in the context of the Modern for, ultimately, the source of the government must now dictate which of these conditions, namely, 'equality', if it be admitted that such does exist, or the simple-minded 'appearance' of equality in the [organized] political process, governs the West.

The legacy of modern Western governments, that is, the modern Nation/State, branched from two main sources, neither of which was truly democratic: Hereditary and Elective leadership. Of these two forms, 'hereditary leadership' was the first 'great' leadership technics of the West, and was seen in the formation of the 'absolute' Monarchy; the monarchy, in turn, was the progeny of the original system by which 'the people' chose their king by affirmation; the 'rule' of 'rule by divine right' came much later. Elective government, akin to what our early efforts on this continent would show us, was based on the 'leadership principle', that is, based upon merit: merit based on 'character', 'personality', and 'example' which was the day to day habits and conditions of life that created the 'character' of the person chosen, and by which the people felt a certain affinity. Close living approximation aided in

---

[7] Lewes, G.H. – The Life and Works of Goethe
[8] Brown, Lawrence R. – Might of the West, pg. 482, Joseph L. Binns, 1978

this effort; we have a harder time of it, simply because it is 'hard to know' who we choose for our leaders. Constitutional government is a relatively new form of technic, since with time the formulation of 'legal nuance' comes with the complex form of national legal systems, which are the inevitable outcome of 'modern' civilization. Anyone who takes any time whatsoever to observe what is going on around them will, of necessity, see the multitudinous amount of Lawyers and their hangers-on. Lawyers, by definition 'study and practice law' for the betterment of the social politic. When the 'size' of government dictates the presence of so many lawyers, the common man is removed, and then again, from the system which was 'designed' for the common man. A system in which a man could defend himself, without benefit of a lawyer. Constitutionalism was designed to provide a 'simple' set of guidelines for the public to follow. Here, then, does the irony of the moment become manifest.

Constitutional States are seen, today, by the modern, as the growth of 'civilization' over that of barbarism; the Modern does not question the accuracy of this perception – but would, if he were honest. We, therefore, 'the posterity' of those who 'defined our constitutionalism', those of us who 'love' and 'care' for our Nation and its living Culture, must question this perception, and we will.

From Sargon the Great, Hamurabi, Cyrus and Alexander; from Alaric, Charlemagne, Louis XIV, from the Magna Carta to King George I, the struggle between the race-culture and those who formed and developed its technics (i.e., form of government), were continually striving for dominance. This, the continuing struggle [duality] necessary for a people to grow and overcome themselves. When all the smoke has cleared from these various combats, and the field becomes visible to us one again, it allows us to see what was not understood readily by us 'in the eye of the storm'. Each particular struggle between dominant and opposing parties was part of the natural rhythms and cycles of our culture. The people, ultimately, know what is best for their future, even if unable to articulate themselves to others, like the modern.

Each particular form or technic of the past has its 'supporter' and 'detractors', depending upon who considered what is bad or good; it should be remembered that even during the American Revolution it was the thought of the day by most of the 'leading' citizens of the Revolution to make George

Washington a 'King' in the manner of the English, a system that most 'educated' men of the day were conscious of, knew both its good and bad character. The early American revolutionaries were not fighting 'rule by a King', but were fighting the 'how' of that rule. They struggled against an aristocratic system, which had failed them; and which [the ruling system] did not readily understand the tremendous power that open spaces and freedom can give men. The English forgot what their own beginnings had wrought through 'struggle and change', through sacrifice and blood. In this case, like so many others, it was that pyramidal system, or its officer corps, which had become estranged from the consciousness of the many. It is interesting, then, that in the above context democracy, as such, was an illusion — for it was a single head [in both cases] that controlled the body. The previous 'age', just as with the new, had produced great events, and the 'great' men that anticipated them. The paradox was that this flowering had taken place at the very time in which 'complete' autocratic control was paramount.

That the flowering of the West was seen during the lives of men such as Petrarch, Louis XIV, Erasmus, Cervantes and Locke who, each in turn, either made his way in a most tempestuous world, or as in the case of Louis XIV, made his world out of tempest, is an anomaly to the Modern who deems 'equality on all levels' essential to a progressive State. Yet 'democracy' in this era of change and vitality, as an 'institution', was not a reality anywhere. Aristotle remarked in the third century [b.c.] that "...almost all things have been found out", but added that "...some [things] have been neglected, and other which have been known have not been put into practice." And so, the great experiment continues in each and every age. Doubts and ambiguities continue to be a part of the continuing story of the West. As such, the West continues to have second thoughts concerning the changing of the guard, of which post the Modern dutifully protects; the Modern is afraid of losing *his* hegemony over the thoughts and minds of those who make up *his* democracy, *his* civilization. Moreover, why should he? Is not the West already civilized?

Civilization, just as in the cycle of birth, life, and senility, is that senility, that ossification of the 'soul and body', which points the way of death. It is, and is ever, the simple static control, *of* control. If this control, this civilization of the Modern, truly represents the volksgeist of the Western race-culture, such as we admit today then, it is truly, the race-culture that is decadent. Its demise is assured. The only remnant of the great Roman was his 'judicial' legacy; of the

Greek, only his 'classicism'; of the People, nothing. Therefore, with time, shall the West also be. Each organism in turn, evolving into another phase of birth, life, and senility; of its cycle of change. We, as a people, should not be afraid of this probability however, but rather acknowledge its potentiality; and if we are not afraid to do this, when it comes, it will come with our understanding and conscious deliberation as to its merits or demerits. Ragnarok may come early, or it may come late, but when it does come, it does not have to be the end of the world.

Let me say, here an now, that I am not 'anti-democratic', yet, since we, our Western Culture, have evolved into – now out of – a democracy, let us be fair and concise on this subject peculiar to the West, specifically of America in which we live, and to whom I generally address this work. We, like our race-culture before us, have grown into this setting (i.e. government, social conditions, financial, etc.), it is not a 'do or die' blueprint of our established condition of life; "…neither race alone nor its setting can account for the outcome, but the two together in their interactions."[9]

In this light, let me once again remind you of the 'primary end', which all people create government and social technics, and that is to confront and meet the needs of its own life, establish conditions for its continuation, and protect and nurture it. Any organism that does not protect itself from destruction does not deserve, nor will it, survive. This is simply Nature's Law. In a democracy, it is the [theoretical] 'will' of the majority consensus, which dictates the terms of its own existence and, as we have seen, if that people is not conscious of that particular 'presence' then, that force [i.e. will] of its 'system' will, of necessity, decide for them.

A People's will-to-express is directed, not to the ambiguous expression of thought or action but, rather too, and for themselves, their kind, and those to whom they share similar values and specific characteristics by which, in turn, they distinguish themselves from other peoples. This living, breathing *organism*, is the race-culture. Its purpose: To live more completely, to live in fashions that are natural to their spirits which, long ago, proved itself worthy to best suit their disposition in achieving their aims in life. This specific nature will carry itself in the 'root and stock' of its people which, in its determination

---

[9] Simpson, William Galey – Which Way Western Man?, pg. 182, National Alliance, 1978.

to carry on, will endeavor to pass on to its future progeny the same characteristics, and to 'establish' them for the future; in the hope that the same way they looked at God, the Universe, Nature, at each other, would never die. This would allow themselves, as well as their children, to maintain and advance themselves against their enemies, and retain their social forms which would not only last long, but would be satisfying to their taste and instinct.[Ψ]

This actualization is not simple stability, far from it. Stability always becomes the stagnant principle. By and of itself, it is never enough. A healthy people, a 'true' higher culture, wills not only to last long, it seeks to be itself for as long as possible meaning, that certain upheavals will be necessary to continue that actualization. A vigorous people will always preserve its identity. Any government, be that 'democracy', 'republicanism', 'oligarchy', 'autocracy', or 'dictatorship' that fails to bear this end in mind, is bound to fail: It is no longer healthy. It is passing from its dawn, into its twilight. It has entered into its own 'transvaluation of all values'; it is now decadent.[β] So, we see in the

---

[Ψ] Cf. Carl Jung's – Instinct and Unconsciousness – Viking Press, for a profound study and discussion into this quality. I have referred many times to this process in human development, and must reiterate the tremendous advantage of one who is able to know himself or herself in this fashion. It is the 'still, small voice' of human kind, which allows us to travel to the stars, to build great empires, or to simply look at one's surroundings unlike the other animals. We may have added reason, as such, but the quality of instinct, that metaphysical manifestation of the inner soul of man, must be brought out of the black hole in which it has been thrown, and brought back into our political and personal lives. Instinct presupposes survival, for how have we survived for so long if not actively using it? Trust your instincts; be loyal to yourself, which is your race multiplied a million-fold.

Let me add in passing as well, that amongst the 'aryan tribes', that of the Celtic peoples, in particular, share a highly tuned 'sense' of instinct. Poetry, Art, Trades, are so highly based on 'mystic' intuition, to mark them as 'unique', if not a 'higher' type of *'intuitive types'* amongst their brethren. The Germanic elements are highly evolved, just as are the more northern elements but, for whatever the genetic/spiritual reason, the Celtic People's have been gifted with this ability to 'discern' qualities: the qualities of 'dreams', of the 'mysticism' of elemental confluences, and generally, the *mood* of individuals. There is so much more – but that is for another time. FLS

[β] Decadence shows a lack or inability to maintain a 'moral' imperative. It is 'decline' in the purest and most elemental sense; it is a 'process', which acts over a certain period of time to change the fabric and the 'face' of the nation or people in question. The Modern has foisted this state upon the West with much ado, since he is self-indulgent; he supports the same in others. Being 'self-indulgent' to a point is certainly 'human', it is the *uninhibited value*, the excess, which is so negative to the value and

West. The 'force' of the democracies of the West has brought consistent and constant change to their environments. To a point, this has proved positive, yet every 'duality' must have balance. Through historical observation, one can see that every healthy people have 'hated', 'feared', and resisted change necessitated by constant 'readjustment'. When this [cultural] change continues beyond a balanced equilibrium, that unconscious perception of self, it becomes a shock to both body and soul; it truly becomes a 'culture shock' to use a well know euphemism. Like a tree, matured after long seasons of growth, for generations, one cannot pluck it from its rooted place in the earth, move it, again and again, and expect it to remain healthy, or even to live long. So, it is, with the race-culture of the West. It will resist this method of control, of disease. It will erect barriers against ideas and bodies foreign to itself. It will not allow those that are not part of their blood, customs, mores, and traditions to exist amongst them. Can an Oak then, be grafted with a Redwood and remain an Oak? It is the same with those of the West. Either it must preserve itself and its distinctive character(s), or it must, and will, cease to be a People. The passing senile democracies however, have done this very thing!

The primary imperative of any people is its own survival – above *all* others. This is the 'natural' state of Nature. This is the 'way' of Nature. This is Life, like it or no. To this end should that same people's government exists for. Any other need is unacceptable! To dilute the higher-culture with foreign race-cultures and ideas is to subvert the very goals and worth of Western man, which is, and has always been, the ennobling of man. For if, Western man fails in this endeavor then, truly, all mankind will wallow in the filth and decadence of death. The Modern admits this, but only 'obliquely', through the canard of international politics; he is loath to admit the racial/cultural implications of our unique systems, for this would 'alienate' his alliances. He

---

spirit of Western men and women. Morals, as well, is problematic today, since we do, as a people, have a 'sense' of morality' it is akin to metaphysics, yet is more quantifiable, insofar as we have 'codified' such morality since our beginning, and 'traditionally', we have abided by those precepts, but today, we are not allowed, in many cases, to follow traditional moral direction. Tradition, as an 'institution' is what the modern reacts to the most, for it is through Tradition and Hierarchy, that system of levels, of 'bearers' and 'non-bearers' which aids and guides the 'people' for long durations. A people who admit a certain 'status quo' which is alien to their origins, will always live a 'dual' life, a *schizophrenia* which will, ultimately, destroy them, if not corrected. FLS supports his allies, because it is 'good for business', at the expense of those he claims to protect and serve. The modern serves too many masters. Since the turn of the 20th century however, the West, as a people and culture, has been directed to do this very thing, against its will and instinct. The West has been led astray.

The 'great experiment', for that is precisely what our own American beginning is founded on, is being held up to the masses as a 'continuing' experiment – this means that up till now, it has not worked out exactly as it should. Somehow, we are to comprehend some 'bigger and better goal' to be reached, in spite of what has gone before. Somehow, we must seek a 'better' goal: To that One World. To that One People. No more Higher Culture, simply man as 'mass-man'. The driving force of the modern is that of mediocrity. The leveling of man is assured against that spiritual height of the ennobled man. This is the end of Western man if allowed to continue; it is the end of his government and all associated institutions brought about by his millennia of social evolution. It must be remembered, it must never be forgotten, that institutions, morals, spirit, education, in short, a culture may, with time and restricted 'interaction' with its past achievements, lose its way, become less than what it was, simply because it has 'forgotten' what it was. Hence it is more than invaluable for each of us, you and I, to inculcate, teach, and instruct ourselves and our children, in those unique and varied 'trades' – carpentry, plumbing, architecture, engineering, agriculture, science, farming and technology – and all the diverse elements requisite for our day to day survival, and the future survival of ourselves as a People, without the disparate and temporary support of foreign workers/skills.

It is, perhaps, at this point where the going gets rough for some spirits. If we have disagreed at all up to this point, it is nothing compared to what lies ahead. The differences we may share may be caused by our own distinct reading and decipherment of what has gone before. This may simply be a matter of 'values and perceptions'; it may simply be a matter of taste. No matter. I must forewarn you, the reader, that at this juncture we may not be able to pass together through the mountain pass ahead: He who does not wish to face, completely, his own way of life, or that of his kind, is without the needed intellectual concern for 'value'. Without 'this' value, he immediately places himself in the same category as the 'rabble', of those persons whose every word and outlook and, yes, whose very world-outlook, reveals that they seek only after peace, security, and contentment; of those who are afraid to be strong in the higher qualities of life; those who ever ask to be excused from any requirement upon them for self-discipline or thoroughness of life. If you are this type of person, alas, the difference may be too great to surmount.

With such a person as cannot see this value, no common cause can now be made. When one calls 'something' white, while the other calls it black; when one calls 'something' good, while another calls it evil, it is time then, to part company – accepting no compromise. To those of you however, who would search for truth, I sincerely hope that you will join in this continuing travel.

iv.

Democracy:

The People's Choice?[*]

Democracy is a term used often and loosely in the modern West.

The 'movement' or 'desire' of a People to gain control of 'government' (i.e. system, form, or technics), and put that government into their own hands, seems always to be connected with, or to follow on the heels of, a failure of some 'aristocratic form of government' whose sole duty it was to protect their closely connected tribe, state, or nation (i.e. race-culture) but, in its *failure* to protect and uphold that selfsame race-culture, fell from grace in the sight and perceptions of their People – their race-culture. It also points to the value placed on Tradition, for if the people have been quiet, peaceful, yes, even happy, then that 'particular' form of technic which has led that people was 'good' in the only way that one may rationally judge it. No matter what that technic is called. If their happiness was changed to anxiousness, or fear, trepidation and hopelessness then, one is only honest when he claims that the 'promises' of his leaders or government has gone unfulfilled.

As stated before, it is the prime purpose of any form of government to '*secure the survival of the culture and people which, in fact, had created it*' and formed its

---

[*] [See] discourse of Socrates and Thrasymachas – The Republic – Book I. Cf. Classic Club Series, Walter&Black, pg. 233-53.

technics through long millennia. The antecedents of the West is not, unlike the Modern would have us believe, from the Levantine, Africa, or the Orient proper, but from our own root and stock. Nowhere is this illustration of greater insight than that of the historic democratic movement in England and France.

Liberalism may be assigned to the former, *Rationalism* to the latter.

In the West today, the 'synthesis' has been to combine the two: Liberalism+Rationalism=*Democracy*. All three deny the existence of an 'aristocracy' – at least in principle – which provided that all who belonged to the 'culture-class' had social value in relation to their peers, above that of the common man. This equated the 'social' with the 'political'. *The synthesis of 'liberalism' and 'rationalism' did essentially the same thing; 'democracy' simply placed the 'social-class' at the mercy of the political.* This was, and is, simply a new political ascendancy. It is the 'aristocracy' of the Modern. The 'old values' now, conveniently, replaced with his.

Democracy is a *feeling*.

Democracy is not an 'equality' of form or, necessarily, of law. Equality equates with 'opportunity'. The leveling of all class distinction, social value and the like, is not what the 'idea' of democracy was originally intended to convey. Indeed, as a part of the rhythm of cyclic evolution, democracy is always in flux, with its goals ever changing and adapting itself to each and every occasion. The cycle of democracy reads thus: *Revolution/Consolidation/Imperialism*, then back again. Yet, this is still only part of the democratic tradition – not the 'tradition' of Napoleon, he was a *true* democrat – but of the 'democracy of the mass'. It can be argued with some validity that this was good, for it forced the 'mass' to choose sides, as was the plan of one of its antecedents – Solon – who expected men with a 'democratic choice' to *participate* actively [!] in such a system. However, such is not generally the case. The mass, without real leadership, usually allow others to mold their own opinions being bereft, as it were, of any real goal or 'world view'; if such exists in the majority, they lack the will or ability to *articulate* it. This, of course, is human nature; the mass will always give the 'power of choice' to someone else's vision.

Most people, given a sedentary lifestyle, peace, accumulation of wealth, and the various studies of higher learning, will become, with time, used to such comfort, in *extremis*, thereby becoming sheep, corralled easily, and sheared when needed; a circumstance not very independent, or likely to achieve any lasting character, which would make them stand out for emulation. We would generally call this 'group' cowardly indeed. In this context, as with all governments, democracy seeks that political control over its social order with which it need to lead. When this happens, the mass is afforded that much sought after panacea of democracy: each man is the same as his fellows, with no distinction made between the two; no distinction based upon 'breed', or 'intellectual achievement', or any other consideration.Ψ The 'aristocracy' of the Modern reigns supreme.

Ψ There is some merit to the allegations by some, that modern democracy has become the 'new' communism of the present age. The 'egalitarianism' of Karl Marx, for instance, or Lenin's political dictums concerning 'aristocracy' and 'monarchy' included the 'democratic' ideal of the 'masses' which, taken to the extreme, ushered in the enslavement of the very mass the communists claimed to speak for. Laws of an extremely *excessive* nature 'forced' the mass to accept the 'leveling' of their society in the name of 'progress'. No Hereditary or Traditional institutions were allowed to remain, since it was 'through these selfsame institutions' that the 'people' had been denied 'choices' of their own; to be sure, the decadence of the existing leadership was obvious, and cannot be discounted as reasons for such wide-spread discontent, but to replace the old with democracies of the mob, is to say that the only prescription necessary for an ailment is poison.

The Dialectics of Hegel [George Wilhelm Frederich Hegel, born 1770, Germany] was essentially in opposition to the 'marxist/lenninist' doctrine but, nevertheless, was studied by the revolutionist of both the Menshevik party and the Bolsheviks in Russia were not the logical dynamics of 'negation' and 'knowledge'. Hegel was fascinated by the works of Spinoza, Rousseau, Kant, and Goethe and by the revolution of France. Modern philosophy, culture, and society seemed to Hegel fraught with contradictions and tensions [the 'struggle' in 'natural law'], such as those between the 'subject' and 'object' of *knowledge*, mind and *nature*, 'self' and 'other' [*inner and outer man*], *freedom* and *authority*, *knowledge* and *faith*, the Enlightenment *and* Romanticism. Hegel's main philosophical project was to take these *contradictions* and *tensions* and interpret them as part of a comprehensive, evolving, rational unity that, in different contexts, he called "the absolute idea" or "absolute knowledge".

According to Hegel, the main characteristic of this unity was that it evolved through and manifested itself in contradiction and negation. Contradiction and negation have a dynamic quality that at every point in each domain of reality – consciousness, history, philosophy, art, nature, society - leads to further development until a rational unity is reached that preserves the contradictions as phases and sub-parts of a larger, evolutionary whole. This *whole* is mental because it is the mind, which is able to comprehend all of these phases and sub-parts as steps in its own process of comprehension. It is rational because the same, underlying, logical, developmental order underlies every domain of reality and is ultimately the order of self-conscious rational thought, although only in the later stages of development does it come to full self-consciousness. The rational, self-conscious whole is not a thing or being that lies outside of other existing things or minds. Rather, it comes to completion only in the

The history of 'aristocracy', proper, is quite different. We in the West, specifically of this northern continent, do not like any form of aristocracy – after all, was not our very birth delivered 'caesarian' from this very Mother? It nevertheless holds true, that for thousands of years, specifically, it has been this type of ruling body, either through some form of heredity or selection [i.e. *election*], which has lasted for the longest periods. Think of Venice, for instance – *a thousand years* – and of Egypt – *three thousand!*

If this form of 'technics' has lasted long therefore, is it not thereby entirely justified if one infers from the evidence that this form of technic has maintained the confidence and loyalty of the race-culture? Conversely, history has shown that Aristocracies have failed, and given place, finally, to democracies. However, what exactly does this say? What 'rule of thumb' can be measured in this constant? Does this not mean, like anything else, [including democracy], that this or that system was worn out; that its technics were fixed, thereby resting in a state of 'static control'? That this or that system was decadent? Is this incidental, or simply the 'way-sign- of senility? It most certainly does not prove, one way or the other, that any one system is better or worse than the other: only its *effects* are judged good or bad. It does not prove in any way that an 'aristocracy' vs. 'democracy' is better than its opposite. The ruling body of any race-culture is *elite*, no matter what system employed to keep those who rule in power. It is, and will remain, no matter what system is employed, the intelligent, vigorous, and most gifted of the 'organic strata' (i.e. those of its blood) of persons who make up a Folk, that will form the *core* of any system of its race-culture. The race-culture *naturally* leans in this direction when it is healthy – no matter what the race-culture. It relies upon itself, and to those that are an organic part of itself. It is this strata that has '*de jure* ' right to lead, but is not always *tha*t strata that *does* lead. Let us expand on this subject risking, perhaps, the valued attention to this premise so far:

Dualistically, nature has always considered systems and forms to be 'one' or the 'other'. There is 'white/black', there is 'sun/moon', there is 'sky/earth'; there is 'male/female' and 'sunrise/sunset' terms which, until recently, held distinctions, which the Modern, seemingly, is unable to grasp. He thinks in terms of grey, of the multiplicity of 'possibilities', the 'minutiae' of reasoning become absurd. Aristocracy, as a 'form', admits a 'duality', insofar as one can see a 'top and bottom', leaders and followers.

---

philosophical comprehension of individual existing human minds who, through their own understanding, bring this developmental process to an understanding of itself. FLS

If it be honestly admitted, elites of one type or another, like cream, rise to the top; in the ancient past of our Western culture, this point is self-evident. But here one must put aside the 'better known' aspect of what is the common usage of 'elite', or 'aristocratic', especially if one limits himself to a 'standard' definition, and delve a little deeper.

In the ancient West, it was not material wealth, its martial skill, or even its priestly castes, which made, or rather, created a sense of *elitism*. Our pursuit here is at once deeper, and metaphysical. At once *psychic*, those of our ancient past, regardless of the level or caste in which one was born, was the sacred ability to 'initiate', *to be initiated*, to 'ritually initiate' that person or persons into a particular *caste*. It was the 'rite of passage' proper, placing emphasis on the religious implications and metaphysical forms in which an individual now 'sensed' that this initiation had claimed him forever; that his service was now blessed according to his role in life. Practiced for so long, it became 'institutional', and was at the very heart and fabric of the West. In the world of Tradition, nothing was more sacred than the spiritual influences that the 'rite' could influence through its 'action' (i.e. through the 'ritual' itself). The Brahmans of India, for instance, even though scattered throughout its country could, nevertheless, command such respect, almost reverence, enjoying a 'prestige' greater than any tyrant or ruler, because they had attained that 'interconnection' with the spiritual that the masses had not.

In Greece, China, and Rome the 'patrician' class, the nobility, the 'aristocrats', were characterized by possession of knowledge and practice of initiatory rites that were connected to the 'divine' power emanating from the founder of a particular Family. This, in turn, was passed down through, and into, the progeny of future generations. It is this 'supernatural' element which, essentially, became the foundation of the 'idea' of aristocracy, as well as legitimate royalty. What constituted legitimate 'aristocracy' was not merely biological, not only blood or racial selection, but also 'sacred traditions'. In Germanic and Northern races, as well as the Far East in the ancient classical world, the feeling was the same. Blood was a part, but the main part perhaps, was the 'second birth', that element of mystical significance, which separated a 'divine' from a 'non-divine', hence it was that the plebeians of Rome would never attain the status of the patrician not because of blood, but because the plebes were denied the 'rite of passage' in a 'ritualized sense'. This may not strike the casual student of history as important, but if one were to compare its 'universal' brother, the 'church', then one can readily understand the mystical importance of 'baptism', which at once 'transforms' the individual, and 'secures' a *relationship* with God himself. One may trivialize this 'rite', as not all are Christians, but they would do so at their peril, since it 'lives' in the hearts and minds of millions. It is in the above context that one must look to the origin of the 'aristocracy' of the past. Like the plebeians of Rome, it was their 'lack' of *cult*, which separated them from the patrician nobility; the same can be said of the 'christian cult' vis a vis, the non-christian by way of baptism.

In the Teutonic nations we find this 'metaphysical' tradition, insofar as the 'chief' was, at the same time, both 'priest and king'. Not only this, but a claim of 'divine' parentage was the *coup de grace* amongst his people. This set him apart from all other 'families' since he was gifted with 'divine' characteristics. Even when compared to a military leader, who was always looked to with admiration, loyalty, and reverence because of his selfless sacrifice in battle for folk and tribe, it was the 'class' of priest/kings which held ultimate sway, going so far as to 'initiate' themselves if need be. This process was hardly for the weak however, and included isolation, trials of life and death; outside of this, a 'person' was considered [as] a member of the 'women and children' until, and not before, he had passed through his initiation. This included the king himself. Aristocracy came from the 'rite' of 'male passage' from one level into the next, without it, he was of the herd.

In our modern time, aristocracy, like royalty, has merely taken on the more 'secular' and 'political' manifestations of the 'mystical'. The origins of Aristocracy and Royalty were based on 'character', 'race', 'honour', 'valor', and 'faithfulness' [*noblesse' d' epee*, and on, *noblesse de coeur*]. Much later, these criteria were discarded, as was the privileges of 'blood and tradition'. Whether or not this quality is lacking in our modern age is, at this moment, not the point, what is the point is the 'structure' and 'form' of the aristocrat; how, and for what reason the aristocrat existed at all.

It was not the 'intellectuality' of peers, but of its 'spirituality', which made this class so predominant. It was never a matter of 'knowing the law', or how *technical* a class of men could be, but rather the 'spiritual' trust and direction 'within'. In an attenuated form, the Knightly Orders of Nobility continued 'tradition' proper through its initiations and rituals, one but considers the Teutonic Knights, Knights Templar, the Order of St. John, just to name a few, and created warriors who were both 'priest and king', and served as judicial, martial, and ecclesiastical leaders: in short, this was an 'aristocracy' based on the ancient laws of the West. Tradition, Honour, valor, and sacrifice were all part of a 'great' tradition which, when entered, made them 'just that much more mighty' than the common man. These men, indeed, were *uncommon*.

The aristocracy of the past, that is, the 'elites' who the people looked to for leadership, were special; they were special as a class; and they were special because of the seriousness required as part of an 'overall' duty to those who were entrusted, in a 'sacred' sense, to *their* care. In modern times, when the West was coerced into disassociating the temporal authority from the spiritual authority, and instead replaced it 'solely' with the electoral, thereby allowing the sacred 'institutions' to be open to 'inferior' types, and the lower social strata, it opened the door to the modern 'impure' aristocracy of money. As time progressed, oligarchies, royal hangers-on, and the like turned more to the whims of the modern *demos*, the mass; no longer was the natural 'aristocrat' a trusted and competent leader. Greece, Rome, and now in our modern technics do we see the effects of these descending phases of senility.

Aristocracies are a *natural* phenomenon.

All cultures, in their own way, host both the leaders and followers of the recurring generations. The point herein espoused is that equality is an illusion, and that 'all' societies have their elite. In our 'modern' aristocracies, we look to the 'kings' of Industry, Oil, and commerce instead of Blood and Spirit. The 'aristocracy' of wealth may do good things, may provide jobs and the like, but they lack 'spirit', and most will agree that these men are in 'business' and would laugh if they were asked to conceive of 'business' as sacred or spiritual.

Wealth, as such, is not what concerns us here, but the areas in which this sense, not of 'duty' or 'sense of honour', or even 'obliges' is not the purview of the merchant class, therefore, to consider as a 'class', the monied classes as more that mere purveyors of 'exchange', then we must look to *others* as our 'sacred leaders' in some other class. Utilitarian democracy lacks the 'warrior' sense of 'faithfulness and honour'; it is replaced with a material and economic character, which implies directly that personal convenience and material interest belongs to the merchant and not to the 'aristocratic'. Aristocracy has given way to the plutocrat; the banker has become larger in life, than the warrior. How we *view* the relationships between our leaders and ourselves is what will mark the once and future West.

Now back to the prime discussion at hand.

Democracy, *as a trend*, is only the way-sign of disintegration.

To those of you who are already shouting 'down with the authoritarian state', or 'down with the 'rule of the few', let me say that a people, a race-culture, may be 'systematized too much by any form of government or system, but it can never be ruled too wisely or too well. Should not the 'rule of thumb' of any people be to *never abolish the very best government that they can devise?* This should be self-evident. Should the 'labels' and 'catch phrases' count for more than the essence of the Race itself, whatever the race? If these labels and phrases suffer the host body to such a catastrophe that it dissolves the *very basis* for its foundation, its blood and tissue, then, whichever name they call their system and whatever form it takes is not, in any realistic determination, the *best* government for that people. Notwithstanding the modern's intention of 'baptizing' the world in its image of ritual sacredness, the fact that nations must bow the knee to what *passes* as 'democracy' under the point of the sword, is the height of hypocrisy and financial imperialism. Those members of the West should take great care should their 'experiment' turn on them.

In our modern situation, with new medicines, forms of travel, communication and the like, the breakdown in a healthy 'upper-strata' of leadership seems to be, in fact must be, the slow ever present evolutionary growth of its population. This creates and exacerbates the existence of two poles of consciousness: *ability* and *mass*. Rule by the *few* or Rule by the *many*. It must, of necessity, come to this.

Europe, for a period of twelve hundred years, maintained its population. In one single century however, between 1800 and 1914, it jumped from 180 million to 460 million. In this country we saw the same in America. Professor S.J. Holmes of the University of Southern California has stated that *"...the U.S. population rose from six-million to seventy-seven million,"*[10] a rise numerically of twelve-fold! This influx of immigration saturated the existing institutions (i.e. traditions), thereby unbalancing the equilibrium between the poles of ability and mass. This suddenness was so extreme that these same institutions were unable to assimilate these 'new americans', and direct their energies in a comprehensive fashion. The sheer power this new mass possessed was virtually irresistible politically. *Rathenau* described it as the 'vertical invasion of the 'barbarians', since its very height in numbers would now dictate the direction of government.

Rathenau, however, was not predicting this observation on the fact of sheer numbers alone, but was drawing a distinction between the numbers and the fact of such alienness brought to these shores by these new immigrants, when compared to the existing inhabitants. Even those of Western stock, upon entering the 'new world' faced many new complex life-styles, which actually retarded their ability to enter into the existing life-styles of their American brethren. This was 'assimilation' in the pure sense of the word; assimilation, in

---

[10] Holmes, Samuel J. – Human Genetics and its Social Import, McGraw, 1936, pg. 293.

a state of nature, is part of the cycles of interactions and fecundity necessary to extend one's culture. It was the 'non-western' elements which did not, and of necessity, could not, assimilate, and to this day have not assimilated, which has proved the dichotomy between the 'diversity' of the Modern, and the 'diversity' of those of Western stock, which made up the early American settlers. These divergent elements of the West such as Italy, France, and Scandinavia, Germany etc., assimilated based on their *organic* relationship with their fellow Europeans. America was truly a 'pluralistic democracy' at this point, and many it is that will say this is precisely why 'democracy', American democracy, works. The America of 'yesterday', however, is not the America of the modern.

It is the 'minions' of the Modern, who endlessly repeat the phrase 'democracy serves the whole' as if a mantra, no matter how large the number or diverse its language, race or tradition, thinking that if they repeat this thought, endlessly, that somehow it will prove true. These minions, of course, cite the endless litany of the origin of all Western democracies: Greece. This claim, however, need not detain us long. Indeed, it may be contended that Pericles himself, in the hey-day of Athens, that 'citadel' of democracy, was not the leader of a 'democracy' at all.

Historians such as T.R. Glover and W.R. Agard contend that the political process of Greece was the ultimate in popular government. Yet this perception must coexist with the fact that, conservatively, only ten [10%] percent of the population had political rights at all.

Mr. Agard has this to say:

> "It was a government of citizens met in an assembly, where, without Presidents, ministers, ambassadors or representatives, they themselves governed. They created a beautiful city and a law-abiding people; they united the Greek world or a large part of it; they defeated the Persian Empire in all its greatness and drove the Persians from the sea. They made an atmosphere where genius could grow, where it could be as happy as genius ever can, and where it flowered and bore strange fruit that has enriched the world forever."[11]

Ah! Can you not hear the cacophony of applause, the slapping of the backs of so many yea-sayers, which claim the legacy of the 'idea'? But they forget to speak about other aspects of this ancient democracy of which the modern claims his parentage; for the democracy of the ancients could not have existed

---

[11] Glover, T.R. – *Democracy in the Ancient World* - Macmillan, 1927. Reprinted, New York, 1966, pg. 73.

as we know it now, *without a huge substratum of slavery*. The 'wealth' required was enormous to build such works as the Acropolis; to be sure, one of the most 'brilliant' of Western endeavors, nevertheless, was drawn by methods so 'undemocratic' in theory, yet so indicative of the record of democracy, that of the Imperialism established over the states of Asia Minor and the Aegean Islands, so as to make any contemporary comparison of 'modern' [one man, one vote] democracy ludicrous. Yet even the 'Athenian' example did not provide the utopia sought by the various thinkers and political architects of the time. It too, was fraught with errors, excesses of judgment, and was saved only by the narrowest of margins by *one man*: Pericles.

For over a generation this man, Pericles, it must be remembered, was *not* a common man, but had the 'blood' of many an Athenian Noble coursing through his veins. Thucydides, a contemporary, saw this fact most clearly when he said, "...*although in name a democracy, Athens was 'virtually a government by its greatest citizen.*'"[12] [emph. mine] Even with the help of the man, Pericles, this [type] democracy lived but a short time – it was, in fact, well under a hundred years. The 'Age of Pericles' closed with democracy completely discredited.

Thinkers on the eve of the French Revolution were of the same mind. They had seen seventeen centuries directed to the course of 'the greatest leader', or King [i.e. rule by its greatest citizen].

Henry Sumner Maine, has this to say concerning these [French] revolutionists:

> The Revolutionists held]...the opinion that Democracy was irresistible and inevitable...there had been more than two thousand years of tolerably...ascertained political history, and at its outset, Monarchy, Aristocracy, and democracy, were all plainly discernible. The result of a long experience was, that some Aristocracies had shown themselves extremely tenacious of life...But the democracies which had risen and perished, or had fallen into extreme insignificance, seemed to show that this form of government was a rare occurrence in political history, and was characterized by an extreme fragility.[13]

And again:

---

[12] Glotz, Gustave – Ancient Greece at Work, Kegan Paul,, 1926, pg. 159.
[13] Agard, Walter R. – *What Democracy Meant To The Greeks* – U. of N.C. Press, 1942, pg. 70.

> Whenever government of the many has been tried, it has ultimately produced monstrous and morbid forms of government by the One, or government by the few.[14]

Even long after its completion, following the French Revolution, Mr. Maine is little less impressed with the almost unbroken tradition of [the] democratic process here. Nevertheless, he adds, *"...that not since the Roman empire began to breakdown has there been such insecurity of government as the world has seen since rulers became delegates for the community"*[15] The record speaks for itself; democracy is short lived at best, and at worst, is the solvent which dissolves the body politic from its host.

There is one facet of democracy left to be addressed. That of its *record*. The relationship of this record and the modern application of democracy have a track record, which calls for our attention. It is assumed, generally, that democracy is opposed to dictatorship, but nothing could be further from the truth, and which facts and common sense will prove out. The history of democracy makes it perfectly and unmistakable that some 'form' of one-man rule is the end to which [all] popular government has led. To whit, Athenian democracy was followed by Alexander; the 'Republic' [of France] followed by Napoleon; the Marxist Revolution [of the 'demos'] followed by Stalin; and the Post War II Reich [of Bismarck] followed by Adolph Hitler shows ineluctably the ineptitude of 'democracy' in dealing with problems and situations that continually build under such unstable and 'bureaucratic' hands, and however anyone puts it, 'mob-rule' has proved chaotic and unstable in any number of recent political developments, and which rapidly brings it to its final stage of development, senility. Those who live in the United States, specifically, should pay special attention to this phenomenon. The inevitable breakdown of 'law and order' shows that we have done no better. The 'experiment' of the Modern has proved no better than those of our antecedents.

Looked at through the eyes of 'causality' and seriously considered, the whole charade of mob-rule foisted upon us by the modern and his minions, leads always to the single leader that the masses will follow for good or ill. This, precisely, explains the rise of Roosevelt, Hitler, Stalin, and Mussolini amongst other lesser-known dictators of this modern time period. Honesty, in retrospect, requires us to accept, at the very least, a dictator 'archetype' which the masses depended upon to extricate them from very real or perceived threats to the individual nation and people. After all, it was this very 'type', which had to be created in the above-mentioned examples to respond, as

---

[14] [Quoted] Agard, op. Cit., pg. 64
[15] Maine, Henry Sumner – Popular Government, Holt, 1886, pg. 70f.

each thought best, to each other on a National level. Whether right or wrong, it is, once again, the individual personality, which presides over the National consciousness. It was Hitler's unaltered perception of danger which pushed him to declare himself virtual dictator towards the fiery end of war; and it was Roosevelt who, while being led from behind the scenes, felt it necessary to become virtually the first dictator here at home (second only to Abraham Lincoln) to engage the United States in a foreign war.

One may not condone, indeed, approve of Totalitarianism as an institution but one can but well imagine what it means to stay afloat or die. All Nations will, inevitably, go through some major 'event' which will precipitate the leadership of the One for the protection and continuation of the whole; a leader is, of necessity, forced to make decisions that will affect the life or death of a people; in this condition, almost any means will be tolerated.*

This, of course, cannot be seen as the 'absolute' technic of a higher-culture; yet, we face this challenge [of survival] today, as real as any Germany had to

---

*The most recent happenings in Iraq, Somalia, Haiti and the like, as well as our imminent involvement in Bosnia 'against' our European brothers who are fighting the insidious inroads of Islamic fundamentalists which, over the past thousand years, has continuously been at war with the West [this would also include the many and diverse semitic religious and philosophical imperatives which are alien to our psyche and national will], and is our first inroads into the cradle of our origins since the Second Fratricidal War. The President [George H. Bush], who says repeatedly, that he does not 'require' Congressional approval to declare war, is a 'virtual' dictator [the rightness or wrongness is not at issue here] for this reason, and most assuredly affects our People during 'war' *as a Nation*. But should not these 'national' issues be decided by the People [congress]?

We tolerate this action by a 'national leader' simply because, as stated before, we are lazy and prefer to be led. As long as our interest here at home is secured, there is no reason to involve ourselves with foreign wars; yet are we not still Imperialists? Does this not mean that our 'territory' is simply being expanded? Europe may be playing dead, but before long the jealousy of the ancient powers will be reignited, and America will be caught, once again, in the conflagration of Fratricide, and once again on the side of 'Money' over that of Culture. It may be called Oil or Finance, but it is nevertheless the element which 'internationalists' secured through the Second Fratricidal War as the 'payoff' for American involvement, and will seek to extend itself, and maintain its extended territorial claims against all comers; even if that means the destabilization of indigenous peoples or cultures; such was Viet Nam.

Democracy of the modern is 'tenuous' at best. Think carefully, People of the West, on just where you/we are going. FLS

face a generation ago, and perhaps even greater. But let us get back to our subject at hand.

In our present case, here in America, how are we to account for the unprecedented success of a popular government? First, and foremost in this analysis, we must recognize that we here in the United States, as a political 'technic', as a *government*, have never truly had a 'popular' government. An Athenian 'citizen' in the days of Pericles would never agree that Americans, or any Western country for that matter, enjoyed any real democracy, since the average American does not participate in government at all – not withstanding the ostensible 'voting power' of the average citizen. In fact, it was the founding Fathers' intentions that 'public' voices not be heard above a whisper.

It was that *temporary* and *emotional* 'Public Opinion' which, by its very existence, could never support a valid basis for a stable and long-lasting government. Therefore, the founding fathers created a strong Executive branch, gave [him] it the power to be a real ruling power; the length of term was long [?] enough to make him 'independent of public opinion' and 'sentiment' which, in turn, would tend to control the emotional flux of the mass. Coupled with the average age of senators, their length of office, and the whole electoral system, not to mention the Constitutional implications, made the ordinary citizen at least twice removed from any actual participation in his government. The 'Constitution', in fact, some call a 'living' constitution, removes the average American more than the majority of Americans could have ever imagined, but such is the mass. As with all modern Western democracies, the flags are waved, and the multitudes excited about 'their' democracy, forget the many usurpations of their very 'democratic' ideals by the leaders who have paved the way for the modern democracy of the West.

Let us examine the U.S. Constitution briefly:

To examine the 'living constitution' it is necessary to dispassionately dispel the difference between the 'Constitution' and the 'myths', which surround it. It is understood that 'holy writ' is looked at like we Americans look at the Constitution; yet Sunday-school never inculcated into the psyche of our youth the impact of the Constitution upon our lives in the 'here and now'. The public, as usual, are confused as to what they 'think' the Constitution means, and what it 'does'; what the constitution sets forth can be devoured in less than half and hour, but the *'official'* meaning, vague even to educated and erudite men [professors too!], is always, without question, determined by the government itself, usually through the 'high court'. To this latter, it is the 'lawyer', held in such esteem as seen by its particular public, which serves as such a 'symbiotic' servant to the practice and initiation of constitutional law; often in disagreement, the Court and lawyers argue between and amongst themselves on just how to decipher and promulgate the 'meanings' of Constitutional Law. Regardless of this sibylline document, no matter the majority of Congressional intent, the President, or the Supreme Court, it is the 'government' itself, who determines what the Constitution permits or does not permit, and all this depending solely upon the *circumstances*, in which it will arise. Why is it, that constitutional lawyers, many of whom have spent their entire lives studying and practicing this type of law, are faced with traditional interpretations, with many a *precedent* in their favor, are denied satisfaction by the high-court? The constitution is many faceted, sibylline, and always open to 'interpretation'. This is the 'life' of a schizophrenic.

The high court, in fact, so often split by majority decisions in cases which 'overturned' majority decisions of the past, claiming a self-regulating 'balance of power' amongst the highest lawyers of the land, should bring into contrast just what the Constitution mandates; in fact, these high lawyers are simply there to keep the 'living' document *healthy*! In this case, that of majority decisions, how can the 'minority' be so far a field [or vice versa]? How can the high-court overturn cases in which there were 'unanimous' opinions expressed by the full body of justices? All this, based upon a growing sense of 'new' opinions expressed by a 'new age', an evolution necessary for a new generation.

Perhaps this confusion would be alleviated if one considers that the 'court' makes policy; far from being merely a 'law-interpreting' and 'law-expounding' body, the court consistently 'modifies' *social and cultural policy under the guise of 'applying' the Constitution*. When the court does this, in essence, it 'enacts' new law; common observation, even amongst laymen, can see this in the 'social policy' of the court, no matter what side one is on. Nevertheless, it is the prerogative of the Congress to enact 'laws'; the Constitution 'explicitly' gives this power to congress, which 'speaks' for the People, at least in theory. The People nowhere, enter into the picture of a 'democracy'.

In fact, to hammer this point home, our American Constitution was drafted during chaotic, turbulent times; the passage of this document was forced through the ratification process by means fair and foul under the very nose of a mostly uncomprehending populace. The 'people', then as now, knew very little of the 'reality' of circumstances surrounding the new government, or the new constitution. The claim that the conventions convened were '*by the people*' is spurious at best, as the Modern, as well as well meaning individuals would have the masses believe. *In point of fact, it was white males, eligible to vote*, and specifically those 'white males' so inclined to be interested in the adoption or rejection of the Constitution while it was being devised, who were responsible for the final, albeit imperfect, document. To add to this is the dispute between majorities of the 'states' themselves who, based on the 'people', a number which at best may be guessed at, is approximately, 160,000 [white] males, voted at all during the act of creating the document in 1787, which would become the ruling body of rules for this, our homeland. This vote was close as there were approx. 100,000 for, and approx. 60,000 votes against this constitution. But there is more: of a possible electorate of close to 800,000 eligible [white] males, the population reached as high as 3 millions, twenty-percent of which were non-voting blacks. Women, Indians, Negroes and children, of course, could not vote.

We the People, therefore, comes down to about 60 percent of twenty or twenty-five percent of eligible voters or, if you will, from twelve to fifteen percent of the total 600-800,000 members of the eligible electorate.* So much for the 'modern's' democracy.

The inception of this 'popular' agreement was just the beginning of our so-called popular government. Yet, every beginning begets growth, and here is where the trouble starts. To the 'average' Western man the Constitution stands as solidly as 'holy writ', but shares also the tremendous annotations and expositions, which follow such scrutiny. The sides are drawn, for the betterment of the 'whole'. These annotations are inexhaustible, and would take several lifetimes to completely grasp. The polemics, stodgy or otherwise, is exceeded only by 'holy writ'; and is either misleading or vacuous.

Constitutional study is, for most, totally devoid of excitement. Perhaps, this is best. Yet, in the end, the common man knows very little of 'what' the Constitution is, or objectively, what it 'means' to them. How was it, for instance, that the policy concerning 'african citizenship' and issues held so very dear, for so long could, willy nilly, be changed overnight, simply because a 'constitutional' amendment or 'social legislation' was passed by a 'high court' which, in many cases, seemed to be at odds with the 'majority'?

The American Constitution was not very different from its British Parent. Putting aside the many polemics on this discussion, *our* constitution is different only in the fact that ours is 'written', while the English version is not. Like ancient Rome, it was the 'oral' traditions, which held the power. The only telling exceptions in the document of 1787 are the Amendments, which accompany it. But this addition, as with any annotation, may be added too,

---

* Cf. Jensen, Merrill – The Making of the American Constitution – D. Van Nostrand Co., 1964, pg. 140, for a more extensive study into the particular numbers and avenues of the origins of our beginnings. FLS

expanded, its interpretation widely viewed; its direction this way, then just as quickly, heads another. The power to 'interpret' is the power to introduce *variation*, which is why the euphemism 'living constitution' is so true.

From its inception, the Constitution is but a 'nucleus' of an ever-extending mass, from which all 'material' sense is derived to form 'rules' which the government is then organized and operates. From this document comes legislative, traditional, and systematic adjudications, which direct the Nation. But where are the People?

The Constitution is the *'supreme law'*. Article VI, Section 2 states:

> "This Constitution, and the laws of the United States which shall be made in pursuance thereof; *and* all treaties made, or which shall be made, under the authority of the United States, *shall* be the supreme law of the land; and the judges in every State shall be bound thereby, anything in the Constitution or laws of any States to the contrary notwithstanding..."[emph. added]

Supreme law, then, is not simply the document of 1787, the 'document' so dear to our hearts, but it is also and equally 'national statutes', and 'treaties', made by the President with the concurrence of the Senate. National Law, then, is *supreme law*; it 'belongs' to the Constitution. But this law belongs to 'interpretation', hence, to *variation*. Individuals who have been 'appointed' for life work in conjunction with individuals who, while acting collectively and, ostensibly, speaking for the 'people', have no more public assent, than those other Nine. Perhaps, if rarely discussed, the Plebiscite could take its place once again in democracy.

All the above listed is not to infer that the 'people' *as* a mass, should be participants at all levels of society or government, the above is listed to show just 'what' our democracy is, and is not. The mass is 'ruled' by one authority or another, and the 'document' by which we are ruled is not a popular document in a true sense, since it has evolved into something which we, you and I, have little to say in its evolution. Appointees and elected officials have that responsibility, NOT THE PEOPLE.

Should Treaties or statutes maintained by vague and misleading interests bind the majority of persons who have never had a say in their creations? Let us be clear regarding democracy and the documents we claim 'define' our democracy. However, is there a method to this seeming contradiction of our hollowed sense of democratic values?

Let us continue by observing the Judiciary Act of 1789 for the *fait accompli*.

This 'act' firmly advanced and entrenched Judicial control over that of Legislation. This 'act' vested the Supreme authority in a small Oligarchy: the Supreme Court. Its 'members' are not elected but 'appointed'. We, the People, have no say in this selection at all. These individuals are appointed for life. As with any 'exclusive' body, good or bad, it naturally becomes detached, with time, from the source and culture which created it; their deliberations and acts, which may happen or may not happen to suit the needs of the race-culture are not, cannot be, brought under any type of review [congress has the right, but the process being so formidable and time consuming, will not be enough to change this premise] except through Executive instance who, it must be noted, placed at least some portion on the bench and must therefore, at least in part, speak with the same tongue as the jurists who preside. This system may be good, it may be the best, it may be the rule by which all others should seek to emulate but, is it Democratic?

If it be accepted by most scholars that it was the French Revolutionists who gave us the 'theory' of our form of government then, most certainly, the English experience gave us our practical reference point. It has been noted more than once that our President is similar to the English King. The only difference is the lack of Heredity.* The founders of the Constitution designed their government, as much as was possible in an age of 'anti-monarchy', to resemble the England of the eighteenth century. A time when the King, as well as his House of Lords had *real* power. If American democracy has succeeded, let me say that a possible reason is that we are not very democratic. So, in the final analysis, is democracy the People's Choice?

---

* It may well be true that all but fourteen of our Presidents are related to English Royalty in the first, second, third, or fourth relations.

Rise of The West

Chapter III

The Ennobling of Man

The last race to keep its form, the last living tradition,
The last leaders who have both at their back, will pass
Through onwards, Victorious.

Oswald Spengler

The words above of Oswald Spengler are worthy of our attention. He saw clearly the step-by-step process ineluctably present in the fulfillment of culture to be the ennobling of Man – to the Higher Culture.

Truly, the 'ennobling of man' was, in his mind, the highest mark of a truly great people. For one to understand the seemingly metaphysical aspects of 'survival', and 'ennobling', one must know empirically, as well as spiritually, *the cause and effect* of the mind of Western man. One, of necessity, must be animated with his [Western man] inner most mental concepts: his concepts of Religion; his concept of Identity; his Mystical apparatus – that element which has driven him ever upwards and onwards – all must be understood in its interwoven relationship with the whole of Western man. Hence, it is that Nobility, as a mental attitude, must be groomed and well founded in a higher Culture.

Along with Oswald Spengler, two men are favored with attention here. There are many persons who have aided in the direction of the West, as a labor of love, seriously, and with the hope that the decline of the West would, instead, become the Rise of the West. All these men and women who have attempted, in their own unique ways, to bring to America and the world the plight in which we all find ourselves are too numerous to list; yet all and sundry are owed a great round of applause, for their efforts will bear fruit. We applaud all who have contributed to the onward and upward momentum of a continuing evolution of our higher culture and to its positive impact upon all peoples. These two men were both prophets to those few who listened to the same still, small voice of their inner spirit. To the names Frederic Wilhelm Nietzsche and William Galey Simpson, we owe a tremendous debt.

Both of these men, to a large degree, represent a fruition and distillation of information, coupled with their own unique insights which aided both in the search for truth and hope for the Western world. They are both Prophets of the Rise of the West.

Nietzsche, who had such a discerning eye, as well as the ability to ask the right questions, while continuously providing answers to his queries in which self-analysis is the major component. All this for the betterment of those who search along the same coastline, who turn the same stones in search of the treasure hidden beneath. One may not always nor, assuredly, know or agree with all of Nietzsche's conclusions yet it is simply the study of insight that must be brought to bear here. Insight opens the mind, and enables one too, ultimately, ascend upwards to personal and National competence.

To the other, William Galey Simpson who, through such anguish of spirit and personal ridicule by those very peers who continually exhorted him to 'experience that which Jesus had experienced', was to spend sixty years of his life in pursuit of that essence which is the pursuit of all higher men: *the ennobling of his fellow man*. Few of Western stock have said so fluently [in the English language], so beautifully, what is meant by *spirit, consciousness, humility, understanding, and Fate*. His term 'beyond' which, is his understanding of 'death', a participation of which is compulsory of all of us all, is as deep and humble as any who have put pen to paper.

Both men, to be sure, were searchers of the esoteric, that 'primitive collective soul of man' which, from his very beginnings has been molded and formed by eons of race-consciousness, by his environment (i.e. territory, landscape, upbringing, etc.); his mode of speech, and his belief in god(s). This latter being his means by which he could 'transcend' all those things he could not comprehend, putting a face on the unknown, as it were. This is not to say 'there is no God', but to some, God may be that 'personal' challenge which forces each and every man or woman to face the unknown. It may simply be that 'still small voice' of his inner consciousness. In any event, can anyone today fix a particular [physical] being *as* God? In addition, if one can, can he then determine the course of man *within* the realm and consent of this god? The ennobling of man must then, of necessity, come to grips with that spontaneous spirit, be it god or himself that ever drives him onward and upward. To become noble, one must become *ennobled*. Thus to our search.

Frank L. DeSilva

i.

The Rise of Nobility:

The Death of the Noble Savage?

Rousseau's use of the term 'noble savage' was in connection with man's ostensible relationship between Nature and Civilization. Between man, *himself* and his *technics*. What Rousseau actually meant by this comparison I cannot say; every man, including this author, has a 'pre-condition' for both nature and civilization. In some respects however, I agree with the premise that 'man is better in a state of nature than he is in a 'civilization'. It is only as to that level in the abstract sense that we agree however. The word 'better', it must be understood, is a 'pre-condition' that supposes a 'lesser' point in man's spiritual and physical being. Of the latter, I concede that we have changed 'externally'; that we are modified on a daily basis. However, as to the conscious and unconscious *spirit*, this point is not clear even to those who have made it their life's search.

Of the nature of man, of that 'first man', what were his embryonic thoughts of *good* or *evil*? After that mystical force of fire was discovered,* what did he *see* there, in the midst of colour change, of form change; what was the *sense* he gained by the fellowship of his kind that, like he, was transfixed by the glowing, turning marvel of fire and heat – of man, woman and child that drew closer, even as he, as the strength and breadth of his fire receded, leaving only darkness? Was it this essence that led eventually to his modes of consciousness and mental thought? His god, whoever or whatever, or however it manifested itself, listened to his simple prayers, looked upon him in his daily struggle for existence – pitied his spirit. He praised and feared his first god. He dedicated himself, his progeny, his Empires to this God. The subtle tissues of his spirit enveloped the 'essence' of what were his spirituality, his evolution of mental constraints, and his outlook on his surroundings.

Primitive man was close to nature, as are all primitives, and was closer to a stricter understanding of 'good' and 'evil' as it seemed to him: *what nurtured*

---

* "...[describes] based on all existing evidence, that fire, not just the ability to 'keep' fire, but for the actual 'making' of fire, was not developed in China but in Europe – about 100,000 years ago." Coon, Carlton S. – The Story of Man, pg. 60-1. [See also Origin of the Races – Knopf, 1962, pg. 90-1.

him was good; what denied or hurt him was bad. Simple, yet not 'simple minded'. Through the passing eons, these 'feelings' and 'experiences' were molded by his evolving system of technics, his very own creations that passed eventually into the regimen of Religion. This, then, was the *Institutionalization* of his very consciousness.

This institution provided him and kind with an atmosphere by which each individual could share, with the many, those innermost feelings, fears, hopes, and aspirations. In this fashion, could the collective memories be driven into a focalized direction. Certain it is, that many unscrupulous men and women acquired the ability to direct, in their own ways, and for personal gain, this collective consciousness for ends that were neither organic nor good. But these have always been found out and eliminated.

The original aim however, that specific undying purpose, *the spiritual ennobling of man's eternal soul, hence, that ennobling 'quality' on earth as a 'higher-man' is unshaken,* albeit far removed from the original intent. By this, in the context of Religion (i.e. as in a 'fixed' institution, eschatology, etc.), a term I use hesitantly because of its 'fixed' and intractably modern usage, it is implied that man can become better by the continual application and continuing process of learning to seek out the better self. *Man, 'the individual', must mark the 'higher man'. The race and culture will follow in a natural interrelation between the body and spirit.*

It is a truism that all higher-culture has had the greatest and grandest religions. The 'religions' of Sumer, Egypt, Babylonia, Persia, Greece, and Rome all come to mind. Unlike the religions of the modern West, these ancient religions expressed in their 'form' the natural inclinations and predispositions of a 'specific' racial quality; this, of course, manifested itself in both Tradition and Authority. Religion, however, is not what must be understood here, that is, not in the 'institutional' setting; Religion, itself, is only the *technic* 'utilized', the outer shell if you will, of its spirit of morality proper. True religion is the great Conscience of its particular 'will-to-power' and intelligence that ever marks the higher-man.

This, of course, is a *moral perspective*. In the modern world, morality is a fluid thing; a perspective, which defies boundaries. Morality, however, has much to do with the 'outward' manifestations of individuals, and collective reality. We may ascribe this division of perspectives as between those who understand the 'cause' and those who have misunderstood the origin, function, and direction of that cause. Yet, even though a conflict often arises between individuals regarding perspective morality, the claim can be made, and with much credibility, that each feels the call of 'intuition'* when it comes to the questions of morality. It is often something 'we know'. This of course comes into direct conflict since each individual 'sees' differently.

If one were to consider and contemplate the various 'actualizations' of morality, it will be agreed that it gives a certain power (i.e. tangible), a certain divinity (i.e. intangible), and will, naturally, spread its consciousness to those which inhabit a close proximity to the person or presence that exudes this potential. This individual, this higher man, finalizes this 'aspiration' into the higher *kundalini*, and displays a morality intellectualized as Nobility. These aspirations are finalized in the higher man, who appreciates and displays Beauty, peace, harmony; these are the concepts desired by the higher man.

In *beauty*, he finds the spirit of good, in *harmony*, he finds the definition of beauty and peace, which, in turn, allow him to enjoy his labors, his creations (i.e. his arts, crafts, and all those mental and manual actions which make up its thinkers and doers), and his unexplored spirit. He [the higher man] consistently listens to his 'still small voice', ever driving him, ever demanding answers to that which each man must, ultimately, answer alone, in the very deep recesses of his own mind, his own morality. Man, Western man, in finding and refining these definitions, is constantly evolving into and now out of his 'types' of form (i.e. in a spiritual sense), and his technics which disclosed his 'inner directions', and which also defines his concept of beauty: that which is good. In fact, his 'sense', 'experience', and 'perceptions' of beauty, make up his total 'aesthetic [tangible] experience' through his life and hence, onward through his racial and national extension for posterity. This is the 'morality' of the higher man, what drove him to the greater 'questions' of his existence; not the crass 'sexual' morality of the modern, for this is his 'center', his priori, which makes up his particular Volksgeist.

Through these actualizations, the higher-man always discloses his spirit, his morality, in and through his *aesthetic* sense. Sense, in its true and simple

---

* [See]: Alexis Carrel's discussion in his chapter on 'mental activities' is an important one for the West, and for all cultures. My use of intuition may mislead some readers – it may appear too metaphysical – but one must realize its absolute value in our daily lives, for it effects all decisions, all conscious thought. A personal analysis, in any event, must be first 'qualitative' rather than 'quantitative'. FLS

context, is the native element and substance of *experience*. In this elemental, an aesthetic bias is native to 'sense' being, as it were, nothing but its 'form and potency'. The influence, which aesthetic habits exercise on thought and action should not be regarded as an intrusion to be resented but, rather, as an *original* interest to be built upon and developed. Sensibility, however, contains the distinctions which reason eternally carries out and applies; such as between 'good and bad, slow and fast, light and darkness'.

With this sense, then, 'man' can, if not dulled by his modern education, or his stifled and tedious hours spent at factory, or assembly line work environments, enjoin his spirit and body to shower upon the world what is in his very essence; that which is entertained by the eyes and hands in combinations with each other to promote that beauty inherent in each person: To the Butchers, Cooks, and Mechanics; to the Artists, Sculptors, Carpenters, Architects and Blacksmiths; Stonemasons and Craftsmen of all kinds, and all the various 'extensions' underlying man's Freedom ['spiritual' or otherwise] to establish beauty, peace and harmony. This is the 'sense' of aesthetics and its manifestations.

The modern wills not to accept this position, he rejects this esoteric analysis yet, surrounded by such vulgar monstrosities as 'his' Concrete Cities, with their 'straight tiered' glass and steel edifices how can one 'spiritually' be connected with himself? This vulgarity, when compared to the uninterrupted evolution of our European antecedents, which the modern calls the 'art' of the Industrialized, has denied man, Western man, that simple 'individual form' of aesthetic art; the same art of Da Vinci who, as a single individual, with a set 'aesthetic ideal', was to promote that ideal for the coming millennia to emulate and enjoy with posterity. Being denied this vision, his spirit, what is left of it, does not soar; rather it conforms to that which must suffice for his daily bread.

The underlying morality of 'aesthetics' lies in both the 'creation and contemplation' of its very beauty.

These feelings, or sense in its purest form, with which the higher-man infects others may be quite varied; they may be, as with those characteristics listed above, be considered weak or strong, very important or very insignificant; they may be very bad or very good. All are manifestations of sense – of Beauty – of that portrayal of who or what we are. Such are the feelings inspired of, and for one's own Country; self-devotion, submission to Fate – of God – expressed in a visual 'drama', an 'allegory' written, or spoken. It is the ecstasy of Lovers engraved in that smoothness of sensuality by a hand that first, and foremost, must have that 'sense' of love and sensuality to create, really create, that image through art. Courage, expressed in a triumphant march or captured on canvas in that one second shot of heroism; a simple quiet meditation of one soul amongst many – this is all part of aesthetics. This is the *distinction* that makes up the morality of the West.

To this extent, Western man must receive his due kudos, in which the acknowledgment of the world recognizes his 'unique' ability to express himself in such ways as spoken of above, such as the Arts or Literature, is not simply the only extant talent inherent in him, but that he also values the rich appreciation of those who *contemplate* such precious gifts – such are those who share, and have the West *within* them, in the realm of thought and deed, and therefore each knows that either by sharing of their talents or by simple appreciation and contemplation of such works they, each of them, is a part of all which has gone before. All who are now, and will become are present at either point of creation or contemplation. As individual, he can share that 'value' presented by those of his Kind, and can share in their accomplishments, which he can then pass on to his contemporaries and descendants the thoughts, and inspiration he has gained from those many others before.

Through this expression of values (i.e. the Arts), the specific effectiveness [of Art] must be gauged by its 'infectiousness' upon the individual, in a positive sense, as a building bloc of the Race-Culture as a whole.

As with all failing Culture-sense, our outlook becomes cloudy, murky, a dream in which our mysteries are seen from a distance, not as our ancestors original vision would see, but as the modern wishes us to see them: As a 'relic' of an Age in which we have now outgrown. No longer is the modern able to look upon the work of his ancestors with respectful 'contemplation', that 'essence' of the spirit of an age which was ever and anon a part of that drama of Western man. Of Reims, or the Monastery of Mount Saint-Michael we are told of a 'european' experience that does not conform to our modes of conduct; indeed, we 'must' [as the modern reveals] break this embryonic relationship because of the sectarian problems inherent in them. We are not to recognize the 'nationalist' (i.e. 'tribal') implications of such magnificence, for it was, precisely, regardless of transient problems, that very racial-national *spirit*, which led to the creation of such genius. Our ability to understand such works has ever been stunted by the modern. We lack, in direct consequence of the modern, the ability to understand, really understand, the beauty and splendor of the craft-work required in the construction of such works of Art. The 'technic' he still possesses, but of that simple ability to 'contemplate' the very essence of this work – nothing.

In contrast to the modern, the simple man and woman of the West are continuously 'infected' by this Art. It must, and of necessity does, stimulate in increasing increments, that 'greater mass' of individuals who are subject to it. The 'abstract', the 'obtuse', these 'artistic perceptions' are not infectious – except if only those modern few who are in turn, 'infected' with the modern interpretation of what Nature provides us to learn from; one can, almost without exception, consider this art to be worthless in a proper consideration of Art.

It is not to the 'abstract', 'Cubist or Dadaist' to which such 'art' holds such visceral fascination, that fascination, which binds the viewer as if it was seen for the first time; the innocence of a spirit who has seen 'magic' for the first time. It is the clearness of such visual effects as the grand Cathedrals, or of DaVinci, or Pousin, which expresses such 'human drama' as is Courage, Honour, and Integrity, vengeance, malice, caprice – all this is human, oh so human – and all those emotions which allow the human spirit to soar ever upwards so that by pure mental insistence, the viewer is brought ever to that realization that he has become infected with Beauty; this individual who is 'receiving' is, in actuality, mingling his essence with that of the author of this art, thereby, becoming more attracted and is satisfied by these feelings transmitted which, intuitively, it seems to him, he has known long and felt deeply. This is that which resides within the higher-man: it is his ultimate value. Some call, or will call this feeling 'mysticism' derisively, seemingly, as it were, to detract from its basic value because the modern has no sense of the 'greatness' inherent in the 'race-soul', that deep well of genius, conflict, drama, and beauty.

The modern claims that we as 'specie' are continually evolving. It is 'evolution' of the 'Newman', evolving upward and away from the old ways; he exhorts us all to cast aside the old garments of the past, which will forever hold us 'small and spiteful'. Yet, in consequence to the modern's 'dreams' of this 'Newman' his art, that reflection of our very soul, he fosters upon the world such 'concepts' which entertain nothing but the spirit of revulsion, of compulsion, against the 'higher-man'. The 'shapes' and 'colours' of objects, which should inspire such deeper emotions as Spiritual or National feelings, such is humanity shaped but, rather, would twist and pervert the concepts of 'draftsmanship' or worse, none at all; the blending of 'natural' colours so as to arbitrarily view the 'outline' of characters which leads the poorly trained mind to wander aimlessly in a turbulent sea of thoughts and décor. To what purpose, then, are the modern's artistic achievements to be accounted?

Art, as with all human technics, must serve a higher purpose. This presupposes that 'art for art's sake' is not what the higher-man is, or should be, striving for. Classical art, bound up in tradition and experience in both a mental and physical state, would always 'direct' the viewer, the receiver, in such ways that would instill such emotions as in the sense of 'tragedy', of Love, Hope, Beauty; of Harmony in Nature, of the simple and enduring beauty of 'Woman and Child', of manly virtues: Courage, Honour, Integrity, compassion and enterprise which will create such an environment so as to be conducive to the future of our sons and daughters, to aid in their respective travels through life. Art is a 'friend' of man, as such, should always extend that relationship. There have always been elements that are not in keeping with 'traditional' culture, the modern would claim this title as his own, but do not let him deceive you; to a point, this is healthy and good, suppression must always be judged in the 'long-term', not in the 'here and now'. The 'health' of the Culture, our Western culture, must always be the test by which we abide 'change'. If and when a 'change' occurs, and it is obvious that the 'end' to which this change is bringing to us is 'bad' in a pure sense, then it is the 'culture-bearing' strata which is obligated by the right of a thing, to excise any virus and eliminate it as waste. This is Duty in its ultimate resonance. It is a mystery to the modern.

This 'duty' of a people to itself is a mystery to the modern, yet he seeks to undo what others have done before him in the name of 'enlightenment', of 'reconstruction'. The modern's value is to replace the 'old' values with those of his new values, for it is the calling of the modern to correct the 'mistakes' of the Fathers who, in their own way, make him feel so inadequate, so insignificant, that he, perforce, must destroy their very existence in those memories of them from within us. He fears the calling of Blood in his veins – therefore, as before, he will eliminate all value in the Arts – mysticism must be eliminated and replaced by evocations of the grotesque, the vain aspirations of the idle who know not the beauty of nature and her endless motifs.

In our present state we rarely, if ever, see in 'modern man' that 'quality' or 'mysticism' in either art or religion. Nevertheless, the mystical experience remains one of the most 'shared' experiences of humankind. Indeed, mankind has been more thoroughly impregnated with 'religions' than he has been with Philosophical Thought. "In the ancient city, religion was the basis of family and social ties."[16] To the modern of today, these are symbols of a dead past, and should not be promoted in either art or religion – they but house the 'fragments' of a dead and alien age. He cannot abide this – and would cry out in agony if he understood, the very deep-rooted essence of that which is understood by the simple mind of his fellows, which, as in ages past has defied him, even as it does today, any qualitative scientific analysis.

Hence it is, by all accounts, that the 'search for God', for morality, for beauty and harmony is, of necessity, a personal one.

The Noble man searches for that invisible [mystical] reality through his normal activity of consciousness. He finds both in his 'conception' of the 'here and now', as well as his search to transcend it. Such an individual, it may happen, will be looked upon by many as 'special'; he may be deemed lunatic or hero. Yet this inner strength, this spiritual light which, ultimately, brings to him that divine inspiration through the contemplation of beauty, and to that which leads poets, mystics, and of consequence, the Noble man, to eventually reach that 'ultimate truth' which will, unflinchingly, lead Western man to his final purpose, must be nurtured and instructed in this path. Such is the 'purpose' of Art.

To ensure this purpose, let those individuals who are gifted by the gods in revealing such a path, be aware of this obliges' to their fellow man. It is a true

---

[16] Spengler, Oswald – Decline of the West – Helmet Werner, trans. Charles Francis Atkinson, pg. 378

and compelling call, do not fail to adhere to the dogma of art: To seek beauty and harmony is to become Noble.

The development and nurturing of higher human beings must be the aim of all our efforts, regardless of what particular craft or profession we have advanced to. These are not mere platitudes assigned to please the liberal but, rather, a necessary reality. It is with this single concept in mind that any lasting superstructure of the Western race-culture be so confined. The 'indispensable' element, that certain class of men, which cannot, and must not, be done away with: this, the element of genius.

To be sure, this is the element of 'extremes', yet without them and their unique styles and rhythms, many of our own revolutionary developments would never have taken root; would never have been. These are such men and women with whom nature has endowed with characteristics such as the 'overgrowth of intellectual or psychological capacities', the personal pain of acceptance, or lack of, which all sentient beings need to overcome circumstance. This may cause 'imbalance' in the fabric of society, but is a part of Culture; this is true evolution. This imbalance in the duality of human nature, which is between persons, or personality, or with one's surroundings or norms should be always taken into account: look to the genius and his direction for instruction. If a gifted individual is confident in his position, well and good; if he is unhappy, then let all consider him, for if there is substance and wisdom in that in which he finds his obsession, for all genius is obsession, then this wretched soul must be pitied and aided in those ways which can, and will realize a healthful end. Each individual is different according to those personal understandings of his particular elements of genius which ever drive him on. It is the duty of individuals and institutions to aid him in his path; in return shall the genius provide 'culture' with hope for a better tomorrow.

Any 'disharmony' between those members of the community may be difficult yet; this disharmony results in the continuous evolution of the 'higher-culture'. It is a passion, driving the race on; it is brought to light by those few individuals who perceive their own ideas of the purpose of Science, Intelligence, the clarity of beauty itself. The only check to be given this 'type/class' is that which nature herself would instill in the body of the race-cultural host, which 'houses' this type of individual. If the purpose of this genius is the far-reaching mental vision of the race-culture as a higher organism, it is well and good. If it is not for the good, as seen from past history and tradition, as seen as common sense, then it is bad, and must at all costs, be eliminated. This, of course, sets up that continuum of duality between the 'inner and outer' man; there will always be two camps of thought on any or numerous issues of the day, so it is that 'debate' will always be 'married' to the collective thought.

These passions, these mental activities obviously, depend upon 'physiological' activities, they must, for they are a part of that 'duality' which is human nature, a thousand generations in the making. These passions, of necessity, are those emotions experienced by all of us – common men all – the genius is no exception. Stages of consciousness, that organic part of a man's essence, are changed through those minute chemical processes, which we observe to correspond to those very differing stages of consciousness, which we call 'emotions'. Conversely, physiological correlations are determined by the various and fluctuating states of the body's physical organs.* These mental [spiritual] and physical aspects of the body are both factors in any sentient being thus, the duality of its being, as well as its conscious awareness of itself. One cannot, at any rate, have one without the other and be considered whole.

Let us take for an illustration the Alcoholic: Intake of this widely used substance from stomach, to bloodstream, from bloodstream to the cerebrum,

---

* We know, for instance, that the application of certain external stimuli, such as Acupuncture, stimulates those regions of the body with minute electrical stimuli, transversing the lines, or Meridians that are commonplace throughout the body. In direct juxtaposition to these meridians, the human organs are affected; diagnosis, in this medical practice, is remarkably accurate. A practitionaer in this field will, for instance, look into the 'eyes' and see a problem located in the Liver, and this in turn, will prompt a question thusly: "Are you experiencing episodes of rage or anger?'
Emotion will evoke 'stress' upon certain parts of the body, and will affect the major body organs in turn. Stress, as in wartime, will produce many such manifestations, including deep psychological manifestations which medical science cannot always explain. Balance, as with all things, must be present for a healthy host to function properly. A healthy person, one who exercises regularly and receives plenty of fresh air, will, undoubtedly, have a better chance to survive both disease of the body and of the mind. FLS

accounts for a 'change' in mental activity; so as with all forms of mind altering drugs, even if used in moderation.*

Passions may be, strictly speaking, part and parcel of the sexual drives inherent in Western man, which have driven him ever onward in his search for himself. Sexual drives are born by many influences, and must, of necessity, be considered when analyzing passions or drives proper. This discussion, however, is not the crass symptomatic illusions of the modern, or the unnatural desire to promote its lower forms, such as the repetitive and crass portrayal of our females in caricature or poses demeaning to their natural beauty. There is no value in this, other than sheer animal Eros; as such, without a host to consummate this desire, the effect of sheer eroticism for its own sake, is misplaced at best, and dangerous to both man and woman, at worst.

Religion, as seen in the modern West, has imposed consequences on sexual behavior, which does not conform to 'social policy' or the accepted 'dogma' of today. This is only right and proper. Yet, those mores and traditions of our fathers and mothers of yesteryear have been dismantled, discarded, and replaced with the exact opposite, guarded by the warders of the 'law' who will enforce this new reconstruction of the masses. In consequence, the proverbial pendulum has swung from the right to left (this has been present for at least one-hundred years, in an ever so slowly evolution of change) creating the new rhythm by which we all must dance; from strict conformity to complete license. Freud was only one of many who promoted this new sexuality. In this respect, Freud was a 'tradition' maker, and employed various techniques to emphasize 'his' (and others) views on the matter. This wide and diverse group of individuals created what is now known as the 'school' of psychoanalysis.

Freud, as the erstwhile 'leader' of this school, begat a strange assortment of followers. In particular, one famous disciple, Franz Boas, boasted an assortment of "friends' and 'social scientists' who were anthropologists; this

---

* Physicians, in today's society, are well known to prescribe medication, which affect the 'symptom', not the cause. In many cases the miser caused by this disservice is incalculable. This is not an indictment of modern medicine, yet it is offered in the hope that doctors of the West will, when faced with a disease, look to other methods of healing rather than medications alone. FLS

slowly and inextricably became the new school of Social Anthropology, which was, immediately, at odds with 'traditional', or forensic Physical Anthropology. From its early days, forensic science took a back seat to the new school, and many major universities soon catered to this new science. Not only here in America, but Europe as well, was inundated with this plethora of new scientists. This has become the supremacy of the modern, that he has 'undone' aeons of generational tradition; no one can deny the accomplishments of persons such as this. Yes, let us admit that it is this 'school' of thought, which belongs to the modern and his followers.

Yet, even in its dim and ambiguous 'sociology', there has been some light, albeit dim, shed upon sexual instinct as it relates to various parts of the human psyche. Both Freud and Boas were flawed to say the least. Freud, in the first instance, worked only with the demented, abnormal, and stunted individuals that had little or no bearing upon normal persons, other than to point out the 'exception' that proved the rule. It is true, that one must examine extremes to find a focal point, but one must also have a reasonable acceptance of what that 'medium' of normalcy is, also. Without the proper bearing, a ship must, of necessity, be set adrift upon an unknown course. Boas, on the other hand, delivered the realm of 'physical science' to that of the non-historical. To the dust-bin of antiquities were placed the study of genetics and eugenics, the study of evolutionary social history as it relates to races and race-cultures as products of environmental factors only; all subsequent human progress was, in fact, due to environment which was accident only. But what, in the platonic sense, creates these accidents? The modern wishes to remain supreme, regardless of the reality or sane appraisal of this natural life of ours.

Sexual drives, held in check by individuals of strong self-discipline, are made stronger by these same [sexual] passions. These individuals release these passions, these energies wantonly, but never irresponsibly. Generally, all "[the] great poets, artists, and saints, as well as conquerors, are strongly sexed."[17] These drives should not be fixed, unless the behavior of persons or individuals becomes so pronounced as to be detrimental to others less versed in the values necessary to control their public behavior. If, at the outset, these drives (here we speak only of those natural interactions between man and

---

[17] Carrel, Alexis – Man the Unknown – Harper&Bro's, 1935, pg. 143.

woman) cannot be accepted by traditional institutions then, it must pass into the realm of renewal and change. The man who seeks to become ennobled, must utilize every opportunity to become master of himself in this, in itself, this requires that he chance new areas of his mental and physical passions. All life, in the final analysis, is change 'within' that natural rhythm of life itself.

Look to the Future for change.

In our ever increasing vision of world instability, the break-up of the 'family' unit, that is, between a man and a woman, coupled with the West's negative birthrate, it seems, more probable than not, that passions long suppressed, and artificially 'reintroduced' by the sexual revolution, so-called, are now seeking their rightful release. We do not speak here, as before, of that 'free love' or pernicious desire to fulfill oneself at the expense of the other faculties of perception, but that deep inner sexuality that marks a balanced and higher individual: it is Romance, in its deepest, and most sincere form. A comparison in naïveté, hardly, for all things depend on one romantic notion or another. It is the spark, which produces great 'love', and it is romance in which the soldier sees his countrymen and their future; greater love hath none, than would give his life for his friends comes to mind. But, in fighting against the modern's picture of the world, the West has taken a serious and dangerous road.

With the numerical advancement of females over males in Western countries, it is increasingly likely that traditional mores and codes of conduct will change. For political reasons, as well as the various natural evolutionary cycle dictates, such attitudes against polygamy, or other non-traditional means to 'increase' the [Western] population will be introduced. These possibilities, of such large-scale import, will be unsanctioned by the church or other state sanctioned 'religions', both of which the modern has rendered impotent and anti-nature. In terms of polygamy the church, such as it is, will condemn this practice; yet at the same time, they [the church] will publicly 'sanction' the interaction between the homosexual as to be 'natural', or least accepted, which is one in the same, in the role and function of church duties and embraced as a 'part of the family'; in consequence, to have a right to choose his own moral law. The church not only accepts this, it codifies it. This is now the status quo of most Western countries.

To the oldest and most affirmed of the commandments, that of replenishing the earth, the modern cries foul.

The non-producing life-style of the 'homo-erotic' is, in the modern's sense, the 'natural' alternative to the earth's over-population. This, however, is beneath any more comment or consideration by sane or rational people. Let us, then, return to reality.

In today's world, 'woman' can ill afford to wait until that 'Mr. Right' comes along, since the mathematical probability exists that her chance is being relegated to insignificance by the sheer lack of male (i.e. western stock) attachments. The fact that her 'first choice' will be highly competitive in nature with other females of her own [western] kind, and just as beautiful as herself, will make it all the more uncertain as to her position in the world of romance, family, and procreation. It is a sad, albeit true position, that it is 'necessary' to provide, economically, a stable and fruitful family in an environment that does not favor nor promote the necessary value of Western life, such as certain monetary enhancements for childbearing, certain incentives for marriage (e.g. five year residency in a Home proper, with the opportunity to purchase after a reasonable time) and the like, rather than the continual denial of same, while at the same time increasing the roles of immigrants who, through no fault of their own, continue to add such an alien flavor to this country, that those of western stock cannot only compete, but question their very survival. The woman who wants a career, love, and sexual alliance, may find that being a member of a family of 'three' or more may suit her, as well as al of their needs in ways that would be literally impossible in the present system.

Children, those persons to whom the modern pays such platitudes, but who receive nothing in return but 'forced' *mis*-direction and instruction, would benefit as well from an untraditional relationship as mentioned above. Born into this 'type' of environment, a small child would be certain to receive that 'special' motherly care so frequently abandoned in modern society; and since a family of two mothers would provide more than adequate care and parental orientation simply by the Mother who 'chooses' to stay home and raise her children, a need and duty which many young women feel impelled to do, but are denied by the denizens of this modern culture and its proponents. Such other duties that are requisite to any relationship are incumbent upon the other partners, and should be delegated with that thought in mind as to invigorate the home life for the betterment of all concerned.

The man, also, would benefit. Confident of an environment that was sound, or better, stable, in the daily activities of his children; he would, also, have more than adequate time for pleasure and the daily comforts associated with it. This is no idyllic postulation, for the Father must, of necessity learn, or at least practice the coordination of all duties expected of by the other partners, as well as himself. This task, to be sure, will take tremendous amounts of energy and responsible application to his family; only a strong man (as well as strong women) will choose this path. It is, after all, the primary strength of the man, at least his specific part in the duality of nature, that must be reconditioned, refined, educated, and fashioned in those directions which will then allow the Family the opportunity to produce its finest fruits: that of the future in the presence of our children.

These unions, while not meant as a 'blue-print' for the future increase of western stock will, nevertheless, with time, be sanctioned by the individual States of the West, if only to replace the enormous loss of Western life, which has been inflicted upon those various western peoples by, and through the practice of abortion which, to date, have murdered some sixteen to twenty millions of our unborn children of western stock.* The number, of course, is more than likely much, much higher since every year many of these numbers are hidden, coloured, or otherwise dismissed from those that seek to ferret out and ascertain what the facts truly are, and who honestly care about there brethren, and who wish to have a simple and forthright discussion regarding these matters with their fellows.

To the business of 'replennishing' man, I am sure, will take up this burden readily. He must, however, be taught (at an early age) that his responsibilities lie not only with himself, but with his progeny, his children, and that there is no such a responsibility as that of the nurture and direction, which will establish their future; that these sentient beings are developing in that nascent stage of life which requires the attention of both male and female, but in this

---

* Of the approximate 1.5. Million women who have had abortions in the year 1987, 63% had never been married; 18.5% were married; 11.2% divorced; 6.4% separated. As to Religion, 41.9% were Protestant; 31.5% Catholic; 1.4% Jewish; 2.9% other; and 22.2% listed no religion. As to Race, 68.6% were White; 31.4% non-white [Associated Press – 7/4/89] X's this rate since Roe v. Wade. FLS

day and age, has been the purview of the woman. This 'stage' requires and demands the Father's attention. Husbanding, as well, the role of man and woman together, must be learned and prescribed, as it was traditionally, despite its many perceived limitations, and regardless of any personal pleasure he might seek from this 'type' of union. Sexual experience, unlike that of the modern, is not his main priority. This construct of a potential direction for the West is not intended to be any 'free for all', or 'free love' of the past, between the various components of western society, but as a stable and confident approach to a future which ever seeks those answers so as to survive intact.

All these visions are, of necessity, pure speculation. Indeed, it may be asked just where this line of thought is going. The only answer to this is this: If we [Western stock] are to reach our potential as a people, as a Race, as an individual, if we are to gain nobility then, we must utilize all sources to that end, all our reserves of energy in the completion of that ideal to become better. This means, as well, that we excel physically and spiritually. In terms of procreation, utilizing multiple spouses, the simple mathematical probability would assure that united blood of genius would be realized. In this day and age, it is the genius that is most needed, not the mediocre that abounds so numerically in positions of power today. This, of course, is a quick 'genetic' programme, and must not be confused in any way with an extensive or long-term arrangement for the careful selection of mates who, by their consent and knowledge, would promote the birthing of higher individuals: physically more sound in constitution, and readily more adaptable to the needs of their people and culture. This, also, is the Future. It is for the rising West.

But let us continue.

In consequence to those positions stated, or unstated above will, in turn, multiplied by a hundred-million, create an environment which is healthier and more vibrant than any culture made up of the feeble-minded. This point is axiomatic, yet how many individuals who consider themselves a higher-man, mentally understand, really understand, that the quality of the psychological state of any social group defines, in large part, the number, quality, and its 'will-to-express' intensity of each individual consciousness, as well as its tell-tale manifestations, that is to say, the collective consciousness.

ii.

The Technics of Religion:

Values and Perceptions

Religion is the technic of primitive man's attempt at structuring his innermost feelings, fears, and desires into a working formula. This dynamic, in turn, creates his 'values and perceptions'. Religion, to put it simply, is everything that man himself feels is good, which he then 'codifies', for the betterment of his soul, and by extension, those that make up his culture. Religion, then, is always a matter of mental attitudes and perceptions, but is *always* the product of the race, which has established its foundations.

In the Christian technic, Jesus was good, yet he insisted upon destroying all that the 'good' Pharisees had spent their lives in defending and promoting. His 'actions', as seen by the leaders of his day, were 'evil', not good. It was through his incendiary rhetoric that he turned the existing establishment upside down. This first Evangel created his own technic, his own religion; and those that followed were left with the entitlement as well as the direction of that technic. In both aspects it was, and is, attitudes and perceptions, which make up the Religion propounded by its adherents, for with time, as with attitudes, perceptions change.

If Jesus was a 'higher-man', then to challenge the 'good' of incumbent civilization is, by definition, good. Of course, this cycle is dual in nature, and does not presuppose that just because there is an incumbent civilization, or established order, that to challenge it, and thereby succeeding, is good. This is, on the other hand, a matter of common sense and of tradition. It is moral sense.

Moral sense is, seemingly, completely ignored by the modern and his society. They [the modern] have ignored those elements in any healthy society which is fundamental, namely, the 'common folk', those industrious and responsible individuals who have a healthy knowledge of what is good and evil in their daily lives; past on perhaps, through generations, from grandmother or grandfather, and forever back. The modern thinks them capable of nothing more that what he derisively calls 'simple faith', superstition, and the like.

Consequently, the Modern and his associates are constantly at war with these elements: either 'socially or politically'. The Modern, of course, is rational. One only has to look upon the modern's modes of communication technics, his advertising strategies, or his preoccupation with 'social policies' to see that he leaves nothing to chance: if there is a god, it is Him. The modern may be many things, but obtuse he is not; from the maxim 'train your young in the ways they are to go' the modern has learned much. But the common folk, the vast majority of the gene-pool, know in which ways they should go, regardless of those occasional flirtations with novel change.

Theologians, also, of every shape and size, colour, faith and agenda, have *rationalized* their religions. They have destroyed its *mystical* sense, that sense of the all being as one, the belief that the group consciousness held in check by the 'idea' or 'belief' in something larger than themselves. The higher-man is akin to this mysticism as 'mass-man is akin to organism'. Each is an outgrowth of time and space. Higher man strives ever for the revitalization of the individual and the collective mass. It is his duty to respond to their needs. This is, and has always been, the duality of man, of higher-man.

The Christian West, for to use less than this 'title' would deny more that two-thousand years of religious technic known to Europe, America, and beyond. In this 'space' of time however, Western Christianity has yet to agree on just what, exactly, it is. Schism upon schism has wreaked such havoc as to completely *dissolve* the unity and continuity of ancient Christendom (i.e. the 'Christ kingdom'). These schisms had deep significance in a psychological sense to those recipients of the 'word', be that 'word' heretical or holy. After all, each warning schism claimed supreme authority to mark and guide their proselytes in the way of their particular salvation. From the beginning, whether it was 'high-priest' or today's modern 'bishop', it has been those who have controlled political power of those western political technics, which are driven by the oldest trait recognized in man: Survival.

The deep, inner- soul of man is of the same desire.

Man, Western man, has searched in his own fashion, for those answers belonging to Life, as he perceives it. In his primitive state, that is, before the modern, western man has responded to life in different ways but, more often than not, it has been an instinctual aggression to the forces of nature which, as the case might be, caused him to fear that which would destroy him; that which threatened his survival. He did, regardless of the modern's position that early man was 'devoid' of spirituality, that is to say, that 'he understood his presence in the world'. That Western man believed, really believed in something 'outside' of himself is manifest by every attempt he made to 'record' his presence in the 'art', 'motifs', 'totems' and relics, which he has left. A *legacy* for us to partake in.

Whatever the 'belief' was, is pure speculation on our, the children of these spirits', part. Whether this belief was seen, or performed through say, for instance, a tree, stone, river, or lake, it was an extension of what he believed. This belief was *absolute*. It could not be separated from him; it was all he knew. He 'prayed' and, if that prayer came to pass, well, it was a 'magical' thing; it became, in our words, *mystical*. He gave up his soul, willingly, to that which blessed him, and which had answered by delivering to him his 'need' or 'desire'. This 'mental' state is the 'healthy state' of faith. This is belief, which denies all 'outside' reason. This is the 'faith' of a child.

This, then, is the essence of 'all' religion: Without *faith*, there can be no *value*.

Alternatively, conversely, without value, there can be no morality, this is the purpose stated, or unstated of *all* of man's religions. However, subjective reality dictates that 'morality' proper, as an extension of each individual or its racial components, the race-culture, are subjective by each racial experience, its history, its location/territory, and all the factors, which predispose a People to be who they are, even as we see them. So, the question is now asked, "Are there morals for some, but not for others?" If there are various degrees of morality, or at least a perception of morality, by which, precisely, is the morality, which we mark the higher-man, hence the higher-culture?

Since there are races of men and, hence, race-cultures, differing in make-up and certain outward manifestations, there is, of necessity, differences in both consciousness and its related technics. It matters not, whether environment or genetics accounts for the majority of these differences. One may, with less than unnecessary gratuity, point out that it is quite simple to distinguish between races based upon the obvious examples, or characteristics, of skin colour, morphology and the like when delineating between what we call 'races' and 'race-cultures'. For example, one can well point to the Chinese or Egyptian race cultures as being fundamentally different; this is seen in their Art, politics, or empire-building natures inherent in each culture at any given point that is known historically. To add, is there not a difference between the Teutonic and Amerindian race-cultures as defined in the same way? Of course there is.

Therefore, it is as safe to say that 'morals, 'traditions', 'psychology', and 'history' are way-signs to those selfsame distinctions, as it is to say that 'environment and heredity' are dualities that are needed to make a complete and balanced individual.

The identity of individuals as well as societies is obvious to all who have eyes to see. For the People of the West however, in our myopic understanding of the 'macro-element', it seems to be difficult to grasp, in its entirety, the breakdown, or categories of races and cultures. We do, of course, differentiate between 'races' based on colour; we also differentiate between religious technics along the same lines. We recognize, or should be unafraid to recognize, an inherent, although highly integrated alien personality in those various aspects of 'religious' sense that is contrary or dissimilar to our own. Yet, as we consider things from the 'inside' looking 'out' we fail, to discern the differences between our past and contemporary vision of Western culture, let alone the various and sundry cultures with which we interact. The modern, even with the landscape emblazoned before his very eyes, refuses to see the underlying consciousness of race, and its consequences in the natural setting of history and psychology.

The religion of the West,* constituting the largest majority cohort of white-Europeans in Europe at any given time, based their individual sympathy or antithesis not upon some others 'religion' nor, in any supra-national sense, on scriptural differences, but on 'race-cultural' differences – even if this included 'intra-national' implications. Race, pure and simple, was the *line* of demarcation of our ancestors. This, of course, is in perfect harmony with nature. I agree with Huxley in this regard when he states, "In whichever we look on the matter, morality is based on feeling, not on reason."ᶲ The Scottish philosopher, Thomas Reid, also concurs when he adds, "…for that which makes men capable of living in society is that their actions are regulated by

---

* Most notably Catholicism of 1500 onwards, since this 'sect' was known to the major European governments, constituting 'christendom' as they knew it before the great Reformation. FLS
ᶲ [Quoted] McDougal, William – The Energies of Men – Vol. IV, 1932.

the common principles of human nature," [] and as we have seen, primitive western man had a complete set of predispositions and proclivities to act and react in certain tell-tale ways. He would accept certain thoughts, and reject others. Some may say that this form of society is led and fostered by 'race-prejudice'; yet, I am inclined to agree with yet another voice on this matter, that of W.G. Sumner, when he declares, "The great mass of any society lives a purely instinctive life."[γ] Hence, what man sees as evil or good is right in the only way he knows it and, with time, establishes itself with mores and traditions that may cause conflicts with any one, or numerous other parties which share a close proximity with him, either nationally or personally.

Religion is for the Individual Consciousness, which created it.

Religion, as a human dynamic is not simply an exercise in metaphysics. As we have seen pointed out earlier in this sub-chapter, 'religion' is simply the technics of the 'actualized presence' of the primitive man. It comes from his deep and pure [spiritual] sense, his feelings, his human nature, his very essence which, then, he derives his morality. He senses its vitality to him, its fundamental usefulness to him in his day-to-day activities. He needed no one to 'teach' or 'indoctrinate' his mind with this, no priest or politician, to show him this truth. Even now, today, Western man is acutely aware that these senses, his feelings, affect him at this moment.

Primitive man's religion affected his immediate family, his tribe, and his race in the collective sense. His sympathy and concern was for them, those which made up his environment and his moral condition; it was not intended for the alien – the outsider. This 'morality', for that is truly what it was, made him in another sense patriotic, for he now felt a higher calling than himself, a duty, perhaps felt intrinsically, as a divine duty, to those which made up his immediate world and their institutions. Thus religion/morality included all his passions according to his inner and outer behavior and, also its accompanying prejudices and discrimination relative to his health. Of course, this would take on both the dimension of love and hate as psychological boundaries set him to task in both the creation and protection of his familial entitlement – his territorial nation. In later years, this would of course have disastrous effects

---

[] Glover, T.R. – Collected Works – Vol. I, pg. 451.
[γ] Sumner, W.G. – Folkways – 1906, pg. 45.

on racial composite empires or states that would make war on one another in a series of internal conquests for that same territory or familial (i.e. political) hegemony. This was not to change until man appreciated the value of Nation States to promote protection of the individual, as well as the collective racial state; this made him willing to give his life for the 'state', which, in all reality, was himself, a hundred-million fold.

The modern example of Christian and Saracen is appropriate here.*

- Let the reader be aware that these words were penned in the early months of 1989. What has transpired since then, most members of western stock, living on this northern continent, will be aware of. But the rudimentary beginnings, that earthly 'contest of wills' is far older than this time frame. It would take many volumes to extrapolate the 'cause and effect' ratio by which we presently find ourselves, and to be able to completely understand and fathom it.

Let me simply add this small token to you, the reader, for valuable information and instruction: T.E. Lawtence, better known, as 'Lawrence of Arabia' was a unique individual of Western stock. His English roots suited him well the travails to which life would offer him in full doses. He lived and warred with Arabians of all stripes, and grew to know not only them, but Jews as well, Berbers, and moors; rich and poor, he knew them all. He was engineer, adventurer, and military man. He was also, a keen observer of what 'was going on around him' and he wrote down (and sometimes drew) what he experienced. *The Seven Pillars of Wisdom – a Triumph –* Doubleday, Doran, & Co., Inc., 1935, is such a work that is rivaled by few; the 'complete' unabridged 'politically incorrect' observations of someone who 'lived' life, and was not afraid to say what he saw. The British government did not enjoy this tome at all, and continuously sought to ban or delay its production. It was printed nevertheless, and it would behoove all people's interested in what is going on in the middle-east as you read this, to read from beginning to end, this most valuable work. Let me briefly share a few quotes from the above edition:

"Some of the evil of my tale may have been inherent in our circumstances. For years we lived anyhow with one another in the naked desert, under the indifferent heaven. By day the hot sun fermented us; and we were dizzied by the beating wind. At night we were stained by dew, and shamed into pettiness by the innumerable silences of stars. We were a self-centered army without parade or gesture, devoted to freedom, the second of man's creeds, a purpose so ravenous that it devoured all our strength, a hope so transcendent that our earlier ambitions faded in its glare." (page 29) And more:

"The everlasting battle stripped from us care of our own lives or of others'. We had ropes around our necks, and on our heads prices which showed that the enemy intended hideous tortures for us if we were caught…''Each day some of us passed; and the living knew themselves just sentient puppets on God's stage…'I was sent to these Arabs as a stranger, unable to think their thoughts or subscribe their beliefs, but charged by duty to lead them forward and to develop to the highest any movement of theirs profitable to England in her war." T.E. Lawrence was, in fact, an agent for the British government who, by placing Lawrence in midst of Arabia, hoped thereby to gain ascendancy over the Turks who were allied at that time with England against Germany. In other words, England would, by stealth and maneuver, destroy both an

Both these groups shared similar roots;* both followed the same historicity as regards their rituals, laws, and similar codes of conduct. The conflict, instead of being strictly regarded as a 'religious war', was more properly regarded as a race-cultural war. In point of fact, it was a 'war' between to racial stocks: Semitic vs. indo-European; it was, and is, a home-grown 'judaism/islam' vs. 'aryanized' *semitic*-Christianity of two distinct cultures vying for politico/religious power – and it will Always be this way – unless, and not before, one element is 'completely' victorious. Victory is not subjective, and both opposing sides will saddle themselves with 'any' power, foreign or domestic in their region, to accomplish this. This battle continues today, and it is, make no mistake about it, a battle for 'world supremacy'. The present day involvement, which is generational in nature, in this selfsame region, has brought this nation no outcome, no victory, in the actualizations of these selfsame ideals and goals. One might, if asked, call this scenario an 'endless cycle' of violence.

All 'religious' [moral] considerations are based primarily on this duality of love and hate.

What man *desires* to love, he will preserve. What he hates, man will destroy. This is 'human nature' in its most basic and fundamental confluences. This is a Universal 'life-law'. The 'moralist' will philosophize, the 'preacher' cant; yet it is this foundation to which all human emotion and spiritual balance is predicated. A stable and balanced psychology (i.e. mental outlook) is the end product, if these laws are followed. If they are not, then imbalance, conflict, and instability is its way sign. Any Religion, which does not preach this duality

---

'enemy' and a 'friend', such was the thinking of Lord Kitchner and the financial establishment of the 'City' and most of the 'anglo-establishment' of the day. Professor Carroll Quigley, mentor to president Clinton, has much to say in this monumental tome "Tragedy and Hope" regarding the new 'modern' man in his future worldwide ambitions. FLS

* The Kurdish people, of whom their leader, Saladin, was numbered, share a high proportion of blondes and light-eyed children even today. It is reported by some that Saladin himself was reddish-blond and had eyes of green or hazel. This would indicate the problems of 'fraternity' with which the various 'tribal' enclaves use so often, so as to gain favor with one or more tribal leaders to maintain their own power and control. Racial composites make up a vast mosaic of conflicts and treachery for we, as a Western nation, to find ourselves in such a precarious position; and with allies such a Britain to sweeten the 'victory', how can we lose? FLS

of human nature, is out of touch with its human proselyte, and is working for another agenda unknown to the faithful.

The moral duality of 'love' and 'hate' is our perception of *good* and *evil*.

The definition of good and evil however, is based on reason derived from a long history of Western technics rather than, let us say, from Chinese or sub-Saharan cultures, yet is always inextricably woven with the experiences of humanity[1] in the macro-element of human history. The 'good' is related to justice, beauty, harmony, and all things charitable. The 'evil' then, means ugliness, selfishness, injustice, and mean-spiritedness. In theory, at least confined to our study of the West, Christianity provides us with rules of conduct based upon what remains of Christian values. In addition, 'who' follows these values? The 'mystic' perhaps, or most certainly those who choose the lifestyle of a 'prophet' perhaps? Inevitably, this leaves us with –

---

[1] I use the term 'humanity' simply because the West, being apart in a 'racial' sense must, and does play an integral part with all the other race-cultures; the emulation of each other is not without risk to both parties. But, and I cannot stress this enough; we are *not* the same as the other race-cultures, the emulation of each other is not without risk to both parties. Each must have their own 'space' from which to grow and become that which Nature herself intended. Preservation, for each distinct racial group, is not only fair, but it is right in light of nature and nature's god.
Scientific study has shown that 'space' resides in the mind of man. Nature, as an abstract, does not have boundaries or territory; it is the unique animal, including man, which creates in his mind what boundaries he is to have, or accept. Studies also show that 'confined' space leads inexorably to a limited population, not food supply as Malthus indicated. If this were accepted by academics today, the Nationalistic xenophobia experienced by liberal bigots would show the weakness of their case concerning 'inter-nationalism' as the sole means by which population would then be controlled by their 'social mores' being implemented on a worldwide scale; this would also include their insane efforts at population control – which effects the Western with far more brutal ramifications than those of the third-world. In a normal setting and with normal national boundaries the 'human-race' would naturally gravitate to a more or less standard population size and dynamic, coupled with the natural tendency to fear the 'outsider' would maintain the necessary equilibrium requisite to any and all race-cultures. The basic 'intra-national' problems, which inevitably will arise is a natural part of that particular race – and should not be interfered with by altruistic 'do-gooders' such as in Africa; for as much as Western philanthropists have attempted to create a National State, they failed to comprehend the dynamics of the herd, and sub-herd evidence in all organisms - that of Language, Tribal Allegiance, Religion, and the like which must take its own course in Federalism 101, such as this western Colony had to do in our infancy – something that is still in the process of its own evolution. FLS

whom? Very few can live a life, which requires a man to discipline himself in any manner, let alone one that embraces 'morality' in a dogmatic and hypocritical sense such as that of the modern's Christianity. The noble man, as well as those who wish to become ennobled, must first instill a self=discipline upon himself; he need not rely on any 'outer' technic to supply him with his morality. After all, are the technics of religion, its perceptions, and values, simply an acceptance of things unseen (?) or is it simply the actual personal interdiction into life itself?

One of the most notable of personalities, and one that by most accounts, was the most successful in the spiritual and physical interdiction of Life's rhythmic cycles was he who died on a cross. This was his value, extending through the millennia to our present day. No one person, who claims to be a practicing Christian, can keep this claim until he 'practices what he preaches'. His cross has yet to be crafted.

This 'act', that of dying on a cross, is not a 'faith', but a 'doing', which requires a conscious perception of right and wrong; and if one cannot do a 'right', he will die for the continuation of those who may follow his example. Each in turn, the teacher. This is, and has always been, the mark of the Noble man.

This act did not presuppose 'equality' with those persons who surrounded him, this first Evangel; he was in constant struggle and conflict [nature's eternal imperative] with those around him, those individuals which, ever and anon, sought to silence him. To the modern however, as Christian, his vision of mental, physical, and spiritual equality is ever present. In nature however, we see time after time, and time again, each [man's] perception is unique; even intuition can belie logic when both should be in harmony for a natural balance. The 'articles' of the modern Christian consists of faith, but not of a doing. When the christian 'does' a thing, it is usually hot on the heels of some inevitable emotional response conceived by those whose agenda is in the forefront, and lacking in those noble tenets of intellectual compassion and restraint. Yes, it is in their 'undoing' that the modern Christian shows his lack of self-discipline; they show that lack of authority, which defines a responsibility, or lack of responsibility to themselves and their own survival – that is to say, the survival of their own kind; their own race-culture.

In societies of the West, the modern has led the pack in his example, which he teaches every weekend; he teaches *meekness,* he teaches *charity*; he expounds the doctrines of individual faiths to those persons (i.e. spirits) that neither comprehend, in a Western sense, nor are naturally inclined or drawn to those thoughts and feelings of the West. Certain it is that any one individual or group may emulate to the point of 'expertise', but never really fathom it, that is, in the *conceptual* way that its 'creators' would except, perhaps, in an abstract sense by these persons [spirits]. When there is a response, such as the rudimentary mimicry of Pavlov, the *modern* Christian pounds his chest with songs of platitudes and self accolades; they bless themselves and their doctrines for the 'divine' chance at *'saving a new soul'*. As if any group or individual can in some way create the umbilical tie between Divine Spirit and *human acceptance* of that divine spirit: these same moderns, who are meek to the point of cowardice; the rules of manly courage having been set aside for the possibility of 'heaven' and protection from their own weaknesses

As with all values and perceptions there is, for the modern, that penultimate doctrine of self – of Faith. The one value that determines the modern's attitude toward these issues is *a priori* of the modern Christian – Redemption. This ambiguous reference of things *to be* is their overriding compulsion; it is their will-to-power. It is to the *exclusion* of all other aspects of Life that the modern strives ever to *'spread the word of God'* to all and sundry who have ears hoping, in fact depending on, for their very existence, that this *compulsion* will assure their reward in a heavenly kingdom [for an *erstwhile* job well done!]. The Race, the Culture, or present day mental state of their people, their blood, means nothing compared to that great *reward*. To think otherwise would put the unfortunate 'unbeliever' in the category of infidel or heretic; this dynamic then, becomes the classic 'inner' and 'outer' man concept held in such disrepute by the liberal and his minions of 'modern christianity'. But there is more.

It is, therefore, in the shadow of such as 'redemption', that this spirit, or lack of same, in their potential proselyte, even when contrary to all that is Western, is then in *fulfillment* of their cataclysm. Their mission on earth, for they have no other *ambition* on earth, is to *have nothing whatsoever to do with the earth*, since their life would, and will ever be, in Heaven. But is this really the Christians outstanding motive and authority?

The deep instinct for *how* one must live is a *human* element, that deep wellspring of life's rhythm, which one must follow or die, is Eternal. To experience a 'thing', to enjoin oneself with a 'feeling', *to be born again*, that presence of one who is already [living in a mental state] in 'heaven', this 'feeling' of being *eternal*, is an act of *desire – of wishing for a new 'reality'*. At the same time, that spirit which *is* man, his *human* duality, is inexorably striving to *'become'*, and is drawn downward, to its roots, to the earth itself; to Life. He then feels, somehow, withdrawn, small, incapable of reaching a higher state of being because of 'sin' – his *mark*; that which will always be with him, a slave to himself and his fears. He lives with these two realities: one *natural*, one *artificial*. He wants to embrace both, but cannot master either. He is then put adrift on an Ocean of indecision and inaction. He is afraid.

The Modern can never truly separate himself from this earth. He sees what he sees because he 'needs' to see a 'reality' which allows him to fail – and *then* be redeemed – to follow the same course again, and again, knowing full well that as long as 'redemption' awaits, he may carry on. The Modern has no relative concept of a man's duality, that living a full life [here on earth] is simply a *part* of a larger balance; that there *is* something after death, an abyss which must, of necessity, have something to offer other than blackness. As spirit and inquiry are a natural outgrowth of our evolution, these concepts, while arising through the culture of the West are, nevertheless, alien to the Modern; concepts of an 'after-life', 'cyclic' change, and the like are intrinsic 'racial' beliefs/concepts which belong to those of the West only, being a part of his particular path through his racial evolution. The Modern can then, in his wild aspirations of social change, 'equality', and financial control [for without money he cannot control] work against his own 'instincts' and common sense, for an *aim* which baffles the common folk – but no matter – it is, after all, for their own good; who really cares, after all, if 'mistakes' are made along the way, as long as it works out in the end: one can be redeemed.

Redemption, as a concept, can also share and occupy the reality of an individual in his present life. As an *objective*, as a *goal*, it then becomes a 'value of perception', but only as a prerequisite for a 'doing', and must, of necessity, be tempered with the reality of the needs, feelings, and future life of the race and culture – *his* race-culture. If it happens that one's instinct for one's own survival is negated by such a perception as 'redemption' then, it is unhealthy, it is alien in both thought and concept, and will kill the host. If this view of 'redemption' or its perception however, is consonant with one's own life, that is to say, that he understands its intrinsic meaning to himself, to free himself from the abyss of human guilt, and that his race-culture may thereby be freed with him, then it is healthy. The *Redeemer*, himself, knew this. He knew the difference. He *chose* the Cross, *his* cross, not to usher in redemption as only a 'spiritual' reality, but to show one *how* to live. Through his personal discipline, his personal antagonism against those that would deny his innermost morality, he gave his Life – which we might gain thereby, by his *example*.

This was and is the morality of the primitive – he knew by instinct his method and his destiny – he actualized that which he died for: Himself. Today, we have only His *remnants*. We have only the shadow of what was his will-to-express. Yet, the morality of good and evil remains a part of Western race-culture – although by only a very fine thread, and will most certainly break under the constant strain of the Modern who, by his continual 'dissolution' of tradition, and values belonging to a unique spirit by 'forcing' all comers, all those disparate race-cultures, to attempt to enjoin themselves with it, will inevitably allow this thread to break. Those of the West, those untold millions of souls who, because of their deep-seated instinct are guided by these primal feelings, those selfsame feelings of the first Evangel, are at odds with the Modern; the chasm between the two is ever widening, and no bridge of today's making will conquer the divide. To this faith, to these feelings, the Modern declares: *Blasphemy!* He fears the *faith* of the child.

iii.

The Awakening::

His Ascent

Since the beginning of time, our morality has not changed; rather, it is the technics by which our various epochs have molded themselves, which have *molded* us, changed us, as a people in the process. Upon entering the Seventeenth-Century however, it changed for all time. The *division* between dogma and morality changed the face of Western man for the unforeseeable future – whether for good or ill, it remains with us. The 'consciousness' of man was, forever, given back to him. He was to *reform* himself, and mold a new reality from the old; he saw it as the inevitable outcome of 'infancy' to 'adulthood'. Constraints, as seen by the child are always bonds, chains, which keep him in check, bound to his parents and authority, which ever seeks to limit his aspirations. Children almost always hate, and are jealous of their parents – this is natural law. It is part and parcel of the stages of maturity.

In the numerous epochs of Western man, he has achieved greatness. The Industrial Revolution of our epoch brought him nothing less. His legacy, past and present, marks his passing; his *territory* defines it, yet in direct relation to his so-called 'advanced stage of technics', he has declined in health and vitality on a steady and direct downward path. He lives *longer*, but does not *live* better. The ailments of yesterday have been overcome, only to resurface a few generations [medical advancements not withstanding] later in relation to his, and in direct proportion to his psychology, physiology, his biological make-up, as well as his mentality – his *outlook*. He has conquered the 'virus' and 'smallpox' but, in direct response to this, he has created a completely new horde of mental and physiological problems, which is contributed by his new [modern] life-style in the massive monstrosities known as 'cities'. He is saturated by the various fumes from exhaust of automobiles, factories, airplanes, public dumps and the like; he is surrounded by mountains and valleys of concrete forms which, outside of their obvious 'longevity', are devoid of that 'artistic' element, which marked the West so ineluctably in times past. His mental attitudes, of necessity, are changed by this spectacle and bombard him from all sides. These attitudes, so necessary to a balanced life and psychology, are increasingly foreign to his own instinctual awareness, forcing him to *separate* from himself, never quite able to adjust, and become absorbed into this 'personification of attitudes', which surrounds him. If Western man does accede to these new attitudes, to split himself in two, however, he will surely cease to exist. All organisms seek to extend themselves, in the *original* state, which their make-up was designed.

The personification of the primitive, natural man, is not found in the monstrosities we call cities today. How can it be? For the modern, *city* is tailor made for him and his corporate mentality – his *bustle*, his *hustle*, his *investments*, his *take-over* – all this a 'service' to the 'world' economy yet, nothing to his own kind, his brothers and sisters of the flesh He, the modern man, rests assured that the 'trickle' of his efforts will be spread equitably. The modern is distanced from his own kind, for he does share in *kind*, whether he admits or no, with whom he inhabits the same territory; those selfsame individuals whom he, the Modern had brought to these shores and put to work for some ten generations or more, those whose democratic vote he daily prostitutes himself and his people for. The Modern has fostered and created this 'mass', this collected assortment of humanity for himself, but cannot, will not, ever fully accept them. He *never* will accept them. And what of Western man? For now, he holds positions as tenuous as his relationship with his own kind, those few who remain with him. As a member, in many instances, of the upper strata of management, he feels that lack of contact with the essence of what he, *himself*, is actually doing in the scheme of things. Indeed, his life, his spirit becomes immersed in the *idea* of the corporation. It is all so much *busywork*.

The personification of the primitive, that naïve and simple person, that person in which all forms of nobility is to be found, warts and all, is not found in the *morass* of numbers, of mass, but always in the *pure essence* of [human] nature – that of the child, with the undiluted purity and trust in the world, which belongs to all such generations.

With faith, as we have seen, the simplicity of the child is manifest, for the child *truly* believes; he follows nature's natural proclivities in its constant rhythmic design. The modern, however, has forgotten those things necessary for a balanced upbringing in a child, *his* [the modern] awareness is not that of his antecedents, and that was always expected, if not always attained, to create a superior physical, mental, and spiritual individual. From child to adult, it is the 'life-stage' set with the props necessary for a fuller, happier life, which are defined by the Nation, the State, the county, and the home. These are perceptions of a normal life cycle, created by its own impetus.

The Modern seeks ever to build, to create, as well – oh, yes! – *how* he loves to build; but he does not *build better or more beautifully*. He builds with concepts of beauty which run *against* the natural will of his fellows, of *their* beauty, of *their* culture, nor is he concerned with what his human counterpart feels about this selfsame environment. Whether it is 'good' or 'evil' for them – or even himself!

It is the Modern who has created 'class' as we see it today. Not in nature's natural setting of *strong* or *weak*, *clever* or *stupid*, these are nature's grades; he who fails to make the grade, dies. The modern, in a futile attempt to 'create' something, anything, has taken these natural orders or grades, and has *created* the 'ideal' of one who is 'noble' and called him merchant, this new 'priest' has become the social politician, and has now presented them *as* noble and priest. It is the rising of the West however, that has reawakened that ancient spirit of the higher, yet nobler man. Unlike the Modern and his essence, the noble man cannot depend on his blood alone; he must *create* it himself. He must first *envision* it.

Eugenics is the *science* of Heredity.

This science, in conjunction with the various other specialties (which should be considered part of 'general' health) such as psychology, physiology, obstetrics, gynecology, immunobiology, etc., is the first foundations of the higher and nobler man. Eugenics, either in its passive or active sense, has been the form in which healthy children have passed into the actual world of their parents – holding both the good and not so good of their parents – synthesized in their own make-up, hopefully fuller and better human beings than their parents were; *all* parents should hope for, and strive for this. The failure to breed [ultimately, as said before, marriage is our breeding *institution*] healthy children, was the death of a People; even the so-called primitive knew, instinctually, that a healthy people, and the healthy introduction of future life, was the secret to extension and strength. This assured that a people, any people, would not *perish* from the earth.

There was no good or evil here; there was only survival.

Today, however, we are modern. We are now *civilized*.

It is held that primitive man was brutish, coarse, and lacked that emotional 'civility', which we possess today. But what of it? Could we not, even today, say the same for many parts of the earth, even our own common territory? It was the primitive man, in a healthy state of nature, who allowed those feeble-minded and sickly children to be taken by the natural elements – they were allowed to die – just as nature had dictated.

The Modern, replete with his textbooks on science [and *ethics* too!], history, and theology, has relegated a part, a part with which the Modern cannot deny or control, of those textbooks *obsolete*, and so the *wisdom* accompanying it. The eugenicist has fallen into disrepute. To those who shout this science down, a *caveat*: Knowledge, *once gained*, can never be fully eradicated.

It was after the Second World War, that second war of fratricide between those of Western stock, after that Faustian embryo was smashed (but not destroyed), that the study and observation of eugenics was stilled - at least publicly – and openly led to the Modern's *version* of race and race-culture in his tattered and coloured patchwork of 'environment' *over* that of 'genetics'. Those written testaments of Socrates, Plato, Appolodorus, Herodotus, Pliny, Strabo, Virgil, Apollonius, Shakespeare, even of Caesar, or Alexander for the sheer power of their keen eyes, even these were of no vital import to the Modern on this subject.

The Modern need not worry about the 'facts' of history, he would simply *say* the words, whatever they might be, which he, himself believed, *and presto!*, it would be so. This is what he has done with the words 'environment' and 'genetics'. Savonarola would have been proud! Yet the modern does not, will not, discount completely the knowledge of his fathers, for without it, he would be lost in the maze he has created. He has, nevertheless, allowed eugenics to pass into the void of 'antiquated' Science, something to be denied one person, but utilized in *his* defense if needed. This, of course, created a vacuum in the analytical study of the *origin* and, therefore, the *continuation* of man. This lack of vision has been at the crux of Western man's apathy and dismal present day performance. *He does not know who he is, where he comes from, or how he may become better.*

The second war of fratricide brought many changes to the people of the West. Before this time, none of the 'community' of geneticists opposed the 'science of heredity' in toto; in fact, the spirit of Western man was being lifted by Science, instead of being left in the dark *by* it.

On the one side you had supporters, on the other you had those who were limited by their lack of vision in the face of a seemingly dark and unknown area in which only the pioneers were the ones to blaze the trails and mark the hazardous areas. Some were skeptical in varying degrees, but no one condemned eugenics completely. Those that disagreed, often as not, disagreed in those areas that one might find anywhere if any modicum of human nature is present, not to mention the various levels of 'opinion', 'perspective', and 'personal attachment' would naturally allow. S.J. Holmes, one of the few truly visionary geneticists and scholars had this to say during these times of heated debate and 'Sherlock-type' investigations into the matter:

> "People differ over eugenics because they differ over such subjects as the validity of mental tests, the degree to which environment is responsible for the development of this or that character, the extent to which children tend to be like their parents in mental traits, and question how far social and economic status is correlated with level of intelligence."[18]

In the final analysis, this discussion is absolutely imperative to the Rise of the West. It must be in line with that future which will mark the higher man.

iv.

In extent, which is unparalleled in any other specie on earth, man creates his own environment. He is subjected to many influences exerted by his fellow beings, as well as the concerted efforts of his social standing. These social mores he finds on a daily basis, and will change from place to place, and from *time period* to *time period*. The resulting change manifested in the *cosmopolis* of the modern in no way

---

[18] Holmes, S.J. – The Eugenic Predicament – Harcourt, Brace&Co., 1928, pg.ix, Preface.

confirms that any 'merging' of the cultural imperative, or 'genetic/environment' argument, is any closer to a responsible conclusion by academics, philosophers, or laymen alike. But *we* must, those men and women of the West, come to a conclusion, if we are to answer those issues which will, most certainly destroy us if we do not. Eugenics, as a qualified Science, must have a clearly defined distinction within our 'perception' of science, if the solution is to be crafted that will aid in a rising West.

The Modern claims that simply because our environment has produced gigantic buildings, massive roadways, and interstellar communications, that this also, of necessity, means that we have advanced biologically. In fact, the contrary is true. We see a decline in human health across the board. In every sphere of Western culture we are bombarded with new viruses, bacterial strains develop via importation of people and foodstuffs; hereditary disease increases with every generations. That our Medical institutions of the West attempt to keep pace with these developments, belies the fact that it is not our medicine, in the final analysis, which secures our place in the dynamics of evolution and its cycles, but how well we *adapt* to our surroundings as a specie. This means, *precisely, by and through our genes* – what our parents were, and what we *are*. Without the proper foundation, that which is built of granite, not sand, we will cease to be a viable, *young*, and energetic race-culture – the death knell of all organic cycles. *This can only be seen as biological decadence*; and as the body goes so, also, the spirit. If it is any consolation to the reader, let it be said that every major civilization has gone through this cycle – and perhaps this cycle is a permanent fixture of our historical, and future landscape, but it must be challenged in every age and epoch. Vigilance is ever Eternal.

War, plagues, and personal inclination [instinct] have fostered primitive forms of eugenics for centuries. It has been remarked that the Black Plague in Europe's dark and dismal bout with pestilence, made the populace in Southern Europe more resilient to such disease, however much it may have dissipated through careless breeding since then. To the survivors, for that is the 'legacy' of today's Europeans, their ancestors having survived such a catastrophe hence, the stronger to 'ward off' disease. *A legacy worth guarding*. But nature should not be left entirely on her own to makes the decisions as to who will live and who will die. We, as a people, have the ability to intercede in our own behalf, our own future.

We should cherish no illusions regarding 'mother nature', nor theologians who seek to define that process, which man requires to survive on a daily or lifetime basis. Nature, on the one hand, cares little if the evolutionary process of man carries itself upward, downward, or sideways; if it carries on at all is of no consequence, as long as Nature herself, continues. The Theologian, on the other hand considers, and teaches that the 'Races of Man' are fixed, imperfect though they may be; yet, he believes that all are part of the same 'divine plan'. So, say the Modern's 'fundamentalists'. It must be remembered, however, that only one-hundred years ago, if not even now, that it was also theologians who said (and could prove it!) that Africans were descended from Ham of biblical fame; after that, he was cursed by 'god' and *turned* black. This was his curse for ever.

It is said by these selfsame authorities, that 'all' people of the earth are *one*, each belonging to the same house, since all have shared in the travails of the 'flood', confined together within the 'ark of salvation', hence the 'human race' was secured. The next step is obvious: If we all share the same 'experience' of a deluge, and we survived it in toto then, it follows, that we are the *same* in 'body' and 'soul'. Human 'equality' then, having been bestowed upon those who survived the 'flood' live *this* legacy even today.

Theologians seem to have answers for everything, for everything under the sun; although not always in agreement with one another, they nevertheless condemn scientific and historic answers they claim do not concur with *holy writ*. How is Western man to answer these deep and imperative questions? One must either *disregard* observation, or he is bound to accept *theology at face value*, while attempting to characterized scientific, historical, and social tradition which has been recorded as dutifully as theology by only one 'source'. Hardly a Western approach.

Theology of the modern, for instance, states that *'all people are one'*, that we all share [or should share] the same history, proclivities, desires, goals, and needs (i.e., salvation), because we are all *grafted* from the same 'tree' – by that act so defined as Creation. *Why then, for instance, do all groups, whether one defines 'group' as racial or cultural, demand 'separation', independence, in one form or another, in one degree or another, to protect themselves as each group senses and sees its values, historical epoch, or the individual goals of each particular presence, which is the exclusive property of the specific group which sees itself as under attack or change from outside forces?* Why then, if we are all from that selfsame 'tree', is the 'race-myth' of the origins of each group based on the *perception* of 'self' in the truly Racial sense? The motif of 'creation' *always* consists of the instant individual people being 'the' *adam* and *eve* of their particular 'myth'. Why do individual peoples remain, and prefer to remain aloof, alone, from their neighbors; from any and sundry other cultures? Is not the modern continually berating his fellows for the consequence of Western man's introduction of his culture on those poor souls who lived in peace and harmony? If this point be conceded in even a cursory and honest fashion, is it then not as equitable to be concerned about the *soul* of the West, its own 'people', in the same fashion? If the introduction of foreign gods, values, perceptions, and needs were dysfunctional for the noble savages of the world, what about the 'nobility' of the world?

Isolation, in the imperative concept and reality, of race-culture, is a natural symptom of the condition and division of human behavior.

Let us continue and add to this point: One may also include such natural divisions as *hair colour, skin colour, hair texture, and eye colour* to number just a few obvious signatures of division. These simple divisions, naturally occurring in nature for reasons developed over aeons of time, create spontaneous 'isolation' amongst the specie of man. In fact, the differences of 'mankind' are so great that one could classify these various 'types' of man as different genre altogether. Does not modern science divide the species of animals and plants? Why not man in the same sense and manner?

We can hear the modern and his minions loudly bleating: *equality* now, *equality* forever; but does that make it so?

The minutiae of difference introduced by the labeling process developed to name and divide certain animals and plants may involve such areas as the structure and form of feathers in birds, and the scales of fishes which share an intimate relationship between the organs and their internal systems. If these distinctions exist in the immensely complex world of animals then, why not in man? Would not, if a Zoologist were asked, classify a Caucasian and an African as different specie by the same rules he applies to animals? The answer, to be sure, is plain enough. But let us add a little more:

> "...[The] anatomical and physiological contrasts between human types are far greater than those admitted by naturalists between varieties, and as great as between species. The interval appears even to be greater in some cases, and to extend to that of genera. Thus, the four characteristics which distinguish the goat from the sheep are no other than those which separate certain great branches of the human family."[19]

There is more:

> "So far as the races of men can be traced through osteology, history, [their] monuments, the present volume establishes that they have always been distinct. No example is recorded, where one race has been transformed into another by *external causes*."[20] [emph. mine]

And again:

> "It seems to follow from what has been said...that the facts of human hybridity do not prove that all human races are to be regarded as belonging to a single specie"[21]

All these things and more, create an *ethos* of isolation. Customs, mores, social taboo's and the like, may prevent *anyone* 'outside' the group to breed, interact, or live with any particular group as part of this natural isolation. It may happen that this 'outer group' may simply speak a

---

[19] Topinard, Paul – *Anthropology* – Chapman&Hall, 1878, pg. 506-511.
[20] Nott, J.C. – *Types of Mankind* – Lippincott, Gambo&Co., 1854, pg. 397.
[21] Baker, John R. – *Race* – Oxford University Press, 1974, pg. 98.

different language, have different skin colour, or religious practices; and we may not agree with the seemingly prejudicial value in this concept and practice, yet, it *is* what has made up the various histories and cultures of the world.

It is a safe position, although much maligned, to say that it is colour, which is the basic line of self-defense for the 'group'. This is to say, that if a group wishes to stay the same, to stay *intact*, both in physical appearance and in mental attitudes, it must remain *itself* for as long as it can. It is through 'extreme' exogamous mating [marriages], which create, and allow new mutations to occur which will, inevitably, *change the literal complexion and mental outlook of a people*. These newly combined factors can, in certain instances (e.g. Celto/Nordic, or Germano/Iberian crossings) be considered good, or acceptable – the passing example of the British Isle may suffice, inasmuch as this island people, a Celtic stock, being fiercely loyal to their chief and tribe, nevertheless intermarried with, and fostered relations with, the Nordic invaders with which they had many years of contact, and which changed their 'alpine' physiology in terms of height and bone structure, and added brunettes to their lot, along with a more 'lineal' or mathematical sense of reasoning, this is bourne out by the fact that unlike the 'continental' alpine's, this island people have developed an empire, which contradicts the legacy of the Gauls. The other side of this formulae, may be cited as well, that of the Island of Cuba, which is defined as a Mulatto population, which was settled by mariners of European extraction, and held for many years, only to destroy, or rather 'consume' these settlers, and allow for the re-introduction of the non-European through mixture of the two diverse bloods. Let the reader be the judge in this example.

Even when isolation, considered as a natural or enforced 'social form', is safe to say that man, as a specie, has changed greatly; whether this change has its origins in 'creation' (i.e. *dispersion after the deluge*) or evolution makes little difference. The differences in the races of man are manifest. Commonality, to be sure, is also to be seen, yet one must not simply lump all together, melted as it were, into the morass of the 'common man' of the Modern. This would be to falsify the entire history of the Cultures of Man, and would seek to achieve a perspective that has no real basis in fact or truth. In short, it would be a 'great lie' used by those who would seek to control the presence of the races of man. To this 'great' mission, the Modern ever seeks to complete.

Western man, in particular, seeks always to change his environment. He views himself in the same fashion. Man does, indeed, have the ability to change himself, to modify for better or worse, his conditions of social, cultural, scientific or physiological make-up. Nature lifts her eyebrow in anticipation.

With the present[*] progress of genetics, as a defined science, not as clear and precise as eugenics perhaps, but well on it way, and on its own two feet, we have gained much knowledge on how such changes may be accomplished. Is there a limit to the changes that may be effected by [genetic] selection? This question may be eternally unanswered, for the debate is a heated one. Fixed 'creationists' would say that deviation from the 'parent stock' is limited by the act of creation itself. Conversely, those who ascribe to the evolutionary processes at work in man are convinced that no limits may be placed upon modification of the species through variation and selection. As a rule, improvement in the specie is accomplished quite rapidly, yet tends to stabilize to almost a walk within several generations. Each particular stock is affected differently in the extent that it can be modified upward. Thanks to such men as Galton and Mendel, we know that Hereditary Diversity is responsible for modification – whether that be upward or downward:

> "If a species contains a great deal of hereditary diversity, or is, as the geneticists call it, heterozygous for many factors affecting the character in question, it may readily be changed by selection, and the limit of modification is not so easily reached."[22]

So it is that man, because he is of a diversified heredity, is a highly modifiable animal. It is true that the most diverse races of man can

---

[*] See article [Smithsonian, Feb. 1990, pg. 41]: 'James Watson and the search for Biology's Holy Grail' – an ongoing fifteen year effort to map all the genes of every human chromosome.
[22] Holmes, op. Cit., pg. 8.

interbreed; their independent progeny produce offspring which, in turn, can reproduce. Hence, *inter-race crossings* produce limitless possibilities for the production of 'new' varieties of human kind. One must, however, take into account that these 'crossings' may produce breeds [of man] that are superior to the highest existing breeds and, as well, such breeds that are inferior to the lowest of existing races of man. Indeed, almost any amount of creating may be reached through such diverse crossings.

Through variation and selection for instance, we are able to produce albino's, six-fingered hands and the like if we wished; but this would be simple carnival tricks, not to mention the affrontive demeanor facilitated by nature and common moral sense were we to attempt this for no other reason than to simply 'do' this creation – to satisfy some aspect of our ego. The higher duty of man however, is to become noble; thus do we have the science of eugenics and genetics. With this knowledge, we may strive to create strong bodies, mental aptitudes, and inherent spiritual qualities that lay dormant among those of the West.

There should be absolutely no limits placed on the acceptance of Eugenics other than common sense and moral imperatives. Through recent studies as diverse as Olympic and National athletic committees and championships, the recognition due as to the part played by genetics in 'superior' athletes is enormous. Such examples of male and female participants in these events will include well known figures such as Arnold Swartzeneger and Cory Everson, who have been praised by competitors and critics alike as being the 'perfect' athletic specimens; geneticists, as well, remark that their bodily 'form' is favored by 'good genes'. The professional athlete knows that his/her endowment with success is partly his own doing, but the rest, is that natural edge given him by his ancestors who passed the rigors of 'selection' and 'variation'. Somewhere in his/her line [family tree] they had ancestors who were marked by large shoulders and chests, coupled with a strong back for pushing and puling motions; through various isolated areas geographically, his ancestors climbed high mountains, rowed long-hulled ships, or swung axe and hammer to achieve, with time, those *traits* which were then passed on to their progeny – their future generations. These are good [practical] traits.

Like all aspects of human nature however, *good* is only part of a duality in nature. There is no exception in eugenics. Traits can, and will always be, both good and bad. Of course, these may be and, of necessity, are subjective to either the individual or group represented based, also, upon the subjective analysis of the 'other' group. In either case of 'subjective' approval, these 'traits', whatever they may be are, or can be, bred into man. Conversely, they can also be *bred out of man*. Among the bad traits accountable to heredity, there are 'manic-depressives', 'insanity', 'epilepsy', and the feeble-minded. All these cases can be attributed to the Mendellian frequency rates mapped out by Mendel. In these various cases, especially those of insanity and feeble-mindedness, the high probability exists that inherited factors are consistently present. When, as the case may demand, two feeble-minded individuals decide to mate, owing that both contain similar defects in their make-up then, in all likelihood, they can expect [through the Mendellian frequency rate] that a majority of their offspring, also, to be feeble-minded, even as they; the exceptions, which will, in all probability occur, does not mitigate the fact that the 'trend' will be, also, that of a 'negative' not a 'positive'. Indeed, a natural *antithesis* abides in all of us on this subject. In point of fact, the policies of most Western nations prohibit the mating of 'insane' people; therefore, so should we also consider the sound and determined reasoning, which supports the contention, and reasonable observations, which make it clear that 'feeble-minded' individuals be included in that number.

The 'natural' fate accompanying all 'civilizations' is to *rise* and *decline*; what makes exceptional cultures is *how they live*. Our civilization and culture may, perhaps, escape this common fate because it has at its disposal the unlimited resources of science. But science deals exclusively with the forces of *intelligence*. Intelligence, as *a priori*, deals exclusively with the forces *of* intelligence. Intelligence never 'urges' men to action unless it is in the abstract; only through 'emotive' energy can this action take place, however much intelligence plays a part. Put another way: Intelligence 'may lead' one down a particular path, but would never 'rationally' put one in harm's way – only the duality of *emotion* will lead to this end. Only *fear, enthusiasm, self-sacrifice, hatred,* and *love* can infuse with 'life', the *products* of our mind, which will allow *for action*, to either 'defend', or 'attack' as the situation warrants. This is Idealism in its truest and purest form. It is what the 'post' fratricidal warriors and academics of the West had hoped for; to create, and infuse the same 'idealism' in the hearts and minds of the people of the 'allies' as had the Germans and the Italians with their people. They hoped that the 'democracies' would succeed in this endeavor for the 'good', where the 'others' had succeeded for the 'bad'. Ironic, is it not, that it was the parent nations of these democracies, which were now to receive the brunt of her children's anger and misdirection. The vacuum thus created by the destruction of the 'idealists' in Europe has not seen a return in the West of the Modern's making. There is no fire, no passion, in the heart and soul of the West today. It is to that ambiguous 'world-order', and to those who would create it, that ever seeks and clings to a 'faith', of any stripe, and then fed to the 'un-washed' masses. The power of the genius, that true and perfect culture of 'personality, is aborted before any bud may flower. Any 'similarity' of this reasoning present in the West today is not, in the context implied in this work, applicable to any modern western statesman or government.

Like all organisms however, the West seeks to *save* itself from destruction and has already secreted that special seed necessary for its future growth; it has already been placed in that place, forgotten by the modern, and will thus revive its ancient memories in the most unlikely places, or in those very places considered most likely, but unseen.

To the Noble man, wherever he may be found, consistent with his desire to better his fellow man, as well as with himself, his utmost concern lies most heavily on the mental abilities of his race-culture, with his blood. This includes both the 'reasoning and intuitive' aspects of human psychology. Intelligence cannot be taught in school, it can only by *disciplined* and *refined*. Through a rigorous application of eugenics, a more healthy and vibrant race-culture can be realized. This is the duality of a Noble People. Like Art, it is to *beauty* to which a healthy people are drawn. To 'ugliness' then, are healthy people repulsed. Physical beauty is no different, for it is the 'obvious' bait by which the *impulse* to procreate is born.

Science terms young and beautiful vitality as 'paedomorphy'. This is defined as the 'radiance' seen in the youth of a vigorous people; that fresh rosy-cheeked flame of idealism and unconquerable spirit held by youth of indomitable horizons. We are drawn, as individuals, and as a group, instinctively, to young and healthy partners. This has determined the largest fecund rate for the longest period of time; that is, young 'races' and individuals start young, and thence procreate for longer periods, making the 'national character' a young one. This breeds vitality, that excess so much needed in the future West.

Over the thousands of aeons, which have passed into history, this has simply been the evolutionary *wisdom* of survival.

Early man, for instance sought, or over a period of time did seek, the healthiest, strongest, and most beautiful of his mates to continue his kind. Ugly, sickly, or unhealthy, obviously, would not attract the finest and best to extend the specie in proportion that the healthy would or could. In fact, Culture depends directly on our 'biological predilections'.

We term 'biological predilections' as *taste*.

Taste is *personal*, and *instinctive*. It is bred over the millennia and ingrained into our social mores, art, and forms of affinity we all share in our human experience. It is 'racism' in its purest form – not the crass impostor *called* racism by the mixed mass of the Modern; his *multitudes* of diversity. The foundation of race-culture, of this racism, is genetic to be sure, and is the wellspring of 'how' a race sees itself. It is self-evident and natural to all save the Modern. The example by which, for instance, certain elements of the Orient's admiration for 'blondes' which, at least in part, reflects their admiration of the [Western] technics of our Military and Industrial power; a fact which does not keep this tenacious race-culture from attempting to supplant these powers of the West with their own might and power. And the African, in like fashion, who does not love or admire this power but, rather, hates this emblem of power and achievement. There is a natural harmony here, which the Modern ever seeks to hide from those he would govern, and that is found even these extremes of 'love' and 'hate'. Sex appeal, vitality, and health, are all seen from the subjective eyes of the beholder; and *himself* the mirror, reflections of what he, himself, sees. This, in any event, is a matter of taste. It reflects the inborn quality of *distinction*.

Physical beauty, in a general sense, reflects intelligence. Mental achievements correspond to that of physical achievements in general – the modern 'myth' of the dumb blonde not withstanding. The antecedent probability exists that mind and body are associated by heredity; science indicates* as much. This was generally accepted prior to the second war of fratricide. To the Modern however, this concept of heredity is distasteful precisely because it competes with the egalitarian dogma of environment *over* that of heredity – hence the assumed 'equal and fair' representations of all peoples. While the Law, to some degree, can 'conceive' of equal and fair treatment, its *force* and *form* is defined by the very genetic inheritance, which has formed its very foundation (e.g. *Anglo-Saxon common law, and Dane Law, not to mention our usage of Greek and Romanic Law, which is the basis for all Western law, comes to mind. FLS*). Difference does, however, exist amongst the various members (i.e. governments) of the West, not to mention those not of western stock. These differences exist despite the numerous attempts, sincere though they may be, of various individuals, governments, or groups, which would make it so. The tremendous mosaic of the earth and her peoples fly in the face of the Modern, despite the foreign attempts of 'patchwork' designs created by minds that are far removed from waking reality. The 'betrayal' by the governments of the West in Bosnia-Herzegovina[1] – at best a

---

* See Indices for a list of a 'Who's Who' in the field of genetics, anthropology, and the like who promote the concept of heredity in intelligence *over* that of strictly an 'environmental' factor. FLS

[1] This issue of 'ethnic cleansing' with which the Modern has held out for the Western world to see is another lie. In point of fact, it is an 'extra-European' affair, and has afflicted the West for several thousands of years: the 'religio-racial' implications of Islam v. Christianity. In a purer sense, it is the age-long conflict between Semitic [even of 'indo-European'] and European forces. The geographical implications of the

temporary reprieve – at worst, a trend which will overthrow the West as we know it; the storm which has appeared upon the horizon of our shores is in direct response to the Modern's injection of 'compromise', misplacing the historical epochs of our tradition, and filing them with the other 'antiquated' forms of traditional knowledge, is a good case in point.

In due course, genius is also a product of heredity. The Family, as 'unit', being a prerequisite to a sound environment, and strong constitution, is attached with still more importance in this context. A sound family unit will, in accordance with the laws of heredity, be well suited in *type* and *disposition*, if they are to produce a more well-proportioned and higher individual who is physically and mentally superior to both their parents. In the country of the origin of this work, America, we have seen a steady and ineluctable decline in those

---

Balkans is too complex for this work, but do not fail to see the interactions between those members of an Islamic tradition and, thereby fail to see the 'Christian' tradition which is, and shall always be, in conflict with it.

For the government of the American West to 'slip' so badly, by taking the 'egalitarian' position of 'protecting' a certain side *against* the 'founders' of civilization in this area of the world is, to say the least, the worst sort of political and moral machinations which, as time has bourne out, has set the course of this, our Nation, into the very real possibility of a collapse of Western hegemony in an area which has historically been the bulwark – the wall if you will – against the very 'ideals' which has put us at odds with the other nations of the earth, rather than supporting our allies/people to stem the rising tide of fanatical religious incursions into our own territory and beyond.

Historically, it may be added, the West has always had a symbiotic relationship with the Arab – his religious technics not withstanding – and has a shared historicity predating Al Farabi, and Ibn Fadlan. We left them alone, and they left us alone, if not coming into contact on those occasions which the West, under some design or another, sought a 'misplaced' connection with the territory of the Arab proper. If we are to take sides in this region of the world, let us maintain nothing but a 'neutral' position upon the region, whether we are in total agreement with them or not; for our lone 'ally', Israel, certainly does not 'always' do those things which are in the best interest of America, or the West in general, yet we continue to advance one over the other. This is the 'cycle' which the West has 'committed itself too – but for who's benefit? Let each American, and each individual member of the West question these policies, and decide for themselves which answer should be given for the 'advancement' of the West, and to each 'localized' region where each calls his home. Truly, if we fail to address this issue, in its comprehensive form, our grandchildren will be shedding their blood, soaking deep into the sands of shame and uselessness. FLS

intelligent and well proportioned matings (i.e. conformation, height, weight, hair and eye colour) which will assure a more vital and vigorous people, of higher intellectual capacities, and nobility of 'spirit'. Their inevitable progeny, likewise, have suffered. Since the 'sixties', this deceleration of intellectual momentum, as a trend, has manifested itself in almost every stratum of American Education and I.Q. levels:

> "When people die, they are not replaced one for one by babies who will develop identical IQ's. If the new babies grow up to have systematically higher or lower IQ than the people who die, the national distribution of intelligence changes. Mounting evidence indicates that demographic trends are exerting downward pressure on the distribution of cognitive ability in the United States and that the pressures are strong enough to have social consequences.
>
> Throughout the West, modernization has brought falling birth rates. The rates fall faster for educated women than the uneducated. Because education is so closely linked with cognitive ability, this tends to produce a dysgenic effect, or a downward shift in the ability distribution. Further more, education leads women to have their babies later – which alone also produces additional dysgenic pressures."[23]

The above statement does not shed new light on the subject, many before these authors have given their lives in the pursuit of truth, and paid very dearly for making them known, once again, to their fellows. The two authors quoted above, have suffered in their own right for speaking what studious research has told them. This subject, lest we forego our train of thought, is based more on a 'demographic' model, and we will attach more interest to it later on. We find, essentially, the same 'trend' wherever we turn among the professional and intellectual classes. Lawyers, professors, engineers, ministers, inventors, bankers, artists, educators, military men [who the nation depends upon for national protection], writers, all represent 'stock' which make up the masses of our nation.

---

[23] R.J. Herrnstein and Charles Murray – The Bell Curve, Free Press [Simon & Schuster] 1996, pg.341.

Professor Dublin, writing long before the above-mentioned authors, stated clearly that this 'stock' as a trend was marching downward, because of a lack of fecundity. For the moment, let us add:

> "There is only one conclusion to be drawn: these groups are not reproducing themselves. These people and their stocks are quickly dying out and their place is being taken by a new generation who are the offspring of our fertile immigrants... We are now making the stock out of which the new America will arise... Whether we like it or not, the people of America will look different, act differently, and be different from those who made our country great. And all this because of the facts of reproduction and heredity."[24]

Let the reader make up his or her mind on the above-mentioned statements. Look around; see with your own eyes what is true and what is not.

American 'education' is the laughing-stock of the Western world. At best, our educational system, taken as a whole, is a *fraud* – we have allowed a system to evolve which is 180 degrees from barely a hundred years ago. The 'development' of pre-school and elementary level children shows a distinct and dramatic indication of just where, or how low we have become. The tremendous emphasis placed upon 'behavior' in the classroom, such as the typical sign-post found on many a classroom wall, exhorts each and every student to be mindful of the diversity, and equality of each and every student, keeping the students ever suspicious of those who stand out, who are marked by their high-level of achievement in mathematics, English or the lineal and abstract studies, thereby marking them different. This applies pressure in the 'downward' momentum; there is no *excellence*. There is no *genius*.

This is pure Indoctrination.

The indoctrination of these youths at such tender ages [6-13] with mental attitudes and perceptions such as 'telling', 'saving oneself', 'siding with the teacher' against his fellows and the like, has changed

---

[24] Dublin, Luis I. – Birth Control – reprinted in Social Hygiene, 1920, cf., pg. 8.

the *pattern of individualism* to that of the 'collective', something that most of us were taught was a 'communistic' or 'fascistic' principle, and that, at all costs, we should avoid. This is nothing short of *'authoritarianism'* based on political correctness. This social modification has affected untold millions of young people who trust, implicitly, those in adulthood and authority with which they interact.

The concept of *individualism*, like any 'ism', is fraught with an extremist inclination; the concept of 'family or tribe' was *always a priori* when faced with an outside threat – this did not disallow an individual from having an 'I' associated with *who* he was; he was protected in many cases by laws and religious concerns which shared equanimity with the secular state. It may not have been perfect; we are far from being perfect. To 'stress' the importance of 'i' over that of the group however, is more than just passing interest. *American schools are putting our children at risk*. This *risk* is the lack of integrity, will power, self-esteem, and, most importantly, loyalty to oneself and his peers, and makes for a cowardly and sheepish population. What will we think if put to war, if a foreign force, much larger than could have been conceived, attacked our shores, and our mettle tried, our 'national' soul put to the test? Will captives [even our soldiers are not immune] become broken because of the 'timid' conditioning received at American schools? What, exactly, would be the national reaction to a conquering force, deprived of food, shelter, and family – who would capitulate, and who would defy the conqueror? This is, of course, the most extreme of circumstances, but a nation and people are known as 'great' only in adversity, or in the pure genius of a Golden Age.

The answer to these questions lie at the root of the race-culture: our offspring. It is not only to a sound environment, replete with the regimens of self-discipline, but to those *elements* we, as parents, leave *in our children*.

Self-discipline, as spoken of here, is not that 'castration' sought or promoted by those pundits who preach and encourage 'paranoia', 'gang warfare', or just 'fear' in general for the purpose of 'controlling' a population. Our children, any child, should follow leadership, this is the job of parent and teacher alike; but when those certain children or child show a tendency to be rebellious, curiosity/inquisitive, or drawn to areas of interest far and above the other children (e.g. those who seem 'predisposed' to show only interest in mathematics, vocational trades, literature or science, etc.) then these selfsame children should be molded and directed in these 'specific' areas of interests at a higher state of indoctrination. This point *assumes* that either the parents or the teacher is aware of these proclivities, and acts upon them. If Americans continue to remain apathetic, bordering on stupidity, then this awareness is suspect; but if we are to demand meritocracy rather than mediocrity, we must become aware and aid our young if they are to develop a balanced psychology. If we are to encourage achievement, then we must encourage these young minds to reach out, not randomly, and become directed with that disciplined *reasoning* which all young people require to become adults.

Here then, is the crux of the matter: lack of self-discipline, integrity, and the devolution of academics in our educational and national political levels, is directly related to the heterogeneous mixture of our American *social/political* attitudes. This has become the legacy of the *'egalitarian'*, of the Modern.

It has been the Modern, that crowned prince of equality, the egalitarian, while striving to maintain some personal vision of the 'world-to-be', has shown little regard for the *essence* of Western man's race-culture, and has opted for one of the biggest frauds, yes, criminal conspiracies ever wrought against a people: for once the *homogeneous* population becomes fused with that of admixture, with heterogeneous importations of very diverse kinds, the Western element loses, with time, all its natural affinity and knowledge of its original stock. With this loss, so also, the various proclivities and 'tendencies' which mark us as 'unique'. Racial 'hybridity' is the ultimate end of these diverse crossings. With time, after several generations of constant amalgamations with diverse racial types, the Western stock as has been known historically, becomes immersed with, and becomes a completely heterogeneous – or mixed-race – grouping. Light complexion will defer to dark and, with time, the complexion of the host race will change demonstrably. Put bluntly, 'white' will lose to 'black' and with time, all traces of the original stock will be lost. Mental attitudes diminish in direct proportions to the racial admixture of any parent stock. It is imperative, therefore, that all future parents decide on a mate best suited to themselves in *temperament, looks, and corresponding mental outlook, if they are to produce superior human beings better than themselves*. This, of course, is mandatory for all races.

It is not education, alone, which will overcome our crime and juvenile problems. Education cannot turn a feeble-minded child into an honor-student; conversely, it is apparent that a bad school system can destroy even gifted students with their mediocre curriculums. It must be both good genes, as well as good basic scholastic education.

What a child inherits from his mother and father is extremely important. This cannot be overly stressed. The son receives more from his father than from his mother; the daughter, in like fashion, receives the best of her mother. If the son is to receive more, not less, from the mother then, the mother should be as close to the equivalent of the father as possible. According to Francis Galton's law of antecendent heredity, an individual receives on the 'average', one-quarter of his attributes from any one parent; the other three-quarters is received from the other parent and the immediate/remote ancestors. The study of the geneology of 'great men' [see Galton] has afforded as ample evidence that the higher the frequency of intelligent mothers, the higher the rate of superior men of genius. Applied to females, it must of necessity bring to bear similar results. A legacy of this kind stays with such a child for life.

The intelligence, or lack of same, of any child remains fairly constant through life. "If a child is [feeble-minded] stupid it almost always remains stupid."[25] Science and observation have given us this information – not just scientists of the past – in our present state of information, it is a demonstrable fact. The Modern however, not to be outdone, has started his schools of 'psycho-analysis', 'psychiatry',

---

[25] Holmes, S.J. – The Eugenic Predicament – Harcourt, Brace & Co., 1928, pg. 70.

and most recently, the 'science' of 'psychophysics' to prove that the above observation is not the case. The dim light of 'fact' however, is appearing once again. A well-known 'psychophysicist', Dr. David Lykken, for instance, maintains that criminal behavior as such, is not inherited; but that 'certain' kinds of temperament are. Dr. Lykken:

> "A child who is relatively fearless, adventurous and insensitive to punishment is likely to seek excitement in the kinds of places that get him into trouble."[26]

Dr. Lykken's position seems to be 'outside' the purview of the Modern in terms of 'equality' – yet he does, and so many of his peers – do indeed, support 'inequality' in *some cases*. Unique, or individual predispositions by definition, amounts to an 'un-equal' relationship between individuals. Let us, then, look closer to what the good doctor has to say.

In the first stated observation, that of a *lack* of intelligence, we are speaking of genetic dysfunction; in the case of *temperament*, we are now speaking of a combination of genetic influences and predispositions which, in fact, *create* a temperament. In the first case, feeble-mindedness can be discerned at birth, even before, and should be corrected. In the case of temperament, environment does play an important role; crime can be enhanced by squalid living conditions, and the arbitrary and unfeeling power of the State – such as the British - have shown us. What Dr. Lykken has pointed out however, is that of the developing 'psychosis' of environmental conditions *over* that of what is inherited, in terms of temperament [a pre-condition in any event, and genetic in nature]. In other words, even though genetics is implicit in human growth, the Modern still would have us determined, ultimately, by our environment.

But let us carry his point further:

Dr. Lykken's school of thought indicates that it is the 'temperament', that is, those traits of fearlessness, adventure (i.e. courage, curiosity, bravery, loyalty and the like), and insensitivity which make one, more

---

[26] [See] Article in Instauration – Cape Canaveral, FL., January 1991, pg. 31.

likely than not, to become involved with the undercurrents in modern society – that is to say, with Crime.

In point of fact however, when we analyze this position more closely and carefully, the very traits which are pointed out as 'bad', are those very peculiar traits or 'temperaments' described by Dr. Lykken and his particular school of thought, are those *very traits so absolutely essential for a people to excel in a world where fearlessness, adventure, and insensitivity are diminishing before our very eyes*; and even more importantly, without which our ancient fathers and mothers would never, could never, have achieved what they have to this point in time: mastery of the oceans, space travel, astronomy, a reasonable control over his environment, and has continued to develop these things 'peculiar' to the West, up to this very generation. But let us not forget the last, and most important trait/temperament, which the modern ever seeks to deny us hoping, it would seem, for us to lose this trait entire: Courage.

Are such traits/trends 'unworthy' or 'unqualified' to exist? What *does* this mean to us, as a western race-culture? Do we, as a sensible and decent population really want or need drugs used to 'tame' our children? Have we really lost touch with the excitement, the vitality, to be young? Do we ever seek, nay, demand, that we possess a sense of 'serenity' and that if we cannot have it, we will then 'force' it upon our young because we, ourselves, are unable to achieve it in our own lives? Is 'childhood' then, doomed to extinction? Have we become so 'civilized' that Jim, upon returning from Treasure Island, be treated as an overly aggressive youth, having allowed his temperament, his traits, to evolve which, in turn allowed him to survive his travails and hardships, allowing him to live and be scrutinized by these psycho-pundits and told that he is now a menace to society; must he now be drugged, or at the very least kept from civilized company? This is, essentially, what is being done; if this school of thought is allowed to continue, our progeny will be persons not worthy to survive or receive our admiration.

Now, in consequence, the observable facts are that environment and predisposition does indicate the direction of individuals and groups.

So, it is, that we must not throw the baby out with the bath-water as it were. A caveat however; since temperament can be very illuminating as to the direction of young people, so it is that racial groups can, and does show predispositions that are liable to be seen as criminal or anti-social. The implications here are manifest, and supported historically by Science, namely, that as a culture of long-standing, Western culture has a right and a duty to *preserve* what is good for its future. This means that if the race-culture feels threatened, or if in fact is under assault, then it is only fitting and proper to develop behavior that will provide that protection needed to fulfill the requirements of its longevity. What those temperaments and behavior are to become, remains the key element in the Rise of the West.

Here again we face the *premise* of equality, equality across the board. How do we, or more precisely, the Modern, rationalize the tremendous expense exercised annually to educate the feeble-minded, the retarded, the imbecile? Worse, to *attempt* to 'educate' these poor souls *within* the public school system (!). This 'form' of educating, not entirely without merit, for who would deny a sense of compassion to these individuals, is done at enormous cost, and requires countless numbers of well intended teachers, therapists, and doctors, and is consistent with Western man's feeling of kindness to those who 'have not', and will attend to those of the West until, and when those trends/traits are no longer present in our population. Many, however, want to know more than this; what do we do with the *normal, intelligent, and gifted children* who inhabit the same space as these others? In fact, a healthy, normal, or superior child has very little spent on them relative to the cost of 'un-healthy/abnormal' children per capita. Where then, is the *doctrine* of equality considering the effort put into the one group, altruistic though it is, and that of the effort, or lack of same, put into the other categories?

If it be accepted that lower intelligence be entitled to a higher rate of education, at least a more intensive education, should not the gifted, also, be given the same and equal market share, relative to the same 'share' given to the abnormal? We must, as a distinct race-culture, answer these questions if we are to survive and excel.

It is true, more often than not, that great men do not come from dull-spirited boys. The Modern, in his typically nefarious way, tries to respond to the supposed unequal treatment of these less fortunate individuals by claiming the 'rule' of higher education to impress upon those of his fellows the need to *create* normal *from* the abnormal. But, I.Q. potential does not increase with the higher gradation of education – it only enhances the raw material present. There is no "art by which an individual with an I.Q. of 80 can be converted into one with an I.Q. of 140."[27] This necessarily brings up the question of 'testing for intelligence' since it is common in today's academia to challenged 'testing' as being culturally biased and unfair to those non-Western elements amongst us.

Intelligence testing means many things to different people, yet one thing is certain and unassailable, and that is that testing gives us a means of *detecting* and *measuring* the differences and inequalities in men. Not only schools and colleges, but also the Armed forces and government agencies, coupled with Industry use intelligence and aptitude tests to 'grade' and 'sort' human beings in order to discover the approximate limits of their capacities. It is argued now, as before, that the capability an individual manifests may be less that his inborn potential, which may have been suppressed by an unfavorable environment or obscured by other factors. This is conceded as fair.

Intelligence testing is objective, as contrasted to subjective, measuring devices. They [tests] yield quantitative results. Like all scientific experiments, the intelligence test provides answers that can be verified or refuted by *'re-testing'*. I.Q., which stands for 'intelligence quotients', is the ratio of a subjects test score to the average test score to the average test score at his age-level expressed as a percentage.

The I.Q., accordingly, makes allowance for the normal development of brainpower with growth and maturation. The normal situation is for an individual I.Q. to remain fairly constant, until he reaches the age at which his mental faculties begin to deteriorate. Brain damage, disease, a repressive environment, or simply an abnormal growth

---

[27] Holmes, op. Cited. pg. 76.

pattern may cause significant variations of the I.Q. from the norm; 'overlap' of intelligence tells what percentage of populations 'a' equals the average score of population 'b'. Where the [psycho-metric] intelligence of the two populations groups becomes equal, the overlap is considered to be, or should be, at fifty-percent.

Small differences in I.Q. are quite significant when comparing different populations. This holds true whether we are concerned with race, nation, class, or education. Even small differences in average intelligence are associated with very great differences in the *very high* I.Q. ranges This means, simply, that a decline in average [psycho-metric] intelligence of only a few points will equate into a much *smaller* population of gifted individuals. This latter group, the very highly gifted elite of any population which does most of the world's creative works, shapes entire nations, creates civilizations, and most assuredly, determines whether nations endure or fall, must be maintained.

These Stanford-Binet sorts of intelligence tests, and used in America, put emphasis on reasoning, and abstract capacities, and it is therefore, *not* culture free. And 'why' should they be? These tests have come out of the thought processes and preconditions peculiar to the West, to *its* culture, and are necessary to *its* continuation and advancement. So, in anticipation of the Modern's cry of foul, let me say that no apology is necessary. In giving these tests, we are not concerned with ascertaining whether an individual group is capable of taking part satisfactorily in one of the sub-nations of Africa or the Orient, but with ascertaining competence for life and existence in our own 'civilization'. Western culture, wherever it manifests itself, in whatever geographical location it lives, is a world made up of Western blood – of white men and women related by blood and temperament. We, through aeons of evolution, our ancestors, up to the present day, have created it. It is an expression of *our* ideas, *our* values, *our* instincts, *our* needs, and *our* aims. The struggle and creation of this 'nation' of America was such an affirmation. The primary duty rests upon us, alone, those of Western stock, to keep it alive; to extend it further, for the people of the West too be. Therefore, we have the *right* and the *duty* to protect ourselves from destruction. In testing, therefore, we assure that the principle ideas, aptitudes, and temperament be fostered and maintained for the betterment of all by continuous advancement, and evolution upwards to create better individuals.

Education must be of the highest priority within the Western nations. An intelligent son or daughter do not inherit 'knowledge', this must be a vital part of the environment of 'higher learning', true higher learning. Mediocrity must not be allowed to continue. Our curriculums must remain 'western' in origin; it must promote the sciences of Western thought. It must promote the 'spirituality' of free religious thought as has been brought down to us by the great thinkers of the West. Education of the mind must, of necessity, be coupled with the education of the eyes and hands. These trade skills, which our ancestors have given us, are rapidly going the way of the alien; to *their* sons and daughters. Certainly, one has but simply to look at the fields of the machinist, carpenters, iron workers, sculptors, artists, as well as all types of cottage industries such as medical transcription, insurance billing, telephone, and public service personnel; computer 'coding' and the associated 'new technologies' associated with computer programming which, at one time, made each man or woman independent, artistic, and in touch with the past which had passed this or that skill to them. All this and more *is* education. This is all part of higher learning. The Brain is the key.

Without mental ability, without that abstract [sense] ability to envision great civilizations, where would we be? Would we really be content in the great primordial forest, thinking of nothing but the sunrise…eating…and sleeping?

Blumenbach, the famed naturalist, provided a thesis that has merit even today. He states: *"The mental varieties seem equal to and sometimes greater than bodily varieties of man."*[28] Brain size used to be considered in strict terms of relative size – we now know, for instance, *that the critical importance is the development of the cortex*. And this in direct

---

[28] Blumenbach, J.F. – On the Natural Varieties of Mankind – London (1781), Bergman Publishers, 1969, pg. 389.

proportion to the layers, or overlapping folds of brain tissue. All this points directly in favor to those minds that are predisposed to be creative in aptitude. Creative thinking and intelligence depend largely upon the convolutions of the brain – small convolutions mean that idiocy is present. This is inherited. No amount of education, not even by the Modern's standard, can help this poor soul, other than to function in a world in which he is totally alone, restricted in his movements; he is unable to grasp the reality of his presence with the exception, possibly, that his reality is suited to his needs.

But what of our needs? Does our reality really suit our needs? The study of the brain is a racial study. It *qualifies* race, ability, and precedent. The proof and reasons for this area of discussion is myriad, too long for this work and, so, we will pass it with a wave and a nod and continue.

The Modern preaches against the immorality of racism. Classifications, like those listed briefly above, while being scientifically sound, and are observable in everyday settings are, nevertheless, considered racist pronouncements by the Modern and his egalitarian cohorts. The Modern considers himself 'un-racist' – that is, devoid of any individualism based on an identifiable issue such as race-culture or biology – he is *non-racial*. He, the Modern, is free to express his equality without fear or favor. He does not wish however, to embrace the non-western on a personal level, but simply to prove his 'theories' of equality. Nothing, however, is further from the truth than the theory of 'equality'. How is it, for instance, that one man, as compared to another, is demonstrably different, sometimes in the extreme?

The modern egalitarian stresses the educational factors of 'nurture' over that of 'nature'.

That the *early* period of a child's development, training, and growing years are of the utmost importance and consideration in a systematic process of education is self-evident. No one, who is honest, may dispute this truism: that this time-period is the burgeoning matrix of a child's *character*. It is also a truism that a child, even with special training, cannot go beyond his allotted mental power given him at birth, that is, inherited. Therefore, if this truth be accepted, the best stock that may be produced by Western man and, specifically the American-West, *must be attained by the highest twenty-five percent of its race-cultural host; not the lowest twenty-five percent.* To our advance or decline, depends on the types or type of person(s), which survives and propagates at the *fastest* rates. This is a fact that must, without qualification, be accepted as the way for future Western men and women.

Sexual *selection* is of prime importance. Men marry women who are beautiful, intelligent, healthy, and similar in temperament. Women, likewise, choose as their mates' men who are handsome, intelligent and, *in their eyes*, superior men. Pigmentation of the skin is also of importance – in a racial sense. Vitality, life, youthful vigor, all is requisite in the mating and romance of partners. It is historically true that fair colouring, for thousands of years, has presented itself in the 'protector mechanism' spoken of so often in ancient literature. This is, for all intents and purposes, a stratification of hierarchy based on skin colour amongst people of the same race; Europeans have followed this pattern for thousands of years. Greece, India, Persia, or southern Europe, all have followed this rule – *the fairest at the top*.

Small, petite, and fair women have attracted the first pick of the men. Tall women, which is relatively rare, find mates in contrast to the above; their choice is relative, since their choice has already be made by nature and will more than likely find a mate of her equal standing. Tall women are the exception, which proves the rule, relative to 'averages' in this discussion, so we will continue with the main thrust of the matter. Health, as stated before, is of primary importance, and influences the mating habits of all peoples. In Western females, it is the rosy-cheeks of a light-skinned woman, which brings out the primal essence of Western men, indeed, of all men, that transcends the explicable.

The face of beauty draws all comers. Lips, eyes, nose, eye-brows, body and facial hair, all are set off by light complexions – the soft juxtaposition of hues blending with the sexual organs as well; the nipples and labia, two areas which exemplify the *Eros* of the female form are unique in Western females. All of this combining to attract the male of her kind. All of this, and more, make her beautiful; it makes her *wanted*. True it is that the 'white female' is sought after by every race of man imaginable which, when looked at through the eyes of the West, may elicit a certain just feeling of satisfaction. The fact remains, however, that the numerical number of men of 'western-stock' has significantly depreciated with the passing of years, abortion, homosexuality, and the 'increased' number of men of 'non-western' stock who are very willing and able to compete with Western men for the right to mate with Western females here, in America, indeed, the Western world.

Beauty does not stand alone, but is combined with a *spiritual* presence, which promotes and extends a unique value – we call it sexuality – the Greeks, *Eros*. This is a biological phenomenon rather than a purely 'cultural' one, that is, biology proper is the liquid, which is poured into the vessel of civilization, which allows for a 'degree' of sexuality to become prominent, or taboo. Biology is a prerequisite for the purpose of procreation; beauty is a requisite for the *enticement* necessary to bring a couple together. In Western literature, the theme is unchanging: the gods are drawn to Beauty, and the mortal form of beauty is considered as beautiful as are the goddesses which inhabit the various temples and habitats familiar to our ancestors – this helped to shape what 'we' consider beautiful. We still marry, today, based upon factors, which, essentially, are physical first and foremost; secondly, we marry based on mental or other considerations. Today's modern women and certain men may consider this crass chauvinism but, to survive, we must procreate, and beauty is the prime consideration.

Sadly, in our modern age, specifically in the prime of marriageable groups, the college campus has shown a demonstrable decrease in the amounts of couples, which are finding permanent marriage arrangements suitable to their needs. Careers have taken precedent. This amounts to a form of [forced] celibacy, which affects the 'career' minded individual. In direct proportion to this trend has been the phenomenon of the 'single generation' and, as well, to the *decline* of the Western birthrate. The proportion of men that marry is greater than that of women – but even these tend to marry later in life. These men, of no little consequence, add very little or nothing to a higher birthrate; and these particular men belonging to that superior stock so much needed for our future [!]. The professional classes, at any rate, are always prone to marry later in life. This is racial suicide. This is the *decline* of the West.

Studies* into this subject are myriad, the time spent on 'research' is why the average person is generally unaware of the technical proof, which can be afforded the premise under discussion – the other side affords their own 'statistics' to add to the weight of their discussion. The *way* in which 'marriage selection' is proved, however, is that *like marries like*. Look around, and see if this is not the norm in your daily activities' remember, the exception proves the rule. Tall tends to marry tall, small with small. This, of course, breaks up the population into a separate and diverse biological 'caste system' that, while fundamentally sound, in such cases as intelligent/intelligent crossings, becomes dysfunctional when we allow, for instance, feeble-minded to mate with feeble-minded. In the modern West, specifically in America, the advent of 'equality' surpasses the laws of nature, and has been promoted over that of an otherwise healthy race-cultural instinct for survival; but a [artificial] desire to absorb those of alien racial, and mental stock, which has been equated with intelligence, to promote said equality in his haven of the cosmopolis of the city – the ultimate in artificial technics.

Indiscriminate mating, whether through 'inter-racial' crossings, or simply through mating of 'unequal' [mental] types, is a sure sign of the decline of a healthy organism and must, ultimately, perish. The celibacy of healthy and intelligent men and women or, conversely, that of crossing these superior traits with inferior ones, is racial deterioration pure and simple. "Whatever influence this factor has, or can have, is indirectly through its effect upon the *birth-rate*, since the kind of people who mate determines the kind of children who are

---

* See, for instance, the study by Anthony Ludovici – The Choice of a Mate – London, 1935. See also, by the same author – Woman: A Vindication; and The Child: An Adult's Problem – London and New York, 1923, London 1948, respectively.

born."[29] [Italics mine]

The fact, which is being stressed time and time again in this work, even if ad nauseum, is that the higher decline in birthrates has been in the higher social classes – those beautiful and intelligent members of our race who are, by definition, *rare* as well – but who are also the traditional *culture-bearer* class. This is not extenuated by money or education, although both play a part, but rather through breed, that long succession of good mating which has produced higher and gifted children and individuals. From these, come the most gifted and intelligent children and, ultimately, are those specific individuals who will see and lead the generations to come into a future that, hopefully, will be grander and healthier that ours. This puts the culture of the West in a position to testify as to the facts of our present state of existence; we are called to the witness stand.

The very character, which is in our blood, of the West, has been decreasing steadily in this fashion for a century and a half. Limiting the birth rate artificially, unlike the Malthusian checks and balances regarding pestilence and famine, land mass and agri-growth, have caused a serious imbalance for the West. On a world-wide scale, the West has artificially promoted the survival of 'peoples' whose condition of life is, or has been predicated upon the natural proclivities of their environment, their adaptability, and the cultural destiny of the their antecedents. The 'west' brings them *survival*.

Instead of allowing the weak or infirm to be separated naturally, we of the West enforce this 'Orwellian' concept of health and *existence*, at the expense of that quality of Life; the over populous centers of the third-world are replete with disease, poverty, and cycles which destroy a healthy balance because the city, specifically, cannot support a population, which is multiplied by Western medicine which, then, artificially, promotes growth at the expense of a *quality of life* – this Western 'involvement' is well intended, but is sadly lacking in vision and common sense. It is, or has become, the *'ethos'* of the 'world', of that particular 'christian charity' which has been at the

---

[29] Holmes, op. Cited, pg. 74.

forefront of this movement. It is, in its entirety, a 'one world concept' closely akin to that of Babel – another experiment in equality, which was found lacking.

It is this essence of 'globalization', of world capital and intercourse, and what will come of it, which has birthed this decline in the virtue and vitality of Western civilization, and which puts the survival of the West in jeopardy. This is, inevitably, the contest between those who would promote the economic global empire of what certain leaders in the western world attempted one-hundred years ago or more; to stimulate a burgeoning 'industrial' revolution in the modern Western States, and between those who, while acknowledging the economic considerations, nevertheless hoped to achieve a certain degree of independence and self-sustaining innovation at home, before thinking of inter-national trade over, and above, that of their national interests. After all, this is how America, in particular, has *become* great.

As is expected, the hypocrisy of these selfsame individuals is manifest. These modern intellectuals and governmental servants go boldly into the public venues and business centres and regale the common man and woman regarding 'sexuality' and demean the natural births of their own stock – the Modern would rather relegate these new humans to the dust-bin of history, or that of the abortionist; meanwhile, maintaining the standard 2.3 children for western-stock, while allowing the third-world to produce three times that amount. This dynamic is a continuous ebb and flow which settles once and for all the question of who will have a place in the Sun, and who will fade in the shade of a world increasingly smaller and less productive. Listed below, is an example of what author Richard McCulloch calculates as the ebb and flow of what he calls the Nordish [Western] elements of the world to *be*:

NORDISH POPULATION IN MILLIONS

CENTRAL   PERIPHERAL   TOTAL

Europe:	135	210	345
Outside Europe:	125	60	185
Total:	**260**	**270**	**530**

McCullochs's calculations concerning the Nordish elements 141.1 millions among Americans today, out of a total population of 248 millions, the rate of increase for the Western population is offset by a –14% [1984] birth rate, and since the above mentioned calculation, the Western birthrate has been offset by even greater numbers. Of the Russian element, and a total population of 258 millions, there are approximately 110 millions of Nordish elements.

McCulloch's views, indeed, are sobering, but there is more. Below, are his essential calculations; it is strongly suggested that you read his study for yourself. Here, then, are the statistics for the United States:

	1880	1981	Births in 1989
U.S. POPULATION*		50 MIL.	248 MIL.
Nordish:	83.5%	57.0%	47/0%
	42 MIL.	141 MIL.	
Congoid:	12.0%	12.0%	16.0%
	6 MIL.	30 MIL.	

Hispanic: 16.0%	0.6%	11.6%
	0.3 MIL.	29 MIL.
Other: 21.0%	3.9%	19.4%

*Largely Alpine and Dinaric whites in 1880, but heavily

Mediterranean, Mongolian, etc., by 1989.

To the keen eye*, the above table shows, dramatically, the *shift* in the

---

* As has been said earlier, statistics are problematic, but we will use them, albeit rarely, to add to an obvious point. Whether these numbers effects you in your daily life, does not matter, your circumstances may be a little more removed, or protected; nevertheless, it is to the largest of our population centers which will affect the nation at large, and us as individuals, simply because the political clout of the 'city' is so much more marked. Overall, in a 'world' sense, look at these numbers as part and parcel to a voting bloc, a world voting bloc, and ask yourself who has the *most* votes? Yes, numbers mean power in a democratic sense, and this is our bottom line. Without our weapons, the non-western elements are the majority – it has always been this way – and the West will have to confront this whether it will or no.

The *pan et circus* of our modern society is no different than that civilization from which this phrase was borrowed. All civilizations, that is, that stage in which Culture has passed over aeons of time need, at some point, to control its population, to direct their thoughts and aspirations in a coherent form. By definition a mass can as easily become a mob, therefore, a mob must be directed if it is to be controlled, if anarchy is to be limited and the 'state' survive.

Keeping people 'occupied' has been the problem of leaders for thousands of years. The Western peoples, above all others, are not a static people; therefore, it is difficult to control them, to keep them occupied. They have a tendency to create and invent; to congregate, and divide themselves into 'thinking' groups and cliques, this is never good for a government or 'state' which wishes to keep the population busy. It can however, dilute a 'portion' of the population, thereby keeping these tendencies in check. This may not be a 'romantic' view, but it is precisely what happens when you mix or dilute any host population. The West, has insulated itself for many thousands of years, we have risen and fallen according to our destiny, our

American-west *as* race-culture today; it is precisely from this *reserve* that all the future men and women of the West will, inevitably choose, or will be forced to choose, to mate with. The sheer weight of numbers will force the so-called 'biological hand' to be played out and, along with the Modern's cry of 'equality' will determine the future make-up of this, our western Continent. McCulloch, in further studies, states that about 530 million members of the Western 'nordish' elements, or about 10% of the world's population, accounts for about 0.5% of the babies being born. It would seem, therefore, that it is the 'western' race-culture, which is the 'true' minority, the minority par excellence in the world today – yet, the Modern is silent, he has nothing to say on the matter.

Where, then, are we heading?

Many, of course, will discount any and all figures, or lineal presentation [as listed above], as irrelevant to any 'moral' consideration regarding the relations between those of Western stock, and those of non-western stock. Their 'axiom' is, "…do unto others as you would have them do to you," and they are sincere in saying this. Yet, if mutual parties do not agree on just what is *good* [for one] and *bad* [for the other] to qualify the relationship, both will lose a degree of respect and confidence, thereby leading to the inevitable: Breakdown.

We all should, as inhabitants of this earth, have the strength of character to respect each other; to acknowledge the inherent individuality which, truly, makes us diverse and special, extending the

---

own peculiarities; it is what has happened over the last hundred years which make certain of us wary, concerned about our fellows, and their future. Re-population, or replennishing of our Western stock in those areas historically Western, needs to be addressed if we are to *secure and maintain* our political and racial hegemony, our territory, and our national *character*. In short, we must e*xtend* ourselves, through procreation, if we are to see a Sun continue to rise over the legacy of our fathers – *if we are to continue to be who we are*, and for a period longer than our present generation. FLS

Rise of The West

mosaic of the earth onward, toward the destiny nature has allotted us.

This is not now, nor should it ever be, predicated upon any 'political' agenda or affiliation, but on the respect due each race-culture as *sovereign* unit – making up the organic representation of the cosmos – the *essence* of the totality of the Universe. Hence, if the various races of man and their incumbent technics would ever seek to respect the other in like fashion then, all the destinies of each people shall be fulfilled as was intended by nature and nature's god. The eternal Cosmos never sleeps, its rhythms at times lucid, other times stormy, yet all determine at which level they may make a peace with this power outside of oneself, playing the eternal game of chance and successes. This is 'harmony' in the truest sense; it is the search for personal and cultural Nobility. In today's world, nothing could be further from the truth of our reality.

The ennobling of man is a fragile thing.

In today's world, the Modern has sacrificed, seemingly, all the higher ideals: Art, Beauty, physical perfection (which includes the highest mental state as well – a continuous duality), and spiritual connections with himself and his kind. He has, as well, sacrificed his future progeny on the alter of Molech – denying them the same opportunity to be what he has the potential to be (the modern "Be all that you can be" is a perverse 'teaser') – ten-thousand generations of race-culture destroyed for the sake of an *'idea'*, an 'idea' which, despite nature's laws, will demand us to cross *all* borders, destroy *all* remnants of the past, which make us what we are. Slowly, very slowly, the Modern immerses himself into the decadence of *mass-man*, his identity a thing of legends, of wayward mythos – something that has no bearing on the present (!) – after all, he is *the* modern man.

The Modern man is continuously lost in the tempest of his technics; his bearings are unstable. The landmarks he has chosen seem to drift with the tide of an ever increasingly hostile environment. His rudder is broken. Indeed, even if it were not, he has forgotten how to sail – his Fathers, having built this ship, are now dead – and he, the modern one, having never paid heed to the patient tutoring of his fathers, is now without those skills necessary to raise the mizzen mast, his sails fluttering without benefit of compass or harbor, disallowing him the power to get to where he wants to go. The days of living on the courage and strength of his fathers are over; he is going to die. Worse still: he knows it.

We, those who question the technics and direction of the Modern, are on another quest. Let the Modern pass from the earth with a bang or with a whimper; to those that consider themselves worthy of becoming 'higher-men', our search, our hope, is picking up momentum. If we are men, we will follow our instincts unflinchingly: the survival of the embryonic West demands it. On then, toward the open portal of the future, if you dare to follow.

Rise of The West

Chapter IV

The present is loaded with the past,

And pregnant with the future.

~Leibnitz~

"The origins of America contain her future," so spoke Francis Parker Yockey philosopher, lawyer, and *seer*. His magnum opus, *Imperium*, displayed a skill and love of, and respect for, the race-culture of the West – his West, as well as our own. He believed that this 'northern continent', America and Canada, originated as a colony of the greater culture of the West. In this, we must agree, for the very roots of its beginnings and origins *are* from the European continent.

Mr. Yockey, one of many men and women who saw, even as we, that America was and is, simply an *extension* of Western high-culture; a creation of its European antecedents. And so we are. Indeed, Mr. Yockey felt that, spiritually, all Western race-culture's like that of South Africa, Australia, America, Canada, and the several smaller 'colonies' are linked, and derive their world outlook and plans, their ideas, and inner imperatives from the same root. Yes, we *are* linked; bound together as corn is to sheaf.

Like many of us today, he could not understand the many factions vying for political supremacy over the other when, in fact, all belonged to the same biological unit, thereby effectually amputating each others limbs by such practice, and therefore denying the whole, a healthy and subtle body. He felt, strongly, that the dysfunctional aspects of these various arguments between relatives were to the detriment of all – since *all* must share in the same inevitable fate of a connected West. America and Europe do, indeed, constitute one large familial bloc, which have definite demonstrable interplays that effect, each other, and the world.

Here now, we shall come to the area(s), which will define what has been presented before:

America, so long a part of the technics of the West has split, as it were, from the ancient history of our *common* stock. Since the onslaught of the second fratricidal war, the battle between Intellect and Money has been won; it has been won by *money*, and the intellect therefore, has suffered.

It is intellect, that peculiar part of a person or a race, which creates mores and traditions; a 'people's' *worldview* is *both* from this same source. Our common history, as a Western people, has gone through severe trauma since the turn of the 20th Century, with several 'world views' vying for supremacy. Money is simply the forum, which makes one or the other view acceptable to the masses; yet, money, in and of itself, does promote, or rather, those who wish to maintain their hold on it, those manifestations, which are necessarily destructive to our culture. In any event, America, as a distinctive Western colony, has abrogated its historical tradition *as* a Western culture, since this victory. Instead of a grand and unified 'history', we have an idea, a 'constitution', or a domestic outlook (not a national outlook however), which drives us ever on. As a People however, *we lack a soul*; implicit in a soul is the ability to look at oneself as a unique individual, separate and apart from other individuals, yet supporting those obligations incumbent upon members of a distinct family to form a complete household. In such a feeble attempt, America says it shares as a world-view the concepts of 'democracy; but here at home, 'national democracy' is a catchword for an *idea* of what we 'think' democracy is. We believe this so strongly, that we are willing to fight, to commit to War.

Our Wars have always been wars of [*or over*] democracy *as* idea – not simple geo-political manifestations of, or between money, power, plutocracy, or any other device or mechanism, which makes up the organic substance around us. The slogan of America: 'making it safe for democracy' has been, and is being heard around the world. It becomes not democracy, but the *tyranny* of the mass *over* that of the higher man. If it takes guns and money to 'enforce' an idea of 'liberty' and 'freedom' to others less versed than us, is that, then, 'democracy'?

The thoughts, ideas, questions, and potential reactions to those perceived attitudes and perceptions developed in this work are, perhaps, considered by many to be hostile to the present state of affairs – so be it. We have, however, in a progressive setting, discussed the origin and purpose of the race-culture, the culture of the West, of which America is but a 'portion' of that legacy. We have discussed at some length the relationship between its people, government, and religion: each a technic *particular* to the race-culture. We have discussed the *force* behind their respective responsibilities to 'themselves' and their 'government'. The discussion regarding eugenics which, while being antagonistic to the Modern must, of necessity, be explored; indeed, much material abounds on this subject that cannot be ignored, at least by an 'un-biased' individual.

We all, to one degree or another, acknowledge that the world is full of problems, on many fronts, and is now high time that we address those concerns with courage and foresight. If we do not, we shall be relegated to the status of a third-world nation, with third-rate citizens trying their best to cope with domestic as well as foreign situations. The latter, it may be observed, is accepted as already *being*. American National elections have seen dramatically a decrease in popular [democratic] voter turn-out; the presidential election in 1990 saw 52% of Americans voting, giving that President 27% of the popular vote (with 23% of the electoral vote), it is obvious that it is more than apathy. Where is the national spirit of the 'new' European renaissance? Where is the glory of the old pax Americana?

Let us consider Europe. After years of systematic failures by their national leaders to address social realignment, economics, moral-technics and the like, it was inevitable that the race-soul should manifest itself in the race-cultural explosion that has rocked the world. The 'cold war' is over – if there ever was one – it was, in actuality, the 'stagnate' principle at work spoken of earlier that has proven the denial of culture. Covered by an alien presence, the race-culture of the west in Eastern-Europe has spent almost fifty years in isolation, kept apart from the destiny-will of their own kind; indeed, the Soviet Union could never have kept the culture's of the West apart.

America is following this same path.

Unusual in form, the spokesmen for the American West pointed out, in days past, of the awakening of the European as a 'gentle' revolution. Predictably, in this country, as the progeny of this selfsame Motherland, we are being pointed, inexorably, to an exchange of values, perceptions, and technics that has, for the past one-hundred and fifty years, held this same [European] people in a state of stagnation, humiliation, and instability, which has now begun to actualize itself into such a metamorphosis, as the rising of a *new* West.

Within the context of the preceding discussion, we have endeavored to present a technic in *thought*. This is necessary to study and research the organism we call Western man. We have not covered 'education' proper, business, religious doctrine, or social responsibilities in its 'minute' forms; however, these will come, of necessity, from an informed and noble individual. This work is not, and cannot be, a doctrinaire 'how-to-manual'. In this context, the propositions and potential possibilities enumerated in the following pages will be as concise as can be delivered through the science of history as applied to our [American] future. Indeed, all the forgoing enumeration's are proceeding even as you, dear reader, are absorbing these very thoughts. They are taking place all across the heartland of this, *our* America, *our* West.

Frank L. DeSilva

i.

The Ascending:

Nationalism and Race

From man's earliest beginnings, there have been two main factors inherent in his struggle to understand and promote his essence. Of these factors, the first we will consider has presently been filed in the dustbin of history, and has been placed in the category of the 'passé', the un-useful. The other, having gone through so many manifestations and evolutions in our human history, is now generally looked at as bigotry and fanaticism. We speak, now, more of the *intangible* and *tangible* elements relating to our human experience, for all races and cultures share this duality.

Of these two 'factors', we shall ascribe to the first, Race; to the second, Nationalism.

Of Race, we have discussed the many varied nuances and manifestations regarding its existence and life. How 'individuals' *look* at race varies from location, religious attitudes, race-cultural imperatives, and governmental agendas (which account for a high proportion of the modern attitudes, *socially*, in organized states); this is especially true in the Western nations, since we have had a century of experience in propaganda, social instruction, and public education.

All the above are 'prerequisites', for and against, the social institutions of the human experience.

To 'nationalism', we attribute the *unseen* in the context of boundaries; the lines of demarcation placed and set by peoples immemorial, both geographically and culturally, which predetermine a *set consciousness* in any, and all particular peoples. This, of necessity, is a spiritual technic, which has been *actualized* in the outward manifestations of an organized people, be that familial, tribal, or cultural/national states of being.

To 'race', as has been said before, we attribute the seen, as it naturally relates to the physical body, to 'type', and common sense, which relates to a common known 'factor' of humanity. We discern these manifestations in many and sundry ways, each person making their own analysis based on their own preconditions, perceptions, prejudices, or instinct; this is as it should be: this is Nature's Law.

Once the *consciousness* between these two prime factors however, is lost, or worse, relegated to 'those things of the past', one must finally take a closer look, a look which, today, has much social weight attached to it. But why should you, the person, the reader, care one jot, or tittle about this ambiguous, dark, and unpopular issue? The answer, while obvious to some, will take a little getting used to by the population at large – strange, since just one generation (!) ago, it was considered as being the foundation upon which all had existed, by which the comforts and technologies had arisen in the West – the answer: Because You are a *part* of it, you live and breathe along side others who, like you, have a similar background, a *look* which shares common ancestry. Your soul, deep down inside, beats to the same rhythmic cycles of *birth, life, and senility*. The same cycles of thousands of your ancestors, to whom *you* owe your very life. Even now, as you read this, every breathe you take reminds you of what you are, what you can be; look outside – yes now (!) – what do you see? Living dwellings, houses, apartments of every shape and size (even of those who are not as fortunate as you); but there is more. Look at the lawns of green turf, those sections of concrete, wood, or wire dividing up each particular property, plots, or tracks; of whole City blocks. Now, just *what* do you see? No, do not look at what you *see*, look *behind* what you see!

For each illustration, for each actuality, there is an intangible; some would call it a divine plan. Call it what you will, but nevertheless, there is a *will*, divine or not, which marks one man, one lawn, one fence, one line of shrubbery from the other. What the common man may see is superficial – after all, perchance, he did not build these structures, nor have anything to do with the design – he simply 'inhabits' them. It is like asking the question: Where does water come from? Some would say: The faucet! One looks only at the manifestation of a thing – You must look deeper. This is the invisible, that intangible boundary, which primitive man, as well as the Modern, experiences. Frankly, there is no escaping the primal feeling of *ownership, control, personhood, and nationhood.*[Ψ] Each is part of the same presence: individuality. Indeed, this very feeling was the match, which set aflame the continent; the fire, which set us, as Americans, free. So, as with a man's house/castle, in the truest and purest sense, is the *smalles*t form of nationalism.

This simple 'nation state' is part of our daily lives; it was passed down, through many generations, to us. It is part of every

---

[Ψ] In early America, it was essentially a movement of individuality, of the *freedom* to attain something *unattainable* in their respective nations of origin. Speech, as such, was not the great motivator – land ownership was. The 'concept' of a man and his castle was a pipe dream to immigrants coming from Europe; to them, it was to be 'tenant' forever.
The men and women who chose to come to the 'new lands' sought many things, but it was the burgeoning idea of commonwealth, of community based upon those individuals who were willing to harvest their labors for an idea, which would protect their sovereignty over their own 'homestead', owing to no man or government for the privilege. *Thomas Hobbs*, and *John Locke* had spoken long and persuasively in this regard, and many were willing and able to take up the mantle. It may well be true that men will fight for women and gold, but it is just as true that men will *die* for Land, for living space. The idea of 'taxation' of personal property was repugnant to the original settlers; representation was considered only sparingly, and only in those areas, which had amassed a certain affluent citizenry, that is to say, merchants and traders, that which makes up any new and struggling township. Taxes on mercantile products were seen, by some, as commonplace, since all government of the people needed some revenue to maintain the illusion of governance. The concepts of land ownership were absolute. If a man could work it, it belonged to him and his. This made a man, of necessity, a vigorous, proud, and recalcitrant individual. To be sure, this was a problem to existing institutions and governments. To our own, it has proved just as difficult.
If the King of England had sequestered a man's home, and called it what he would, the man, and the surrounding population would, absolutely, consider this theft of the highest order; in the same *sense*, the 'system' which would take away a man's property for eminent domain, or any other reason is, without equivocation, theft. The early fathers answered the King with a revolution because they were willing to die for an idea, an idea which said that the individual was more powerful than even a king, when it came to his personal property.
In today's world, in this modern America, the shadows of despotism have reached deeply. The individual has been replaced by the corporate unit, by the mass of complacency. FLS.

neighborhood. It is part of our cities. In fact, our major centers, ironically, of our modern cosmopolis are, decidedly, the most nationalistic. Territory defines just who we are, and in our major cities is seen the most diverse, jumbled, and dominant themes of nationalism. For instance, the massive and blatant symbols of power, which highlight the cities of America, are not without their own symbols of power and control, which sit beside the red, white, and blue. A name, a flag, these describe just *who* this empire belongs. Each is personal, denoting that essence, which steers the ship of state. When one looks upon each symbol, there is, inherent, an intangible essence of power. This, observable fact, is downplayed by the Modern.

The Modern, like all hypocrites, preaches equality to the mass man. This dictum is hammered into the social construct. Each day, upon waking, the mass man is hounded by the conscious and unconscious directives of the State, that there is no 'I', just the 'we', not the We as the People — but as 'we' of the mass slave — each a member of a world order, which is safe as long as its denizens maintain the daily grind of the commonplace, the know-nothing, the slug.

How utterly absurd! How degrading!

The striving for *excellence*, indeed, the sheer struggle for survival, not to mention that absolute *supremacy* over their competitors is simply Western man's spontaneous imitation of nature's perfect technic of survival through variation and selection. And as we all know, the *fittest* survive. Adaptation does not occur without, firstly, a fight for survival, at least in Corporate America, where the ruthless exchanges of power is also part of their personal ethic. This, also, a part of nature's eternal cycle. This *cycle* is seen, also, in the exchange of power, control/ownership, and culture (or lack of it) in the Nation as a whole. But, if sight is the issue, the clarity of the nationalist is paramount.

Nationalism *is* patriotism. As has been said before, the family, as 'unit', instills those values of leadership and group responsibility in the nascent stage of national responsibility — *this* is Patriotism. It is the patriots *reason* for being; it is in protecting and establishing those things, which he was taught and, hopefully, believes in as being right and noble, enough so, that he would give his very life-blood for its extension. The true patriot, as nationalist, contains all that is carried in the soul, the race-soul, of *any* given people. There are no boundaries, racial or otherwise, in the love that an individual feels for his own kind, for the laughter of the children bourne by his sisters, and the faith of his fathers he shares with his brothers. His faith, his very senses, which *begets* his feelings, such as that of primitive man, follows his morality in conceptualizing such things as tribe, duty, loyalty, honour, and all those things, which make up the 'greater self', that extended part of 'what' he is, or at least sees himself as. He exists, and remains, *as* a part of the total familial cycle. This is the *highest* form of citizenship.

In today's world of politically sensitive phrases and sound-bites, of 'domestic' this and that, nationalism, especially in this day and age, is both hated and romanced; it only matters just what side of the table you are seated. The nationalist sees himself in many lights, even here, in America, we have our own sense of what nationalism is; the proof, however, is the very real sense of duty, that divine duty, to his own kind – his own people – his own race-culture. This was how the *Pax Romana* was birthed. Very little of it remained as she lay dying.

Few people could proclaim this dictum more eloquently than Sir Arthur Keith, when he says of the nationalist, *"[The] Nationalist mind is most deeply concerned with the integrity and perpetuation of its race. What is most feared is its death – death by absorption."*[30] This was also addressed by Oswald Spengler as well, when he stated his perception on nationalism, *"Every culture possesses its own conception of home and fatherland, which is hard to comprehend, scarcely to be expressed in words, full of dark metaphysical relations, but unmistakable in its tendency."*[31] *[emph. mine]* The Modern, however, is still unable to grasp this. Yet, the rise of the

---

[30] Keith, Sir Arthur – New Theory of Human Evolution – Philological Library, 1941, pg. 348.
[31] Spengler, Oswald – Decline of the West – Helmet Werncr, Abridged, Trans. Charles Francis Atkinson pg. 174-75, 1962.

West has already passed him by.[φ]

In every quarter of this nation we call America, the signs of nationalism abound. We remain, however, a nation of 'phrases', 'sound-bites', and visual contradictions. To most, America is a 'patchwork' of people – the Modern's theory of the melting pot – he would, as well, have us believe it actually works. The fragile, almost imperceptible realities of the various, but distinct race-cultures, is continually washed, 'white-washed' by the Modern, in terms of *his* 'melted-pot'. Like with many of the phrases of the modern, glittery catch-words like 'melting-pot', 'democracy', 'equality' and the like, have meanings known only to those who have *created* its modern meaning. The nationalist, however, has a more far-reaching vision of reality.

To those unclouded by the machinations of the Modern, which includes his phraseology, fancy as it is, will know, or at least feel, the decadence of it; the principle is *stagnation*, it lives and breathes in the cosmopolis of his design. The conglomerate of the mass, this, the Modern loves. The hustle, and bustle of the mindless, endless, spectacle of humanity: the more *diverse* the better. The Modern has

---

[φ] Euphemisms, such as 'fatherland', denote ideas that are not fashionable in polite American society these days. Father would, of necessity, denote a 'specific' meaning as seen by those in power, who wish to 'control' these deep seated emotional ties; in its place, various phrases have been inculcated to replace it; the concept of 'homeland' as intended by this work, is susceptible to any misdirection as any other word we would choose. In today's environment, such words as these have been dusted off, re-packaged, and sold to the mass *as* fatherland and homeland; a cookie cutter look-alike to those who obey the new masters. They follow a new Pax Romana – the great Idea – an idea which, paradoxically, has been designed to appeal to every tribe, ethnicity, and corporate unit – at least a *part* of each.

The common man, that man, precisely, who represents the strength or weakness of a Nation, is not a part of this modern homeland, he sees the world through the eyes of his past – his grandfather, father, or township – in this vein, if asked, this thought would, perforce, be at odds with the ruling masters of today. His homeland is his *family, his tribe, and his race.*

Of course, this speaks for those of Western stock. In wartime, as we see coming, a portion of each culture will initially sign on; the true test is the stamina of the long term, and how long this initial fervor will last; for all foreign entanglements will push the populace to a dividing point. Nationalism is concerned with home affairs, not extra-national ones. FLS

roots very deep, and his tree must be fed. The carpet seller, the street barker, the negotiations, the swindle. These are *his* roots, and he relishes the fact that he is *better* at it than his fellows.

To the Nationalist, melting pot means *absorption*. Precisely, the *opposite* of the modern. It means, simply, to the pure nationalist, absorption by what is seen as foreign, not just different, but *foreign*, as in *opposed* too. It is instinctual to the common man, as such, it defies description or definition, for he is not a philosopher or etymologist.

The nationalist fears instinctively the foreign racial component, the foreign ideas of his 'religions' and his concepts, which are not part of the soul he bears, the soul of *his* West. This is predicated on a racial memory, *not* education. A people, an individual, who seek to be *who* they are for as long as they can will, at every opportunity, seek to *isolate* first, and foremost, and *maintain* isolation, rather than risk absorption, and its incumbent annihilation. If, this cannot be done, then they will fight, or die as a postmark to history, unworthy to survive.

The Modern, however, has survived precisely *because* he is coward. He is also a hypocrite. It was he, after all, who brought the modern slave-laborer to these, our shores. The African, Asian, Polynesian, and amer-Indian, which would work for wages, and often the whip; money and the whip, both to fuel the engine of the Modern. It was not the Modern who cared for the simple man, or his needs; he cared not that this invasion he had instigated, was becoming a festering sore that spread into the host body of the American West.

This tragedy of human displacement, as much for the slave laborer, as it was for the indigenous 'western-worker', created a new sense of nativism. It brought nationalism in a continuing evolution of form and substance. This was the direct consequence of the Modern. Yet, he [the modern] was already its master. Remember, if you will, the displacement of those of the Western race-culture from the very beginning of the Modern's first great experiment: Indentured Servitude. This title, alone, was the greatest of hypocrisy. The modern would have us believe that it was only the 'negro', the 'chinaman', and so on, that ever suffered the bonds of servitude, but fails to address, as always, that it was those of the West that founded and colonized this American frontier. It was, indeed, and colonized specifically with *white slaves*. *"In the British West Indies slavery was instituted as early as 1627. In Barbados by the 1640's there were an estimated twenty-five thousand slaves, of whom twenty-one thousand seven-hundred were White (Calendar of State Papers, Colonial Series, pg. 528)."*[32]

Such a delight to the nefarious multicultural modern is the fact that Negroes had *owned* white slaves as early as 1670. It was in this year that the Virginia Assembly enacted the following law: *"It is enacted that noe negro or Indian though baptized and enjoyned their owne ffreedome shall be capable of any such purchase of [white] Christia*ns."[33] True it is, that men, and women of Western stock, had been enslaved by their fellows since the early 1600's. The Modern, even then, was part and parcel of his fellow racial stock – he worshiped the same god, looked the same – yet he was to enslave those less fortunate; he caused them to be whipped, persecuted, kidnapped, and murdered by their own brethren. These taskmasters, all, the antecedents of the Modern. The genetic memory lives, today, in the hearts of their children, ever seeking to portray equality, but ever loving the sense of superiority over those he feels the need to control and direct; after all, it is for our own good! In response to this treatment, resentment arose. In consequence to the spiritual and political realities, many movements arose to qualify 'equality' as between 'christian' peoples, namely, white Christians, as it was unlikely that the religion of the West was to be passed to any others. It ran the race of debate and dissent up to the Revolutionary War. It has continued ever after.

In the annals of America, The War Between the States, was the first major attempt to *control* the power of the Modern. Soon after, during the rush to 'reconstruct' those wayward and independent Southern States, thousands of *"…immigrant ditch-diggers and the railroad armies…"*[34] came to supplant those of Western stock which, in the

---

[32] Hoffman II, Michael A. – They were White and They Were Slaves – Wiswell Rufin House, 1991, pg. 4.
[33] Ibid, page 7.
[34] Sumner, W.G. – FOLKWAYS –1906, pg. 29-113.

immediate and long-range account, would have benefited the nation at large and, most importantly, would have allowed some semblance of real equality, as real as any equality ever is, for the race-culture that had the most to benefit by hard work and a stable environment.

The response however, was quick by those of the West. The response was the *nativism* of the 'Yellow Peril'. Unfortunate it was, that this natural instinct for survival spilt over into areas of passion that included those, also, of Western stock. Yet, where those of similar stock have reabsorbed, the former, those not of Western stock, have not, nor ever will be absorbed, however many laws are passed to accommodate their presence, voluntarily or involuntary.

It is at this juncture that we, again, find the Modern. He waits. He patiently approaches the growing believers of nationalism – he strikes, bayonet well fixed, he preaches the doctrine of a 'kinder and gentler America', while the suppression of natural instinct and desire is a daily occurrence. It is seen and felt throughout this Western Continent. The Modern, however, forgets the wise and introspective words of Rudyard Kipling, *"the eyes of the awakened Saxon,"* truly, *"are level and straight."* They know of the treason: they *see*, *hear*, and *feel* its passage.

The Modern has betrayed the race-culture of the West. With few exceptions, members of the West rarely speak of this aloud. Only those few who feel compelled to rise to the occasion are ever noticed – their destiny is the *fire within* them. Treason exists. It must be driven out, if the West is to survive and become healthy again. Each member of the West must start with himself or herself, as individual; it will then pass to others. By his own actions, the individual multiplied a million fold will overcome the Modern.

The Modern fixes his *idea* to a culture of his own creation. Indeed, he *has* created a culture. He seeks to fashion this culture after the examples of the past; but he has failed. He seeks to emulate the ideas of the great Reformers, the great levelers – such as Rousseau, but the modern lacks the unified cultural idea inherent in a greater vision, that actualization of the race-culture that would, of necessity, define its very presence. Of America, of her original colonizer's, their way of life was to *dispossession*, dispersion; their vision acutely rearranged. They, those children of the West, are taught, every day, that their legacy of manifest destiny denies them substance, creates of them the image of impostor, and interloper; that their legacy is vile conquest, their European antecedents criminal thieves. The Modern continues this picture of his past, because it serves his interest – demanding ever and increasing compromise with his once beloved servants and slaves. The Modern has no idea larger than himself, or his needs. This is his Culture.

Nation, also, is an Idea. So spoke Francis Parker Yockey in his monumental work *Imperium*; but it is more. It is Soul, it is People. It is neither abstraction nor fantasy. Nation *is*. The nation, as organism, has dreams, thoughts, and manifestations [deeds], which mark the body as a whole, as a unique element in nature. The Nation, truly, cannot exist in nature without its self-manifestation of Folk, or people, that *organic* substance, which endows the politico-technic of the nation to exist as *more than idea*.

The Nation is broken up into strata of mass, the biological underpinnings of the mental understanding of the 'greater idea' – *the* Nation. At the lower end of these biological strata, you have the elements that do not, truly, share the spirit of the nation or its ideals – such does the Modern share. At the highest strata, you see this spirit, this soul, in the art, philosophy, literature, and architecture of the race-culture *as* idea. The monuments it leaves, it leaves as an organic *continuation* of its essence. In the world of art, who could question, for instance, the Western influence in the 'oil painting' of 1500-1850? This art is distinct, precise, and has meaning known to both simple and educated folk – it is bore a presence to a reality, a universal spirit that was shared by the race-culture. The invading *types* of American paintings and architecture have been fostered by the Modern; he has been its *greatest* champion.

The Modern champions the concepts of diversity in many areas, including Art, and languishes in the *espris de corps* of surrealism, the homo-erotic manifestations of 'art for arts sake' in which the tempest created by the assault on tradition and traditional artistic value is, or becomes in the process, the only *real* 'expression' of mention. In contradiction, the traditional *realistic* interpretation of Western art (i.e. David, Pousin, Girodet, DaVinci, and the like) is relegated to second-place, with the blue-ribbon being handed over to the various 'native' American artists, African art, and generally *any* art *not* Western. The 'basis' of Western Art, allegory, myth, and religio-cultic interpretations, are deemed 'static', 'stiff', 'chauvinistic', or developed from a sense of unique and absolute world vision. Yes, the abiding truth is that the Modern 'hates' the West, for it truly is *not* of his blood.

If it be acknowledged that the Modern is a child of the Enlightenment then, one must also assume that he is the disciple of Reason. Such is the legacy of the West. Reason is a 'mechanical' process, and as members of a race-culture who advances the 'process' of reason, we can claim, also, a certain symbiotic relationship. Yet, without that process of intuitiveness, there remains a vacuum; we would be eternally unbalanced, if we did not utilize and *think* organically as well, in fact the abstract reasoning potential is what has set apart the Western thought process from all other competitors. This is what the Modern lacks and promotes: he creates bigger and better machines, computers, and institutions, but has forgotten that better half of himself; his *spiritual* continuity. While this may seem a rootless thing, it defies mechanical reasoning – yet it can be observed – as such men as Spengler, Gibbons, Yockey, and Brooks have shown. The final and positive proof of spiritual continuity is, as shall always be, Race, which defines Soul, which then *becomes*, Nation.

Since the Modern has denied the existence of a race-cultural 'soul', he then continues and expands the position that, of necessity, a 'nation' is anything *but* Race. It is *his* Idea. It is his nation of *reason*. He twists the notion, the expression of Nation, as the most rudimentary understanding dictates. He defies the expression and articulation of form – at least for the Western – for he denies the existence of either its *expression* or *form* as a viable institution in this modern day. To the

Modern, nation means *mass*. He loves the conglomerate, the literal and stupendous volume of humanity that is controlled in its daily manifestations, such as seen in any major metropolis – the bazaar, the barker, the merchant – this is the *kinship* of the Modern; this is his 'democracy'.

Let one argue or no, that this is good or bad, healthy or unhealthy (this too, is democracy), yet this *ideal*, that of mass *over* substance, leaves no Nobility nor any sense of aesthetics; it certainly does not allow for any one group to arise with a *higher ideal* – this would lead, inevitably, to the *betrayal* of *his* betrayal, that of his 'equality'. OH! that great leveling!! The sides are picked, and this great leveling, the antithesis of the race-idea, of nationalism, and will be rejected by its descendants as long as there is the reality of Race.

In this modern age, the wants, needs, and cries of desperation are rarely heard if uttered by anyone conscious of the race-idea, of nationalism. If one is able to hear, even a *whisper*, of these needs or wants, in-between the tears of these nascent expressions, it is too late. It is Reaction. The trauma has already been inflicted; the resonating emotional duress has cut deep into the race-soul; the blow to the human psyche is too profound to articulate. It does, however, seek relief; it seeks *survival*.

Nationalism is a *product* of organism. Moreover, it cannot be disorganized, since it has no organization [with few exceptions]. It remains fluid, and organic. To the Modern, this is catastrophe, it is the flood, which washes away everything, which he has ever striven to create – creation of and from the *destruction*, which had preceded it. There is only one 'ship of state' in nature – this is survival. It is nationhood. It is the eternal imperative of all ages; it is the eternal *succession* of young and old.

Nationalist are *always* young.

This 'spirit' of youth may be mental, physical, or ideological. This *youth* is the way-sign of the nationalist, insofar as the impetus for nationalism comes from a sense of romance, idealism, and such vagaries, which accompany youth; in short, the technics of the nationalist consist of a burgeoning sense of experimentation – of one's coming of age. The Modern sees this as juvenile behavior, and resents the political manifestations of this type of romance, for he feels it will supplant him. It is very true that in most cases, the nationalist seeks to *reaffirm* what is traditional, what he [the nationalist] sees as the better part of the past – the golden age of his experience – but knows that he cannot salvage all of it. The Modern sees this as fanaticism.

Like all young people, there is a certain shock value associated with the 'doing' of youth, and the intellectualizing of the elder. The nationalist shocks the complacent Modern out of his cultural stupor by bringing to light, by reaffirming, the original idea, the primal origins of their shared beginnings, to the forefront. These manifestations may be recognized as ideological, racial, cultural, or civil discontent. It may very well bring out emotions long suppressed: hate, fear, survival, love, and sympathy.

Hate, because those who are supposed to be looking out for them, those who have been entrusted with the power to protect and serve, have abrogated this duty, have given the halls of justice and leadership over to the enemies of their kind. Fear, because the nationalist can see clearly the underlying betrayal of his national borders, the abuse and rape of his economic system, and finally through the cowardice of the body-politic of the Modern in allowing the disgraceful dissection of his ancient traditions, either through the written word of his forefathers, or the direct interpretation of the nation's laws and precepts. Survival becomes his highest priority, and the feelings of love and sympathy for his fellow man becomes ever the benchmark of his aspirations. The Nationalist, in almost every case, sees a betrayal, by those in power, in whatever the Age who, as *guardians*, decided to change or redirect those things, which had gone before; in other words, to make a change *against* what was seen as right for generations. As seen by the Nationalist, these changes had not come from any continuity of interests, or over a slow evolutionary period [seen in hundreds of years, not in dozens], but rather through the impetus and social construct of the *personal* wishes of individuals, rather than the needs of the People at large, devoid of contact with the real world of the living, outside his marble halls, and insulated by his money and sycophants. Such breaches of longstanding Tradition were the elements of France in 1789 – which brought about a victory in revolution by its adherents – at least the victory of 'mass' over 'quality'. The Modern, alas, has not understood this past so apparent for he continues to *rationalize* his position.

While the Modern *rationalizes* his position, the Nationalist *reacts* to his. It is instinct.

Granted, his emotions tend to place him outside the accepted sphere of influence of modern society. Indifferent though they [the mass] may be, being of the same race-soul, nevertheless, is drawn to it as well. They share the same instinct. Yet, as if it were deaf and dumb, the mass feels indifference to what they 'feel' intuitively as evil to their way of Life – they react in the same fashion to those that would *act* against those things felt, even if seen unclearly, that affects all in its path. Persecution, prison, and loss of life result in the actions taken by the nationalist against the Modern – for *he* has the power.

To the mass, the Modern still attaches such 'code words' as patriot, constitutionalist, legitimate power, etc., to instill a sense of continuity with the past. The mass will not see just how far they have been controlled, for they are kept busy with work, worship, and raising families; after all, they seek nothing of the truth of the matter, they remain, simply, *content* with things the way they are. The mass, generally, are oblivious to the sequence of birth, life, and senility of their waking consciousness. The mass rarely will accept the fact that their legacy is dead, they too, are afraid of the rising West, for it is ancient, unspoken, and cloaked in guises that have long gone untaught by the powers of the Modern.

The Rise of the West is always precipitated by a foreign organism being *inserted* into the host body. This insertion, and the accompanying acceptance, weaken the *will* of a people, and is the *symptom* of death and racial instinct. This will, inevitably, lead to the deterioration of all public life and social intercourse on the level of spiritual consciousness. The once high levels of race-conscious leaders abdicate, in favor of the Modern. As 'private men', they retain the semblance of national power. Everything, then, remains the same – it stagnates. No *new* ideas, no *creation*, no effort! The necessities of life are placed in juxtaposition with pleasure, the age-old pattern of *pan et circenes* of all decadent empires. This, then, produces the voluntary abandonment of the race-cultural creation that, over ten to twenty generations, and countless millions of souls that have given their ultimate sacrifice – their lives – in building this very race-culture from the deep abyss of history, and have then cast aside their sacrifice, and that of their ancestors, for bread and pleasure. This leads, inevitably, to the hatred of whoever or whatever practices and encourages the mass to entertain regimens of sternness, creation, and a sense of the future. With all this, through its many machinations, the absorption of the cultural or racial alien is secured.

In large enough numbers, or equally quantitative in relation to position[s] of power, a change becomes manifest. This may appear small or incidental in relation to the vast majority of a particular race-culture, specifically a Western one in this discussion. It may appear innocuous in the local community or larger city. The local religious 'center' gives way to a *new* element, demonstrably different from the traditional western religious technics. Insignificant, it exists *beside* those institutions that have been a part of the cultural presence of the West for thousands of years. Soon, more begin to follow; soon there is a *merging* of the alien element, becoming larger politically and race-culturally. No longer, may an individua of the original race-culture, respond to his ancient beliefs – *pluralism* now overshadows the 'restrictive' duties of a particular religious technic. This merging appears on *all* levels of society; like an octopus, its tentacles wrap around every idea, every greater idea, and strangles it. It does not kill; worse, it does not let it *live*.

Over the horizon, those of the West see the last great ideal of the Modern: *Mediocrity*.

Mediocrity, as any rudimentary analysis will show and, by which all *common* aspirations are gauged, is the *renunciation* of all greater ideals, of effort; *to all values relating to worth*, worth of any kind whatsoever. It is a great leveling value, that massive 'common denominator', which leads only in a circuitous route to the original source, stagnation.

To the race-culture, then, it strikes at the heart. The incumbent leveling of the individual racial components, and its genetic foundation, is manifest. The ancient and steady watch placed upon *blood*, upon *breed*, is now open to all comers. The dilution of generations of race-soul will be seen within a few generations; there is no race *in particular*, only the even, dull, and the mediocre. This is seen, all too frequently, on any street in a major city. (The reader need not look any farther than the center of his own town of any significant size; even the small and furtive 'farm town' is not to be forgotten in this equation – and this the most telling, since it is in the small rural settings that the youth of the West are the most capable of receiving the instructions of their peers and parents.) All this, of course, leads to a 'democratic liberalism', a complex of social constructs, *making* everyone equal: women are men, men are women. The human element of *difference* and *uniqueness* fades away into the will-o-the-wisp of the Modern.

This 'complex' originates with the Intelligentsia. It is, and has ever been the bolshevism of the 20th century.

It is the so-called 'cultural elite', the denizens of money and the overstuffed pomposity of those who 'claim' to be educated, who are, also, those who *surrender* and show any *sympathy* whatsoever to the enemies of the West, cloaking their effeminate natures, behind the podium of academia, or the titles of paper nobility afforded to them. It is *liberalism* in a truly 'liberal sense', which would teach, as a common imperative, to treat others than yourself as you would be treated – Western evolution is replete with these various experiments, which demanded that individuals be cognizant of nature and her human counterparts, by which all would then live in relative peace and harmony, confined in each and similar political technics. This was the golden-rule of our ancestors; a practice, which has worked, and worked well, amongst those of the West. This, like all Western values, has become a liberal reality, but has been twisted, and is now based on Revolution and Institution.

Intellectuals *always* played a pivotal part in this evolution. They look to their own for instruction; and if there is a will, a will which comes not from the halls of invidiousness but, rather, from the well of the common folk, a paradox occurs – instead of taping and sharing the common experience* of their kinsmen, they would insulate themselves *away* from those persons who require their expertise the most!

The [modern] political liberal knows, or should know, the elements of *thesis*, *antithesis*, and *synthesis*, those elements so necessary to the struggling character of any people; and this innocent character, which can be manipulated and controlled by persons more astute than his fellows, uses this manipulation at every opportunity.

The traditional reason for liberal philosophy had its origins in a nobler state – *to protect those who have been wronged, this is true liberalism* – it is only his *excess*, which puts him, the common man, in danger. As the demise of the intelligentsia draws ever near, the weight of burden placed, artificially I might add, upon the liberal becomes even more fraught with excess. More 'statutes' must be introduced which, by its very nature, becomes *restrictive* to the populace as a whole – the battle for liberty and freedom becomes the tool by which the Modern seeks ever to enslave. The new-speak of the Modern: the more the protection [restriction] the more the freedom [slavery]. Look to the examples of the French Revolution and the Petrine Nobility of Russia for a ready-made example of what has happened over the past several generations. Neither of these examples, from the top down, knew of their decadence.

Such do we see here, in America.

A single example of a Modern American, Emma Lazarus, who demanded that the poor, wretched, and unwanted should come to

---

* Here now we speak of a *common* denominator, a *common* Race, and *common* racial experience, [i.e. as was the United States up to the Second War of Fratricide]. FLS

these, our shores, should remind all of us of the absolute stupidity of such an acclamation. Any person of average intelligence would remonstrate that such a position, not devoid of compassion or intelligent consideration, would absolutely object to the placement of wretched or unwanted persons in their environ; this does not mean, of course, that just because a person is without means, or is wretched because of his native predisposition economically, or is even unwanted by their respective nations, that this must mean that they cannot contribute to our own experiment. It does not. What is meant here, for the possible obtuse reader, is that the maxim of *strength* and *intelligence* is what is necessary to a vibrant and healthy nation and its future prospects. The Nationalist, as with all common-folk desires, and considers the position that 'all people' be allowed, indeed, recruited, to these, our shores, is a *betrayal* of the original intent of their peculiar institutions and traditions, of which, and foremost among the Nationalist, is that this spectacle, by its own weight will, and has trampled, those traditions and institutions placed here, by our own experience, for the benefit and *extension* of the people of the West. The Nationalist wants no part of this suicide.

These esoteric trappings of the nationalist, understood instinctually by the common man, are ridiculed by the Modern, and his minions. Heartland, fatherland, motherland, all these euphemisms, and more are decried by the Modern as antiquated or relegated to fanaticism yet, the Modern cannot refute, at least not in any believable fashion, the facts of waking consciousness. *The disintegration of America is obvious to all who have eyes to see.* From every level of American society, this reality is manifest.

The traditional Rights of our political experience, namely, the Constitution and its myriad renderings of writings and treatise by men of sound discourse and political insight, which have created the common American experience, abound for us to compare, in a modern sense, what *was*, and what has *become*. Add to this, the understanding that, for many years, the 'bearing of arms' was considered [by the People] as a natural and normal part of our American experience; this 'bearing' was not restricted, and the common militia was armed just as the present military of the day –

the forces militant were of the same stock, fought for the same territory and promised rights – therefore, to be armed, was as right as rain. Hence, it was to the surety of the Promises made by Compact that the right of Arms was construed to maintain said promises. Men, to secure and maintain these rights, must be *willing*, and have the *means*, to fight for these rights. Anything less is fantasy and romance.

I dare anyone to look about them, and answer me: *Have these Promises been fulfilled?*

Add to this, as well, the denial of Western thought and action on the screens of our various media. Who can honestly deny the tremendous change seen daily through the massive amounts of information/propaganda, seen by millions of citizens of the West, that is to say, information, which just forty-years ago, would have been relegated to the dustbin of perversity and unmanly behavior!

To this sense of taste and beauty we see very little left; and with this loss so, also, that sense of shock, that instinctual *revulsion*, and worse, do we see the loss of a unique *perception* of beauty. From a purely Western point of view, the natural beauty of the blonde, brunette, and red-head actor and actress, comes their replacement with black, swarthy, and foreign persons so as to *change the perceptions of ones own self* as seen through the eyes of someone else's making. The Celto-Nordic ideal of early America is now replaced with the ebony hue of the African. To the twisted understanding of 'ethnicity', as opposed to race, and the forced acceptance of a serious loss of territory for the men and women of the West (yes, this means here in America!) both politically and geographically to foreign race-cultures, this has spelled defeat; it is decay.

Otto von Bismarck, the Iron Chancellor of Germany, remarked of the latter, *"A nation that voluntarily surrenders territory is a nation in decay."* In other words, a People who does not *show* the strength to *hold* a territory deserves neither land nor freedom. This may also be a naïve form of federalism, but it speaks well of that *organic* process by which a people rise or fall.

The Nationalist, in a pure sense, does not concern himself with territories outside his own national boundaries, or racial technics. His concern is for *his* Nation; not some international, money orientated 'world order' such as the Modern aspires too. The Nationalist is not a Colonialist, such as is the British legacy. He, the nationalist, is ever concerned with *his* environment, *his* domestic governmental policies, *his* family, and *his* root and stock. This leads, inevitably, to the tendency of separateness, of the Separatist and his related movements.

Separatists, also, have their antecedents in American history. The year 1789, you may remember, was the most pronounced act of voluntary isolation – of separation – that marked the middle ages of the Western race-culture. As we have previously discussed, isolation is one of the primary ingredients to race-building, hence, the formation of a higher culture. The National Origins Act in this country was designed specifically to enforce that racial homogeneity of twentieth century America. The denial that ethnic groups are not assimilable is ever a sore and heated contest between Modern and Nationalist – the Modern rationalizes the 'humanity' of man – his waking consciousness is a dream. The Nationalist *is* rational.

ii.

The Contest of Cultures

The articulation of Culture, such as in the race-mechanism, is three fold:

1. It is the Idea itself;

2. Those that transmit the Idea;

3. And those to *whom* it is transmitted.

The latter is the *mass* – but *not* mass as a diverse racial composite – a mass, rather, that represents a *value* of worth, of refinement, of breed, such as was seen in the first 150 years of this American commonwealth. This is not, specifically, the mass, which belongs to any social state or construct simply, *as* mass. What we speak of here is the mass of nobility, honor, morality; a mass who feels intrinsic in its aspirations of property, self-respect, and the common rights of others – in short, an educated mass in the 'common' principles of [Western] beauty, peace, and harmony; those who ever seek to improve themselves and their specific culture, without diminishing any other culture outside their own. This is the main body of a Culture; such was Athens, or Sparta; Rome was, or at least became, a liberal *mobocracy*; another proving ground of the Modern.

Those who transmit those elements listed above, and specifically those who transmit the *idea* are the brain, the central apparatus of man. These are those who are intelligent, but not necessarily those of the intelligentsia. These are the protectors in the purest sense, their innermost compassion is for their own kind, and their families; they consider themselves, indeed, by others as well, as above the rest, but are the 'true' equals of the mass, for they are intrinsically and organically linked, that is, of the same kith and kin, the same blood. This Idea, then, is collectively the *soul* of the race-culture. It is ever present, and its articulation is seen in the rhythms and cycles of the race itself. The Modern laughs at this concept. He prefers Mob. Canaille. Indeed, what else can one expect from the plethora of divergent racial stock intended to confuse those of Western stock?

The Rise of the West is marked by the great divergent racial stock and contestant culture inherent in each. In microcosm, America has already been played out, just as the 'union' of Soviet Republics which, also, promoted *this very same* stupendous leveling of races and cultures. In macrocosm however, America presents a unique study into the *rise* of culture over the mediocre. True, since the early 1900's, America has forgotten just who and what she is, but, as we shall soon see, it has been simply a lull in the organic cycle of birth, life, and senility.

As the American race-culture entered the twentieth century, it carried with it the *remnants*, of that health and vigor, left over from its attempt at *deliberately* setting itself apart from the tyranny of an overgrown central power. Although the separate bodies of political dissent had been destroyed, the *race-culture* carried on the battle. The *'government of reconstruction'* [the same power today] had a firm grip on the rebellious elements encamped in the political battlegrounds of the day; they did not, however, have any real control over the collective elements decidedly in favor of the 'idea' of separatism. This ushered into the *consciousness* of the rise of the West the desire to *remain apart*. This was, at first, relegated to feelings of inter-race-antithesis*, the negative aspects of 'tribalism', but soon spilt over into the dormant, but ever-festering feeling of betrayal by the central government, a governmental technic [Kingship] which had stood for almost a thousand years. It was race-antithesis, as a *sense*, however, that remained the 'watchword' of American politics until shortly after the Second War of Fratricide.

Miscegenation, as both an idea and practice, was held in contempt during the latter part of the nineteenth century, and late into the middle of the twentieth century. Slowly, at an almost imperceptible rate, through two fratricidal wars, the race-consciousness of the American West became imbued with a sense of worthlessness and loss of direction. This is obvious in the decadent understanding of the 'pacifist internationale' which, while selling America *on* war, *used* peace as just another catch-word, such as had been used, and is used today, as 'the *last* war', 'a war *against war*', and the best to date, *'the war to end all wars'*, and the like, on the intelligentsia which was the only class that mattered, and would soon be taken in by this utter non-reality.

The mass of American western stock, as a collective consciousness,

---

* In this case, 'early-Americans' vs. the 'stable-British', while being a common racial stock like those disparate nations of the West today, nevertheless, through concepts like 'freedom', 'democracy', 'territory' and the like, *became* political and personal enemies; they became such enemies that the sacred blood of this noble people was spilt wantonly, and 'codified' the 'american' feelings of independence, sovereignty, and culture for generations to come. FLS

did not for a minute believe this hypocrisy. After each successive war for 'democracy', the people of the West became, increasingly, more disillusioned, became more acutely aware of the *constant need* for the 'improvement' of the negro and all minorities included in the now disparate, American West – or so he was reminded by those in power, by the Modern. The race-culture of the West always felt revulsion, antipathy, and enmity between the overtly racial divergence in race-culture's different from his own; to miscegenate, was to disappear, to *cease being what they are*. But this was precisely what 'his' government was asking him to do, indeed, what he was being *forced* to do, since the actual and implicit approval of *social intercourse* with the alien was tantamount to the tacit, if not actual, approval of *sexual intercourse*. Indeed, this is the reality; even the race-cultural distorters cannot keep what the 'eyes can see' away from all the people, at least not *all* the time.

This has brought *impasse*.

Let us be clear on this issue. The Framer's of the Declaration of Independence had envisioned a dream, a dream of equality *under* the *law*; of happiness, and of harmony. It was, without a doubt, no matter how many protestations of the Modern and his minions, was predicated simply, and *only*, upon the race-culture of the West – this means, precisely, predicated upon the world outlook, historicity, and genetic make-up of the assembled European delegates who drafted it, and further, was penned with *their own understanding*[α] of just *who*, and *what* the 'people' was intended to be – this is incontrovertible [Simply read *your* Constitution!]. This attempt, at creating a formula for the *direction* of men, was one of the greatest working attempts of 'self-rule' in our race-cultural history.

In some respects, it was short sighted, and why not – no one can conceive of every facet of a projected experiment. The twentieth

---

[α] See the Preamble to the Constitution: "We the People of the United States, in Order to form a more perfect Union, establish Justice, insure domestic Tranquility, provide for the common defense, promote the general Welfare, and secure the Blessings of Liberty to *ourselves and our Posterity*, do ordain and establish this Constitution for the United States of America." U.S. Constitution. [Italics added]

century was so far removed from their conceptions of the world that when the culture distorter became entrenched, the written instruments of the past were not entirely capable of handling the new problems of the West. The Framer's, especially Thomas Jefferson, were aware of the evolutionary changes of nature as well as societies, but nothing could have prepared the way of America's future in its entirety. Men like Jefferson were aware of the potentialities and relationships of 'amity' vs. 'enmity', in a political sense – hence the value placed upon the system of 'checks and balances'. The 'race' factor was a constant in their day, and was seen by the Fathers as a lasting constant, for themselves, and for the future in which they had worked so hard to prepare. The factors today are vastly different.

The natural amity/enmity of inner and outer man has gone through many phases in the cultural history of the West – to say nothing of the various people's of the planet who have emulated and constructed similar documents based on these Western constructs – some of which have been foreseen, others unforeseen. The Modern, after the Second War of Fratricide, had just about completed his massive experiment in 'equality'; the burgeoning flower of the Western race-culture had been aborted before its time, and its void was now to be filled by the 'democratic value' of the *smallest* over the *biggest*. Bayonets marked this crucial point in 1954 and continues to this very day. Ever since, the Modern has raised his clarion call of 'human rights', of 'civil rights' as an expression of a legal mandate, above and beyond, that of the Western race-culture. β

β The most controversial aspects of these policies involved busing children to schools in dangerous neighborhoods or previously integrated schools, or busing them from integrated schools to partially-integrated ones. Opponents claimed busing compromised the quality of the students' education. Declining property values due to white flight further decreased the quality of the educational systems. Most forced busing programs met with persistent complaints from parents of all races due to the long rides, hardships with transportation for extra-curricular activities, and separation of siblings when elementary schools at opposite sides of the city were "paired," (i.e. splitting lower and upper elementary grades into separate schools).

Busing and desegregation orders have in many cases led to white flight into suburb school districts or private schools. As many forced busing programs only required integration of schools within a particular city, forced busing led to a decline in the population of many large cities (especially those with large African-American populations) and helped fuel the rise of suburbs, which were largely immune to forced busing due to their smaller size and ethnic homogeneity. Suburbs were also immune due to the case of Milliken v. Bradley wherein the Supreme Court declared that busing between separate school districts (such as between the inner city and the suburb) was impermissible. Rust Belt cities in particular experienced the largest population declines, with declines of fifty percent or more between 1950 and 2000 in Detroit, Michigan, Cleveland, Ohio, and Buffalo, New York. It should be noted that these cities were already experiencing population declines before forced busing came into effect, but that busing increased the rate of decline. In Boston and California, where land values are higher and property tax structures less favorable to relocation, it is more common for parents to enroll their children in private or parochial schools.

In the Boston metropolitan area, the term "forced busing" is primarily used by critics of a remedy prescribed by Massachusetts US District Court Judge Arthur Garrity for perceived racial inequities in Boston public schools in a 1974 ruling. Garrity's ruling applied a state law, called the Racial Imbalance Law, that had been passed by the Massachusetts state legislature a few years earlier, requiring any school with a student enrollment of more than fifty percent "non-white" to be balanced according to race. The ruling ordered schoolchildren to be transported (presumably by bus, hence the term) to schools in different neighborhoods, in order to eliminate the racial segregation that had come about.

The conflict in Boston over busing primarily affected West Roxbury, Roslindale, Hyde Park, Charlestown, Dorchester, the North End, and South Boston (the latter being traditionally Irish-American but also having a sizable Polish/Lithuanian community). It also affected the mostly black community of Roxbury. To a lesser extent, schools in Springfield, Massachusetts were also affected by Judge Garrity's order, but the plan caused little overt controversy there.

The State Board of Education took a differing view, agreeing with the Boston School Committee, chaired by Louise Day Hicks, that if any segregation did exist, it was residential, i.e., caused by families' housing choices, and not planned.

The integration plan aroused fierce criticism amongst many Boston residents. Opponents personally attacked Judge Garrity for hypocrisy. Garrity lived in a white suburb; thus, his own children would not have been affected by his ruling.

There were a number of incidents of protest that turned violent. In one case, a black attorney named Theodore Landsmark was attacked by a group of white teenagers as he exited Boston City Hall. One of the youths, Joseph Rakes, attacked Landsmark with an American flag, using the flagpole as a lance. A photograph of the attack on Landsmark, taken by Stanley Forman for the Boston Herald-American, won the Pulitzer Prize for Breaking News Photography (known at that time as Spot News Photography) in 1977.

Today the Boston Public Schools are eighty-six percent African American and Hispanic. According to the 2000 census, Boston's white population is 54.48 percent; whereas Boston's black and Hispanic, populations together total 39.77 percent. It seems most white parents prefer to send their children to private and parochial schools as opposed to the integrated public schools. Boston's South Boston High school (now the South Boston High complex) was declared "dysfunctional" by the State Board of Education.

The above information is utilized to reinforce the perception of the Modern, insofar as the rhetoric and platitudes he generates in the words of 'freedom' and 'liberty' are true only for his minions; the Mothers and Fathers of these American cities are protecting their rights, their children and, so far, have failed to receive the protection of the Modern, who claims to be the Pater familias of Western culture. FLS

To be sure, these 'so-called' civil rights 'acts' qualify, to a greater or lesser degree, all citizen's of this country to equal protection under the law, and has been beneficial in regards to the *perception* of justice, but has not proven itself to those of Western stock, as *being* beneficial to *us*. Yet, to attain this degree of legal 'civility', the Modern rose to every occasion, used every sundry device of manipulation, restricted millions of Western stock from voting [post war of Succession], and designed legislation to accumulate the voting power of the non-Western voting bloc. The Modern promoted the artistry of 'guilt'. This artificial guilt syndrome has unconsciously allowed the collaboration of the mass with bureaucrats: the Priest Craft of the 'now-you-see-it, now-you-don't', metaphysics of the Modern. Right or Wrong, the civil rights acts of the past were done above and beyond the *will* [of the West] of the people. OH! To the Modern's touted democracy!

There are two systems of Constitutional Law being used in America today. One system favorably sponsors minorities, and the other system affectively bewitches whites. A well known example of abuse in the civil rights laws can be understood by the fact that European Americans are not required by civil law to sell their houses to other whites; but refusing to sell to a minority will bring an immediate retaliatory suit against the property owner who is white, even though the reason the owner may be refusing to sell to the minority in question is far removed from racial inequities. The only way a jury could possibly decide and determine the owner guilty of 'racism', when refusing to sell his property to any minority in question, would have to have been determined from reading the owner's mind. This is not traditional Western *de jure* law in practice.

It was in 1906, Professor Sumner of Yale made this statement: *"[that] Black and white in the United States are now tending to more strict segregation."*[35] This was not simply from laws, such as Jim Crow, but was the organic imperative of all race-cultures. The white European was dominate, fixed to the American landscape of its own making; not much room was left for any contending culture's, even if they

---

[35] Sumner, W.G. – FolkWays, 1906, page 113.

had voluntarily submitted to the contest. It is the same today. The entire planet is fixated with ethnic/territorial imperatives that deny the hollow promises of the Modern. Instead, demands from all quarters of the world, and America, reiterated the complexities and denial of racial and cultural assimilation.

To those of the race-culture of the West, assimilation is rejected out of hand. Exacerbated by today's 'fast-paced' technics, assimilation funnels its way into every strata of the West. The changing attitudes, mores, and legal jurisdictions are felt by everyone. It was stated in the end of chapter III that complete assimilation by, to use McCulloch's term, the "Congoid" and "other" elements in this country with that of Western stock, would completely dilute the present 'white stock' to such an extent that, even if racial equilibrium could be reached after such a devastation, it would take perhaps 20-30 generations to reproduce the same quality, such as was in the original stock; and this with absolute control over selection. But, the solution to this potential catastrophe is simple: if one sees, if one believes, then he may supplant such a situation by acting on the problem before it becomes so over-powering that nothing can now stand in its way.

A simple example of assimilation and antithesis should suffice: *"[the Negro] willingly assimilates, for he sees to marry a white is to go up in the world."*[36] A Jewish person, on the other hand, as has been observed before, *refuses* as a race-culture to assimilate. Thus, and it must be perfectly clear, that all or certain culture's will, at some time, share a position of antagonism between each other – each reason is particular to the specific needs, codes of conduct, or values placed on race. In the case of the Jewish individual, it is to his benefit if he does *not* assimilate; it is mandatory for his very survival that he *remains* what he is, for he too, is the *extension* of his past, and the passion by which he views this relationship is known to everyone and sundry. This is Nature's Law.

The Western man and woman, is faced with the same decision, a decision that has been deleted from his options by the Modern. He is

---

[36] Keith, op. cited., page 406.

faced with stigma and antagonism by the Modern, and yet persists in rejecting the possibility of assimilation with the negro, Chinese, Indian or any non-Western elements – the exceptions which, perhaps, not uncommon in today's atmosphere is, nevertheless, the exception rather than the rule, regardless of the tremendous weight of any government to promote and encourage this betrayal. The clash of cultures on this level is inevitable.

The West has always tended to look upon its technics and its people as superior. Whether this is a subjective fact or not, is irrelevant. The *fact* that the West *sees* itself in this fashion is, nevertheless, the reality here. The reality is that *all* cultures see themselves as superior to someone. The natural antagonism between the biological inner and outer man is a disruptive factor in national and political life. This situation, however it may develop, is best left for the Statesman to ponder and control (but by all means *not* a politician). The politician, the Modern in 'disguise', has no conception of the accumulative power his decision on these matters will endear on the political face of his present presence. His future is marked by simple *control*, rather than the more deliberate and balanced program, which would correct the massive momentum of the cultural clash of the West with foreign elements. "Nation building is a specie of race building."[37] The modern has forgotten that a successful nation, like a successful race, like a winning team, must have a balanced and workable relationship in accordance with all the talents and healthy qualities inherent in human nature. A house eternally divided, cannot and *will not*, stand.

The Modern, as well as millions of his adherents, see his pluralism, his *tyranny* of the few over the many, as his divine duty. Since race, as a polarizing influence, degrades his position, in relation to power, he must, then, *control his geo-political environment*. He passes off this control as law and order. But first, he has to destroy all the laws and [social] order that went before him.

It is accepted and understood that a Race, a Civilization must, of necessity, have 'boundaries', both physical as well as spiritual. The

---

[37] Ibid., page 100.

physical interface of laws becomes the established means by which a people/culture may proceed fluently into a transition of an orderly and sustained environment; this is 'control' with a sustained compassion for those under this authority. This process is called, among other things, Law and Order. But, law for one man is anarchy for another; order, likewise, is subjective, insofar as order to one man is tyranny to another. What, then, is the *difference* between law and order?

Law, by definition, are those *codes of conduct* so prescribed by those in the ruling capacity of any given culture or civilization, which guide, direct, or mold that particular group to *act* and *behave* in an accepted manner. Deviation from this norm is 'anti-law'. The purpose of law, and there is no other *value*, is to *maintain control over any specified or unspecified number of persons which form a community, State, or Nation*. This simple analysis is basic to all forms of organized social constructs. Order, then, is the absolute *value* of law.

Order presupposes a mental attitude existing in one or more persons that envisage an atmosphere of *continuity* and *organization* within the body of an existing social order. This definition shares some kinship to law, yet it does not confine itself to this definition; rather, it shares a more organic and natural impetus from the cognizant awareness of the race-culture which has, of itself, defined its mores, traditions, and 'accepted' values, which are consistent with the survival of the specific social order. The Modern however, cares nothing for *tradition*, he is the great leveler.

Laws, ipso facto, create criminals. Dysfunction in any given social order is construed to be, as likely or not, liable for criminal activity. This, however, is not necessarily the case. Like Prohibition, the new 'anti-smoking', 'anti-weapons' laws, and other numerous *classifications*, which *create* criminals where there were none, is not a system of 'law' per se but, rather, it is the application of *behavioral control*, or modification of same, that has been designed to enhance a 'new system' of social change across the land. The Modern, in his vision of the world, says not to worry: He promises that it will bring that social harmony, peace, tranquility, and equality of the *new world* – the new world order.

Laws are necessary. Yet, laws can, and do, of their own impetus, become 'anti-law' if, for instance, a 'law' or set of 'laws' becomes untenable to the very culture, people, or existing State by its sheer 'weight of conduct' (i.e. discipline, force, methods, etc.) With time, this weight of *law* becomes, of necessity, the tool of breakdown within its normal sphere of influence, the nation/state. The overwhelming influence of these innumerable types of law brings not order, but anarchy. It is, in the final analysis, *the end of order*.

Law seeks to establish a mechanism, which would *circumvent* any action, which would, in his mind, beget reaction that, in the end, would become dysfunctional to the whole. This is good. However, once built into the mechanism of the social order, laws will increase, *never decrease*. In this case, it is only nature's way to cull out those areas of control/change, which hamper the growth, and vitality of the host culture. This is the contest of cultures in *microcosm*. The imbalance caused by this inevitable relationship brings with it friction and, ultimately, violent exchanges between any number of different groups, individuals, or special interest groups. Law then, in its abstract sense, becomes useless, based on the perceived human elements involved – existing turmoil is only exacerbated by the continued application of the *classification* of law.

Order is the prerequisite for the survival of any organism. Moreover, order is a man-made manifestation of the highest *perception of organism*. It comes from the discipline of 'self', and can only be carried out in the larger social groups if the *spirit* is unanimous. In a heterogeneous population, simple diversity [of foreign bodies] is enough to throw the entire organism off balance. The attention paid to 'control' is *increased* in this environment. Those who rule in this environment are constantly on the move to enact laws that will, hopefully, disrupt any activity as seen by those in power, which seeks to destabilize their authority. The Modern sees *order* in terms of *control* only.

Control, and the *means* required to achieve it, are not forms of *equality*. Force is the superior element – be that force 'fire-power', 'legal jurisprudence', or control of the institutional means of representative government (e.g. the ballot). This form of control, perforce, relegates the mass organism to impotency. In the latter case, in many instances, when the voice of the common man is stifled, and words fail to carry any weight with the ruling class, it becomes necessary, in a natural organic sense, to react in a hostile fashion against those areas of concern, which have not been addressed by those in power.$^{\psi}$

Laws cannot *contain* reaction. The purpose of law, as stated before, is to control behavior. When this cannot be contained within the perimeters of past tradition (i.e. the force of patriotism, etc.) an increase in *law*, as seen by the *law-makers*, must be present in the system. If not consonant with the spirit of the traditions and concepts of the founding body however, these 'law-makers' become *the* dysfunctional element in society. It would seem, however, that this is precisely the response that the Modern has anticipated for those of the Western Race-Culture. It has been planned this way.

Containment is the key. Unlike Europe, America has a 'so-called' tradition of law and order based on the Modern's concept of that

---

$^{\psi}$ One must simply look to the examples in the Middle East at this time ['89]. Certain elements at war with the leader of Iraq and his governmental technics, seek ever to destabilize that power, which seeks to repress them and *their* will-to-power. The Kurds and Shiite are sub race-cultures, *within* the Iraqi State, and look for a way, any way, to form any alliance whatever, to *secure* their freedom as they see it, from that of the existing system. The powers of the West, sympathetic for many different reasons, are inclined to destabilize the *present* government in return for favors unspecified if they are to aid these people in their 'fight for freedom'. In any event, the case can be made that the 'voice' of the people has been stifled, and in logical course, the battle of words will soon become a battle of bullets and willpower.
The West, will, most certainly, imbue its allies with the clarion call of this 'fight for freedom' and garner some advantage. Sides will be drawn, and it will be on one side or the other that each will decide. In this case, the point here is that the 'underdog', the 'minorities', will overcome the master with the aid of 'outsiders', the forces of good in this case. But, if the forces of good were, let us say, the Chinese or the Soviet Union, without benefit of Western influence, how then would we, here in the United States, view the injection of military intervention in a region so vital to our interests? How would we, then, view the 'rights of the minority'? More poignant still, how would we view foreign intervention, which would supply and arm a division of the population here, in our homeland? If voices cannot, or are not allowed to be heard, then, is it any wonder that such forces should seek to mobilize? FLS

which we, specifically, as Americans, hold dear: that of Democracy. As with all ruling authority, however, *power and control* are factors that must, at all cost be maintained. This is natural law. Containment of the population then, is imperative – such as was Shay's Rebellion, the Whiskey Rebellion, and the War Between the States in our early history – all challenges to the Federal perception of government have been denounced by Force, not by the general will and desire of the social group (i.e. race-culture) but by the ruling power who *spoke* for the populace. The right or wrong of this reaction is not is question here – just the *action*. The action in question was not done simply to maintain those in power, or strengthen their base, but rather to simply maintain the *status quo*. Today, the Modern acts no different. The Modern has offered, as the status quo, the egalitarian principle of *mass as the ultimate achievement in society*. This principle of egalitarianism is seen as more *stable* and *reasonable* to the Modern than, let us say, the stability and supremacy of the original Western stock, above and beyond, the other diverse and divergent racial elements present with them. This is true for both America and Europe's status quo.

The Nationalist of Western racial stock faces the same consistent elements of *status quo* – on either Continent. The 'american' flag, the symbolic representative of that long and honorable tradition *of* nationalism, as a *symbol* of America, is no longer the symbol of the original presence of the Western race-culture. Let us be clear on this point: The 'symbol' of America no longer functions in any real sense as it did in its inception. This symbol, this flag, was a symbol of War – of that hostile act of belligerence and warfare against kindred, related by blood – Western blood. It was between *white brothers*. The fact that non-white elements played various parts in this conflict, on one side or the other, is of relative significance. The symbols, political technics, and the like, were founded by, and for, *one people* – alone.

The symbol of the flag represented an *intrinsic stability inherent in a unified effort*. This effort was War – an act of betrayal against a body politic, which had led the Western experience for five hundred years or more in relative unbroken succession. But it was more; it was 'order' without law, it was law based on consent – not of the people, this a common fallacy – *but in harmony with them*. The cycle required to maintain this development was a continual trust and acceptance of both *government* [ruling body] and its *charge* [race-culture]. The acquiescence of this race-culture to the domination of any government (and why not – leadership is also an organic process) was consonant with their needs; it was not subservience to any dictatorial power. In fact, the race-culture was prepared to accept George Washington as King – something the Modern has forgotten, for a King was the ultimate recognition of the race-culture – *the race-culture personified in the leader*. The vast Indo-European history had proved this a working system. This 'history' of race-culture shows that systems are chosen because they work – for a short time, or a long time. Each a prerequisite for the individual presence at *that time*.

Containment is not the key to any and all perceived or real social ills. Safe and satisfactory *diffusion* of that ill is, however, difficult at best, if the general host population is diverse as seen in both the United States and the Union of Soviets. The Soviet example, however, has acknowledged the separation of these divers race-cultural states. It is recognized for what it is – distinct racial types, with distinct imperatives necessary to the survival of each. American security interests however, have proceeded to maintain these parallel situations through containment of the body corporate. The inevitable resultant breakdown of law and order is already obvious for a least the past fifty years. It is to our national *insecurity*, which has fostered this containment. We have, of course, reached the breaking point – for both Western and non-Western elements.

The Modern element has only succeeded in maintaining *law* – he has failed to maintain *order*. In all outward manifestations of [American] society, there is nothing but chaos. This breakdown will not be seen in its true form in the local paper – it will, however, be seen in the 'public school yard', in the discernible, albeit natural division of neighborhoods, and the 'browning' of the metropolitan politics. This, too, is natural.

The natural outcome of increased non-Western birthrates, coupled with the ignorant stagnation of the upper twenty-five percent of the Western social group, has simply intensified the awareness of the

American white stock. World-wide it is even more obvious – five-hundred fifty millions of whites, versus the six to eight billions of non-Western stock makes it all the more clear, to those with vision, that the White western world is losing more ground every day. International law, like domestic law, is a travesty. The law of The Hague, or the law of America? Neither sees itself, as outside of the common man – America, however, should pay attention to both the European model, as well as their own legal evolution.

We, here in America, as a race-culture, indeed, all Western countries, are but a *microcosm of the world*. It is a natural fact that all races, and distinct cultures try, and endeavor to maintain, an orderly existence to fit their needs. Some are, quite obviously, more successful than others. Success is relative to the needs and desires of that particular people. We are no exception. Any attempt at furthering that goal, or particular goals, should be gauged as effective or ineffective by the amount of honest achievement realized by its particular host culture. What does not work on a local scale cannot work on a national or 'world wide' scale. This is self-evident. Would Rousseau, for instance, seek to change the direction of 'his great experiment' if he recognized the end product as dysfunctional? Should we accept the leveling of all people's to that of the 'noble savage' as a proper goal to be realized by the entire world?

Individuals must make their own decisions. But, as a race-culture, this must take shape in the collective response of the mass – not as mob – but as culture. Do we, as a race-culture demand that we, ourselves, be enslaved by containment? Do we recognize 'order' as being a part of the innate natural rhythms of a single race-culture? Do we really believe that the Modern's presentation of equality is a panacea to all our social ills? If we do not follow the Modern's way of thinking, then, what shall we do, separate? What path do we follow? Can we, as a People, change our presence? Can we change our reality? Does it need to be changed? The Rise of the West has answered these, and many more questions. The die is cast.

Should our answers prove contrary to the Modern, should we use force to change it? The Ferrier, for instance, used fire and steel, coupled with the strength of [a] hammer to form *a thing*, in this case, a horseshoe, and must use force to conform the unwilling steel to the shape *he* wants. So, even we, ourselves, must not be afraid to use the force necessary to form events and circumstances to conform to what we want, and to the forms, we need. Creation is the key! Unlike our forefathers, are we now afraid of the lightning?

iii.

Race Building

It has been said previously, that nation building is a relative form of Race-building. And so it is. Like a winning team, one that can not only run, but also *win* a race, it must have a workable and balanced relationship with the talents and healthy qualities inherent in the nature of one People, or race-culture, if the nation or race is to grow greater than the smallest of its parts. Let us use South Africa as such an example. Yes, South Africa, that land of harsh elements, rugged byways and highways, savagery, opulence, wealth, poverty, corruption and honor. A land that, by the Modern's definition, is better served by the 'diversity' of racial inclusiveness rather, than it was before, a mainstay in the Western evolution; the White Tip, nestled in a far corner of a Black Continent.

On the great expanse of the Continent of Africa, on her southernmost extremity, exists a white *tip*, a remnant of Western Culture, expansionism, and manifest destiny, and there resides a 'colony' of the children of the West. A legacy of four hundred and fifty years of settlement, wrought with empire building, abuses, canards and hope. It has been the same throughout the epochs of man. From Hamurabi to Napoleon, all empires have risen and fallen, dependent upon the vagaries of time and space; of destiny and consequence.

As a Western nation, South Africa has been lost to a generation of

Western stock who never knew the power and glory of attaining something through raw struggle, or the majesty of creation for the sake of itself; for the dream of Commonwealth and social instruction predicated upon thousands of generations who had facilitated the legacy of their past.

South Africa, as a Western nation, is descended from a common racial Western stock – our own root and stock. For hundreds of years, this branch of the euro-folk has struggled to improve their lot, and fulfill their destiny as they felt the Almighty would have it. Through all the years, which have seen these white settlers on this continent, they and their children have learned the rhythms and cycles of living required to master and contain their environment. They have learned to survive.

Africa is a land of extremes. No moderate can exist here – it is either hot or cold. One takes a position/side, or one does not. It was a harsh brutal existence. Yet, this branch of the euro-folk has become as modern in terms of its technics as are any of our other branches. In Africa, as elsewhere, survival is *power*. If you are not the fittest, or most capable, then you will be overpowered. The democracy of the Modern has been rejected out of hand. Pluralism would bring disaster. Hence, it was seen that a National government was best suited for this people of European descent.

After a violent war between Europeans of British extraction and the original Dutch settlers, or Boers, as they proudly call themselves, several governments came and went, finally a consensus was agreed upon which would demarcate and totally separate the white and black races sharing close proximity in the territories of South Africa. In microcosm, this colony shared the same frustrations and real political reality of a 'mixed' national state. Such was America during the same time period.

In the 1983, all this changed in South Africa. In reaction to rising discontent between black and white, a new system was attempted to ameliorate the violence. It was at this time that the NP [National Party] submitted a proposal that would allow for a 'tri-chambered' parliament to exist. This system consisted of one House for whites, one for coloured, and one for the Indian. Since this change of government, the South African euro-folk have been effectively controlled by non-Western stock. No legislation may be passed by the 'minority' whites, without permission (i.e., by concurrence of majority vote), from these non-Western Houses. The president may, if he so desires, veto any and all provisions he does not accept. Thus, the ancestors of the original people of Europe, which founded this colony, represent only one-third of the *real* political power.

The past leadership, such as H.F. Verwoerd, who came to power in the 'fifties as Prime Minister, began the application of 'separate but equal' to the diverse race-culture's present in South Africa. This facilitated the extension of not only white townships, but black independence as well. Each now had the chance to excel on an individual basis. This, of course, was unacceptable to the Modern. Verwoerd was assassinated in 1962. Since that time, the Modern, that nefarious race-culture distorter was in power. The Modern demands that 'apartheid' be dismantled – even though it ceased to exist many years before this. The only apartheid laws that are still in effect are the denial of blacks to vote in Parliament. When this happens, there will be no government of the euro-folk. The colony will have surrendered. Whether they stay or not depends on many factors.

The euro-folk of South Africa have made the same mistakes as other Western Cultures have made time and time again.* First, instead of utilizing the often slow, but consistent work force of the original settlers, they opted to use the ignorant and subservient native population. The second mistake is that of *maintaining* that presence. Greed, plain and simple, is responsible for this element. Bigger farms, bigger ranches, and the like, call for more labor; rather than use components of the same race-culture, they opted for the

---

* Correspondence to the S.A. Ambassador [Prof. Koorlof] with this author, detailed a single theme: the labor force in S.A. must be moved to a completely white European force; the call to Europeans with the incentive of wages and land must be paramount in securing talented, trustworthy, and assimilable workers. As with most Western governments, the need for 'cheap' labor, is the harbinger of death and dilution of the national will.

continuation of the 'cheap labor' force. Like Rome, it has failed miserably. But, this is not what we wish to discuss.

The fact that South Africa is a viable Western technic is seen in her Industry, Agriculture, and the like. She is a producing nation. This is grinding to a certain halt. The infrastructure has been torn apart. No longer is she a distinct race-culture any more. She is almost a 'democracy' – that is, of the Modern. The final act however, is yet to be played out – and this will be the most violent scene to hit the African continent in a thousand years. It can already be seen.

Voluntary conscription [2 years] is at its highest peak in years ['88]. The white youths of South Africa flock to the enlistment centers. The Police forces are another matter. Like any large cosmopolis of the modern, it is difficult, at best, for a loyal white to work for a system that he sees daily destroying what he was brought up to love and cherish. Resistance [civilian] groups are growing daily. Violence is a daily occurrence and breeds more continuously. Some whites have reached the breaking point. Case in point: Hendrik Strijdom.

In the heart of Pretoria, [Nov. '88], this twenty-three year old ex-policeman, killed seven blacks, and wounded fifteen others. The American press gave this much attention – what they failed to cover was the fact that, a day earlier, Mr. Strijdom had planned to assassinate President P.W. Botha if he had released the communists ANC [African National Congress] leader, Mandela, a man responsible for hundreds of white men, women, and children being bombed, hatcheted, burned and shot. Hendrik Strijdom was found guilty of murder. When facing the judge in his case, a Justice Harms, he was asked if he had anything to say, he calmly addressed the court, and stated he would do it again if given the chance. OH! How the Modern screams in horror at this attitude. But, what made a man of twenty-three years of age act in this fashion? Certainly, the modern reader is traumatized by the very thought, having not yet faced such barbarity in his own country, as had men such as Hendrik Strijdom – the American West's only true experience of this sort was the War Between the States – the Viet Nam War fought from a distance, seen only through the television news, or the print media, which is even more removed. The Modern sips his latte' and considers this.

The court record shows that in [1984] he had joined the police force. Shortly thereafter, he helped to quell a riot of over a thousand black, but not before, they [the mob] had killed a white nurse. To add insult to injury, as well as show their contempt for the [white] woman, and her reproductive organs, they [the mob] built a fire between her legs. The second grisly scene this young man had to endue was even worse. A second nurse, burned alive in her car; after he [Strijdom] arrived, the body had been partially eaten (whether by man or beast is not certain). These horrible situations, which were more than prevalent, were to haunt Strijdom terribly. He left the police force and joined the *Vereeniging van Oranjewerkers* (Union of Orange Workers).

Hendrik went from job to job, dispossessed from his kind. Eventually he was led out into the 'veld', that great expanse of wilderness, where he sought the compassion and instruction of the 'lord' in what he should do; the answer, apparently, was to commit himself to a one-man war against his perceived enemies – the black communists. Little did he recognize of the Modern. In his mind, he wanted the world to know that there were 'beoere' still in Africa. This young man selected Strijdom Square – associated with Prime Minister J.G. Strijdom – the Lion of the North. This act, contrary to the opinion's of the Modern, was a act of bravery and courage – not the killing – this was futile given the political posturing, and done from complete frustration in regards to the events and situations that he had no control over whatsoever. His was an act – an individual act – in *defiance* of a system that had taken away his identity, his way of life, and the *life* of his People. Right or wrong, he *acted* with the best of intentions against the 'outsider', the 'agitators', the alien influence levied against his soul, against his Volk.

In response to this event, unlike any party spokesman here in America, was the leader of the *Boerstaat* Party, Robert van Tonder, who said it was not Strijdom who should have to be hanged, but President P.W. Botha and his cabinet. He spoke for most white South Africans in this same situation worldwide when he added:

> The desperate situation in which Afrikaners and all other white South Africans found themselves, the continual murdering of [our] elderly, the inundations of our cities and towns by a black deluge, the impoverishment of our people, the large-scale theft and assaults and the insecurity about our future.

This is a most tragic example of the *modernism* of the West. The *capitulation* of Race to that of 'ideal' is the Modern's telltale sign – to betray instinct and tradition for some worldview – a view, which holds neither honor nor identity. This is also to accept the life-style of the Modern. This is the extreme end to which all nations will succumb; yet, all the various branches of the euro-folk face the same inevitable end who fails to grasp just what the *loss of sovereignty* really means.

To the sympathetic Nationalist of Western race-culture, it is inconceivable that a government, any government, with such decisive ties as the West, has with Pretoria could, and would, facilitate the demise of the only working and energetic Western-cultural technic on the entire continent of Africa. Western governments recognize the status of South Africa *as* colony, of Western ingenuity yet, all refuse to aid this people in their struggle for race-cultural survival. Like the [American] South, it is that 'great leveling' of the Modern, the anticipated destruction of the Western epic, the total Reconstruction of an entire people that is demanded.

The Modern, in the United States and elsewhere, decries the exploitation of the black/coloured races, by the whites in South Africa yet, he does the same to [American] 'south-western' mestizo's, negro's, and Vietnamese for his financial gain – as opposed to hiring whites. He demands that the 'exploiters' be driven out of Africa, and replaced by blacks of the Marxist variety – these, of course, are honorable men. The antagonism between race-cultural technics, between black and white, creates the always-tragic confrontation, and inevitability, of war on both small and large scales. It is the eternal cycle of *inner* and *outer* man.

Ethnic relations, worldwide, are at its most violet stage in the history of the Modern's attempt to 'control' these very same tensions. The

Nationalist, world-wide, sees the fallacy of the 'one-man-one-vote' of the new leveling – since the simple truth of the matter is that Western man is just one-tenth the population of the world, yet produces ninety percent of its wealth. To whose purpose and need then, is 'his' work to be given if, for instance, the world was connected by a United Nations voting system, relegating these choices to the 'majority' vote? The Nationalist knows that *his* 'vote' would be worthless. The Modern, however, rushes to make this a reality despite the consequences to his brethren. The *ideal*, once again, is greater that the sum of its parts.

The Nationalist, like those in South Africa and America, sees the *end* of Culture. The Rise of the West, especially in America, has already taken many steps to correct this treason. There are 'parties', 'movements', as well as *martyrs*, prisoners [political], and statesmen – these, the natural phenomenon of the technics of organism. The battle begins – the battle for Power and Dominance.

iv.

Race Relations

The American West, in a strictly cultural sense, is broken up into *distinct* Nations.

At first glance, many who read this will wonder just what is being said, having no formal instruction other than what little they think they know from television and government 'think tanks'. It is said that there are forty-eight 'united states' [within the Continental U.S.] but that each, voluntarily, make up the Nation as a *political unit*. In a purely political sense, this is apparent, yet, what is spoken of here is the precise components of *biological* nations, which inhabit that political unit called 'america'. Each race-culture, such as Afro-american, Asian-american, Amer-Indian, Mexican-american, ad nauseum, constitute 'specific' [biological] nations which act, perform, congregate, celebrate, and decide political, moral, and social issues predicated upon those that are part of their particular race-culture in question. This is political reality.

The political reality of race-cultural separation is also manifest. It is very commonplace in the language and conversation of every race-culture presently inhabiting America. The Modern has instructed his national organs of communications to ignore these realities in the hope that this slow, ineluctable demise, through *absorption*, into the entire consciousness of America, and just what it has to offer in *return* for this absorption. The 'security forces' of the Modern are instructed to destroy this *idea* of separation, of sovereignty; but it continues nevertheless. The contest of cultures begins anew:

The 'nation' of Azatlan is spoken of by the south-western mestizo-Hispanics; the 'nation' of Islam is taught by the Afro-american; the Asian-american is, already, content with his presently achieved level of separation. The Jewish population, as always, is unassimilated into the body of the West, and is perceived *as* assimilated, and totally a part of the 'americanna' of the West. He, above all else, is truly an 'american' phenomenon. The only real surprise here is that of the burgeoning formula of Western [white] demands for separation.

White [western] Nationalism is at its highest incident rate since just prior to the Second War of Fratricide. In that case, Americans of European descent, denounced the aggressive 'alien' position of involvement in a foreign theatre against a Nation that was, and is, very close in make-up as our own. The feelings of the associated numbers of present day White-Nationalists is of a different sort. His present day 'spirit' is imbued with a feeling of consciousness that transcends the 'old form' nationalism, that is, Conservatism. The Nationalist, unlike the conservative, sees his position as having deteriorated to a point that is unacceptable. The conservative still believes he may battle and win a duel with the Modern in the political technics of the great leveler. He has been *deceived*.

The Nationalist, however, does not choose to take the bait, no matter how beautiful the lure. The Nationalist is, and will always be, a part of that 'working class' which, on a daily basis, sees for himself, in the street as it were, just where the Modern is trying, and in most cases, already has, taken him. He is not part of the monied aristocracy. It is *he*, and he is aware of this, that must shoulder the responsibility of fighting for his race, with his very hands, if necessary, for the future of his family, his children, and his culture. The Modern, always prepared for this eventuality, declares War.

It was the Prussian tactical Officer, Carl von Clauswitz, who declared a "defensive war," a "winning war." The Nationalist, as always, has started from behind, from a position of defense – a legacy of his fathers who had not the stomach for utilizing those means necessary to stop this change in his environment. The Modern has declared war. The Nationalist is defending himself. Even the 'conservative' has felt the brunt of the Modern in his [the Modern] reaction to the growing elements of resistance. From every corner, the conservative feels betrayed, his ox has now been gored, the wound too apparent, too deep, to reject the obvious. From his timid exploitation of religion, to his childish belief in democracy and liberty (as is portrayed by the Modern) – it cuts across his whole field of vision.

The conservative now denounces the Modern.

They have, as significant elements of the conservative apparatus, begun to question the Modern's 'legitimacy', to demand such extremes of judicial process as confiscation of [all] weapons, especially the small concealable handgun, which is designed to eliminate intruders of all types, including the Modern if necessary.

The Nationalist, as well as the Conservative, questions the Modern's sanity. To the issue of 'gun control', the elements of the nationalist and conservative come closer than on any issue. In both cases, they recognize that guns, ultimately, are for one purpose, and one purpose only – that weapons, in general, as well as specifically, are designed with one purpose in mind: That weapons are designed to kill *people*; and is clearly defined for all to see. Sporting, as such, is a smoke screen by the conservatives, to ameliorate the Modern, to keep him at bay.

Since our primal epoch of development, man has sought various means by which to defend *and* attack. Without this ability, Western man, perhaps, would have ceased to exist many aeons ago. Man is *martial* by inclination, and remains peaceful at least half the time – the other half, is either actively pursuing "war by other means" or pursuing war, period. Any *use* of weapons *after* that primary use [listed above] is, purely, an *individual* choice, such as hunting in a purely 'sports' sense. The *right* to 'keep and bear arms' is shared by both the nationalist and the conservative – the only real telling difference between the two is that the nationalist knows, already, just *who* the enemy [of these rights] really is; who the enemy of his traditional freedoms are, and to where they gravitate. The conservative does not want to see, or admit, these enemies exist at all – for he is afraid, and rightly so – that these same enemies are a part of his own ranks. The Conservative is content in watching from the sidelines as the nationalist carries on the fight for his [the conservative's] liberties, while, at the same time, this self-same conservative helps himself to the *victories* and *spoils*, while at the same time, distancing himself from any losses – 'conservatives' are well known to 'leave their wounded on the field of honour'. But, in recent days, a few stouthearted conservatives have ventured out beyond the 'traditional' norms of conservatism.

No longer is the conservative of *one mind* concerning his belief in the Modern and his governmental technics. A concerted effort, having been traditionally relegated to small nationalist 'factions', once considered outside the Western race-cultural mainstream, have now designed a 'national' programme to 'educate' the mass as to its loss of power and legitimacy. The Nationalist forms a wry smile as to this approach; he nevertheless accepts the conservative's coming of age.

As stated before, the common ground between nationalist and conservative has been, and is, for the most part, the issue of 'bearing arms', but for different reasons. The Conservative believes in the documents of the past to *maintain* this 'right'; the Nationalist believes that there is no 'right', *other than the right to choose for himself the 'right' to self-determine his role in relation to his surroundings.* If the reader will take, good naturedly, another reminder, let it be this, and ever this: If there is anything such as a 'god-given right', it is up to *man to enforce it* (!). *Man* has made his political State what it is, not god. The Conservative awakens from his slumber – his attacks against the positions of the Modern multiply daily. But nothing has reached the crescendo of battle cries, as has the issue of 'the right to keep and bear arms'. This whole position was ably penned by two separate [conservative] authors in two separate conservative periodicals. Their positions, frankly, were revolutionary in scope – something that, as of late, have been relegated to nationalist publications (usually very small, well written, but not read widely) and not part of the mainstream.

The first, author Roger Koopman, spoke directly to the Western race-culture when he stated: *"The people, not the government, possess an absolute right in the area of gun ownership"*[38] This statement transcends all political boundaries of both the conservatives and nationalist. What is new in this area of political maneuvers, implied or stated, is the attack on the technics of the Modern – the Modern's *perception* of Order has run afoul of the mainstream. Mr. Koopman goes even further by stating these rather provocative words:

> What these folks [government technics] stand for is a total reversal of our Constitutional system, where rights and powers become vested not in the people [race-culture], but in government. They promote an alien…mentality that turns the citizenry against itself by convincing us that we should trust the government and *distrust* out neighbors. [emph. mine]

What a statement from a Conservative!

It is that 'alien' mentality with which the nationalist is very much at odds. That of the Modern. The Nationalist is, by far, more vociferous in its attack against the Modern than is the conservative – but without the larger media aid of the conservative it is apparent who still holds the upper hand. While the childish argument continues, the Modern closes his grips upon both; his governmental technics continue to reserve for himself the right 'to maintain weapons in the

---

[38] Koopman, Roger – Second Defense – Outdoor Life, February, 1990, page 61, 99, 100.

hands of *his* militancy, *his* police force, *his* national security services. This, above and beyond, the majority of those Western people's who demand the same right, also, but who, as of this writing, have not the power to *enforce* their will.

The issue is not, nor ever has been, over 'gun ownership', this was simply the clarion call of the Conservative, the 'sound-bite' for the masses. The issue is Freedom, pure and simple. Freedom to maintain a *race-cultural* imperative; to *protect* Family; one's Home, self, and ultimately, *the freedom to defend oneself from the tyranny of a technic, individually or collectively, of any infringement of one's Liberty by a foreign or domestic power.* Period.

The Nationalist realizes that defense against all predators is a *law* cognizant with nature. The nationalist knew, and has always known, that the issue of gun ownership was his first line of defense - that the issue of 'sporting arms' was the pleading of the conservative to the traditional governmental technic, like a son pleading with his father for favor, for his 'inalienable rights' when, actually, the basis of his pleadings were based upon documents of the past, which at the outset, *granted no rights*, it simply verified, as a device of communication, *recognized* and *battle-won*, yes, those hard won rights decided in *struggle* and *contest*; decided by blood and sacrifice. Through Blood and Iron; through the *contest*, of culture and civilization.

Lessons like these are designed to instill a certain value intrinsic in the very learning. The conservative has forgotten "*...that this nation was born in a revolt against the legitimate authority of a long-standing government that had gone progressively sour until violent revolution was the only escape possible.*"[39] But the conservative will not hear of such a thing – he is loyal. But, to what? What loyalty does he owe anyone that would take his most treasured and important necessities? What will he do? Here is yet another conservative answer:

> The thought that there might come a time when peaceable gun ownership (and even members of the NRA) must take arms against the U.S. Military and their own local police is anathema to nearly everyone. The possibility,

---

[39] Koman, Victor – The Real Reason We Own Guns – Guns and Ammo, February 1990, page 32.

however, must be faced."[40]

Ponder the above statements – carefully. Americans preparing for possible armed conflict? This must be the ranting of a paranoid nationalist. But is it? Do we not, rather, see a rising, a reawakening of a spirit long dormant? What is it, this rising amidst the 'kinder and gentler' America? Do we, both conservative and nationalist alike, feel the soft rustling of a midsummer breeze, or is it the whisper of the growing hurricane? Does *culture* begin to resist its technics? The Modern considers the entire issue of guns, and their 'destructiveness', as being just a part of the reactionary elements incumbent in the ignorant, uncivilized mass. He promises, as only a snake can, to prohibit only assault-orientated weapons - since this 'type' weapon only serves the purpose of murder. This type of prohibition is always the Modern's way.

The 'prohibition' movement created criminals. So also the 'drug dealer' of today; so also the 'gun owner' of tomorrow. Crime is, as has been stated before, created by definition, not necessarily by the *simple act*. There must, of necessity, be a *value* prior to the consignment of any criminal stigma. Value, in its pure form, is subjective – the course of its development is mapped by its proponents – *might is right*. The weaker elements must accept the consequences of a loss of power – he accepts the *privilege* of power. The 'gun owner', 'nationalist', 'modernist', etc., is also facing the same classification – whoever is the fittest, or most capable, will survive. The reality of judicial conduct in any major city in America which, as is widely known, already classifies gun owners as criminals, and is utilized daily by the Modern. Innocents are now, ipso facto, criminals. What will the Conservative do then, when the security forces come to his home, demanding the receipt of any and all weapons in his possession? The Conservative cannot face this inevitable reality (or, in the opposite, will gladly allow members of the 'state' to pilfer, search, and confiscate *any* weapon, which the state may deem unacceptable as *a matter of course!*). One can sense the furrowing of the broad brow of the Nationalist.

The average Western individual, at least in the large cosmopolis of the 'city', goes blank when pondering this thought of impending alienation between

---

[40] Ibid.

himself and his traditional protector. He forgets the first imperative of the original revolutionaries which may force them to consider the possibility that *"they may have to choose between owning their guns and facing the full implication of the Declaration of Independence"[41]* ...that, whenever any form of government becomes destructive of these ends, it is the right of the people to *alter* or *abolish* it. Some, it may happen, will meekly give up these rights, the right of primitive, *free* man, horrified that they may have options, which require any *real* action on their part – others, however, will not submit. What then, will be said of those that will not? Criminal? Insurgent? Seditionist? Revolutionary? Will it be legal? The Modern begins his assault; *he cringes in fear at the culture he thought long dead.*

Intrinsic in this discussion is the *survival* of the West.

Gun ownership may be, to some, a side issue – and so it is – yet, intertwined with that very survival. It is *not* 'guns' per se, but the *actuality* of survival. A murder in defense of one's family, nation, or race-culture (this is done in any *patriotic* war) is *ethical*. Anyone who proscribes this act is considering something *other* than the personal intrinsic ethical instinct of self-defense. It is the most *primal* essence of survival; the platitudes of the 'state', which arbitrarily seek to circumvent the individual imperative – the Modern claims that this will maintain order, and take away the emotional element – well and good, as far as it goes; but to consider, let's say, the rape of one's infant daughter, *that* father or mother has the 'right' to be emotional – and justice by either the hands of parents or family members prior to the 'state' spending millions of dollars is, somehow, to say that 'justice has *not* been served'! It is only by *whose* hands, justice is to be delivered. In like fashion, the nationalist sees the separation of the West from all aliens as imperative to the survival of all he knows. This is *his* ethic. This is *his* Justice. The survival of his race-culture is ethical; its destruction, *unethical*.

National 'unity' is a *will-to-express* technic of Culture. Once that 'unity' defined by race, tradition, mores, etc., fails to exhibit its high-culture, in its will-to-express *life cycle*, it is finished. This, in relation to the entirety of Western history. For all intents and purposes, a *new evolutionary process takes place*. The technics, values, and imperatives in the Western culture have changed – but

---

[41] Ibid, page 33.

Western man cannot place his finger in the problem. He is *undecided*. Nature, however, has nevertheless, made the decision for him. Indications of this decisive change can be seen in the 'ethnic relations' within the race-culture of the West.

Here we draw the analogy between 'gun ownership' and the right of 'separation'. Both can be categorized as a battle for the consistent understanding of 'inalienable' rights, those that are provided by nature – but maintained by man – which, after long ages, has become written in the pages of historical survival. The proof was in the *doing*. The Modern has taken this proof, twisted it, and perverted it. His vision of 'unity' has fostered the amalgamation of all peoples; of the *perversion* of an experiment intended solely for the race-cultural extension of *one* people. The Modern's actualization: Babel. The confusion of tongues, of Cultures. The *confusion* of racial identity.

While the political understanding of 'unit' is sound in relation to the American technics of the past, that is to say, in relation to the bonding of 'states' and the like, in a unified cohesive unit, such as a living organism, the Modern has transformed it to include all the elements, diverse though they are, of far reaching and alien cultures, and then forced them to mix *as* 'unit'. This is his social experiment – not the experiment of our Western Fathers. It is a fabrication intended to beguile the Western; to re-learn, to reconstruct Western man, in the *new technic* of 'political unity; this, of course, is the very reason for such feelings of racial separation in the West. Racial and political determinism is the watchword of today's thinking.

To some, the future 'ethnic/political' relations are horrifying. To others, it is welcomed as natural, inevitable, and sound practical race-culture politics. To those moderns, which are fearful of this trend, they mask themselves with self-righteous condemnation of all those who seek a different path. They point to the 'democratization' of Eastern Europe. But that should not deter us long, if at all, since it is precisely because eastern Europe was breaking apart along racial lines that any change in the political environment was necessitated. The role of *money* was secondary. Race was primary. The once great Soviet Empire, like her mirrored sister, America, has finally realized that ethnic 'groups' (i.e. Biological nations) must determine their own future and political realizations – based on their organic needs and will-to-express.

The Modern knew this, does know this, and is precisely why he has kept the West confused, continually fighting himself over who is going to be the greatest democracy; who is going to bend over backwards in helping all others but that of his own kind. To those in America, the Modern would have us believe that Europe will be weakened by the apparent separation of its individual collective states – nothing could be further from the truth! In reality, the Western race-culture of 'old' Europe will become stronger than it has ever been. The casting aside of years of forced assimilation has, or will produce, a nation of truly epic proportions. The Modern shudders at the thought.

Isolation tends to mark the race-culture with *will, strength, and a will-to-power* that will, with time, create a positive destiny. In this light, must America, also, decide its own destiny. But only if America, truly, remains a higher-culture. If she is not, then the coming isolation from her sister, Europe, will dim her epoch making flame to that of a dead ember.

The Balkanization of the contiguous 'states' within the boundaries of these United States is unacceptable to most, if not all those that carry the flame of the Modern. To all and sundry, the cry is heard: 'to all *one* god', 'to all *one* people', 'to all *one* government'. This is, and has become, the rallying wail of the Modern; this is their *imperative*. They must, their power depends upon it. Yet, the ancient drive to realize, to actualize a particular race-culture with the necessary developments required to succeed in a vast world of competition is the kind of struggle the Modern will, at any cost, keep Western man from attaining. The Modern, however, is wearing thin; he fears the technics of *organism*. The Cosmopolis, that crowning achievement of the Modern, has been split between the *visible* lines of racial demarcation from their very inception, and the visible realities of equality and diversity in the coming Babel of the 21st Century.

In the past, this presented little problem – he [the Modern] controlled his environment – now, however, it is controlled by those 'individual' racial units who, with political power have, ipso facto, created a balkanization effect with no thought whatsoever of their future excepting the single imperative of breaking up the political state of the Western. The Modern, of course, supports and aids in its implementation. In the 'cities', they already have *control*. Their very numbers demand this control – *the mob now in control*.

Democracy, once again, serves the Modern, yes, and even the Western who created it, and allows his technics to pass from him to the *mob* of the Modern. The Western [man] cannot complain. Nay! He must welcome this passing – it is, after all, the 'people's choice'! Freedom of choice, however, cuts both ways, but not always in those ways predicted. The Nationalist as well, has made his choice.

It is now true, unlike any time in our history, that large segments of the Western race-culture of America has realized the loss of political power as a 'race-cultural unit'. Let us be more specific: members of white European stock have not only decreased numerically through abortion, self-denial, and intellectual decisions to 'decrease' family size, and fundamental encouragement of non-European immigration over that of European immigration has, most assuredly, put the 'white race' at an untenable crossroad: his extinction as a 'voting majority' is already here; and extinction of his racial sovereignty follows close behind.

Let the Modern say what he will; let him denounce this position until he is blue in the face; the fact remains, that Western man has neither the *power* to change a thing on the National level, nor the power to *claim* any sovereignty other than what his 'status' as a de facto citizen of the republic – with rights and privileges granted by those who hold power over him – even by those who neither know his past nor have any inclination or knowledge of how his future must be formed and shaped to guarantee his future. Western man, those white Europeans of America, are facing a future directed by others.

The Western fecund rate, the ability to create and raise children, is ever decreasing, and now forces one to contemplate the reality of a non-western increase in *real* numbers, which equate into a *real* increase of voting power – this simply is the way of nature. The collective 'units' of the various diverse race-cultures feel the present presence of their *own* power; the resultant spin-off leads, of necessity, towards separation. So, also the Western. Where will this trend lead us? It is the question of a new century; of a new future – Destiny awaits *in vitro*.

The birthing of a new order, of a new destiny is apparent in all we do and see. It must be addressed now, for if this continent is to be sustained as a Western race-cultural unit, as well as a 'safe haven' for the other existing units, it must be determined to just what *extent* this trend is manifested, indeed, as to just how far along we already are. More importantly, in the long run, is the understanding of what this fulfillment of separation and diverse individual unity will bring to *our* culture and race, that is, the Western Culture and Race.

Broad predictions can be made. Anything other than predictions is highly unlikely. As was stated in the first part of this work, however, we can learn, if we have eyes to see, the lessons of the past for the organization of our future. The great *cause*, the seemingly insignificant apparatus, which turned the first gear in the machinery of the race and culture can be identified by the very application of causes – the practical *result*. Its technics are never to be isolated in the context of 'this' or 'that' was the *cause*, but rather in the overall outlook of the entire personality of the particular presence being analyzed. The Future, likewise, may be seen in the light of the past and its *continuous presence in manifesting itself in Industry, Political technics, and its Military endeavors*. The disposition of the past is the manifest spirit of any age – as change evolves slowly, the recognition is, therefore, also slow and, consequently, may take several centuries to be analyzed effectively. Only during the siege of revolution may one ascertain, on a daily basis, the future of this or that particular culture.

Therefore, as in this case, generalized predictions may be made in the expectation of a 'high certainty' as to the eventual outcome of this present discussion. The long-range prediction, of course, is symptomatic of a lesser degree of certainty. Deviations always occur – this is the *great cause* – the working prime lever of the machine of change in the period of, say, a hundred years or so which may, or may not, fix any one or numerous predictions to a set course. The trends we speak of now is based solely on those experienced here, in the United States of America, as well as based upon her international conduct. These predictions, as well, are predicated upon a 'liberal' policy of immigration towards non-western elements; any tightening of this policy will slow, but not stop, these predictions. Predictions are *not* prophecies. This is, rather, a safe series of probabilities and possibilities as seen in the present presence. Here, then, listed below, are such predictions as are warranted in this work:

1. **ETHNIC TENSION WILL INCREASE RATHER THAN DECREASE:**

This simply recognizes that Whites will begin to show less and less sympathy for nonwhites. Their feelings of charity and aid to these groups will be limited to the altruistic, and philanthropic principles. Ethnic factors and values will be ever more prevalent in the political arena; the deadlock realized from this positioning will create ever more conflict, and prolong the process of governmental stagnation. Separatist movements will increase.

2. **AMERICAN FOREIGN POLICY WILL CONTINUE TO DETERIORATE:**

Internal conflict will rise above the level of any party to handle; this will raise the International specter of instability, and indecisive political technics. In the International view, the American political and cultural outlook will be more and more of a 'third-world' manifestation. These manifestations will conclude with the 'international' outlook of military/political imperatives which, at this date, would be 'anti-american' if put into practice. How the American people respond to this remains to be seen; apathy will be consonant with cowardice and betrayal, and action to deny this [internationalism] will be condemned as betrayal to the principles of the Modern and his minions.

3. **ETHNIC 'MOVEMENTS' WILL CONTINUE TO GROW IN SIZE AND POWER:**

The path and direction, laid out by 'black power' movements, will continue to gain increased dominance in the realm of minority reality. *Hispanics [mestizo] will gain the most impetus from this manifestation of power* by 'asserting' those desires in *maintaining* the same space as their hosts; this *desire*, having some 'historical' validity, will only encourage and promote more separatism.

4. **COMPETING 'MINORITY' GROUPS WILL FIGHT FOR SUPREMACY IN THE POLITICAL REALM:**

The dissimilar values and attitudes expressed by these minority groups, as well as a predisposed animus toward the Western race-culture will, undoubtedly, cause in direct proportion to the level of conflict, an animosity unparalleled in a modern democracy – since, in this environment, all contending parties will be able to have 'their' voices heard. Unification of these 'groups' will, however, find the value of cooperation with each other, against those of Western Stock. The expression of this cooperation will take on more strident and 'defensive' racism [as seen and promoted by these groups] against those of Western stock.

5. **AFRO-AMERICAN REACTION TO PERCEIVED DILUTION OF POWER BASE BY MESTIZO-AMERICANS AND OTHER NON-AFRO ELEMENTS:**

In the Future, Afro-Americans will realize their limited position in relation to Hispanic [mestizo] political acumen which, after being in the shadow of European cultural technics have gained superiority in technical understandings of Western political innuendo. Problems of just *who* is the 'oldest minority' and, consequently, who will garner the greatest favors of the Western political leaders – (this is perceived as being a 'social contract' between the 'whites', and the blacks for their rather close association between the Western, as seen by afro-americans). It is not coincidental, that 'black' criminal activity has surfaced in areas, which promote such interactions between Mestizo and Asians in numbers, neither familiar nor experienced by African-Americans. This will continue to escalate.

6. **WESTERN AMERICAN [white] CULTURE WILL SHOW A SURPRISING AMOUNT OF RESISTANCE IN VARIOUS FORMS:**

Once passive, whites will become combatants in continuing ethnic violence. Not being politically astute in the areas of 'specialization' areas, such as immigration, housing, and the like, the average white-worker will, inevitably, become more estranged and enraged by the amounts of money spent on 'social reform', and 'grants' of housing and other commodities, as those of Western stock start to feel the loss of what they had come to expect of their 'way of life'; while they, the white American, are seemingly doing without, paying exorbitant taxes, and seeing little in any real return, which affects them, personally, they will soon react. Whites will soon shed the 'image' of black, or any other 'minority' *as* victim – this will allow his [white] true feelings to come to the surface. Anger and resentment in the 'work-place' will continue to grow at an enormous rate. Frustration will turn to anger – for all parties involved – and one or more groups will elicit various responses including, but not limited too, violence against persons and property, political challenges such as 'education', 'jobs' [i.e. once *granted*, never given up], 'citizenship', and nationalist sentiments, on all sides, as to their idea of racial, and political hegemony on a local and national level.

7. **EDUCATIONAL AND CAMPUS HOSTILITIES WILL INCREASE IN DIRECT PROPORTION TO LEVEL OF 'MINORITY' INVOLVEMENT AS COMPARED TO WHITE ENROLLMENT:**

Conflict of twenty years ago between black and white used to take on the picture of 'small' rising against the 'big'. Now, it takes on the picture of 'inter-group' against 'inter-group'. The lines of political demarcation are diminished. Racial antagonisms are increased based on perceptions of the level of achievements between 'groups' and 'sub-groups'. Black students, as with other minorities, receive 'preferential treatment', be it real or perceived, and then fail to 'make the grade'. This further disenfranchises whites. The 'right' to address these issues by White Student Unions, papers, and staff will create issues of 'freedom of speech' and the real ability to use the 'forum' of the Campus for their attempts at recognition as a racial unit. The policy of 'selection' in regards to enrollment of 'special' groups will further alienate the white student. He will sense the shift in traditional norms in every field of education. European studies will decrease – those who wish to follow this traditional 'western' path will be termed racist, and insensitive. All this will sow the seeds of racial discord and anger, and see a loss in actual Western alumnae.

8, **WHITE 'Political' RESPONSE TO GROWING COALITION OF NON-WHITE POLITICAL BASE:**

The political *outcome*, of minority political power, will be predicated upon *which* group holds the coalition together, and what 'alliances' are made, and with which 'sub-group'. In response to this, will be the emergence of a new Nationalist/Racialist Party – or some racially conscious PAC embolden by a central figure – either an individual or an [existing] institution which has a more radical approach to the issues of the day. *This will be a racial alliance first and foremost.*

Religionists will be drawn to one another, or be forced to split that party or institution, which is now representing them. Hispanic 'Catholicism' may prove to be a decisive factor amongst Irish, Italians, or others traditionally of the catholic experience. The 'Poles' as well, would be drawn to their co-religionists – but the racial distinctiveness between themselves and other non-Western stock will force any realignment necessary. The Irish, and Italians will be valuable assets in any coalition; should the Irish prove to be inclined, as have their fathers, then whichever they decide, their religion will be first and foremost, as their sense of 'race' has been contravened by their religious history, to follow their deity. Italians will, as is their nature, follow their passions, wherever this takes them, but are inclined to follow their sense of 'western imperialism' and will be split here in America as to how, properly, to address this issue. All in all, those of the West will, ultimately, choose to participate in a 'working' relationship with each other, no matter the small dissenting minority 'within' Western culture, and support the growing sense of Western *identity*.

Continuing 'legislative' dominance by minority pressure groups will force the growth of this 'white coalition', and will receive the support of the military over those 'interest' groups, which have facilitated the breakdown and massive social experimentation of the armed forces. This would be needed, of course, to qualify the largest amount of 'public' perception as to the legitimacy of political change. The trappings of military 'order' will draw the white-mass for good or ill. The extent to which the military and civilian forces, both political and personal, will accommodate one another will be gauged by both the 'internal' and 'external' stimulus exerted on either one individually, or collectively. A militarization of the populace will occur spontaneously regardless, as a matter of course.

9. **BIOLOGICAL 'Affirmative Action' WILL FORCE POLITICAL CHANGE:**

The continuing understanding of just 'who' one is will, in ever increasing amounts, force a realignment of historical realities: for White, Black, Asian, and Mestizo. This understanding, of one's root and stock, will cause continued imbalance in the day to day working relationship of any one or all-existing racial groups. Of course, this 'type' of polarization is natural and must be fostered by each individual 'type' – assimilation by the weaker group, or group that refuses to acknowledge his past will occur, inevitably. The Western race-culture will be the most powerful since, as has been shown before, he is capable of solidifying his power base more quickly when threatened from the outside. His past is marked by more marital conflict, and his diplomacy is usually relegated to violence of the most extreme nature. The expression of 'racial' memory will take on greater and larger meanings as time goes on.

10. WHITE 'Ethnic' REVIVAL:

As Western whites, increasingly, see themselves as a *distinct ethnic group,* threatened by invading cultural aliens, coupled with the submergence of their own racial stock to that of other diverse groups, *their* particular 'reactions' will imitate, in large degree, that of *traditional* 'ethnic groups'. They will *react* violently to racial slurs, job discrimination, inter-racial couplings, and will therefore assume a more demonstrable kinship with 'their own kind' as has been accepted in the past with non-Western 'minorities'. Ethnic 'revival' will be largely Cultural, and will not take on political shades until they have first made their cultural needs manifest – more likely than not, in the 'streets' or in the traditional 'institutions' of the country. From this reaction will come the *political manifestation* of Separatism, seen as the only method of survival.

11.   MESTIZO 'Ethnic' REVIVAL:

The greatest possibility of a 'first' separatist movement is seen in the Mestizo population. The hotbed of contention is in, and over, the Southwestern portion of America. New Azatlan is already a part of the 'cultural' mind of the southwest Mestizo – it is, after all, the ancient historical homelands of his ancestors – the Aztec Indians, who controlled a Mexican Empire prior to Cortez. Religious leaders (such as Father Florecio M. Rigoni), looks at the mass immigration of Mexicans across the American borders as 'a peaceful conquest' of territorial lands. Some may think this fanciful thinking by an aspiring culture who, those of the West, have had little feelings for one way or another, as their religion boasts of 'the love of mankind', and thereby rationalizes this transformation. The Mestizo, on the other hand, believes strongly in this possible realization. There are two main reasons why the chance of success is high for this race-culture:

a. There is some justification of their ownership, rooted in relatively recent times. They, at one time, controlled the Southwest as a People and Culture.

b. There is simple evidence that Mestizos will be a numerical majority in all or large part of the Southwest in a relatively short period. If the latter happens, and there is an almost certain possibility that it will, then Separatist sentiment will certainly thrive. The French in Quebec is just another example of the way this contest is about to play itself out.[]

12. BALKANIZATION OF THE WESTERN CONTINENT INEVITABLE:

The 'break', of even one traditional race-culture from the norms of the United States, will create a domino effect that will not subside unless tremendous force is utilized in its suppression. This is not, however, the worst-case scenario. A more dramatic, if not less popular, would be a continuing 'state of war' carried out by guerilla's in a small scale civil war. Terrorism would be the watchword of the day. The examples of Lebanon, Sri Lanka, India, and Northern Ireland will suffice to make this point. Even in forms not as

---

[] Note: The fact, that the present American government has approved the 'fast track' to Mexico, as of this writing, should make all those of Western stock raise their heads in anger and demand an explanation. With the close proximity that Mexican mestizos and American-Chicanos have in both culture and geography, it is certain that any 'extra' positioning of these groups by the government, will lead to the rapid deployment of these kindred people's between Mexico proper, and those American 'centers', which house the greatest numbers of Mexican mestizo immigrants and Chicanos. This will reinvigorate the 'old' contacts between agitators and leaders of every persuasion – marking, even more so, the difference between the opposing groups. This may well facilitate a situation much more militant than that of Quebec. Mexican mestizos *will* fight when the time is right. At the very least – in the case of a positive Separatist movement – the southwestern mestizo will demand autonomy on levels not seen since Pancho Villa. The Modern, it would seem, is trying to placate these elements by their fast-track proposals. For those that think this possibility of annexation, of separatism, as illogical, let it be remembered that our own revolutionary leaders and people, were certainly not logical to take on the entire British Empire for something as esoteric as 'freedom'. Whether we, those of Western stock, accept the aspirations of the immigrant Mexican mestizo, or other non-Westerns, it is, nevertheless, part of a racial imperative, which will, and does seek, release. FLS

concrete as total separatism, the probability that the various groups maintain a more than rigid conglomerate in the large cities of the United States is highly likely. This will be *de facto* separatism.

13. OPEN U.S. BORDERS WILL ENSURE THE DISSOLUTION OF TRADITIONAL AMERICAN IDEAS OF 'Federalism':

This is over and above any real 'nationalism'. America will be truly International in scope. The 'open border' concept will bring a two-way traffic, which will usher in the new [American] and will usher out the old [American]. This 'may' create the largest white flight in the history of the Western race-culture, or they may stay and fight for sovereignty like has not been seen since the first wave of Aryan invaders crossed the eastern steppes. The consequent loss of scientific and educational levels in America by the latter situation would completely rearrange the face of this continent.

14. THE RISE OF A 'New' WEST:

This manifestation will be regarded as 'revolutionary' by the powers that be. It is, however, a necessary prerequisite to the continuation of the Western race-culture, either as a distinct 'ethnic' group, isolated, and sharing a possible 'portion' of this Western Continent, or as a racially dominant legislative bloc – this latter, however, will not be necessitated if the present trends continue. The new conscious Western man and woman will, most assuredly, demand their part of the pie – what is left of it. He will face growing opposition from the established order, which, after the levels of determination will convince those of Western stock of their betrayal. Military and civilian contacts will continue to facilitate joint ventures and, when that 'personality' becomes known, will voluntarily commit to each other's cause; the presence of 'money' will manifest itself in, and from those American interests which have succumbed to ventures of International Finance by forcing their economic interest to go abroad, thereby denying their own people work and sustenance. Militarism, coupled with money, will bring about the venues certain to establish Culture over that of the mechanism, of civilization, and will eventually be overcome by Culture created, formed, and lived by those of the West.

These predictions, as said before, are broad in scope. To face the facts as we see them is to be honest with ourselves, as well as to the future of our [white] children. To drive all the foregoing home however, let us add this: The *fact* that non-Westerns are numerically growing is evident; the *fact* that political power is based solely on the *majority of the voters*, regardless of their race, is supported by the ideal of 'democracy' – a Western concept – and will, eventually prove the maxim of 'one man, one vote' is the essence of modern democracy – and the *end* of the Western Culture on this continent as we know it, as well. Forcing these various 'groups' inhabiting this continent to be *like* the Western race-culture will only add fuel to the already burning fire of Nationalism and Separatism.

The feelings of Nationalism and Separatism are felt by all groups, regardless of its racial makeup. The present system only artificially suppresses these feelings. In America, the 'traditional' minorities such as Blacks and Mestizos will continue to localize their political *unity* and increase their demands for a larger and larger role in their political destiny – this is only natural and expected. The eventual coalition [between black and mestizo], while not very palatable to either party will, nevertheless, be realized – if only to take a shot at political mastery. To *not* take this gamble, for it would truly be a gamble, would show that their ability to match the Western is of an inferior nature. However, between the two separate ethnic groups, the Mestizo-Hispanic is the more technically advanced; hence, it will be the dominant *culture*.

The tendency of ethnic 'units' in demanding 'equal' time politically, economically, *and* culturally will increase in proportion to each individual units size and social needs. What the Western [man] cannot, or will not give up will, most assuredly, *force the needed cooperation spoken of above*. In the present democracy [of the West], the right of every voice to be heard will be protected – imagine the million voices, the million needs, spread out, demanding attention to their individual concerns that will, and presently, is, sucking the life-blood from the entire apparatus of the present system. The majority 'rules', no matter what majority [coalition] this represents. African Americans, on the other hand, will rightly feel betrayed by any upsurge in the mestizo-Hispanic power base. Any 'historical' consideration that has benefited the black race in the past will be of no account to the newly powerful mestizo-Hispanic voting bloc. Independent and powerful, the mestizo-Hispanic American will take them to task for inferring preference by *another minority*. This perceived loss of respect and lack of political acumen will force them to conclude, and with some veracity, that it is the Western, that must bear responsibility for this state of affairs; this will only exacerbate the existing ethnic turmoil even further.

A microscopic look at these political factors can now be witnessed in any major American [or European] city, which shares this disparate population. An already existing racial hodge-podge presently exists in the southwestern United States trying, it would seem, to function in the 'democratic sense' of a new world order. This study, into 'new politics', can be seen in the ascendancy of 'brown'; however much this is a political *fact*, the Western now emerges from his stupor of the sixties. The Western man of today is tired; he cares not for the *minority*, for the *victim*. *He sees himself as a true victim* – a victim of betrayal, a victim of a Modern who is no longer a part of *his* West.

The Western perception, real or imagined, that affirmative action has now canceled out his productivity will force his hand. He will, and is seeing, the life-value of *his* family passing into oblivion. He will, with some help from the nationalist, project himself as a *new political force*. If this new found power, however embryonic, will not help him in any way recognizable to him on a daily basis, he will force the Modern to play the final hand: *war in the streets*. The Modern will seek, at all costs, to avoid urban warfare. He already has a plan – a plan, which has been in effect for over a hundred years – that of the destruction of the Western, or any 'nationalist' prone groups or individuals who have gained any credible political favor, through the process of assimilation; the degradation of the racial-stock, which founded this American West. The Modern must, at every opportunity, revamp this idea of obfuscation, misdirection and destruction since, it being unnatural, will always show itself to those with the eyes to see, and must do this *before* the Western realizes just what is taking place in the arena of politics – politics that will affect the Western in the most direct and influential ways. The Modern realizes that if he does not *merge the various ethnic units he will face his own annihilation at the hands of his creation*. Faced with the various decisions he must make, marked with the obvious race-cultural contradictions that are present, he will be shown for the hypocrite his is. His power will fade into oblivion.

The inherent power of all Culture starts with the *learning process*. The traditional Centers of Learning, specifically of our Universities, will encounter major ethnic confrontations. The sole purpose of an educational environment is to learn – this is axiomatic. The increasing predominance of 'ethnic units' will force a radical shift from conventional scholastic thought. It must needs be so since, once again, Western culture is restrictive to many people. The coming change is already seen at such Universities as Harvard[42] and

---

[42] Psychiatry Ponders Whether Extreme Bias Can Be an [mental] Illness – "Mental health practitioners say they regularly confront extreme forms of racism, homophobia

Dartmouth. In fact, as is widely known at this writing, such 'black' leaders as the visual spokesman and politician, Jesse Jackson, has said repeatedly "HO!HO!HO!– Western Culture gots ta go." While, at the same time, those at Dartmouth and other conservative Universities will increasingly become more and more adamant in their *own cultural rights*. Admission rights in such places as University California Berkley, presented by, of all people, the staff administrators themselves, were artificially restricted in allowing only forty-percent [40%] of the eligible Freshmen in academic standards alone. Those not coming up to academic standards were, nevertheless, accepted because the representation of ethnic 'units' was not diverse enough. In 1984, about seven hundred white applicants were redirected elsewhere to make room for minorities.

To 'unify' this prodigious amalgamation, the Modern, typically, has tried the band-aid method of Language. This theory, oddly enough, has been proposed by a stalwartly proponent of ethnic isolation in a cultural sense; himself a child of Asian ancestry, and a proficient spokesman for the 'conservative' cause. This theory runs thus: An

---

and other prejudice in the course of therapy, and that some patients are disabled by these beliefs. As doctors increasingly weigh the effects of race and culture on mental illness, some are asking whether pathological bias ought to be an official psychiatric diagnosis. Advocates have circulated draft guidelines and have begun to conduct systematic studies. While the proposal is gaining traction, it is still in the early stages of being considered by the professionals who decide on new diagnoses. If it succeeds, it could have huge ramifications on clinical practice, employment disputes, and the criminal justice system. Perpetrators of hate crimes could become candidates for treatment, and physicians would become arbiters of how to distinguish "ordinary prejudice" from pathological bias."
And More:
"They are delusional," said Alvin F. Poussaint, a professor of psychiatry at Harvard Medical School, who has long advocated such a diagnosis. "They imagine people are going to do all kinds of bad things and hurt them, and feel they have to do something to protect themselves.
And still More:
"We treat racism and homophobia as delusional disorders," said Shama Chaiken, who later became a divisional chief psychologist for the California Department of Corrections, at a meeting of the American Psychiatric Association. "Treatment with antipsychotics does work to reduce these prejudices." Shankar Vedantam, Washington Post Staff Writer, Saturday, December 10, 2005.

This is just the beginning of the Modern's Priest Craft of the modern age. FLS

amalgamation of diverse ethnic groups will be forced to submit to a *national leveling* based on the *commonality of language*. The [Western] English language in this case. This will, in theory, provide a 'common' ground – on a cultural level! – hence, the prosperity and peace of the entire nation will follow. No lack of skills, no lack of opportunity – such is the utopian dream of the modern.

Reaction, especially in the State of California, has been swift and deadly all across the nation by 'ethnics' that voice their true feelings over a 'loss of National Identity', of heritage. The morass, of this *'new language'*, would deny their children the 'cultural' backdrop of a real people – outside the home; their children would be denied, on a daily basis, the realities of their ancestral roots. The Nationalist/Separatist agree.

The 'conservative' elements, along with the Modern, still seek to press the issue. The Nationalist/Separatist knows that 'language' will bring the 'non-western' ethnic unit closer to him in every day life, while keeping a definable distance between the parties on a social level. *Language cannot change the leopard's spots*. This manufactured idea of the Modern is yet another ploy in his 'grand experiment'.

In its great diversity, the various ethnic units will, ultimately, rely on the coalition political party. This so-called 'rainbow' coalition, to use a present term, will undoubtedly play a larger and larger part in the political 'cat and mouse' games of the democratic process. At best, however, this conglomerated rainbow coalition would be an uneasy one. In its growing political power, the destabilizing effect would be manifest. Every thing would depend on 'compromise' and 'smoothing' the way for these disparate groups. Put to the test however, say, in the cases of a 'national emergency' or war, this system of 'coalition; would be stifled from the outset; it would be besieged with atrophy such as Poland was during the interim period between world wars.

Western response to the above coalition will be a heated one. The response, already in the making, will be, also, a cultural one – call it a Pan-European expression if you will – and it will include all those of

European descent as a voting bloc. This, as with all that has been stated before, is a natural one; it will be as natural to the West as it is natural to the non-western to *form with his own*. The tribal mechanism of Western history is replete with the opposite occurring; but as time goes on, the various democracies will come to grips with the methodology requisite to maintain our Culture – as the culture distorters have in past derailed this imperative we, all those of Western stock, must remain vigilant and never let this imperative recede to the background.

The two largest and most predictable groups in any Western alliance in this potential coalition would be the great Celtic and Nordic elements – combined with German (the single largest ethnic white group in America). The potential problem regarding religion, that is, the technics of Catholicism, Lutheranism, etc., specifically the interests of the Irish and mestizo-Hispanic element is worth some consideration but, in the end, will opt for its racial affinity with its own kind – and put religion to the side, when the case warrants. The Pope, as an 'institution', however, could very well prove to be a dangerous 'wildcard' if any real religious threat presented itself on behalf of the Roman Pontiff. If the West has learned (?) anything, it should be that *religious wars are fought for political power* – the Race, sad to say, matters least in these types of war.

Religious Wars must be avoided between those of Western stock at all costs!

Economic considerations will precipitate the final breakdown of the diverse ethnic units. As the competition increases for jobs, and their related skills diminish, the need for 'outcome', not 'income', will increase. Production in traditional fields will expire, the necessary 'high-tech' areas will lack the competitive edge needed to stay afloat in a world of high demand for high quality material; we will all be expected to accept everything which is *mediocre*. The welfare rolls, already pushed to the limit, feeding on those vast amounts of 'prepared' savings, the greater of these savings by our elderly, and using them to keep the indigent and homeless fed on a daily basis. Even those of the Western race-culture will, and is being forced, to accept this handout. Income will be offered by the 'state', and outcome, as well. No production – just a cycle of burden to the entire nation. The tremendous amount of litigation, which we will experience in this area alone (e.g. those who are on 'welfare', and those 'intending to enroll') is massive, and is only really known by those that are already on this system. The monstrous, 'bigger is better' *pax Romana*, is yet another lie of the Modern, that has been uncovered.

All this, however, has its rising star. The Rise of the West is predicated upon it.

Between the bashing, political or otherwise, along with the obvious fiscal realities facing the race-culture of the West, and the continued growing dominance of the non-Western race-culture to become an 'identifiable' and genuine ethnic group – this will provide them with the legitimate *technic* of political determinism – which, in turn, will provide them with a sense of community, and into a *breeding* ground for political, and racial thought. The realization that *race* and *culture* actually exists and has viable power will bring those of the *biological nation* together; once the significant understanding of 'racial ancestry' is taken to heart, the People of the West, world wide, will consider their political decisions as being an integral part of their daily lives. This will breed true and healthy nationalism. The feelings of a *great white tribe* will grow increasingly as the political events of the United States and the Western world deteriorate.

The time involved in this ethnic tension, and its eventual culmination is uncertain. But it *will* take place. The revival of the West, as well, is seen to have started [by the Nationalist] about seventy-five years ago. Its contemporary zenith is to be seen in the numerous events in Europe, especially in German (i.e. European) re-unification, as well as the smaller states like Serbia, Albania, Yugoslavia, and the entire Balkan Region. The reaction of these states, once being freed from the 'occupational' powers of the West, was to dramatically show the world that Freedom, Sovereignty, and a reaffirmation of nationhood is the wave of the future – this, of course, is contrary to the new world order – hence it will, undoubtedly, cause future tension and possible war between those elements of the West still under alien domination and political persuasion. All this, and more, is the *organic* result of the technics of race-culture. Economics plays a secondary, if not also a supportive role; money is necessary for all great revivals.

The United States, the hearth and home of many sons and daughters of the West, and an integral part of the Race Culture, is also traveling through a revival, a renaissance, which will surprise many. America is unavoidably being drawn into the same awareness, as is the European commonwealth. How we, as a People and 'political technic' deal with this eventuality is what will determine our future — it is the *presence* of our Tomorrow.

As always, any race-cultural revival is purely cultural, that is, *spiritual*, almost intangible, and is seen only with the 'eyes that see'. Many have seen the trends; many have experienced the Modern's vision of the future. Those that share this reality are already demanding separatism at once. Those, which advocate complete 'separation', are small, numbering only a few million [many who feel this way, yet lack any real *substantive* ability to show this feeling are, nevertheless, manifest; the 'common man' has no real way to *share* with his fellows in the present climate of political control — dissent *appears* not to exist). However small, one may use these numbers as an *indicator* of a reality, rather than an existing, functioning, reality. In any event, if any so-called 'rainbow' coalition becomes dominant in the future, with or without the aid of the present government, it is a foregone conclusion that opposing Western technics of the same caliber will be manifest.

The Modern cannot conceive of any separate nation on this continent, yet he is coercing, intimidating, and fomenting this exact phenomenon in Europe at this very date. He calls it the great coming of 'democracy' in once totalitarian systems, while he, at the same time, practices the same totalitarian dictatorship. The Modern is a hypocrite. His hypocrisy stems from the original idea of *universalism* — of all beings being brothers in the sense of 'community'. His idea, or more rightly, the 'idea' of Montesquieu, was the crystal clear rationalism of separation of powers, a separate but equal *idea* which has been discounted by the Modern in every other sphere of political dialogue in this century, to accommodate a smooth transition into the realm of a *living* world. Like all rationalistic thinkers, however, its reality of life-process is muddied by a *natural* reality. That reality, as always, is the continuing *un*-equality of man.

The Modern's hypocrisy extends even further. The *idea* of State is a technical apparatus, which the Modern has never fully understood. The idea of 'state' as a component of national survival was not part of the original conception of America – the elements that the originators of the first Thirteen Colonies had to contend with was not the [same] elements of that in which the 'states' of Europe had to contend with: America had no boundaries, no hostile nations,)other than small indigenous Indian tribes), no inner, long-lasting Monarchical intrigue, in fact, the American situation was totally different in composition in regards to *all* traditional concepts of origination of its European past.

The European concept of 'state' was Idea – the *idea* of 'state' in America was a geo-political/legal/economic/territorial concept without perceived values of destiny, aim, or purpose other than its simple existence within the political Federalization of controlled anarchy, which was the present value in almost the entire confederation of original states. Manifest Destiny would come later; it would appear from a utilitarian need. There was no defined superstructure, there is no defined superstructure, in America today, which presupposes, in fact will guarantee the rights of each state, a state, that is, in the sense of a European commonwealth which, in turn, will protect itself from a possibly hostile Federal 'central government' that cares not for the indigenous culture politics of the individual state – not withstanding the simple realization that each state must have its own agenda based upon its territory, culture-ethic, and geo-political needs and desires. A Federal system, unlike a Monarchy, is only the glue, so to speak, that must bind the entire political organism together only in a State of War, or in such cases as to unify certain laws basic to the instruction and welfare of the entire nation. This, of course, by the consent of 'legislatures' and their independent governors. Instead, we have the essence of 'state' *as* monarchy – but Monarchy without *blood* or *breeding*.

Central to the *idea* of State, is the *idea* of Nation. The difference here, as seen by all nationalists, whatever the race-culture, is that nation *is* race. In all areas of America, one sees this reality. The so-called mestizo-Hispanic 'movement', calls for an independent mestizo nation of Aztlan; Louis Farrakhan teaches the belief in The Nation of Islam which would provide for the independence and direction of the majority of the black race. This is seen, also, in the manifestations of the Western culture as well – Robert J. Mathews, the white nationalist revolutionary leader killed, in the prime of life, by federal military detachments in the Pacific Northwest, for organizing a White American Bastion in which, as he and others saw it, the sons and daughters of Western kind could come and live, set up a government, and fulfill the destiny each felt was to their own making; this, because in the present system, it is unacceptable to practice one's faith in a congregation of one's own kind, to promote and actively live in a community which is, for all to see, made up of persons who belong to one's ethnic bloc. This was, in short, a Territorial Imperative in the northwestern United States, and is still a bone of contention within the nationalist communities in this country and the federal government. As the conservative elements in the existing governmental technic become ever more disgusted with the ways things are turning out, the more the chances between the nationalist and conservative elements fielding a political candidate become acceptable. This may, or may not, cover the issue of separation. But, if the minority 'separatist' movements, as said before, continue to press for the recognition of 'their rights', and ultimately they will, if they have the *will* to suffer for it, those of the West will be sure to follow in the same fashion. If the converse is true, that is, that the West breaks away from the 'federal state', the minority race-culture will, without a doubt, have their issues discussed as a matter of course.

The example of Robert J. Mathews needs to be followed up in terms of the *future* West. His example, in a strictly Western race-cultural sense, was one of militancy. Militancy is in harmony with the needs and desires of fledging race-cultures; it is also consonant with the natural law of *organism*. The Modern has failed to understand this – he understands only in part, and the part he understands, he wishes to destroy. Instead, the Modern has given the artificial and plastic realization to his subjects the fantasy of the brotherhood and equality of man – *regardless of the spasmodic and natural inclination to be distinct and separate in their culture*. Any deviation of this, *his* norm, is considered 'evil', revolutionary, and anti-social – worse, to the Modern it is anti-democracy!

The Nationalist believes in democracy, that is, in a system, which treats all men fairly *under the law*. But, to be treated fairly, which is, at best, still a utopia, it is necessary and mandatory that all citizens inherent in this democracy be of the same race-culture – one race, one law. The equal respect of other race-cultures would be incumbent upon any responsible government – as long as each race was itself *autonomous* and *recognized* as such. Only through this fashion of the 'inter-state' idea can any lasting *peace and equality be achieved for the future*. Under the Modern, the only peace that can be realized will be the peace of *'control'* – or control by *force*; it will be *his* peace – his and no other. Each race-culture will have to bend to the will and desire of an ideal, which, in all likelihood, will be contrary to his own natural inclinations, and desires.

In all this, and more, the rising West is a reality. It was said early on in this work that man, Western man, could not master himself in his ultimate search for *truth*. Yet, there are those that have mastered their reality. These are those with the vision, with the ability to see in their dreams, the reality of tomorrow. They see their families, their people (as a distinct race-culture), and life itself as something special, an integral part of themselves, as a *conduit for those that come after*. These individuals consciously seek it, they grasp it straight on, twisting and turning with every natural rhythm of life itself. It is to their vision that empires depend – that the *life* of a People *may continue*. To those alive or dead, we owe our thanks and dedication. To the struggle and purpose of the unsung, we dedicate this work. All we can do now, all we have ever done, is to *recreate* the reality of our original making – that which has been taken from us: *We, the masters of our own Destiny*. *We* are the cause and effect; *we* are the race-culture. *We*, you and I, are the beauty and harmony of the ages; our purpose is to *become* noble; to *affirm* our origins; to reach for the stars. *This, the West must do or die.* Thus does Nature ever teach.

Frank L. DeSilva

Chapter V

The Rise of The West

The time for petty politics is past;

The next century will bring the struggle

For the dominion of the world – the

Compulsion to great politics.

~Nietzsche~

All of the preceding considerations, questions, analogies, propositions, and possibilities have been presented in the hope that the people of the West, including this America, will realize, and become aware of this rising, this ascendancy of Culture over that of civilization, the macrocosm of the *institutionalized* common man. For, in all reality, this rising has happened already. The waking ascendancy of *real politics*, its essence, is manifest in our daily happenings, in our hustle and bustle, these little, but so essential, *human* elements, of our very lives. This is the same *essence* of ages past. It is the essence of need, desire, and will-to-power of *all* citizens of humanity – it is organic – its Life animates in all our outward forms; it ignites our imagination and stirs deep waters in the memories of our past. It belongs to *struggle*, that which all organisms are formed in the crucible of contest and survival. This essence will be, *is* being marked, by the very struggle between the race-cultures of the World. It truly has brought the compulsion to great politics.

Politics is the *great* technic of Nature. Nature divides the mediocre from those with merit; from those that are skilled and unskilled. It establishes supremacy of the one, over the other – this can be the individual or institution – this natural law ever is, and will be: the *one* will survive, and *one* will die. This is Nature's Law. Politics is, or should be, the greatest of compulsions to emulate, where possible, the rhythms and currents by which nature seeks ever to instruct and guide. The examples are myriad; as students, in this great experiment, we have the ability to seek instruction through the records of the past; we can receive instruction from the various individuals who have had many years bestowed upon them; and finally we have the instruction of *common sense*, which we utilize on a daily basis. Nature is a part of us, and if we but listen, and recognize that low soft whisper of intelligent reasoning, we shall see our path, clear, and undeniable.

Nature, herself, is not lineal but, rather, rhythmic, flowing as a tree in the wind, bending with the changes in the continuing evolution of the cycle of life. The presentation of this work is in keeping with this cycle. This concept alludes to times and places; to happenings we see passing in the twinkling of an eye – the lineal lacks the subtle rhythm and continuity of the organic growth inherent in the real world that surrounds us; this, the orderly cycle of nature.

The cycle of birth, life, and senility accompany each and every great civilization, not the least of which has been ours – that *great family* of Indo-Europeans, which founded and, still maintains, the greatest living history and working Culture yet experienced on this planet terra. Modern historians however, over the past seventy-five years, have concerned themselves only with this traditional 'school room' variety of lineal history, circumscribing the root cause and effect of actions and events that affect civilizations as it affects the individual. Distortion is the inevitable result of failing to address history as a living, breathing, manifestation of life: *Culture itself, becomes ambiguous.*

The *lineal* portrayal of history leaves our vision of the past distorted, ambiguous. These many, and diverse pictures, delivered in sequence, numbered, dated, and clouded by time, leaves us confused; the simple enormity of historical data simply boggles the mind. These clouded perceptions have been handed down to us by well intentioned authors of history but, limited by design and the seemingly chaotic, unpredictable value of chance, have delivered to us only *half* the product. For the most part, these authors have failed to recreate, for the most part, such events and situations that would take into account the very essence of the Age and Civilization of which they study. With the few exceptions of Spengler, Yockey, Adams, and Gibbons there has been little or no attempts at this recreation of history that would define our Western Culture, that is, the Race, if we say this a million times over, that is the *creative* force behind all that we know; it is the organism which pumps the blood into the body to continue life. Without this understanding, History, and all its various forms of philosophy, ethics, and the ancient value placed upon the present, and its reporting, would be a dead thing, it becomes, as with all dead sciences, simply a 'specialization of content'.

Visions and perceptions of our life seen, albeit dimly, have surpassed our wildest imaginations while confounding, at times, our most able scholars. These men search, they study, they become redundant with historical fact, dates, and actions mimicked by those before them. The living organism of the race-culture defies their assaults, precisely because they fail to acknowledge the very nature of organic life: *a root, a purpose, a people*. Moreover, to *what* do we owe the living reminder of the past – to the monuments, the living literary achievements, the art? This, all this, was left to us by a People. Our People! To the Fathers and Mothers who created us, we, you and I, are but their extension; we represent their lives, their presence, *in our own destiny*. In the coming and going, each of us tell of that small, yet significant story; the seed for *our* children. This people have their manifestations of God, of Life, of Religion, and a definite vision of the world – it is our distinctive *volksgeist* – that was made manifest by, and for the race-culture. This was *their* creation. It was intended, as a matter of course, to be seen and utilized by their children, their Posterity; it was to *prepare* and *perpetuate* their kind in a progressive setting – both in the present and the future. It was to carry on the life cycle of the *Original birth*. This, a living history that will outlast time itself. The visions of our ancient life survive as history to us – it is the continuation of the present presence of our past. Only through an understanding of Life, and its organic application, can history have any true significance to us who, at this moment, are but the living history of our tomorrow.

With the Rise of the West, we *acknowledge* our history – no longer afraid, guilty, or misguided as to its past, present, or its future. We have left the Modern, we, the Sons and Daughters of our gods have realized the ancient symbols of our present, and see it as our gift, our legacy, and our salvation. The symbolic metaphor of birth, of creation, of Life itself – our Life – will be that which we are to pass on, that extension of ourselves. Our future, truly, and irrevocably, depends upon *blood* and *soil* – not concrete and glass. It depends, and will ever depend, upon understanding *who* we are, and to that *essence* of nobility, which makes us more than what is termed, common; it obliges us to *obey* duty and honor. The opposite, that of the Modern's understanding, is the 'value' of words for their own sake, and that of the lie of equality, not under the law, but in the natural, harmonious, legitimate 'diversity' which does, truly, exist in nature, much to the disappointment of the Modern.

The greatest achievement, as seen by many, of this Western Culture, has been the never-ending search for *truth*. Not by the various forms of governments, or rulers, wherever they may be, but by those peculiar and special individuals that form the essence of the entire race-culture. It is to these few, to the men and women of vision, that we owe the Laurel Wreath of victory. Yet, for these same 'moderns', the continuous thread of the life-blood of this culture has been diminished, for they acknowledge not the 'spirit' nor the soul, of those who are born with that essence which makes them stand above the rest. They see but will not believe. They refuse to acknowledge the driving, sometimes brutal force used to make all this a reality. They seek to change it, to mold it for the mediocre – as if the mediocre could ever hope to hold it! The West, however, has risen without him.

The Rise of the West is a living certainty. You, dear reader, are a part of it. Whatever the part, play it well. Destiny serves no master – *it is mastery*. Each one is a part of the total. From the Halls of the past, you are, still, the greatest of monuments: *you* are the living history of the greatest age to be seen since the dawn of man. Too you, belong the questions. Too you, belong the answers. The Rise of the West depends on you; do not fail in your attempts to create.

i.

The Birth:

Which Way, Western Man?

Which way, Western man?

This, above all other considerations of the Western race-culture is the *greatest* of imperatives. How many before us have asked this question: *Just where, are we going? Who, is to take us there? Is [present day] 'democracy' and [present day] 'equality' the way-signs of a society that is bound to succeed? Is the 'quality' of our species worth the effort? What 'method' or 'form' shall we endeavor to emulate, or create for that matter, to enable us to achieve nobility of character?*

In the coming century, what is to be our *goal* as a nation – or as a distinct people – which will mark the change in our spiritual values? As a society, America in particular, are we willing to 'give up' certain rights, natural and inalienable, for the benefit of a new 'world order' that has never asked, nor in fact, consulted the mass, not as mob, but as race-culture, to voluntarily submit to a separation from the traditional bonds of 'federal' union – to accept the balkanization of the various ethnic 'blocs', so as to facilitate the independent and sovereign 'destiny-will' of each and every group? Western man sees…but will he be heard?

Which way, then, goest thou, Western man?

If we accept, from the first, that a rising West is a *spiritual manifestation*, not to be confused with a 'religious' one, and that this spiritual awareness manifests itself in various ways then, all of us, share in the burden to answer the above [and more!] questions. This defies the Modern who, in his search for rationalism has relegated all individual spirituality to the excesses of a by-gone era; indeed, this must be the case, for in all birthing, the consciousness of a primitive soul is like a fire. Once the consciousness envelopes the new idea of its actualizations, it will hold on to it, like a vise, unvarying in it perception of its future, sure in its value of the present. The flame of its birth marks, forever, its passion. The passion, however, of a new order, must be tempered with the reality of the present presence as well as those of the past. We know we are all heading in some direction – whether it is up or down, sideways, or long-ways remains to be seen. It could, without end, go on indefinitely, unstructured by any human hand, or it can be *actualized*, by direct interdiction of those who *see* this future; these people may presently be in power, or they may be those that have yet to attain power. Who, then, should we believe in, or support? Do we support those who 'presently' speak for us, to those that have power *over* us? Do we, as people of the West, demand a change; a changing of the guard? If we do, if this feeling is to manifest itself in a positive and constructive way, *who* would be best suited for this life mission?

Yes, the birth of the West is a spiritual one, but not for long. Its substance will continually gain physical shape. It will attempt to channel into its 'declarations' those philosophies, which best reflect *its* mood, character, and desires. These declarations may take on the trappings of religion, philosophy, or of politics. The judicial applications of the Modern will reflect the continual discontent that is becoming more apparent between the factions of the Nationalist/Separatist. The momentum of 'great' politics will continue. Democracy, as we have traditionally known it, will flounder; the pinnacle of leadership – the Dictator – will emerge. Thus has the cycle begun.

The Religion of the West, namely, Christianity, will fail in its attempt to reorganize its status – this is not to say that the tenets of this philosophy will disappear, but the manner in which it proceeds will be of a novel nature. No longer will the aspects of 'universalism' be sacrosanct to the *mass*; no longer will the vision of the 'tomorrow' be for the others – it will ever be for one's kind; for one's people. This feeling will not be limited to the West; it will, and has already started, to cover the entire planet with a, seemingly, justifiable antipathy for the 'outsider', for the *alien*. There will not, nor ever has been, peace on earth. Peace will never come until the West, and every other nation recognizes the inherent difference in each other (this includes the tribal divisions of the West itself); when this happens, there will be a calming effect, an economic burst of energy dependent upon the entire restructuring of cultural groups, based upon the realization that they must either compete on an international level, or withdraw from any type of United Nations idea, and work on a more *regional* basis, solving the problems of *their* territories, on the same extended regional basis of natural law. The West, having its own particular problems, must concentrate on these, not on the passions, and legitimate problems experienced by non-Western elements. Trade, from an 'international' point of view, may be restricted initially but, with time, will level out, entering the common market based on real substantive concerns.

The West, as a distinct race-culture, cannot rule the world [this does not mean that, militarily, we could not, for a while, control it, but in the end, it would, as it has done before, *destroy* the party responsible for the effort]. The Modern, of course, thinks he *can* – and worse, *he thinks he should*. Indeed, he feels that it is with his ingenuity that the world demands a 'one world order'. Nothing could be further from the truth. The ingenuity of the West is in its ability to *learn* from these innate gifts, and benefit from these accomplishments, based solely on just what is *natural* for them – the non-Western elements may be forever weakened by the absorption of these Western technics; if the Modern cares at all, *where* is his compassion? This has always been the legacy of the Modern. Babylon is always his capitol. The mob is his ideal, but not his ward. They must fend for themselves

The West, in its infancy, will be nothing but *great* politics: Dictatorship.

The illusion has always been that we [in America] have been democratic, but we most assuredly have not. The major forces of the

West, Europe and America, have always utilized the ruler ship of the elite – whether that elite be Economics [Plutocracy], Aristocracy [rule by a blood-right], Oligarchy [rule by the few], or Industry. It will remain ever so. The great stratum of the mass is needed but, only, as seen by the Modern, to fill the rank and file of the mediocre; the *bottom* of the great pyramid. This, of course, is natural – but the Modern has twisted it, subverted its very principle of organic necessity. The mass, under the tutelage of the Modern, has turned *into* mob, into the *unthinking*. This has brought the inevitable Dictator. This will be the *actualization* of the rising West. Whether this be good or ill is not at issue here; what the point of interests here is, is that this will *begin* the evolution of a new order – one the present generation, and this writer, views with some suspicion *and* anticipation. It will force all to choose a side; and not all decisions will be done with quiet contemplation and discrete analysis. It will come as Storm, and who, amongst us, can hold the lightning?

To many, this whole concept may seem an evil. Dictatorship has always left a foul taste in the mouths of all that have not come under the ruling parties ideal of the world. However, it should not be seen as the *end* of the world (in terms of cycles). The direction of one man, or one Party for that matter takes, is not always to the detriment of a people or a nation; of course, the converse is true. If the individual or [individual] party is not directed upon the course that would set the natural boundaries on civil matters, ethical matters, and the like, then the West is in for big trouble. If the latter is the case, then the mass, for this usually is the case, will choose to confront evil – for it is the 'welfare' of a people to which the good must be relegated. By such confrontation, the race-culture will, for the first time, achieve the status of Nietzsche's *Superman* – that is, they will be going *beyond* 'good and evil', by the sheer fact that their decisions have *created* right in the only way they perceive it: *that which promotes their survival is good; that which denies that survival is bad*. A simple, yet logical conclusion.

This *new* West is not for the poor, downtrodden, or the helpless. It is for the superman, the overcomer. It is for the overcomers, the strong, and the willing. It is for an army of one, as well as an army of *believers*. It is for those men and women who are not afraid of the lightning – these individuals will grasp it, hold it; they will mold it to their desires for their children. Let us, then, seek to understand the *spirit* of the 'superman' to fully understand this concept coined by Nietzsche himself:

> Ye lonesome ones of today,
>
> Ye seceding ones, you shall
>
> One day be a *people*: out of
>
> You who have chosen your-
>
> Selves, shall a chosen people
>
> Arise – and out of it,
>
> The Superman[43] [emph. added]

And more: [The Superman is]:

> The Roman Caesar with the Soul
>
> Of Christ.

This, then, is the actualization of the Western future. It is the embodiment of the power of the earth; it is the spiritual embodiment of the consciousness – the qualities of compassion, love, respect, and the inner understanding of nature, and her eternal laws. Both must be balanced, working in unison with one another. It must work for *itself*,

---

[43] For more information on this study see Nietzsche in toto; also see: Superman – chapter III in P.D. Ouspensky: A New Model of the Universe, Knopf, 1934.

before it can work for others. There will be no 'band of brothers' who is not of your kind. This will be the rule of survival. The earth will be harnessed for the continuation of the race-culture – but only in those quantities that will assure the survival of both. Nature will not long endure the rape that is presently taking place across the planet. The infant West will always acknowledge this, and divine those methods, which will be in accord with nature's laws.

It would be a mistake to assume that all men will become that which can, of and by themselves, overcomers of 'good and evil'; this has always been man's *pathway* to perfection. There will always be those who will rule – either by right or might – and those that will follow.

Those that will rule in a risen West will rule by virtue of their productive worth – that is, those who have established a natural order through those means best suited to the race-culture. The mass, those that are ruled, are ruled by their knowledge and consent. They will both be distant, apart, and distinct; this is natural law. Unlike the Modern's conception of law, this relationship will be based upon mutual respect, both parties articulating the same form and function – like the natural involuntary respect the 'eyes' have for the 'hand'. Like the 'brain' has for the 'feet'. What good would one be without the other?

It would be a mistake to assume that *all* men are equal. This will enrage the Modern who, while talking of compassion and equality under the law has lied, cheated, and manipulated the mass to believe this, while he, the father of lies, does everything in his power to do the opposite. He takes away their liberties under the *pretense* that law and order must be maintained – when in actuality, he simply insures that his power is secured for all time. He knows that there is no such thing as equality. There never has been, excepting, perhaps, the *enforced dictatorial control over peoples so as to effect equality under an Iron Heel.*

The goal that a people set for it creates the avenues or means by which these goals are to be attained. This does not mean, then, that *equality* of mutual respect will not exist in the West, quite the contrary. But, to reach that point, where our culture must be in the next hundred years, will demand the rigors of discipline, self-denial, and eyes, level and straight, which will not deviate from the set goal of uplifting our people from the dregs of the Modern's technics. An *absolute* authority will *have* to be set up – just as the modern is setting up his Authority. The West, will have to cultivate the ideals of Christ, *and* Nietzsche, if it is to overthrow, and create a new world, out of the chaos of the Modern.

A new world must, of necessity, have its own unique foundation. So, also, with the rise of a *new* West. The demand by, and for this new West will be, first and foremost, homogeneity. The study of history and causality shows, conclusively, that all great nations, cultures, and 'states', have been of one 'greater' people, that is, the majority of people confined to, and by a State, is one connected people, both genetically and culturally; *these have lasted longest*, produced the greatest religions, the greatest scientific discoveries, and the longest lasting racial memories (this includes the mores, religious and economic histories, which have aided in the *extension* of that people). We are not talking here of that 'pure race', on the contrary, we are talking about the generations long task of *making a people*. This can be done in several ways:

1. Isolation of the host race-culture; segregation.

2. Inbreeding – that is, of closely related peoples *within* that people.

3. *The constant application of values and traditions for the longest periods of   time.*

This will, as has been seen many times in history, mold a group into a relatively 'pure' *people* – lacking in all the negative implications in today's environment. This, and only this, is the basis, the foundation of a healthy and vibrant People.

The above analysis of race-culture in its purest sense can be examined closely in the race-civilization of Egypt or Mesopotamia – both shut in by great deserts and the sea; Rome and Greece by its peninsulas. Japan, Britain, Crete having their Islands. Where nature herself was not conducive to this isolation, man designed massive walls to surround him; the Chinese became the ultimate isolationists, and now are seen as the strongest, and purest, race-culture extant. The West, even now, feels its shadow pass overhead, unheard, but by a few.

Open borders, as we have been instructed to see them today, open to any alien presence and beliefs, were abhorrent to the vital, living cultures, those that have made any significant headway in the morass of human history. The Egyptian who, as we know, had already been through a thousand years of evolution – the First Dynasty being the most imperative, recognizing and practicing the 'original' intent of the people who created the essence of the Egyptian civilization – and whose 'world monument', the Pyramids, were the canvas by which they would continue to apply their faith in the future. Thebes and Karnack were relatively insignificant compared to these in a strictly material sense, and all the while, maintaining their unique racial imperative. The Hebrews, as well, having acquired Jerusalem, with its technics, history, and population intact, developed an otherwise strong, almost fanatical belief in *their* people, *their* god, and *their* will-to-live. The Hebrews brooked no mixture of their Blood outside their own kind. The ancient, and modern denizens of the Middle East, even to this very day, look at any concept of Universalism as a detriment, a pariah, and an act of national suicide. Only the West continues to believe in its own death.

History goes on to show, in many cases, that once the feeling of aloofness becomes diluted, intermarriage between outsiders necessitates an increase, never a decrease in actual participation, and this fosters the eventual destruction of the host culture. The acceptance of out-crossing of divergent racial couplings, such as seen in the extreme examples of the Black and White races, is followed by higher crime, debasement of moral considerations, and the ultimate betrayal of the essence of the original founders, whose idea it belongs, and their posterity, which the present culture was based upon. If this moral trespass occurs, then it is death to that people. The Culture, whoever that culture was created by, always declines; it never rises. No amount of skepticism by the Modern or his minions will wash this away. This is both anecdotal, and historical fact.

Cultural diversity does *not* promote solidarity. Every branch on the tree is continuously fighting for supremacy; each demands the sunlight necessary for its survival. Survival, of each and every organism, will demand this struggle. You cannot legislate the mechanism of survival – one can only crush or control this mechanism.

The Birth of the West will bring *racial solidarity.*

The Family will follow this birth. For long years now, the Family has been under attack by the Modern. Through social programmes, propaganda, and movements, which foster 'anti-family' agendas, it has fallen by the wayside. Family, however, is older than all our previous experiments with government and its associated technics, including Religion. The Indo-European, the Western man, has always proved this to be the case. We have said much concerning the genius, the individual leader – but before him/them, as well as after him/them is the Family. The West, feeling adrift in an ocean of uncertainty will go back to the basics of life and its origin: the Family.

The Birth of the West will bring back Family *unity* as the *basis for a sound society.*

This basis will also bring back another basic: it will bring back the natural understanding of a People to its relationship between itself *and* the earth. That greater understanding of a more *personal* interaction with the elements that surround us. Families will, once again, be rooted to the earth. The Modern and his technocrats laugh at this, but there is more: Homesteads, instead of pigeon-holed apartments in smoggy, dirty cities will become the way sign of a new West. On this point, there is no room for compromise: A man must have a place, not just a living 'quarter', which provides him shelter from the elements, but a living space which will *support* him, and his family, as well as those of his blood that will come *after* him. Every individual needs an area, a Farm, Homestead, whatever one wishes to call it, where he is able to follow his predilection in his chosen area of work, which he has chosen (or which has *chosen* him) to support his family. Even farther, and more removed from the Modern is the fact that this man may support his family indefinitely, subsisting on the land itself (this, of course, will be fought by the Modern; he will claim that we cannot go back to an agri-based system – what he really fears is the loss of 'slave labor', which he has become so enamored with). If, for one reason or another, an individual chooses to sell either his labor or his goods for extra capital, that is his right; but, if he does not *choose* to sell his labor or his goods, he remains independent, neither sharing his goods with the state, nor deriving any benefit form the state other than his basic *citizenship*. This Homestead, or farm, will never leave the family; it will be a *perpetual* holding of the family – unless, for some financial reason or obligation, must resort to the sale of only a portion of the property – which would, then, *guarantee* that at least some portion of that property would always remain, even with a poorly constituted individual, and give the *next generation*, his children, a chance to repurchase the property. Man must, at all cost, *remain* a part of his earth; he must not be *forced* to pay a fee for this right, year after year, to a state or government or its bureaucracy which, in many and acute cases, *speaks for him not at all*, and of most import, was won *for* him, by *right of conquest*, to secure an environment most beneficial for their descendants.

This Homestead, or simple *living space* provides, in varying degrees, a fortress against that oft times tempestuous world, the uncertain future of economic determinism, and the like, by which he can call himself master. He may not be as great as the next man, for such is the inequality of man, but he will be great in the eyes of his family, those that love him, those which comprise his daily aid and support in that struggle to live. This will create a new generation of individuals who, looking the world in the eyes will, at every turn, meet the hazards and gratifications inherent in life; he will face success or failure as have all who have come before him, honestly, and with courage. He will be known by his strength of character in the face of adversity, and by the way he *accepts* his role in relation to the earth and its elements.

Some may say, and by now, have quite possibly said, that this is a picture of a non-reality; of some ancient dreamer. Some will even question the political reality of a man, indeed, an entire nation dedicated to this lifestyle. Well, all that can be offered in this regards is this: A populace which is busy, happy, and productive will, of necessity, bring the same stability to its political state. Not by the many and numerous voting rights, what does *that* prove (?), and now, even as you, the reader, read these words, what *good* has it really done? Only in the very real sense of a National Plebiscite, on issues pertaining to issues of War, Foreign Policy, and issues relating specifically to the Nation as a whole, does any voting 'rights' really amount in any telling force. The government will still function; its measures of control still granted by popular consent, and the day-to-day operation of central authority will still maintain its momentum in relation to the race-culture.

On a larger, and much more long-term view, the landscape, literally, of the American West will, of necessity, be changed from a 'city' central idea, to that of the village, town, county, and [regional] State. All decisions made, affecting the most basic needs, will be made by those residing in that particular local area [or State]. The central government of the new West will not invade the natural balance of *order* or *law* within the confines of these communities, town, or villages. This central government *will enforce no law* that has not first been legislated by the *local* governments. This, along with the Homestead, will bring the *original concept* of freedom as envisioned by our Fathers of old.

All of this is related to the *solidarity* of family life. With Industrialization, and its 'machine' pace, the family unit, the family *organism*, has been diffused. No longer is man dependent, today, upon himself and his neighbor but, rather, upon the 'corporation', the 'empires' of control and finance – by which, *all* must depend upon for their daily bread. Individuals, and groups, seem incapable of stability – families move, willy nilly, from place to place without thought of *root*, or *stock*. A nation of nomads we have become, not knowing where to go, or just *why* we are moving! I will say again, if it be a thousand times, that no culture or civilization can be greater than its oldest institutions. The Modern, who rejects this opinion, and casts his ballots with all that *is* modern, I say that he will follow his path, continuously, until he dies from the stink of it, and *we too*, if we but follow. The new West however, has already chosen its path.

The men and women of the West have already seen, albeit dimly, that society is a man-made, passing institution – man was not made for society, but that *man* made society. Any structure, or form by which man must live under must first and foremost be in his best, and deepest rooted interests. It must be consonant with his deepest emotional ties. Personality, being the collection of 'emotions', is established with the aid of *a society* – it promotes either healthy or unhealthy responses to life and the conditions that surround it. What has the Modern offered us? The daily mass centralization of factory work, the faceless, nameless activities of the corporate empire, working for someone you have never seen, nor reaching a goal you will never know. Is not the greatest catastrophe ever to occur to a people, that of the nameless, faceless, inanimate machines, or individuals, which have *supplanted* the individual person as a being worthy of independence and worth? Yes, it is.

We have been robbed. Our personality has been taken from us. But, to restructure what we have lost is to demolish the existing and growing control of the Modern's school, factory, and office, rejecting, at least in principle, the entire 'plan' of the Modern's technologicalization of our culture. It is the change in conception of human progress that the new West addresses. It is a vision of becoming, not of stagnation. At any rate, can we expect to continue the *rate of expansion* as we have done in the past? Are 'fast-track' solutions best suited to our best needs and desires? What does the Modern offer besides this? Our Industrial base will never be the same again – and perhaps this is a good thing – as long as we are still able to manufacture those elements necessary to protect this nation, and provide the mechanization necessary for the survival of our working class. Let us be realistic, if corporate America would seek to 'increase' the industrial base, *for what purpose*, would it be resurrected? Let us design our future now, while we still have a chance. Perhaps, in the near or far away future, we will quantum leap in some science that will put millions to work, at least for some 'seeable' goal, for the good of the culture, but what then? It is a matter of timing.

The Birth of the West will bring national order based on the *independence* of its smallest units.

The new West will also hold 'equality' on a different level of understanding. The Modern has held, in fact still holds, to the 'fact' that all men are born with the same potentialities from birth – this is the Modern's revolutionary outlook; it is the attitude of the 'Christian' as well, at least the Christian of the modern 'churchianity' persuasion. These 'types' *want* to believe, in fact, *must* believe, that all men are equal; this is from the same assumption that all are born equal. This, of course, flies in the face of historical and scientific evidence. The 'religious' implication of the equality of man is a *need*, a *faith*, which may, indeed, transcend all other motives. With the exception of redemption, as a faith, the *belief* in 'equality' is at the very heart of their worldwide revolution. It seems as though these modern worshipers of equality purposely achieve a great leveling so as to *bring themselves up* – the cry of equality does nothing but demand that any superior person or group step down; thus, *are we all equal!*

The Modern 'cries out in the name of *love*' for all to become believers in his new faith – the doctrine of the true mob. His religion, upholding love above all else, relegates their 'god' to the leveling of an understanding that they *themselves* share. It is a *god in their image* – love conquers all, even reality. It is not an overstatement to say, that in this context, that to the many Christian advocates of equality, *the belief* in human equality, is more essential to their peace of mind, to their value in living, than the idea of 'god' himself! Rather than give up this belief in equality, they would *give up 'god' himself!* The superiority that comes from the co-religionists of the modern Christian is so essential, so sublime in nature, that it must be had; it must be demonstrated even if it flies in the face of fact and the human condition.

The contention of the Modern is that he must disparage *heredity* in favor of environment. The controversy centering on this duality has come only from the camp of the Modern and his followers. Physical and Social Anthropology have been made to fight one another, two aspects of the same science, competing for dominance, not in the healthy arena of scientific study and debate, but in the unhealthy arena of the political muckraker, the political theorist; to Propaganda. To Franz Boas, and his ilk, belongs the modern establishment of equality. Not simply to one man, but to an agenda of certain men dedicated to promoting this value, contrary to nature as it is, so as to level the entire Western value in the process. The new West spits in their face!

The new West demands that *quality*, not equality, be the rule by which all are gauged. Attention, would, of necessity, be paid to those who show, or will show [eugenics] the *highest promise of quality*. This, as stated before, must start with the family, and individual perception of worth. Opportunity would not, then, be given to anybody that asserted it as their 'democratic' right, but to those that show, in the here and now, that they are capable of using it. The present day 'scholastic system' does the exact opposite. Instead of promoting the intelligent, vigorous, and gifted student, the mediocre, un-gifted, and lazy are afforded the same [equal] attention as the former – this taps the energy expended by individual Teachers, dilutes it, and denies the individuals that will, and must needs be utilized for the betterment of the nation. Even in a homogeneous environment, this must be practiced. No one would, of course, relegate the average student to a life of ridicule and atrophy. These, in turn, would be promoted as their merits warrant – opportunity would be available to all, but opportunity based upon the general need. Does not even the evangel, Jesus, have this to say: "To him that hath, shall be given." This is the opportunity of merit: Let a young person ever prove that he has increased in mental and spiritual vigor before he is given any more merit than he deserves. Through the *test*, comes the *prize*.

The *product* of such a being, such a student, will be a man or woman with self-reliance, self-discipline, and courage to be different from the crowd. Independent, he will strive for those things that are beyond him, for those things that are attainable only through his vision – for the *betterment* of his people and nation. For those men and women who do not achieve that highest of levels, it is of no consequence, knowing as they must, that still, in every eventuality, that they hold a place of their own, being *worthy* to hold it, and doing the very best they can with what they have. Whether one has five talents, or only one, he must do with it/them as best he can. This agenda, as are all programmes of this type, defines the ability of the top to the bottom, from the last man to the first, and energizes them all [this is real equality!] with a feeling for destiny, of worth, and of value. *A noble nation is made up of noble individuals*. Whether one is a menial worker or a governmental leader – both are, and will always dedicate themselves to the greater good and fulfillment of their race-culture. Both will be held accountable.

The Birth of the new West will bring Leadership.

History has shown that the 'equalitarian' denial of strong, indeed, any leadership, the need of leadership, is sheer folly – the Modern loves his parliamentarian fiasco, his round-about way of delving into the realm of decision making, his lack of any real, spontaneous, or significant decision makers. Without leadership, real leadership, a nation will, and must of necessity, fall into chaos, and disintegration. This leadership must be well endowed, a class by itself; it must ever seek to follow the best path available for the security, and protection of its people. It must protect the weak against the strong [this is law], it must assure the orderly and judicial running of the judicial system; it must ensure that mass means of information be safe-guarded so as to protect the race-culture from those culture distorters, those that ever seek to debauch the sanctity of existing traditions, mores, and spiritual essence of the populace. This leadership must ever seek to protect the soil, the air, and the water of the environment. Above all, it shall ensure that the quality of our genes, of our future stock, be protected at all costs. This, it will hold sacred – *no* law, will be higher than this.

This leadership, in particular, shall protect the race-culture from the greatest element of destruction yet – that of the power of money.

Harmless as 'currency' is, the element of greed and power will always beckon those of small minds, those that see only the elements of power and control. This power of money is not necessarily simply those of uncommon wealth, but the simple power to circumvent those legislative actions that are, or were formed, for the betterment and extension, of the race-culture. When this happens, and it always does, the will, direction, and purpose of a people are destroyed.

World money, based on control of individual national wealth, destroys all national borders, destroys all sovereign popular government, and denies the independent will of any one or more race-cultures. Industrial nations, such as America, are controlled by systems of credit; the system of credit used today is vastly concentrated. All the present growth, or lack of same, is controlled by a handful of men — it doesn't matter *which* men this might comprise — who are directing this nation, as well as a majority of the world's nations, above and beyond that mandated by the individual peoples. Conversely, this handful of people could, just as well, lead a country into an era that is unparalleled in the history of man. Leadership is the key.

Supreme leadership is *never* held by the mass. They may, in certain political environments, control the outward manifestations of government, but it is to the few, or the one, who has the means, if not the will, to keep money, usury, and all the machinations of 'money', in check. It has, ever and anon, been such.

An example of such leadership may be seen in the way Louis XIV handled *his* money power, articulated in a man — Nicolas Fouquet — the nation's [France] Minister of Finance. This man, Fouquet, was chief of all the heads of credit, such as may be said of the House of Rothschild a century latter, or of Morgan, Rockefeller, or Warburg in this country. Louis, either honestly or dishonestly cut this powerful man off at the knees. Finding evidence that Fouquet was brazenly corrupt, and defrauding the people, the King had him arrested. A trial took three years, tolled heavy fines, and exiled Fouquet from the country. Louis, however, commuted the sentence — he gave him much more! Louis imprisoned Fouquet, knowing that if this man were allowed to continue this present contact with international finance, he would be back stronger than he was before. Fouquet, being imprisoned, spent nineteen years in an inaccessible fortress.

This example may seem cruel, in fact, was very cruel. It may seem despotic, and it is. However, to destroy such an animal as International Finance can become, Louis knew that he must behead the hydra – and this can only be done by a swift, and merciless death to the beast. King Phillip [the Fair] did the same to the Knights Templar. Whether one agrees with the life and times of Louis XIV, it could never have been done until, and unless, he had first *destroyed* the only power capable of standing in his way – money. America may well be beyond any recognizable point of redemption in this area, indeed, the world may be forever in its grip, but it is still the foundation of every true, and free nation to establish their own currency, based on their output and needs. No one may assume power until he has first obtained the power of money. Anyone who has obtained this power is King!

The Birth of a new West will bring *control* over finance.

As the new West begins to grow, its maturity will follow various forms that have gone before. First, it will establish itself through warfare. Second, it will begin to demonstrate that it seeks self-fulfillment in its workforce, its relation to its family life – between men and women; between marriage and children.

In the context of 'war', we do not mean, necessarily, the combat of arms, although, in the long run, at least to keep a People from relying too heavily upon material things, upon ease and luxury, war is positive. Indeed, War brings out, in some, the truly *heroic* individual, the chivalry of courage in the face of a foe, or the *compassion* of the victorious over the vanquished. We do not speak of the Modern and his 'view' of warfare, where women and children, undisciplined troops and ignoble dictators are slaughtered. The West will enter the fray like Frederick Barbarosa, Napoleon, Cromwell, and Mazzini – not herded *en mass* before the flags of money and idealism which, at best, show nothing after the fought battle, excepting the conquest of might *over* weakness. The soldiers of the West will go to war for a cause, enthusiastic in their personal desire to fight for their national interest – and that interest will be manifest at every turn – not for some ambiguous 'world power', or united front where no one but the behind-the-scene players knows just what is to be attained by this warfare, but what will benefit *themselves*, and their *posterity*.

The 'workforce' of the new West will be diffused, spread out over the entire area of the continent. Homesteads, Farms, and Cottage Industry will flourish among those of the West. It will not produce enormous amounts of surplus, it will not be able to support the present governmental life-style; it will not be able to support the 'world-order' as is presently envisioned. Yes, those who do not have the capacity to surmount their own environments will never attain the status of 'producer nations' in an artificial way, some will lose enormous amounts of population groups – but, after the initial pain, will, from there on, live within their means. Just as we, here in America must, and will do. In a reasonable fashion, our surplus material will be sold on the open market, just as Europe, Japan, England, and Russia will do with time. Just and honest investment between these nations should, and will be, fostered. Foreign exchange, however, should not become cumbersome to any one or more national states, that is, material will be exchanged only on an *as needed* basis. No flooding of the markets, with third world production, into our own, no exhausting control or limits to import/export commodities. The pace of the race-culture will be slowed, man will once again gain the ground he has lost to the pace of the machine – following *its* lead, rather that the other way around.

The Home, that center of political government, of production, and community ties will be reestablished. In an overworked industrial society, this institution has been pushed aside: no longer the center of vital Crafts and Arts – what is being produced in the 'home shop', on the 'workbench', is of diminishing importance, both economically and personally. Where the family was once centered, balanced, it is such that a man [and woman] must sell himself to a power over him, which has tended to mask him with that same faceless appearance as a million others. The woman, also, can no longer teach her children the beauty of handy-crafts that have been passed down for generations – leaving our children to marvel at 'minute rice' and other 'automated' trivia. The Home has given way to the disastrous imitation of *schools who try and take the place of Home* – giving them activities which, at home, were natural, but are cold and artificial in the setting of the Modern's 'daycare centers'. The old people who, in times past, used the remaining years of their lives in useful pursuits, limited though they may have been, at home, around the son or daughter, the grandchildren, giving meaning and substance to their remaining years. The new West demands this dignity for all members of the Home.

ii.

The Life

I recognize only two nations, the

Occident, and the Orient.

~Napoleon~

Cultural life, its organism, is the most outstanding aspect of the race-culture. The Age of Cultural Politics is the way sign of the West. Indeed, it marks the planet for centuries to come. America, like all white European nations are tied, womb like, to its European mother – the land where our ideas, our religions, our laws, and our economics have had their origins. Blood is stronger that any other factor – excepting, the Modern and his minions. The political thoughts of the coming age are one of absolute politics, of absolute power. Never mind the 'kinder and gentler nation', that is illusion. The center of vital interests will be finalized in a grand Pax Ameruropa, an alliance of those traditional interests, which have brought the Occident, as Napoleon envisioned it, into a working, functioning race-cultural *technic*.

This technic will perpetually be a source of struggle between the East and

West. Between the Occident, and the Orient. It will be a race-cultural imperative: Law, technics, and Social Organism, all will reflect the realities of great politics. Wars, either of an economic, or military nature [wars of *conquest*] will be fought purely between European and anti-European forces. It will be wars of *hegemony*, of power politics and social [i.e. cultural] dominance. Nothing has changed in a millennium, nature will carry on, the struggle between positive, and negative will enforce its will whether anyone likes it or not. The West is preparing for this conflict.

These Wars will be of long duration. They will not resemble the 'regional', or 'co-regional' wars of Europe of the past. These wars will be Absolute. Wars of *total* victory, or total death. No 'world order' can stop the inevitable – not even money can stop it – it may slow it apace, but it will never stop it. The 'codes' of war will change; indeed, we have begun to see this change already. The battlegrounds will be the same, but the tactics employed are revolutionary. Total commitment, total victory; prisoners of war, for all intents and purposes, unknown – death, the lack of compound space, and all the rest will bring a new view of 'international prisoner status' – fight us and you will die, surrender and you will live. There is no right or wrong – the enemies of the West exist – it will simply be.

All this, and more, will come from the unity of the West – its component parts will fit together, knowingly, or unknowingly, in a web of cultural vitalism unknown for millennia.

This, in all its entirety, is Culture. It is the swaying and moving of an organism. It can be seen in War – or in a Poem. It can be seen in an office building – or in a Church. It may be seen in Sculpture – or it may be seen in a rifle. These, and more, are the actualizations of the race-soul; the development is relative to the Age in which it finds its destiny – its Epoch. It is the essence of the present presence; it is a spiritual connection with the Soul.

The Modern has battered the soul of Western man. His technics of a crass, selfish, and brutish nature. When one thinks of a 'cultured' man, one does not think of the Modern. One would, on the other hand, think of nobility, of character, of courage, of something *above* the norm. The soul, present in this individual, is magnetic, charismatic, quick, and healthy. The Modern, an individual of small soul – that is, sightless, faceless – is limited to few horizons; he lives for himself because he can envision nothing greater. The Cultured man, the extraordinary man, puts the greater essence before him – even his own life. The West, in this *new* life, will be a 'cultured' process, learning from the past, but seeing nothing but the future. It will belong to Western man and woman, neither apologizing, nor recanting this realism. Thus, will they live their life honestly, bravely, surely, and *absolutely*.

In the absolute age of politics, it is natural that the best brains go into politics and war. War/Politics is absolutely the realm of heroism. Sacrifices done, in the service of Culture, are never in vain. War and Politics, after all, is always an expression of Culture – it can either be for the good of culture, or for its demise. The rationalist of the modern variety refuse to believe in Idea, he would think it foolish and stupid. Organic reality however, does not obey the force of rationalism, in its absolute sense, but rather, strives for the concept, the idea – leaving the rationalistic leveling of the mediocre. The noblest of all are the heroes; those that will *die* for an ideal – others, of course, will *live* for one. These, all of these, continue nobility, digest it, and pass into the *culture-bearing stratum*.

The stratum of 'culture-bearing' men feels the essence of their Age; they know it exists, even before it triumphs. They are often met with violent death, simply because they see before all can see – such are all great men. Their time is not yet, but soon all will follow, and call it natural.

And so we have it, Democracy stands *opposed* to Authority. One will ascend, while the other descends. What the West will, ultimately, choose, remains to be seen. The new West will, however, choose *value* over that of mob rule; it will embrace Culture over technics; it will love nature, and hate the unnatural. It will recognize the various way signs and follow, come what may. The new West will over come the Modern, the decadent, and realize his destiny. His rising will be as an earthquake. It will shake the foundations of the world. The new West will embrace the sons and daughters of his past; the sons and daughters of the present. Soon, after the old has passed away, the children of the future will rejoice in the knowledge that this new West is their own, that they owe no one but their sires. Proudly, they will enter a new epoch, a new sunrise, golden with opportunity and reward – all the sacrifice a necessary element in their maturation.

The stratum of Culture increases with the increase of population so, also, its opposite. Quality versus quantity is ever the way sign of Life or Death. The life of the West depends upon this understanding, even unto its tenth generation. Western man must ever believe this, or ever succumb to the morass of the Modern; for he loves the unclear, the mediocre, the small; he hates the noble, the courageous, the unselfish, the independent, the superior; he hates the authority which would confine him – yet, expects all to obey his lead, his commands. The Culture-bearing he hates. He is always envious. This, all this and more, the Modern would tear down, and if allowed, will continue to do the same as he has been. The new West, will never allow this.

The new West *is* Culture. It is culture *over* that of civilization, for the former is the real manifestation of a People. The People, in turn, must actualize themselves in their leader – whichever *form* of Authority this takes. The life of the culture must balance itself between the authority of the leader and the led. The West must find its own rationalism, its own essence of reality.

The Life of the West will never die. It will never die as long as its blood remains intact. In its continuing evolution, its technics will change, its organism of culture bending its way to form new life-cycles, new horizons. For the present, and for the foreseeable future, it will live a full life, heavy with the burden of struggle and sacrifice. Old orders may die swiftly, or they may die slowly, yet there will remain remnants of the past; even a past we wish to forget – this will take generations to finally put to rest. The future, however, belongs to the rising West. The warmth of its shinning rays may already be felt, enriching the plant-like urge of the growing organism. It is *our* Future. It is *our* Destiny. *It is our West.*

Frank L. DeSilva

Afterword:

An Appraisal

The foregoing work was done in the Hope that, the men and women of the West, would see, as I see, the need and vision for the future, which is so imperative today. The *continuation* and *extension* of everything we hold dear, everything our Fathers and Mothers held dear, depends on us, you and I. The spirit, which animates us, today, is but a flicker of that soul, which came before; we have a *duty* to reanimate what was vital and imperative to those who have gone before. What we do after that is strictly a path, which we will walk, for better or worse, to fulfill that destiny, which has been given us. That destiny is ours *alone*; it is a *spirit*, which only those of the West, will understand.

Spirituality, however, is a personal thing. The rising West however, is not only for the individual; it is for the Race, and its Culture-bearing stratum. Like the 'world order' of today, the new West will sweep away all foreign matter, which has attached itself upon the body politic; it will be a cleansing. It will not, and cannot be, Universal. The lies of the Modern will fade, slowly, and then more rapidly, until he is replaced with a new dogma, a new hope. The several factors involved in the rising West will become plain, to those of the West, it is self-evident: The West will recognize its genetic heritage, predisposed and naturally occurring in the host of the West. What we gain thereby, however, will more than likely be shared, or at least offered, with the various nations of the world [this will be the remnant of recent past, of the Modern], but it will be rejected. It is not part of their soul. It will, with time, become an alien thing, unsuited to those not of the West. This, of course, is natural, and will be understood by those who follow Nature's law.

What or Who, then, should the West follow. Should we follow Hammurabi, Moses, Jesus, or the Philosophers? Should the traditions of our northern Folk, the Eddas, be followed? Should the spirituality of the West be confined to any one Institution? Can we, in any event, reshape the technics of the past? What imperative should we, as a People, follow? Should our value be 'of this world'? On the other hand, should we transcend the earthly and nestle, childlike, in the realms of 'heaven' and the 'world to come'? After all, as has been said, 'where a man's heart is, there also, is his *vision*, his *value*, his *importance*'. This, then, the spirit of Western man. This spirit, the *power* behind all great cultures, has also seen its greatest Religions.

Good and Evil are symptomatic of every Religion, of every Culture. Hence, the question: What *is* good for our People? What *is* evil for our People? For some individuals, the search is for something outside 'christianity' – that substance, which embodied the original teachings of that first evangel, Jesus, and not simply the *de facto* relationship of the modern religious technic of the 'church' is their prime motive – still they search. If we seek a foundation by which to reaffirm our spiritual direction, our spirituality, what, then, do we replace it with? Can we, you and I, *overcome* ourselves? Can we, you and I, create our own 'good' and 'evil'? This, of course, would be the great doing as Nietzsche put it. Do you believe, are you able to *envision* this actualization? This is the question: Are you willing to try? Let us, then, *resist the evil*, and *embrace the good*. Thus, to our rising.

The Rise of the West will have its many champions; it will have its many casualties. It can count many to date. However, not all can become the flaming stars of Martyrs, Heroes, and overcomers. Those, and there will be many, who feel drawn to this destiny, should follow it; those who know, deep in their heart of hearts should, likewise, be content as participants in the great technics of the mass – not the unthinking mob – but realizing the fact that they are driven by those motives of courage, selflessness, and desire, utilizing these different functions to achieve the same ends. This will be the greater stratum; for we cannot *all* can be a flaming star. Let us, then, become as an ember, glowing warmly; not bright to the eyes, but *hot to the touch*, a thing which *smolders*, a thing, which even the giants are afraid to touch.

Such an *element* must we be. To be sure, we may be moved from time to time, from place to place by opposing elements seeking, as it were, a safe place for which the heat may dissipate. The opposition, these so-called giants, must be careful however, for one misstep, one careless fall, will cause the rushing wind to ignite us, bursting forth in all the splendor of a consuming fire. But is it only the fire, which brings such deep dread in the hearts of the Modern? Or do the opposing elements recognize something larger, more primitive, as the harbinger of the Storm? Aye! Even more!!

Like all prairie fires, it seems that nature herself, always, is prepared to eliminate waste, thereby causing a rejuvenation of her elements. Yet, as is the way of nature, it is inevitable that a rescuer will appear, a greater presence than the fire itself. So the giant knows. As with fire, our passions will be inflamed, it is like a consummation; the clouds gather. We can all see it. We all await its power and presence. The Thunder extols the strength and purpose of the storm. Yet, it is not the storm, which will save us; nor is it what the giant fears. It is, and ever has been, the Lightning! The very presence of the gods – of God!! It changes the face of everything. No longer are we mere rivals for the hottest spot in the flame of ignited passion, no longer does the Giant attempt to extinguish the flame. The lightning illuminates, it crashes with vitality and purpose. Those who are of the Lightning rejoice; those that are not of the Lightning fear, and reject it.

Out of this fire, this *passion*, will arise a purpose, a Will, which will match the Lightning. It will go 'beyond' all that has gone before. It will be at one with the Universe; and will recognize its part in the '*passion play*' that is Nature. It will be 'high noon', and *all* will see. This Will, this leader, will be a friend of Western man. He will utterly destroy the giant – that modern assortment of sycophants, dreamers of control, and those who hate, utterly, the strong, courageous, and superior elements which guarantee the future; yet the Modern will be dashed to earth by this Will; his crash to earth will put out the fire, but *not the purpose*. Those of the West will always share that purpose, as long as there is air, fire, water, and earth. We will cross over with he, who, carrying the Lightning in his right hand, while in his left he carries the Hope of a People yet to be.

The Rise of the West is now complete. Look! Can you not see…there…through the mountaintops, ancient and familiar, the first rays of the Sun…it has risen, warming the cold valleys and souls of the West?

****
*

The way sign of the West is not its Money, its massive buildings, and its warships. It is Race, and again Race – those hidden elements of nature – what our children *will be*, what *we are*. It is everlasting, as long as we protect it, nurture it. It will grow as we grow, or die as we die. The creative power of the Universe has given us a special place in the eternal cycle and rhythm of our People; but like any talent or gift, we must utilize it, make it more that what it was in its original state. *We, all of us, are the caretakers of our own blood, our own Future.* Woe to those who squander it, who pollute it, who leave the seed of the gods to wash away in the streams of the alien. A curse be on our children, and our children's children if we do. This I see, this I believe. Those who are called will hear this voice, whispering, calling incessantly to each child of the West. To you, the overcomers, belongs the entirety of the West. It lives in you, through you, and no other. May you live long, and continue, Western Man!

Which Way then, goest thou, Western Man?

Author's Addendum
(December 2005)

One cannot be sure of anything.

But life, itself, is not that *insincere*, for it leaves many telltale signs of its passing, if one but just considers the way signs, which surround him. In doing so, one may rightly adduce what the future will hold. As you, the reader, consider what has been put to paper in the preceding work, it is felt that this addendum be included, both as a way to correct anything which has been inadvertently left out, or which can be added to by the normal increase in current information. This will include 'new' material sources, or additions to sources or information which, when this work was first envisioned and outlined, was unavailable to the Author while in the collective control of the federal government. The sincerity of this work, and the truth it wishes to impart to those souls who seek to find an 'answer' to questions which, for the most part, cannot be found in today's collective consciousness is freely given to those of my Folk, my blood, who search for truth. Insincerity becomes the thrashing ground for those intellectuals of the Modern who have, since this work was envisioned, continued to betray and hurt the sons and daughters of the West.

Since the inception of the Rise of the West, many, many circumstances and events have propelled us, Men and Women of the West, into currents of past, present, and future decisions, which will affect us for many years to come. And our Children.

The perceptive reader may have adduced that this work was written during a very tumultuous era of world history; and that, specifically, America, as another incarnation of what is termed Western Culture, and bears the weight of the modern 'world outlook' as regards the leadership role of this country as a major Super Power, and leadership through its ideals and media perceptions. America has been embroiled in altercations all across the planet; its 'police actions' are well documented and continue to this day. Politically, America is developing a *modus operandi*, which is, and has defined the foreign strategy of our nation for generations to come.

Those of us who are living this legacy, both for and against, have mobilized for the battle to come; for it is coming. The ranks of the Nationalist have formed and reformed. The dilettantes of the intellectual left have been reborn into the 'neo-cons' of today's Conservative. The nationalist of yesteryear finds himself secured by an alliance of the old 'democratic' parties who, like their predecessors, are concerned with *rights* and *privileges*. The irony is not lost on those who follow or practice technics, which seek to correct and maintain a future, which is sound, healthy, and continuous.

The scope of the Rise of the West is broad and will be continuing fodder for debate and structure. This small effort, like many before, both small and large, is simply the attempt to discard the inevitable, and replace it with substance, harmony, and beauty. I fear, however, that history, that hoary old mistress, will manifest itself in the same fashion, which our forefathers fought so hard to see that we never faced again. Human beings, being what they are, simple and trusting, will follow only those faces, which they deem 'normal', being seen on the nightly news, distant, and unassailable by mere mortals, will follow the path of least resistance; and this, the path of our destruction.

When we, you and I, look around and see the presence of our present existence, what do we feel – WHAT DO YOU FEEL? When we drive through our 'hometown', or that town to which we moved ten years or more ago, just *what* changes do we see? Have the small storefronts, nestled comfortably and securely look back at us unchanged, unbroken? The graffiti, which covers most of the banners and sidewalks belong, don't they, having been created from the 'essence' of others not quite like us?

Do we notice the elderly, those that we may have seen at church, the local restaurant, or grocery store, walking unafraid on our streets? Have we noticed their 'passing'? Is the complexion of the local fuel station attendants the same as when we moved here? Does one really listen to one's children when they speak of 'theories', of 'dogma', or racial 'incidents', which bombard them at school? Do they ask for our aid, or simply talk around us, because of the knowledge that 'we can't *do* anything'?

When was the last time we visited our parents in a 'retirement' village, instead of knocking on *their* door in our *own* house? When was the last time we spoke with a man or woman, wizened with age, and recounted with them the events of the past, and after hearing the picture painted by their words, wondered aloud "*why have things changed so much since then*?" Why is it that working-class whites of Western stock load their working trucks with men far different than ourselves? When we consider and, perhaps, wave good-by to our Sons and Daughters of War, bidding them safe return from lands inhospitable, dangerous, and deceptive, do we know, really KNOW why they go; and to that noble sense of *nobility*, to what *purpose*, here, now, and in the future, is this sacrifice requested?

What is the West?

We hear so much about it, being both a mantra by those who seek to encourage a 'point of view' or who wish for you, and I, to see an antagonist, an enemy, by which to conquer and destroy. We see denizens of the world pound the pulpit, who cry in their shrieking and pleading voices, their demands, that *they* are the West. The claims on the 'history' of the West are unbounded; we, you and I, owe everyone but, seemingly, ourselves. Is this fair? Is this right? And if we acquiesce to these claims and call it 'our idea', our morality, what is our future?

When we speak our platitudes of historical decency, honor, and morality; of chivalry, duty, folk/people, to what *end* do we plead this '*identity*'? Do we wipe the blood from our children's noses or plead with them to not get into another altercation over the 'past', what *once* was? When our children speak to their living grandparents, and ask what it was like, or 'what would you have done' and, after receiving their answer, the feeling of regret felt deep within your heart what, then, do you teach them about the West?

Is the West an Idea, which has lost its substance; or is it a living reality of what you are, what you *want* to be? What? You cannot be what you feel deep inside? You say that you are unable to '*be what you want to be*'! But the West *means* 'freedom' for all; so how can this feeling be, digging deeper and deeper into our soul, so pronounced, this feeling of helplessness? The leaders of the West are our people, chosen by god, are they not? Every breath they take is another influx of hope is it not – that is what we hear every evening – hope, after all, has been the life blood of our fathers for generations. If the West, as is posited in this work, is to survive then, you and I, all of us, must first, and foremost, create a vision of just 'what' the West is, today, and contrive this paradox to conform to just what we want it to *be*.

How do we accomplish this? Personally, I am not sure any more. There was a time, like many of us, that simply belonging to the party of the traditional thinkers, the Republican Party, was all that was necessary; Ronald Regan reinforced this for many of us. It was a good shot, the 'party'. Institutions, however, are larger then their proponents, or their followers. In any event, *both* parties offer the same thing; both are multi-culturalists, hoping to 'embrace' all-comers who, as was the message of the past, come here to be 'equal' under the law, under the Constitution. Both, in part, seek to maintain the *status quo*, to find the lowest common denominator, which will allow the edifice, the monstrosity, of their creation to continue without a hitch. Both offer – what? – the right to be taxed, and taxed without consent; for if our money is taken from us, by either party, and spent on those 'projects' which, for whatever the dearly held belief, is not consonant with our spirit, with our needs, and given away, willy nilly, regardless of the desires of WE, the Western peoples, then we but plunge the knife into the throats of our own selves, and our own children. Is this not the case? It is not a matter of not caring, it is a matter of caring, and deeply, about OUR future, OUR children, OUR destiny.

So, what, then, do we look toward too in our present system? Do we create a 'white people's party'? A 'pan aryanist party'? Do we mobilize our 'churches' – OH! I must have misspoke – for having places of worship, which comprise parishioners of Western stock, simply because 'we want it that way' is not possible; in fact, it is illegal, and will, never doubt, be prosecuted to the fullest extent by this present 'legal' regime. Do we mobilize the 'churches', I wonder. Do we create local 'youth corps' which would instill historical, spiritual, environmental, and noble pursuits – sorry, forgive me - to mobilize young men and women of Western stock, *alone*, is hateful, prone to division and strife; but not to worry, the Modern has many groups and functionaries which are inclusive, compassionate, and moderate; the only sacrifice we will have to make, should be willing to make, is that we should expect our children to make such diverse friends that will, with time, prove to be mates, lovers, and part of that greater experiment of a beautiful 'one world'. The lamb will lie down with the lion. Beautiful!

I think you get the picture – the *Real* picture of our situation.

For those members of the West who, whether real or imagined, disbelieve this picture of our present presence, let me speak, if I may, for those who are unable, that you may do what you will, you may live with whoever you want - just don't stand in our way, those of us who 'do' want this path – are we not all Free to follow our own path? We trust, implicitly, that those of our brethren who believe in the sanctity of freedom and discourse, of liberty and slavery, will have no problem in standing aside, and who will 'demand' with us, that we be given the chance at 'Life, Liberty, and the Pursuit of happiness' in those ways which seem right in our own eyes…right?

What institutions can we plead our case? Without money, our spokesmen in prison, or financially ruined, our religious leaders but cookie-cutter state spokesmen – who do we turn to? I am not sure any more.

On the other hand…

Since the inception and creation of this work, many things have changed. The Nation, as a whole, has shifted, markedly, into areas that, twenty years ago, would have been undreamed of. Not the direction, as distinct from theory, or dialectical experiments, but the solid, day-to-day direction of the 'consciousness' of the inhabitants of the West, in toto.

In Eastern Europe we saw the fledgling, if not dramatic, increase in the supremacy of Culture over that of the culture-distorters: we think of Yugoslavia, Serbia, Croatia, and all the 'tribal' enclaves which, together, make up a large and distinct proportion of the far-flung West. In this case, to those who know the history of the West, the presence of a anti-Christian, multi-ethnic, multi-racial force was protected and defended by the 'so-called' leaders of the West – America played the prominent role in defeating those forces who, truly, believed in the West, in Tradition, in the Church. Repayment of this treason was the common purpose of the non-western, his religion, and his terror. This can, and must, be laid at the feet of the people of America, you and I, for without our complacency, Mohammed would not now be in the ascendancy, at the expense of our brethren, strangers though they are, yet a vital part of the greater West.

From Scandinavia to France, from Italy to Romania and beyond, the West has made decisions unthinkable fifty years ago; the Turkish invasion is well on its way. Western governments, for the first time in sixty years, seek ever to justify the Iron Heel. Ironic it is, that every day the propaganda of the West instills such ridicule, and venomous hate against 'government', which seeks to stabilize itself by ever more and rigid rules, depravation of rights, and professional armies which can, and will enforce the regimes role of 'protector' of the people. Never before, have governments had such *absolute* control of their populations, and none more than here, in America.

Believe no one who declares: 'Napoleon, Alexander, Hitler, Stalin, these the worlds worst tyrants." Ha! Look at the 'patriot' act for a primer of just what *has* happened, and just what is *going* to happen! Do not let anyone frighten you – THINK! – all of you who have 'given' leaders the right to 'take away rights' have given, through technology, such absolute control of person, of travel, of freedom, that these other 'tyrants' pale in comparison. There is one telling difference, however, between the past and the present: in the past, leaders and tyrants were known by 'how' they treated their *own* People – if they betrayed 'their' people they were tyrant – if they treated their People *good*, they were saviors. It is the same old 'from which side of the road do you hail'. Nevertheless, the 'change' is here. There is no escape.

In response to this, information has tripled, and tripled again. Indeed, the pen is mightier than the sword. It is having serious consequences, and can never be turned back. Too many questions, not enough answers. This forces, or will ultimately direct, disparate individuals and ideologies to gravitate to each other – it is already starting in the circles of the intelligentsia, of Universities and institutes of technology; in biology, in ethnic/racial Medicine. All have taken strides in directions, which cannot be undone. It only remains if the people of the West will follow – or be made too lead.

Change is everywhere.

Soon, very soon, the powers that be will be 'forced' to secure those elements sympathetic to the postulated 'friends' of the west, of whom Nationalists everywhere have common antipathy. This, ipso facto, makes all of us 'enemies of the state'. It has happened before. Hate crimes; you haven't seen anything yet. The Rise of the West demands that its acolytes be ready, that they know their history, and hence to learn thereby. Do not discount your brothers attempt at creating a Political Party, nor the brother who seeks a more divisive path, for all roads lead to the Western shore, our shore, our Destiny. Fear not the wave, which ever seeks to drown you, for your 'ship of state' lies buried, deep, under the crashing waves, seeking to float again atop the sea of Nation, which is our Race, our Blood.

Frank L. DeSilva
© 2005

GLOSSARY

1. Technics — A word that describes a function, either by a Machine, system, or form of Government. A process, either Mechanical or natural.

2. Modern — Connotes a problematical example of 'today's' man; of the thinkers, Philosophers, and government 'experts' which have, and are presently, leading us into a Dark Ages. Its overwhelming connotation is negative.

3. Inner-Man — Describes the essence of Man in a 'intra-personal' relationship with all who are 'outside'. In a Racial sense, it represents all that is held within the racial family. In relation to 'spirit', it defines the essence of Western man to that of non-Western. The duality of nature, hence, inner/outer man.

4. Race-Culture — The relationship between organism and organization. Culture is the organic process by which the Race proceeds into the cycle of Birth, Life, and Senility. It is the total essence; it is the Soul, and what can visibly be seen of that Soul. Race-Culture is organism.

5. Will-To-Express — This is the action in relation to man's ability to challenge his environment, his Institutional technics. It is the spiritual value of his determination; of his ability to survive.

6. Mediocre   This is the definition of the great mass. It is what the Modern teaches. It is his value. It is the leveling of all that is superior that has nobility. It represents the death of Western man.

7. Tribe   This connotes the relationship between a People; its various ritualistic, and traditional role in the making of a larger technic. It is, outside of the family, the microelement of all higher culture. It need not be primitive in nature, but can be highly technical. It is the racial root of Culture.

8. Causality   The essence of the unknown, which, although it cannot always be seen, measured, calculated, and the like, nevertheless, interacts with every organism on the planet. It is *cause* and *effect*; it is *action* and *reaction*. It simply *is*.

9. Melting Pot   A term coined by the Modern and his minions. Meaning is understood if one fits, consciously, into the psychosis of the mob, that un-racial, un-independent mediocre element of the Modern. It is a catch phrase, with no natural meaning, unless one is predisposed to consider it in light of a 'same-race-' setting; like the Germanic, Scandinavian, Anglo-Saxon relationship of the original settlers of this Continent.

10. De Jure   [As opposed to de facto] This is the 'right to rule' by consent; not by simple force of arms – which becomes, at this point, a de facto right.

11. Collective Consciousness

This is the state of mind in which all see, feel, and act in a similar fashion; this can be for long duration, or it can be for a short period. This is not 'mass hypnosis' as many would like to believe but, simply, the energy of a similar People, responding to stimuli in a natural, organic, and fundamental fashion.

12. Democracy — The system of government by which the 'majority' has right to rule. In the world of the Modern, it is that system by which he has gained a monopoly of national power [using elements *outside* of the Western]. The mechanism used here is force; the West, and the entire planet will be 'forced' to become democratic, whether or not the particular race-culture is ready for it or not. In this way, the Modern will always enjoin his will upon all peoples. The majority of 'force' will dictate his future.

13. Nobility — The spirit of honesty, sympathy, and character which allows the individual to travel through life with head held high; with the ability to face any odds, conquer it, and thereby becoming stronger. It is, or should be, the goal of every man or woman who wished to become ennobled. It is part genetic, and environmental. It is the totality of the race-culture.

14. Family — In the traditional sense of Father, Mother, and offspring. It is the duality of male and female; of fire and water. The nation and all culture revolve upon the 'axis'. It is the continuation of the Race.

15. Imperative	Connotes Survival. Importance. A necessary requirement for the survival of the organism. Used in the sense of Territory, and Personal Will.
16. Churchianity	Used to connote the modern 'judeo-christian' essence of a technic which, while traditionally a Western form of religious technic, has been twisted, and is now being used to pacify, inundate, and promote a system of universalism guided by a belief in middle-eastern Talmudic thought – the Law of the Modern. A non-Western manifestation in its present form.
17. The West	This term defines the limitless boundaries of the racial components of the racial body of the Indo-European White Race. It is, once again, representative of organism. Geo-Political boundaries are artificial in this context. A race is a race, no matter where it resides. The spiritual quality of that same people. The connotation is strictly positive.

APPENDICES

I considered many additions for your consideration, dear reader, and I hope that what is added here will create more fodder for thought, and direction.

Over the past twenty years, many of our Folk have come and gone in the telling of this great epic, this evolving West, which belongs to each and every one of us. Many of these persons may have come and gone, and have left little or no telling sign; many others, however, have left a legacy of their own. One such man, of whom I was to befriend, and to be befriended, was David Eden Lane. Many who read this work will, readily, recognize this name. David Lane, truly, is a hero of our Folk. His sacrifices, the depth and conviction of his beliefs, can be matched by few – excepting those of his Bruder, those Silent Brothers, which, in their own unique and corporate body, have given freely their lives, their fortunes, and their sacred honor, which all, with no exception, were willing to give their very Lives. In a relative sense, their lives have been given; although in prison, they have sacrificed their families, they have given up their rights to be present at the birthing of their own children – sons and daughters – and have lost the wives who started out their lives with these men – some amiably, and some not. No matter, all these men, known collectively as 'die Bruder Schweigen', or 'the silent brothers', have never asked for sympathy above and beyond what sympathetic and compassionate people would give from those deep, beautiful, and sturdy hearts, which have, already, shown themselves to these men over the years.

The tale of die Bruder Schweigen is yet to be told. It is filled with adventure, love, treason, loyalty, honor, and courage. It is a story, which has been told by enemies of our folk, and by well-intentioned individuals. But, it has not been told. Perhaps for another age, or perhaps, in the near future. But it will be told.

For now, I want to pass on a simple and dynamic work which was written by David Lane, and sums up, for us, all the men and women of the West, those precepts which, every time I read them, make an even stronger impression upon me.

Study these precepts. Memorize those few which seem to fit your frame of reference, for any one, or all, will make you stronger, more noble, and instill that essence, which die Bruder Schweigen, and their friend and champion, Robert J. Mathews, lived on a daily basis. To Honor. To Courage. To Loyalty!

Frank L. DeSilva

THE 88 PRECEPTS

Until the white race realizes that there is only one source from which we can ascertain lasting truths, there will never be peace or stability on this earth. In the immutable Laws of Nature are the keys to life, order, and understanding. The words of men, even those which some consider "inspired" are subject to the translations, vocabulary, additions, subtractions, and distortions of fallible mortals. Therefore, every writing or influence, ancient or modern, must be strained through the test of conformity to Natural Law. The White Peoples of the earth must collectively understand that they are equally subject to the iron-hard Laws of Nature with every other creature of the Universe, or they will not secure peace, safety, nor even their existence. The world is in flames because Races, Sub-races, Nations, and Cultures are being forced to violate their own Nature-ordained instincts for self-preservation. Many men of good will, but little understanding, are struggling against symptoms, which are the result of disobedience to Natural Law. As is the Nature of Man, most take narrow, provincial stances predicated on views formed by immediate environment, current circumstances, and conditioned dogma. That powerful and ruthless Tribe which has controlled the affairs of the world for untold centuries by exploiting Man's most base instincts encourages this. Conflict among and between the unenlightened serves as their mask and shield. A deeper understanding of the Fundamental Laws that govern the affairs of Men is necessary if we are to save civilization from its usurious executioners. The following are not intended to provide a detailed system of government, but as *Precepts* which, when understood, will benefit and preserve a People as individuals and as a Nation.

The 88 PRECEPTS

1. Any religion or teaching which denies the Natural Laws of the Universe is false.

2. Whatever People's perception of God, or the Gods, or the motive Force of the Universe might be, they can hardly deny that Nature's Laws are the work of, and therefore the intent of, that Force.

3. God and religion are distinct, separate, and often conflicting concepts. Nature evidences the divine plan, for the natural world is the work of the force or the intelligence men call God. Religion is the creation of mortals, therefore predestined to fallibility. Religion may preserve or destroy a People, depending on the structure given by its progenitors, the motives of its agents and the vagaries of historical circumstances.

4. The truest form of prayer is *communion* with Nature. It is not vocal. Go to a lonely spot, if possible a mountaintop, on a clear, star-lit night, ponder the majesty and order of the infinite macrocosm. Then consider the intricacies of the equally infinite microcosm. Understand that you are on the one hand inconsequential beyond comprehension in the size of things, and on the other hand, you are potentially valuable beyond comprehension as a link in destiny's chain. There you begin to understand how pride and self can co-exist with respect and reverence. There we find harmony with Nature and with harmony comes strength, peace and certainty.

5 Secular power systems protect and promote religions, which concentrate on an afterlife. Thus, people are taught to abandon defenses against the predators of *this* life.

6. History, both secular and religious, is a fable conceived in self-serving deceit and promulgated by those who perceive benefits.

7. Religion in its most beneficial form, is the symbology of a People and their culture. A multi-racial religion destroys the senses of uniqueness, exclusivity, and value necessary to the survival of a race.

8. What men call the "super natural" is actually the "natural" not yet understood or revealed.

9. A proliferation of laws with the resultant loss of freedom is a sign of, and directly proportional to, spiritual sickness in a Nation.

10. If a Nation is devoid of spiritual health and moral character, then government and unprincipled men will fill the vacancy. Therefore, freedom prospers in moral values and tyranny thrives in moral decay.

11. Truth requires little explanation. Therefore, beware of verbose doctrines. The great principles are revealed in brevity.

12. Truth does not fear investigation.

13. Unfounded belief is a pitfall. A People who do not check the validity and effect of their beliefs with reason will suffer or perish.

14. In accord with Nature's Laws, nothing is more right than the preservation of one's own race.

15. No greater motivating force exists than the certain conviction that one is right.

16. Discernment is a sign of a healthy People. In a sick or dying nation, civilization, culture, or race, substance is abandoned in favor of appearance.

17. Discernment includes the ability to recognize the difference between belief and demonstrable reality.

18. There exists no such thing as rights or privileges under the Laws of Nature. The deer being stalked by a hungry lion has no right to life. However, he may purchase life by obedience to nature-ordained instincts for vigilance and flight. Similarly, men have no rights to life, liberty, or happiness. Oneself may purchase these circumstances by one's family, by one's tribe or by one's ancestors, but they are nonetheless purchases and not rights. Furthermore, the value of these purchases can only be maintained through vigilance and obedience to Natural Law.

19. A people who are not convinced of their uniqueness and value will perish.

20. The White race has suffered invasions and brutality from Africa and Asia for thousands of years. For example, Attila and the Asiatic Huns who invaded Europe in the 5th century, raping, plundering, and killing from the Alps to the Baltic and Caspian Seas. This scenario was repeated by the Mongols of Genghis Khan 800 years later. (Note here that the American Indians are not "Native Americans," but are racially Mongolians.) In the 8th century, hundreds of years before Negroes were brought to America, the North African Moors of mixed racial background invaded and conquered Portugal, Spain and part of France. So, the attempted guilt-trip placed on the White race by civilization's executioners is invalid under both historical circumstance and the Natural

Law, which denies inter-species compassion. The fact is, all races have benefited immeasurably from the creative genius of the Aryan People.

21. People who allow others not of their race to live among them will perish, because the inevitable result of a racial integration is racial interbreeding, which destroys the characteristics and existence of a race. Forced integration is deliberate and malicious genocide, particularly for a People like the White race, who are now a small minority in the world.

22. In the final analysis, a race or species is not judged superior or inferior by its accomplishments, but by its will and ability to survive.

23. Political, economic, and religious systems may be destroyed and resurrected by men, but the death of a race is eternal.

24. No race of People can indefinitely continue their existence without territorial imperatives in which to propagate, protect, and promote their own kind.

25. A People without a culture exclusively their own will perish.

26. Nature has put a certain antipathy between races and species to preserve the individuality and existence of each. Violation of the territorial imperative necessary to preserve that antipathy leads to either conflict or mongrelization.

27. It is not constructive to hate those of other races, or even those of mixed races. But a separation must be maintained for the survival of one's own race. One must, however, hate with a pure and perfect hatred those of one's own race who commit treason against one's own kind and against the nations of one's own kind. One must hate with a perfect hatred all those People or practices, which destroy one's People, one's culture, or the racial exclusiveness of one's territorial imperative.

28. The concept of a multi-racial society violates every Natural Law for species preservation.

29. The concept of "equality" is declared a lie by every evidence of Nature. It is a search for the lowest common denominator, and its pursuit will destroy every superior race, nation, or culture. In order for a plow horse to run as fast as a race horse you would first have to cripple the race horse; conversely, in order for a race horse to pull as much as a plow

horse, you would first have to cripple the plow horse. In either case, the pursuit of equality is the destruction of excellence.

30. The instincts for racial and species preservation are ordained by Nature.

31. Instincts are Nature's perfect mechanism for the survival of each race and species. The human weakness of rationalizing situations for self-gratification must not be permitted to interfere with these instincts.

32. Miscegenation, that is race-mixing, is and has always been, the greatest threat to the survival of the Aryan race.

33. Inter-species compassion is contrary to the Laws of Nature and is, therefore, suicidal. If a wolf were to intercede to save a lamb from a lion, he would be killed. Today, we see the White man taxed so heavily that he cannot afford children. The taxes raised are then used to support the breeding of tens of millions of non-whites, many of whom then demand the last White females for breeding partners. As you can see, man is subject to all the Laws of Nature. This has nothing to do with morality, hatred, good or evil. Nature does not recognize the concepts of good and evil in inter-species relationships. If the lion eats the lamb, it is good for the lion and evil for the lamb. If the lamb escapes and the lion starves, it is good for the lamb and evil for the lion. So, we see the same incident is labeled both good and evil. This cannot be, for there are no contradictions within Nature's Laws.

34. The instinct for sexual union is part of Nature's perfect mechanism for species preservation. It begins early in life and often continues until late in life. It must not be repressed; its purpose, reproduction, must not be thwarted either. Understand that for thousands of years our females bore children at an early age. Now, in an attempt to conform to and compete in an alien culture, they deny their Nature-ordained instincts and duties. Teach responsibility, but, also, have understanding. The life of a race springs from the wombs of its women. He who would judge must first understand the difference between what is good and what is right.

35. Homosexuality is a crime against Nature. All Nature declares the purpose of the instinct for sexual union is reproduction and thus, preservation of the species. The overpowering male sex drive must be channeled toward possession of females of the same race, as well as elements such as territory and power, which are necessary to keep them.

36. Sexual pornography degrades the Nature of all who are involved. A beautiful nude woman is art; a camera between her knees to explore her private parts is pornography.

37. That race whose males will not fight to the death to keep and mate with their females will *perish*. Any White man with healthy instincts feels disgust and revulsion when he sees a woman of his race with a man of another race. Those, who today control the media and affairs of the Western World, teach that this is wrong and shameful. They label it "racism." As any "ism," for instance the word "nationalism," means to promote one's own nation; "racism" merely means to promote and protect the life of one's own race. It is, perhaps, the proudest word in existence. Any man who disobeys these instincts is anti-Nature.

38. In a sick and dying nation, culture, race or civilization, political dissent and traditional values will be labeled and persecuted as heinous crimes by inquisitors clothing themselves in jingoistic patriotism.

39. A People who are ignorant of their past will defile the present and destroy the future.

40. A race must honor above all earthly things, those who have given their lives or freedom for the preservation of the folk.

41. The Folk, namely the members of the Race, are the Nation. Racial loyalties must always supersede geographical and national boundaries. If this is taught and understood, it will end fratricidal wars. Wars must not be fought for the benefit of another race.

42. The Nations' leaders are not rulers, they are servants and guardians. They are not to serve for personal gain. Choose only a guardian who has no interest in the accumulation of material things.

43. Choose and judge your leaders, also called guardians, thus: Those who seek always to limit the power of government are of good heart and conscience. Those who seek to expand the power of government are base tyrants.

44. No government can give anything to anybody without first taking it from another. Government is, by its very nature, legalized taking. A limited amount of government is a necessary burden for national defense and internal order. Anything more is counter-productive to freedom and liberty.

45. The organic founding Law, namely the Constitution of a Nation, must not be amendable by any method other than unanimous consent of all parties thereto and with all parties present. Otherwise, the doors are opened for the advent of that most dangerous and deadly form of government, democracy.

46. In a democracy those who control the media, and thus the minds of the electorate, have power undreamed by kings or dictators.

47. The simplest way to describe a democracy is this: Three people form a government, each having one vote. Then two of them vote to steal the wealth of the third.

48. The latter stages of a democracy are filled with foreign wars, because the bankrupt system attempts to preserve itself by plundering other nations.

49. In a democracy, that which is legal, is seldom moral, and that which is moral is often illegal.

50. A democracy is always followed by a strongman... some call him a dictator. It is the only way to restore order out of the chaos caused by a democracy. Pick your strongman wisely! He must be a guardian in his heart. He must be one who has shown that his only purpose in life is the preservation of the folk. His ultimate aim must be to restore the rule of Law based on the perfect Laws of Nature. Do not choose him by his words. Choose one who has sacrificed all in the face of tyranny; choose one who has endured and persevered. This is the only reliable evidence of his worthiness and motives.

51. A power system will do anything, no matter how corrupt or brutal, to preserve itself.

52. Tyrannies cannot be ended without use of force.

53. Those who commit treason disguise their deeds in proclamations of patriotism.

54. Propaganda is a major component in all power systems, both secular and religious; false propaganda is a major component of unprincipled power systems. All power systems endeavor to convince their subjects that the system is good, just, beneficent and noble, as well as worthy of

perpetuation and defense. The more jingoistic propaganda issued, the more suspicious one should be of its truth.

55. Political power, in the final analysis, is created and maintained by force.

56. A power system, secular or religious, which employs extensive calls to patriotism or requires verbosity and rhetoric for its preservation, is masking tyranny.

57. Propaganda is a legitimate and necessary weapon in any struggle. The elements of successful propaganda are: simplicity, emotion, repetition, and brevity. Also, since men believe what they want to believe, and since they want to believe that which they perceive as beneficial to themselves, then successful propaganda must appeal to the perceived self-interest of those to whom it is disseminated.

58. Tyrannies teach *what* to think; free men learn *how* to think.

59. Beware of men who increase their wealth by the use of words. Particularly beware of the lawyers or priests who deny Natural Law.

60. The patriot, being led to the inquisition's dungeons or the executioner's axe will be condemned the loudest by his former friends and allies; for thus they seek to escape the same fate.

61. The sweet Goddess of Peace lives only under the protective arm of the ready God of War.

62. The organic founding Law of a Nation must state with unmistakable and irrevocable specificity the identity of the homogeneous racial, cultural group for whose welfare it was formed, and that the continued existence of the Nation is singularly for all time for the welfare of that specific group only.

63. That race or culture which lets others influence or control any of the following will perish:

        1) Organs of information
        2) Educational institutions
        3) Religious institutions
        4) Political offices
        5) Creation of their money
        6) Judicial institutions

7) Cultural institutions
8) Economic life

64. Just Laws require little explanation. Their meaning is irrevocable in simplicity and specificity.

65. Men's emotions are stirred far more effectively by the spoken word than by the written word. This is why a ruling tyranny will react more violently to gatherings of dissenters than to books or pamphlets.

66. The organic founding Law of the Nation, or any law, is exactly as pertinent as the will and power to enforce it.

67. An unarmed or non-militant People will be enslaved.

68. Some say the pen is more powerful than the sword. Perhaps so. Yet, the word without the sword has no authority.

69. Tyrannies are usually built step-by-step and disguised by noble rhetoric.

70. The difference between a terrorist and a patriot is control of the press.

71. The judgments of the guardians, the leaders, must be true to Natural Law and tempered by reason.

72. Materialism is base and destructive. The guardians of a Nation must constantly warn against and combat a materialistic spirit in the Nation. Acquisition of wealth and property, as is needed for the well being of one's family and obtained by honorable means, is right and proper. Exploitation, particularly through usury, is destructive to the nation.

73. Materialism leads men to seek artificial status through wealth or property. True social status comes from service to Family, Race, and Nation.

74. Materialism ultimately leads to conspicuous, unnecessary consumption, which in turn leads to the rape of Nature and destruction of the environment. It is unnatural. The true guardians of the Nations must be wholly untainted by materialism.

75. The function of a merchant or salesman is to provide a method of exchange. A merchant who promotes unnecessary consumption and materialism must not be tolerated.

76. The only lawful functions of money are as a medium of exchange and a store of value. All other uses including social engineering, speculation, inflation, and especially usury are unlawful. Usury (interest) at any percentage is a high crime, which cannot be tolerated.

77. A nation with an aristocracy of money, lawyers, or merchants will become a tyranny.

78. The simplest way to describe a usury-based central banking system is this: The bankers demand the property of the Nation as collateral for their loans. At interest, more money is owed them than they created with the loans. So, eventually, the bankers foreclose on the Nation.

79. Usury (interest), inflation, and oppressive taxation are theft by deception and destroy the moral fabric of the Nation.

80. Wealth gained without sacrifices or honest labor will usually be misused. 81. Nothing in Nature is static; either the life force grows and expands or it decays and dies.

82. Respect must be earned; it cannot be demanded or assumed.

83. Avoid a vexatious man, for his venom will poison your own nature.

84. Self discipline is a mark of a higher man.

85. One measure of a man is cheerfulness in adversity.

86. A fool judges others by their words. A wise man judges others by their actions and accomplishments.

87. In our relationships or interactions, as in all of Nature's Laws, to each action there is a reaction. That which we plant will be harvested, if not by ourselves, then by another.

88. These are sure signs of a sick or dying Nation. If you see any of them, your guardians are committing treason:

    1) Mixing and destruction of the founding race

2) Destruction of the family units
3) Oppressive taxation
4) Corruption of the Law
5) Terror and suppression against those who warn of the Nation's error
6) Immorality: drugs, drunkenness, etc.
7) Infanticide (now called abortion)
8) Destruction of the currency (inflation or usury)
9) Aliens in the land, alien culture
10) Materialism
11) Foreign wars
12) Guardians (leaders) who pursue wealth or glory
13) Homosexuality
14) Religion not based on Natural Law

We must secure the existence of our people and a future for white children.
~David Lane~

Appendice II

Reparations or Repatriation?

We hear much ado, constantly, regarding the positions and cultural diversity of the various race cultures presently living within the boundaries of the continental United States. The reality of a 'majority' race culture is quickly coming to a close. This has, for many years now, been a *cause celebre* amongst the various groups agitating for their individual rights and needs. Among many of these concerns, which are voiced by the various spokesmen and women for these groups, one seems to stand out, especially amongst those common and thinking persons of the race-culture of the West, namely, that of Reparations.

Reparations can be looked at in many ways. To the sons and daughters of the race-culture of Africa, reparations are seen in a definitive form, namely, as compensation for a wrong, or something that is done to achieve this, usually seen in terms of monetary recompense for the time their ancestors spent in slavery. The Japanese have, of course, received a limited apology for wartime internment, which, as in all wars, sees extreme behavior by both sides; the monies paid by this American government were small, and not consonant with the pain inflicted upon their ancestors, yet it was a reparation. American mestizos, of Mexican extraction, also see the viability of receiving something for perceived wrongs, namely, the compensation or reaffirmation of their ancestral homeland, Azatlan.

Each of these groups are *distinct* race-cultures.

Without revisiting the question of who's culture, it seems probable that the question of survival for one, or for all, becomes paramount. The study of the rise of the West has refrained from the voluminous studies, statistics, experts and their individual rationales for why the West has maintained its particular individuality. For the 'mass', I think, the time is passed to intellectually appreciate the conundrum in which they, *as mass*, find themselves. The amount of time watching television, or its cousin, the computer, has dumbed down the present generation to a point, which can see no other reality than that which is fed them on a daily basis, or what desires or needs have been met for the moment. The contest of cultures, to be sure, is being played out.

Many cases can be made of abuse and excess. The West feels the same. No amount of cynicism can mitigate this truth. No politician can gloss over, nor misrepresent these sentiments to those common men and women of the West who live this present 'dream' of the Modern. Men and Women of the West see, also, the finite and ordinary roles of their ancestors, their Mothers and Fathers, as passed down to them, as changed, perverted, and sequestered by all manners of machinations by and through the ever-evolving governmental technics of the age. True it is, that another sense of 'reparation' can be seen: That of a compensation demanded of a defeated nation by a victor. In this case, the West has been defeated by those various and sundry groups and individuals and, most certainly, by our very own apathy, cowardice, and fear, which has led inextricably to the cul-de-sac in which we now find ourselves. The victory, not won on any battlefield, but by and through social programmes, racial reassessment, and historical supplementation has put the members of the West in a quandary.

Why is it, for instance, that just forty years ago, the majority of America was white, minorities, in many instances, were considered a distant, yet present danger, not quite making the national news, and the 'national leaders' seemed to be working for the interests of the majority race-culture, that is, the culture of the West? No matter what, or who's story we hear about discrimination, segregation, poverty, or denial, it is the sense that all those Western feel, deep inside, that has been taken from *them* which truly matters: The loss of something intangible, opaque, and not truly substantive, their own *Identity*.

What we all feel, individually and as a group, is well known. What do we do about it, that is the question which has been asked by at least four generations of our kind here in America. If violence solves nothing, as we are always being told, unless state sanctioned violence by the state is used to topple perceived dictators, or to solve disasters imposed by 'agenda' thinkers of every stripe, in *our* name, then by what method do we extricate ourselves, and secure a future for our children? A political/Judicial answer perhaps?

In this democracy, that is, the 'democracy' which has supplanted the Republic, we can postulate just what our powers really are, or should be; the fact is, each one of us, a hundred million fold, would not have much of a chance in securing the future of our own country, let alone our own family, if it were put to a vote. However, for those of you, those readers so predisposed to consider a change in the democratic fashion, let us here cover a superb attempt at this very idea.

Our Republic, and our Constitution have set about to confront those areas in which The People would have the ability to transform areas of their life, against any governmental intrusion or design, by way of Amendment; as such, showing such a strong and national inclination, could never be undone, such as our First and Second amendments, unless the People themselves relinquished these hard won rights. A people do not voluntarily give up its claim to liberty, unless they believe the lies and panderings of those individuals who would supplant them. A healthy people would fight; a sickly and degenerate people will simply give up.

Yes, an amendment. That is the ticket. That is the democratic way. Let us pursue this line of thought for the future.

Frank L. DeSilva

Amendment to the Constitution:
*Averting the Decline and
Fall of America**

PREFACE

When the fate of a nation is imperiled from within its own ranks, and from aliens who have joined its ranks, and within the space of one or two generations, the society established by its forefathers has been riven from its frame, the guardians of that nation must take action to defend their people from their own destructive elements and repair their defects, or be held responsible before God and man for their inaction. America is such a nation; the 80's are a part of such a generation and our local elected officials are the guardians of whom I speak.

The purpose of this text is to remind this generation of its obligations to its country, to enlighten it in some measure as to its defects and destructive elements, and to present a plan to correct them. Subjects discussed herein may be considered by some to be sensitive and even outrageous, but the incensed and outraged will be those who by their action or at times by their very presence within the nation were themselves

---

* This heading is the working title of James O. Pace's work published by - Johnson, Pace, Simmons & Fennell Publishers, 1985. This section is an attempt, in summary, of the fine work, in which Mr. Pace has presented the very workable construct of an Amendment for the reinsertion of the Western imperative, that truly primal need to extend what is his, the nature of which, is bred within the confines of the West, alone. Since, to date, this is the only credible attempt at utilizing the 'democratic' process to claim what is ours, it is fittingly used to impart this attempt in a democratic fashion to establish the will and intent of those particular Western Peoples who share in the birthing and extension of this great America.

The Amendment, which Mr. Pace has presented to the Western Public, indeed to all who reside on this continent, is a work of clarity and foresight. At present, I am not certain if it is still in print. I do know that it caused quite an outcry shortly after its inception, and received tepid reporting even during its heyday in the mainstream press. In many circles, however, it has proven quite workable, and there are groups, both legal and financial, who continue to work on this premise. As with all attempts in a democracy, the machine moves slowly, all too slowly, for the most part, and always runs the risk of dying on the vine – or in committee. But, its very premise, like it or no, is democratic, and was/is intended to go before the public, be voted on by members of the House and Senate as is the way the Founding Fathers had intended such amendments to be passed.

It is less certain, today, than it was in 1985, that it would have any legitimate chance to receive a fair hearing in the halls of government, those repositories of the 'voice of the People', those who have the best interests of the nation at heart. I will try my best to present, in Summary, the intent of the so-called Pace Amendment for the serious student of change and renewal. FLS

outrageous and controversial twenty years ago.[44] The course of action recommended by this text is a constitutional amendment presented to the several states through a convention called by Congress upon petition by the several states through their legislatures, who would have the foremost responsibility for action, that this text is primarily directed.

The time is now. As President Ronald Reagan said, "You and I have a rendezvous with destiny. We can preserve for our children this last best hope of man on earth or we can sentence them to take the first step into a thousand years of darkness. If we fail, at least let our children and our children's children say of us we justified our brief moment here. We did all that *could* be done." [emph. added]

I. TRENDS IN AMERICA

1. Introduction

America has changed dramatically in the last thirty years. Rapid and extreme change has affected every region of our country and every aspect of our lives. Advancements in such areas of natural science as chemistry, physics, agriculture, electronics and engineering have improved the quality of our lives, have mad us healthier, and have given us more comforts. The opposite side of the advancements made in natural sciences are the changes that have occurred in the social sciences, in such areas as law, politics, religion, ethics, race relations and the structure of our society and activities of its members. Changes that have occurred in these areas are as profound and dramatic as the changes in the natural sciences. However, where changes made in the natural sciences can generally be called advancements, changes in the social sciences cannot be considered such. Indeed, as we will examine below, the order and structure of our society is as marked by decline as world technology is marked by advancement.

In America's quest for a more progressive and better life, many of the advancements made in the area of technology are offset by regression in our social order and structure. And just as technological inferiority will result in defeat in the battlefield and in the marketplace at the hands of our enemies and competitors, social inferiority will result in our conquest by superior or more artfully structured social orders, or possibly by more primitive but more effective social orders, or demise by internal collapse.

---

[44] Here Mr. Pace is speaking of the turbulent 60's in which racial integration was foisted upon unwilling members of Western stock as a 'majority' by the machinations and cowardice of the federal government. Force was used in Arkansas [1957] to force members of the West to accept social change/control as seen by those who change the primitive fundamental construct of race-culture, to the detriment of all parties involved. FLS

In order to determine the current state of our society, let us briefly examine its various aspects and see what changes have recently occurred therein. We shall examine aspects of change in the context of two primary areas, racial identity and standards of conduct. Our racial identity encompass such issues as racial composition and culture. Only racial composition, however, will be discussed herein. Our standards of conduct are divided into three categories, those concerning the family, those concerning the community and those concerning industry. The standards of conduct concerning the family include such issues as living patterns and sexual ethics. The standards of conduct concerning the community include religion, crime, drug abuse, entertainment and litigation. Concerning industry, the standards of conduct include poverty, education and production, and technology. A summary of recent changes in our society regarding these issues is set forth below.

2. Racial Identity

   (a) Racial Composition of the Nation

The statistics and facts relation to racial composition and demographics in America are incomplete in many respects. Two causes of this are (i) the undocumented and undocumentable illegal aliens in this nation, the numbers of which are impossible to calculate accurately, and (ii) the method of classification employed by government agencies, including the U.S. Bureau of the Census, which often obscures racial classification, which often obscures racial classification. No one knows ho many illegal aliens are not in America nor how many enter each year. The issue is sensitive and volatile. Liberal and minority groups cite low estimates while politically conservative groups cite higher figures.[45] Possibly the only way to get a real feeling as to the number of illegal aliens is to visit such states as Texas and California where the highest concentration of them reside and observe the situation firsthand.

Incompleteness in facts relating to racial composition and demographics arises further because U.S. government agencies do not always compile statistics in a clear or consistent manner. The government records various statistics concerning Hispanic [mestizo] and Spanish–origin persons, but has snot been as uniform in its classification of them. At times, Hispanic [mestizo] have been classified as nonwhite, and at other times as white, and currently, they are not divided according to race at all. For example, in the various Fetal Death Ratio, Neonatal, Infant, and Maternal Mortality Rates by Race: 1915 to 1970, the Mexicans were at times included in the category "Negro and Other,"[46] and at other times were included in the category

---

[45] See NEWSWEEK, Feb.27, 1984, pg. 49.
[46] U.S. Department of Commerce, Bureau of the Census, Historical Census of the United States, Colonial Times to 1970, 57 (1975) [herein after cited as HISTORICAL STATISTICS]

"White."[47] Mexicans [mestizo] did not change their skin color, but governmental statisticians changed their classification. Currently, the trend in U.S. government statistics is to include a footnote for data concerning Hispanics [mestizo] providing: "Persons of Spanish origin may be of any race."[48] The inconsistency of this is compounded by the rebuttable presumption that exists in the U.S. government to the effect that Hispanic [mestizo] are white, which means, for example, that statistics regarding Mexicans [mestizo] are often combined with those for Anglo-Saxons. Further, in surveys for government purposes concerning matters of race, the current definition of white includes Middle Easterners and persons from Asia Minor as well as Europeans.[49] Thus, often for statistical purposes, Arabs and Anglo-Saxons are grouped together. For purposes of this text, Middle Easterners, persons from Asia Minor and Hispanics [mestizo] are generally not classified as white. With this state of affairs in mind, let us examine the racial composition of America and today.

In 1950, the population of the United States was just over 150 million, of which more than 135 million were white and about 15 million were non-white.[50] Hispanics [mestizo], because of their small numbers, did not constitute a separate category. The American population was 90 percent white. In 1960, the population of the United States was just over 180 million, of which over 160 million were white, 19 million Negroes, and 1.6 million were of other races. America was about 89 percent white and 11 percent Negro and other races. The 1960 census did not generally contain separated categories for the Hispanics [mestizo], Orientals, Pacific Islanders or other nonwhite groups. There were only three classifications: "white," "Negro," and "Other." Census takers were instructed to classify Hispanics [mestizo] as either "white" if their appearance was white or "Other" if their appearance was nonwhite. Gradually the Hispanic [mestizo] immigration grew until the U.S. Census Bureau felt it was necessary to classify them separately. During the 1970's the documented Hispanic [mestizo] population increased by 61 percent.[51] "Between 1977-78 huge increases of Vietnamese and Mexican [mestizo] immigrants accounted for 95 percent of the total rise in immigration."[52]

In 1980, the population of the United States was over 226 million[53] of which nonwhites, including Hispanics [mestizo], totaled, over 52 million.[54] In other words,

---

[47] Ibid. at 45
[48] *See, e.g.* U.S. Department of Commerce…(1982)
[49] *See, e.g.* employment questionnaires given by California state colleges and universities to prospective professors and lecturers or other equal opportunity employers.
[50] Historical Statistics, *supra* note 7, at 9.
[51] NEWSWEEK, Jan. 17, 1983, at 23.
[52] Ibid.
[53] Newspaper Enterprises Association, Inc., THE WORLD ALMANAC & BOOK OF FACTS, 210 (1983).
[54] NEWSWEEK, Ibid., at 22.

by 1980, America had, of record, become 23 percent nonwhite. These figures do not include an accurate estimation of the undocumented illegal aliens (primarily Hispanic [mestizo] and Oriental) who number many millions more. Based upon the number of illegal immigrants actually apprehended at the U.S. border by the Border Patrol, it is estimated that, in all, over 4 million Mexicans [mestizo] illegally immigrated to the United States in 1983 alone.[55] It should be noted that illegal white immigration to the United States constitutes a negligible percentage of the total illegal population.

From 1951-60, about 1.8 million recorded immigrants came from Europe, Australia, New Zealand, Canada or other white countries, comprising 72 percent of the total immigrants for this period. According to the U.S. Census, from 1971-79, of the 4.6 million recorded immigrants, 22.6 percent came from white countries. 87.4 percent were from nonwhite countries. Taking the year 1979 as an example of recent legal immigration trends, the U.S. Immigration and Naturalization Service recorded 460,300 immigrants, of which 19.5 percent were from white countries, and recorded immigrants. If, for that year, we estimate that illegal and unrecorded Mexican [mestizo] at only 2.5 million and the Asian and Pacific Island illegal and unrecorded immigrants at 0.5 million, that would mean that for the year 1979, America has seen a dramatic increase of nonwhite immigration, with 1985 estimated to have the highest number of nonwhite immigrants enter the United States of any prior year. This trend is not seen to be changing in the near future.

With an estimated 4 million illegal Mexican [mestizo] immigrants in 1983 alone, and a birth rate for Hispanics [mestizo] in America at 102 per 1000, compared with 71 per 1000 for whites[56] (85 per 1000 for blacks), the Latinization of the United States is particularly salient. Estimates of Hispanic [mestizo] growth to 50 million by 1990 is quite possible.

As a result of current U.S. immigration policies, illegal immigration trends, high fertility rates of nonwhites, including Hispanic [mestizo], low fertility rates of whites, and the growing occurrences of interracial marriage[57], unless measures are taken forthwith, in less than two decades, America will be more than 50 percent nonwhite, and in two more decades, white America will be virtually swept away.

---

[55] We now are aware, of course, that up to 12-15 million illegal Mexican [mestizo] immigrants now reside within the continental united states. FLS

[56] Los Angeles Daily News, May 9, 1984 (News) at 1 cols. 3-4.

[57] The technics of 'marriage' could, at some point create a sense of false security, since it is not, necessarily, marriage proper, which is of concern here; rather, that of *sexual union*, period. With the numerical advancement of child-bearing females of Western stock, over that of their male counterparts, and the likelihood of permanent or semi-permanent liaisons between inter-racial couples, the magnitude of the burgeoning births from these unions will be extraordinary, and will add, geometrically, to the changing face of the United States and its Western countenance. FLS

Standards of Conduct Concerning the Family

Living Patterns

[See Text]

(b) Sexual Relations Outside of Marriage

[See Text]

(c) Abortion

[See Text]

(d)

[See Text]

Standards of Conduct Concerning the Community

(a) Religion

In 1957, respondents to a Gallup Poll on the influence of religion in America felt overwhelmingly that religion had an increasing influence on American life. Almost 70 percent felt that religious influence was increasing, while only 14 percent felt that it was losing influence. By 1970, only 14 percent felt religious influence was increasing and 75 percent felt that it was decreasing.[58] According to a survey of the National Opinion Research Center in 1972, 35 percent of the American public attended church or other religious service at least one a week. In 1977, that percentage dropped to 27.6 percent. Prior to 1962, schools in many states had voluntary daily prayers and Bible readings. In 1962, the U.S. Supreme Court declared those acts to be unconstitutional.[59]

(b) Crime

[See Text]

(c) Drug Abuse

---

[58] U.S. Department of Commerce, Social Indicators III, at 515 (1980); American Institute of Public Opinion, The Gallup Poll: Public Opinion, 1972-199, The Gallup Opinion Index, rep. no. 145 (1978).
[59] *Engel v. Vitale* 370 U.S. 421 (1962); *Abington Township School Dist. v. Schempp* 374 U.S. 203 (1963).

[See Text]

(d) Entertainment

[This section involves the issue of mores, or moral character, and how this is affected by the technic of visual and written mediums. The issue, in my opinion, is not, and never has been one of First Amendment issues; rather, it is to what line one holds *oneself* too. The human impulse to sexuality is normative, and continues throughout life, however, to allow ones impulse to direct and lead by the nose, as it were, on a course which serves nothing but license, is not in the best interest of those of the West, nor any other people, as the inevitable result is always to the detriment, and social destruction of the group or individual which allows his senses to control his moral pathway.

As well, let us differentiate from the Western experiment in 'individuality', which has been commandeered by elements who espouse personal liberty, yet utilize its fundamental outcome, to further an agenda which, if not controlled, would most certainly, continue to exploit those basic human needs and desires for their own economic and theoretical agendas. FLS]

In areas of entertainment in recent years, our tastes have become lewd and less refined. Our movies and books typically contain great amounts of nudity and profanity and portray the lowest standard of morality, and our legal system [Judiciary] condones this. An actor, who refused to take off his clothes for a movie scene in a movie already under production, received a Los Angeles Superior Court summons ordering him "to comply with all orders of the producer."[60] Our television shows, also containing profanity, involve protagonists who not only are bad role models, but who are often homosexuals, adulterers, and even perpetrators of incest. Each of these forms of entertainment is considered *mainstream* and for the common man [emph. added].

Americans spend approximately 750 hardcore pornography motion picture houses in the United States, not including those showing pornographic homosexual movies. Thirty years ago, prior to *Playboy's* and others challenge to our stance on pornography, there were no above-ground magazines that were explicit in their pandering to the sexual interests of the public.

(e) Litigation

[See Text]

Standards of Conduct Concerning Industry

(a) Poverty

---

[60] Los Angeles Daily News, Sept. 8, 1984, (News) at 12, col. 5.

[See Text]

(b) Education

According to our almanacs, we still claim to have a 99 percent literacy rate as we had in past eras.[61] Further, larger percentages of high school and college graduates pass through our institutions of education, and our students attend school for many more years than their counterparts in previous generations. Yet, in spite of this, the educational level of our youth is deteriorating dramatically and they learn much less today even though they live in a more complex world. [A]...report, *The Nation at Risk*, asserts that if an enemy nation had forced the U.S. to accept today's low educational standards, "we might have viewed it as an act of war. As it stands, we have allowed this to happen to ourselves."[62]

(c) Industry and Technology

In 1960, America's economy made up 33.7 percent of the world's economy; in 1980, that margin shrunk to 21.5 percent. [table below is note 127; used for effect.]

	Share of World GNP 1960 – 1980		
	1960	1970	1980
US	33.7%	30.2%	21.5%
EEC	17.5	19.3	22.4
Japan	2.9	6.0	9.0
USSR	15.2	15.9	11.6
PRC	4.4	4.9	4.7

---

[61] Newspaper Enterprise Association, Inc., The World Almanac & Book of Facts, 1983, at 575.
[62] *Grading Time for U.S. Schools*, Scholastic Update, Feb. 3, 1984, at 2.

Japan more than tripled its share of the world economy during the same period. Its economy rose from 2.9 percent to 9.0 percent. From 1870 to 1970, the United States almost always exported more than it imported. In the 1970's, this trend began to change.[63]

In 1950, the world production of motor vehicles was 10,577,813 of which the United States manufactured 8,005,859 or 75.7 percent of the total.[64] Japan manufactured 31,597 or 0.3 percent.[65] Today, America produces millions fewer motor vehicles than it did in 1950. In 1981, the world production of motor vehicles more than tripled to 37,550,845 while the United States production declined to 7,942,916 or 21.2 percent of the total world production.[66] Japans share rose to 11,179,962 or 21.2 percent.[67] In 1950, world pig iron production (including ferroalloys) totaled 146,381,747 tons. The United States production was 65,439,769 tons, or 41 percent of the world total. In

---

[3] Almost all common persons who view this situation, view it simply and logically. In the late 70's, anecdotally, I prepared a fence for the yard, I had to purchase fence poles, and chain fencing. In the neighbors yard were several existing, dated, poles which would have allowed for a little more than half of the job; the dated material was stamped 'U.S. Steel' 'made in USA', and seemed a better gauge steel, being heavier and threaded deeper. The other material purchased to finish the job was lighter, did the job, but was made in Japan. Consequently, I was informed that since the closure of American steel plants, we were shipping 'our' steel overseas to Japan, and in return, the Japanese were selling this same material back to us, cheaper than we could have [?] in the first place. However you look at it, someone was benefiting in a larger degree, and that was not us. How many jobs were lost because of this 'national direction'? Thousands, to be sure. Was it worth it to the common people, losing their jobs, keeping local communities tight knit, and maintaining a competitive productive edge with the Europeans and the Japanese? Remember, these decisions came from international financial recommendations, as well as those in our own government who stood to gain thereby. This was just one of the many 'de-nationalisations' to occur within this country that would change the way in which we viewed ourselves, and developed as a growing nation. The issues of 'clean air', 'water pollution' and the like, would have been solved if the Corporate entities saw their very survival at stake; if they were prone to leave the shores of this country regardless, than temporary nationalization of domestic raw materials and resources and industry would be the punishment meted out to these concerns. FLS

[1] Motor Vehicle Manufacturers Association of the United States, World Motor Vehicle Data 10 (1982).
[2] Ibid.
[3] Ibid.
[4] Ibid.
[5] Current Affairs Atlas, *supra* note 82, at 35.
[6] U.S. Department of Commerce, Bureau of Industrial Economics, 1984 U.S. Industrial Outlook 33-1 (1984).
[7] Ibid, at 33-2.
[8] Ibid.
[9] Ibid.
[67] U.S. Department of Commerce, The U.S. Industrial Outlook for 1961, at 164 (1964).
[67] 1984 U.S. Industrial Outlook, *supra* note, 144, at 143-6.
[67] U.S. Industrial Outlook for 1961, *supra* note, 150.

1965, world production was 360,544,00 tons and U.S. production was 88,858,672 tons, or 24.6 percent of the world total. In 1982, the preliminary world total of pig iron production was 550,815,000 tons compared with the United States preliminary total production of 43,136,000 tons or 7.8 percent of the world total.

In 1978, America's merchant fleet with 12 million tons sailing under its flag, is dwarfed by Japan's 29 million gross tons, Great Britain's 33 million, Norway's 28 million, and Greece's 23 million.[68] U.S. shipyards are unable to compete with foreign shipbuilders who offer to build merchant vessels at prices 60 percent lower that it will cost in the United States.[69] With rare exceptions, U.S. shipbuilders must rely on military and domestic shipping procurement protected under federal law. During 1983, shipbuilding declined by 14 percent.[70] The current orderbook for commercial vessel production is at a pre-World War II level. Only 12 deep-draft commercial vessels, 1,000 gross tons and over, are projected to be under construction or on order as of January 1, 1984.[71] In contrast, world orderbook of vessels of 2,000 dead weight tons or more was 1,442.[72]

Regarding consumer electronics, in 1960, the United States manufactured 17.2 million radio sets.[73] Today, the only radios manufactured in the United States are some car stereos.[74] In 1960, the United States manufactured 5.7 million televisions[75], or almost 30 percent of the world's total. By 1976, it manufactured 6 million sets, or only about 15 percent of the world's total. In 1984, the U.S. manufactured even a smaller percentage. During the past 25 years the domestic consumer electronics industry has shifted from being a principal supplier of traditional radio and television receivers and related products to being the minority supplier. Imports account for an estimated 56 percent of sales in the domestic market.[76]

U.S. manufacturers no longer produce monochrome television receivers; domestic demand is met by imports from the Far East.[77] Portable and table radios and audio tape recorders are not produced in the U.S. Production has shifted to the Far East.[78] The U.S. does not produce consumer-type video cassette recorders.[79] Few U.S. firms

---

[75] U.S. Industrial Outlook for 1961, *supra* note, 150.
[76] 1984 U.S. Industrial Outlook, *supra* note, 144, at 143-6.
[77] Ibid.
[78] Ibid.
[79] Ibid.

manufacture dot-matrix impact printers.[80] The U.S. manufactures virtually no 35mm cameras.[81] Only one U.S.-owned company manufacturers motorcycles and it has been losing money yearly.[82]

The rate of savings in the U.S. is the lowest of any developed country. Personal savings rate in Japan is 19 percent; in France, 16 percent; in West Germany, 14 percent; in Britain, 14 percent and in the U.S. less than 5 percent.[83] When business needs more capital than ever, we are selling more stock than we are buying. In 1970, there were 31 million individual investors. Today, there are only 24 million.[84]

(d) Public Works

[See Text]

6. In Conclusion

The above facts unequivocally indicate that America is:

1. Becoming a nonwhite nation;

2. Allowing its Family structure to dissolve;

3. Engaging in rampant sexual promiscuity directly resulting in:

    (a) an elimination of chastity;

    (b) widespread abortion;

    (c) widespread and open homosexuality;

    (d) rampant heterosexual and homosexual venereal disease;

4. Losing its faith in god and its Christian ethics;

5. Beset with uncontrollable crime;

6. Beset with widespread drug abuse;

7. Promoting decadence through its forms of entertainment;

---

[80] Ibid. at 27-3.
[81] Ibid. at 37-2.
[82] Ibid. at 44-14.
[83] W. Wilshard, *supra* note 130, at 317.
[84] Ibid.

8. Contentious and litigious;

9. Allowing the numbers of poor to swell enormously;

10. Losing its national literacy;

11. Losing its technological edge; and

12. Allowing its public works to decay.

II. DECLINE AND RUIN

[See Text]

III. ANALYSIS OF PHILOSOPHIES WHICH FOSTER OUR DECLINE
---- PART ONE

[See Text]

IV. SOLUTIONS AT LAW REGARDING STANDARDS OF CONDUCT

There is no clear-cut method to change our attitudes and actions to enable us to overcome our social ills. However, as mentioned earlier, we can return the structure of our laws to a form that will one again be conducive to right conduct. This would be accomplished by reempowering the states with the ability to govern and solve their own domestic problems.

Over time, the reach of our federal government has grown so long and powerful that it now covers almost every action of the people.[85] It is bulky and overbearing and often restrains effective measures to solve our problems[86], whereas states, reempowered with the right to solve their problems could effect change on a local level and accomplish more efficiently the will of the people. This is the essence of the states' rights arguments that have existed since the constitution was ratified in 1789. at this point, an explanation of this argument is appropriate.

> The question of the relation which the State and General Government bear to each other is not one of recent origin. From the commencement of our system, it has divided public sentiment. Even in the convention, while the constitution was struggling into existence, there were two parties as to what this relation should be, whose different sentiments constituted no small impediment in forming that

---

[85] Milton & Rose Friedman, Free to Choose, 190-1 (1980). See, supra note 348 and accompanying text.
[86] Ibid.

instrument. After the General Government went into operation, experience soon proved that the question had not terminated with the labors of the Convention.[87]

These words of John C. Calhoun, uttered on July 26, 1831, are just as relevant today as they were then, and the issue of federal-state relations is as pressing as it ever was. The U.S. Supreme Court stated in 1975 that: "Surely there can be no more fundamental constitutional question than that of the intention of the Framers of the Constitution as to how authority should be allocated between the National and State Governments."[88]

Despite this debate that continually rages over the extent of federal jurisdiction arising our of enumerated but undefined and indefinite powers, the Constitution of the United States is a truly remarkable document. Gladstone referred to its as "the most wonderful work ever struck off at a given time by the brain and purpose of man."[89]

The Constitution was fashioned by the representatives of "sovereign states" who had met for about a dozen years in a loose-knit confederation,[90] and who saw the need for a more powerful central government. Two cardinal features distinguish the republic created by the Constitution from all other political organizations in existence up to the time of its founding.

First, 'in creating a new government the founding fathers sought to guard against the exercise of arbitrary power through a system of checks and balances referred to as the 'separations of powers' whereby governmental authority is divided between three branches of government to the end that each will serve as a limitation on the others."[91]

Second, "the framers resolved to further limit governmental authority by creating a dual or federal system, be delegating to a central government only those powers which conveniently could not be exercised locally while at the same time reserving to the several states the broad residuum of powers traditionally possessed by governments."[92]

---

[87] Address by John c. Calhoun, in Virginia Commission on Constitutional Government, The Fort Hill Address of John C. Calhoun (1960).
[88] *Fry v. United States* 421 U.S. 542, 559 (1975) (Rhenquist, J., dissenting).
[89] Gladstone, *Kin Beyond the Sea*, North American Rev., Sept. 1878.
[90] This period is calculated from 1776, including the events of the Continental Congress under the Articles of confederation, to 1788 when the call for constitutional revision was issued.
[91] Leverett, supra note 303, at 352.
[92] Ibid.

The U.S. supreme court described this dual or federal system in United States v. Cruikshank[93] as follows:

> We have in our political system a government of the United States and a government of each of the several states. Each one of these governments is distinct from the other, and each has citizens of its own who owe it allegiance, and whose rights, within its jurisdiction, it must protect. The same person may be at the same time a citizen of the United States and a citizen of a State, but his rights of citizenship under one of these governments will be different from those he has under the other...
>
> The government of the United States is one of delegated powers alone. Its authority is defined and limited by the constitution. All powers not granted to it by that instrument are reserved to the states of the people. No rights can be acquired under the constitution or laws of the United States, except such as the government of the United States has the authority to grant or secure. All that cannot be granted or secured are left under the protection of the States.

Further, the U.S. Supreme Court stated in *Hammer v. Dagenhart*[94] that:

> In interpreting the Constitution, it must never be forgotten that the nation is made up of States to which are entrusted the powers of local government. And to them and to the people powers not expressly delegated to the National Government are reserved...The power of the States to regulate their purely internal affairs by such laws as seem wise to the local authority is inherent and has never been surrendered to the general government..."

The powers of the federal government are vested in the three branches solely by virtue of the Constitution. The central government was one of delegated powers only. Moreover, the Founding Fathers felt that the exercise of these powers delegated by the federal government needed to be limited so that the rights of the citizens of the several states were protected. The Constitution was ratified only after assurances that limitations on actions by the federal government would be submitted by the first Congress in the form of amendments thereto. These limitations, known as the "bill of rights," were adopted three years after the ratification of the Constitution,[95] largely as a result of James Madison's insistence,[96] and are considered to be an integral part of the original federal system.[97] Under our dual or federal system, any assertion of power by the federal government must be in accordance with the powers delegated to it by the Constitution. If the Constitution does not delegate the federal government the authority to act, then we need look no further; the federal government cannot act. If

---

[93] 92 U.S. 542 (1876).
[94] 247 U.S. 251, 275-6 (1918).
[95] Leverett, *supra* note 303, at 353.
[96] B. Schwartz, The Law in America 47 (1974).
[97] Merrill, *supra* note 304, at 579.

the Constitution does delegated power to the federal government in a certain area, then "we must go one step further and ascertain whether the mode in which that power is sought to be exercised transgresses any limitation contained in the bill of rights.[98]

Under the bill of rights, the federal government could do no act to restrain certain enumerated rights of the people even if it was action under the color of certain delegated powers. Moreover, the tenth amendment provided "the powers not delegated to the United States by the Constitution, nor prohibited by it to the states, are reserved to the states respectively, or to the people."[99] In essence, this language merely set forth in writing an already existing principle and did nothing more than state the facts that the federal government's powers are delegated ones and are not plenary. If the states, as independent sovereignties, did not delegated powers to the central government by the Constitution, then they retain those powers. By no other means does the federal government attain power but through the delegation of the states. The states' rights debate centers on just how much authority should be vested in the central government and how much should be vested in the people. Advocates of centralization of governmental power accuse the states' rights advocates of being confederates and rebels,[100] racists,[101] and "radical in the extreme."[102] Advocates of a centralized government have traditionally looked to the government as a "mother figure" to solve most national ills, and, until the most recent trend away from big government, had been effective in attaining a centralization of power.

Therein [above] lies the states' rights debate. Centralization and big government on the one hand and division of power and local control on the other. A return to local control will be the vehicle for the American people to effect the change necessary to alter our current course toward ruin. In recent years, we expanded and extended the scope and authority of the central government to such an extent that the continued existence of our federal republic is in jeopardy. "One well may ask whether the states have not been reduced vis-à-vis the federal government, to well below the status of counties in the ordinary commonwealth. All this has been accomplished without the aid of constitutional amendment. If it stands, have we not replaced our Federal Republic with a unitary policy without even half trying to do so?"[103]

---

[98] Leverett, *supra* note 303, at 353.
[99] U.S. Constitution amend. X.
[100] Mason, *Must We Continue the States Rights Debate?*, 18 Rugers L. Rev. 60, 61 (1963).
[101] Ibid., at 60.
[102] Prof. Charles L. Black, Jr., Professor of Jurisprudence, Yale Law School, Cong. Rec. 8263 (daily ed., May 15, 1963), as quoted in McGovern, *Confederation vs. Union*, 9 S.D.L. Rev. 1 (1964).
[103] Merrill, *supra* note 304, at 584.

Long before Justice Rehnquist concluded in *Fry v. United States*[104] that "the Constitution was [not] intended to permit the result reached today; have we not driven another nail in the coffin of the Federal Republic?," officials representing many states met together in Biloxi, Mississippi, on July 27, 1962, and "speaking through the powerful Council of State Governments,"[105] addressed the issue of extension of Federal powers and concluded, as follows:[106]

> "The characteristic of our constitutional government, which has contributed most to the development of democratic processes and the preservation of human rights is the division of the powers of government between the nation and the states on the one and between the executive, legislative and judicial departments of both state and federal governments on the other. Over the years, we have escaped the evils of despotism and totalitarianism. It is only when each division of the whole government structure insists upon the right to exercise its powers, unrestrained by any other division, that the proper balance can be maintained and constitutional government, as we understand it, preserved.

"It is the responsibility of the central government to protect the people from invasion by the states of those rights which are guaranteed to them by the federal Constitution. It is equally the obligation of the states to initiate and to prosecute to fruition the necessary procedures to protect the states and the people from unwarranted assumption of power by any department of the federal government.

"A greater degree of restraint on the part of the United States Supreme Court can do much, but experience shows that it is not likely to be sufficient. The basic difficulty is that the Supreme Court's decision concerning the balance between federal and state power are final and can be changed in practice only if the states can muster sufficient interest in Congress, backed by a three-fourths majority of states themselves to amend the Constitution. While the founding fathers fully expected and wished the words of the constitution to have this degree of finality, it is impossible to believe that they envisaged such potency for the pronouncements of nine judges appointed by the President and confirmed by the Senate. The Supreme Court is, after all, an organ of federal government. It is one of the three branches of the national

---

[104] Douglas, *The Tenth Amendment: The Foundation of Liberty*, 16 New Hampshire Bar J. 286 (1975).
[105] Mason, *supra* note 343, at 60.
[106] State Government 10 (Winter, 1963).

government, and in conflicts over federal and state power; the Court is necessarily an agency of one of the parties in interest. As such, its decisions should not be assigned the same finality as the words of the Constitution itself. There is need for an easier method of setting such decisions straight when they are unsound.

"To amend the Federal Constitution to correct specific decisions of the federal courts on specific points is desirable, but it will not necessarily stop the continuing drift toward more complete federal domination. The present situation has taken a long time to develop and may take a long time to remedy. Accordingly, some more fundamental and far-reaching change in the Federal Constitution is necessary to preserve and protect the states.

"It is the ultimate of political ingenuity to achieve a vigorous federal system in which dynamic states combine with a responsibly central government for the good of the people"

Basically, the power of the federal government just grew over time, little by little, through a judicial activism, which characterized the Warren and Burger courts, but was prevalent in other courts as well. The meaning of judicial activism is attempting to achieve social reform through judicial decision. Judge Jerome Frank described this process by saying that 'judges work back from conclusions to principles."[107] A more detailed explanation of judicial activism is as follows: Judges formulated out of the record and the arguments a tentative conclusion as to what justice and the law require. Then the judge searches for theories and authorities to support the tentative conclusion.[108] Judges excuse this approach claiming, "it is psychologically impossible even to approximated objectivity and impartiality."[109]

The two major constitutional theories by which the activist courts have extended their power to control state activities are the commerce power and the fourteenth amendment. Concerning the commerce clausse*, legal scholars have stated: "during

---

[107] J. Frank, Law And the Modern Mind 102 (1930)
[108] Merrill, *supra* note 304, at 358.
[109] M. Thomas, Felix Frankfurter, Scholar On The Bench 286 (1960).
* Clause 3. Commerce Power: POWER TO REGULATE COMMERCE

Purposes Served by the Grant

This clause serves a two-fold purpose: it is the direct source of the most important powers that the Federal Government exercises in peacetime, and, except for the due process and equal protection clauses of the Fourteenth Amendment, it is the most important limitation imposed by the Constitution on the exercise of 'state power'. The latter, restrictive operation of the clause was long the more important one from the point of view of the constitutional lawyer. Of the approximately 1400 cases, which reached the Supreme Court under the clause prior to 1900, the overwhelming proportion stemmed from state legislation. The result was that, generally, the guiding lines in construction of the clause were initially laid down in the context of *curbing* state power rather than in that of its operation as a source of national power. The consequence of this historical progression was that the word "commerce" came to dominate the clause while the word "regulate" remained in the background. The so-called "constitutional revolution" of the 1930s, however, brought the latter word to its present prominence.

Definition of Terms

Commerce. --The etymology of the word "commerce" [cum – merce (with merchandise)] carries the primary meaning of traffic, of transporting goods across state lines for sale. This possibly narrow constitutional conception was rejected by Chief Justice Marshall in Gibbons v. Ogden, which remains one of the seminal cases dealing with the Constitution. The case arose because of a monopoly granted by the New York legislature on the operation of steam-propelled vessels on its waters, a monopoly challenged by Gibbons who transported passengers from New Jersey to New York pursuant to privileges granted by an act of Congress. The New York monopoly was not in conflict with the congressional regulation of commerce, argued the monopolists, because the vessels carried only passengers between the two States and were thus not engaged in traffic, in "commerce" in the constitutional sense.

"The subject to be regulated is commerce," the Chief Justice wrote. "The counsel for the appellee would limit it to traffic, to buying and selling, or the interchange of commodities, and do not admit that it comprehends navigation. This would restrict a general term, applicable to many objects, to one of its significations. Commerce, undoubtedly, is traffic, but it is something more--it is intercourse." The term, therefore, included navigation, a conclusion that Marshall also supported by appeal to general understanding, to the prohibition in Article I, Sec. 9, against any preference being given "by any regulation of commerce or revenue, to the ports of one State over those of another," and to the admitted and demonstrated power of Congress to impose embargoes.

Marshall qualified the word "intercourse" with the word "commercial," thus retaining the element of monetary transactions. But, today, "commerce" in the constitutional sense, and hence "interstate commerce," covers every species of movement of persons and things, whether for profit or not, across state lines, every species of communication, every species of transmission of intelligence, whether for commercial purposes or otherwise, 586 every species

the forty years since the New Deal, social control has inexorably consolidated in the expanding federal bureaucracy on the strength of the commerce power and the spending power,"[110] and "during the Depression years, the country suffered the spectacle of the court distorting the Commerce clause completely out of proportions so as to drastically expand federal power."[111]

Concerning the fourteenth amendment, legal scholars have pointed out: "the ironical fact of all this is that the so-called enlightened 'liberal' who today invokes the [fourteenth] Amendment for his own selfish aims invariably professes to be conduction some divinely inspired crusade, yet nothing in the history of this country is more immoral, fraudulent or high-handed than the manner in which the Fourteenth Amendment was adopted."[112]

It is not the purpose of this author [James O. Pace] to trace the tortuous precedents concerning the commerce clause and the fourteenth amendment, which have empowered the federal government to control the affairs regulated by the states. Nevertheless, as for the fourteenth amendment, a brief history of the development and interpretation is in order, due to the recommendations this author makes concerning it.

The history of the "ratification" of the fourteenth amendment, which provides in part "that no state shall deprive any person of life, liberty, or property, without the due process of law," is as follows.[113]

> The fourteenth Amendment was submitted by a Congress dominated by a radical republican leadership, which never would have succeeded, had Lincoln lived.
>
> The Constitution requires a two-thirds vote of both houses to submit an amendment for ratification. While the submission was by two-thirds of those present, this two-thirds was obtained only by excluding, under reconstruction acts, representatives of ten confederated states, notwithstanding the fact that the Constitution also provides that each state shall have at least one representative in the House. If the Southern delegation in Congress today

---

of commercial negotiation which will involve sooner or later an act of transportation of persons or things, or the flow of services or power, across state lines. [Note added. FLS]

---

[110] Heldt, The Tenth Amendment Iceberg, 30 Hastings L. J. 1763, 1764 (1979).
[111] Leverett, *supra* not 303, at 358.
[112] Ibid, at 335.
[113] Ibid, at 355.

were to forcibly eject representatives of other states and seek to submit a repeal of the amendment, would anyone seriously contend their actions legal?

Consequently, it follows that the Fourteenth Amendment was never legally submitted.

However, even passing by the illegal submission, it is equally clear that the amendment was never legally ratified. Adoption under the Constitution required ratification by at least three-fourths, or 28, of the 37 states then in existence.

Kentucky, Delaware and Maryland rejected the amendment outright. The amendment has never been ratified by California. New Jersey and Ohio initially ratified it but both later withdrew their ratification. All ten of the Southern states immediately rejected it. The Amendment failed.

Assuming for the moment that the submission was legal, this rejection was lawful and proper under the procedure provided by the Constitution. That should have been the end of the matter. But ['reconstruction'] Congress became infuriated, and thenceforth adopted high-handed measures.

It enacted, over President [Andrew] Johnson's veto, the Reconstruction Act of 1867, which declared that no legal government existed in the 'ten states' [emph added], placed them all under military occupation, disfranchised the white people, and put the state governments in the hands of illiterate Negroes, scalawags and carpet-baggers. In another section, this wholesale bill of attainder* provided that each excluded state must ratify the amendment in

---

* [Note: Bill of Attainder

Definition: A *legislative* act that singles out an individual' or 'group' for *punishment* without a trial.

The Constitution of the United States, Article I, Section 9, paragraph 3 provides that: "No Bill of Attainder *or* ex post facto Law will be passed." [emph. added]

"The Bill of Attainder Clause was intended not as a narrow, technical (and therefore soon to be outmoded) prohibition, but rather as an implementation of the separation of powers, a general safeguard against legislative exercise of the judicial function or more simply - trial by legislature." U.S. v. Brown, 381 U.S. 437, 440 (1965).
"These clauses of the Constitution are not of the broad, general nature of the Due Process Clause, but refer to rather precise legal terms which had a meaning under English law at the time the Constitution was adopted. A bill of attainder was a legislative act that singled out one or more persons and imposed punishment on them, without benefit of trial. Such actions were regarded as odious by the framers of the Constitution because it

order to enjoy the status of a state, including representation in Congress. It was only under such duress that the amendment was finally adopted.

As mentioned earlier, the bill of rights originally applied only to the federal government. The states ratified the Constitution on the *promise* that further restraints on enumerated federal power would be adopted by means of a bill of rights, and this was done. The Constitution contains an enumeration of powers expressly granted by the states to the federal government. This indicated that the Constitution is an enabling and not a restraining instrument.[114] By virtue of this fact, since the states did not restrict themselves in the bill of rights, the various state legislatures were free to act on the rights contained in the first ten amendments as they saw fit, subject to approval by the state supreme court review and not the U.S. Supreme Court.

Accordingly, states could pass laws outlawing what they perceive to be obscenity, pornography…They could empower their school boards with the right to dismiss incompetent teachers without fear of civil rights reprisals. States could impose the death penalty, crowd the jails and deny the prisoners recreation facilities without fear of federal courts ruling that such acts were unconstitutional. In sum, any right contained in the bill of rights could be handled in a manner the state governments saw fit.*

---

was the traditional role of a court, judging an individual case, to impose punishment." William H. Rehnquist, The Supreme Court, page 166.
"Bills of attainder, ex post facto laws, and laws impairing the obligations of contracts, are contrary to the first principles of the social compact, and to every principle of sound legislation. … The sober people of America are weary of the fluctuating policy, which has directed the public councils. They have seen with regret and indignation that sudden changes and legislative interferences, in cases affecting personal rights, become jobs in the hands of enterprising and influential speculators, and snares to the more-industrious and less-informed part of the community." James Madison, Federalist Number 44, 1788. FLS]

[114] *Worcester v. Georgia* 6 Peters 515 (1832); *Brown v. Epps* 91 Va. 726, 21 SE 114 (Va. 1895).
* Note: I personally feel some uncertainty in this area. Since my personal experiences include interaction with the 'legal' system and its various arms, on a federal level, yet am also aware of the particular and individual 'state' excesses in which the public, especially 'prisoners' are exposed, I feel it necessary to point out that, while supporting 'state rights', it is necessary to understand that if a 'nation' is to share both flesh and bone, then a common legal system, such as our already existing Anglo-Saxon/Dane Law, which has already attempted to provide for this Western nation this very example, through many hundreds of generations, to prove its validity and value, both socially and legislatively. In other words, common interests, in the name of decency and justice, should always be paramount in determining the 'federal' jurisdiction or, in any term, the 'national character' through its laws and perceptions of their consequence. *Pater familias*, must always be judged by its consequences. FLS]

The adoption of the fourteenth amendment provided the U. S. Supreme Court with the opportunity to change that. Through a series of cases, the U.S. Supreme Court construed the due process clause of the fourteenth amendment (which was applicable to the states) in a manner, which made the bill of rights also applicable to the states. At that point, the U.S. Supreme Court empowered itself to review all actions by the states in regard to bill of rights issues and pass on their constitutionality.

Historically, "due process" meant that the federal government would not deprive someone of his rights without following lawful procedures. This meant that in order to send a suspect to jail there had to be a duly conducted trial held first. This concept is embodied in numerous laws and ordinances besides the Constitution. The concept of due process was expanded by dividing it into two areas, one called procedural due process, the traditional concept, and one called substantive due process. Procedural due process concerned the legal procedure employed to deprive an individual of his rights.

The procedural due process safe guards ensured that the individual charged with a crime would be assured of the right to such things as:

    a.   Notice of the nature and cause of the charge against him;

    b.   A speedy and public trial by an impartial jury;

    c.   Opportunity to confront witnesses accusing him and to compel witnesses in his favor to appear;

Furthermore, the individual would not be:

    a.   Subject to unreasonable searches or baseless arrests by government officials;

    b.   Compelled to incriminate himself.

These and other procedural rights are incorporated into the bill of rights. The concept of substantive due process was developed to extend the power of the court's authority beyond the mere enforcement of proper procedure when depriving a person life, liberty, or property, to include the power of the court to guarantee what it saw as a basic liberty. At this point, it no longer was sufficient for Congress or the sates to pass laws, which restrict the actions of the citizens. Even if they did so according to proper, established procedure, i.e. due process of law. Every act of Congress o the states which could affect an implied constitutional right became subjects to judicial scrutiny. The courts would determine if a right is guaranteed under the Constitution by implication, and if it was, the court could rule it unconstitutional in the event the court thought is unjust. Hence, the courts, for example, were able to read into the Constitution the guarantees of the right of a woman to have an abortion, even if elected legislators enacted laws to make it illegal. Under other amendments contained in the bill of rights made applicable to the states by the fourteenth amendment, the U.S. Supreme Court has been able to invalidate state anti-pornography statutes, state penal codes, zoning laws, etc.

The result has been that in recent years the power and the rights of the communities and citizens of the various states to promote programs and use their duly enacted laws to maintain their traditional value system has been curtailed by the U.S. Supreme Court and other federal courts as well. Once the U.S. Supreme Court granted itself jurisdiction over state action, it began to cast aside various state action governing standards of conduct as being unconstitutional. At times, it would find an entire state statute to be unconstitutional and at other times only portions thereof.

Because of this social activism on the part of the U.S. Supreme Court, states in the 1960's bean to raise questions about the Court's present day function. Many states were saying that the U.S. Supreme Court, comprised of unelected officials, was legislation laws rather than merely interpreting them.

As it stands now, there is no purpose in maintaining separate state constitution or state laws. On vital social issues, the federal courts have removed the power to which the states were originally entitled to construct and construe their own laws.

There is no debate as to the express powers of the federal government. These are many and are fundamental to a united nation. However, the U.S. Supreme court, other federal courts and even congress with increasing fervor in recent years, have been enlarging the role of the federal government by taking a concept in the Constitution and expanding it to include vaguely related principles, giving rise to so-called *implied* federal rights. For example, Article I, Section 8 of the Constitution provides that Congress shall have power "to regulate commerce with foreign nations, and among the several States, and with the Indian Tribes" Congress and the federal courts reasoned that race relations affect commerce and since Congress may regulate that area, it may regulate race relations to the exclusion of the states. Accordingly, the power to regulate racial discrimination was delegated to the federal government by *implication* and the U.S. Supreme Court approved. Thus, there was no violation of the tenth amendment guarantee of states' rights. [emph. added]

The interpretation of the fourteenth amendment by the U.S. Supreme Court has altered our federal system. The U.S. Supreme Court, by its own social activism, has assumed legislative control over the states and now decides issues of race relations, religion, abortion and many other pivotal issues which determine whether or not a society progresses or regresses. The U.S. Supreme Court thus makes decisions that no state or community can alter no matter how wrong the decisions are and no matter if 100 percent of the population votes to have them altered.

In spite of all we do as individuals to elevate the morality of the nation, our efforts will be thwarted by the strictures of unconstitutionality placed upon the legislatures by the federal courts. Courts, in their attempt to restrict the community of its rights and have mandated the legislation of immorality, and the abandonment of our entire heritage.

There exists a solution.

This [action] would be accomplished by repealing he fourteenth amendment to the constitution and strengthening the tenth amendment guarantees of states' rights. Since the federal courts use the due process clause of the fourteenth amendment to gain supervisory power over the states on key issues, the repeal of this amendment would effectively remove the court created basis on which federal judges rely to regulated state action so extensively. To repeal the fourteenth amendment would be to eliminate the due process clause applicable to the states, with which the U.S. Supreme Court and the federal government have appropriated the constitutional rights of the states. This would mean that only the various state supreme courts and not the U.S. Supreme Court could pass on the constitutionality of these key issues, and they would do this based on the U.S. Constitution and the respective state constitutions. Due process, as applied to the federal system would still exist in the fifth amendment and in federal statutes such as the Federal Rules of Civil Procedure, etc., and due process would exist for the states as set forth in their constitutions and other laws and statutes. The basic rights of the citizens, as they concern the government's obligation to abide by the laws in its disposition of life, liberty and property, will be unaffected. What will be altered is the power the U.S. Supreme Court has assumed to invalidate state action on issues that are so fundamental to a community's wholesome development. The supremacy of the Constitution and the federal government would remain unchallenged. Our country would still be centrally controlled areas of national interest, taxation, military, international affairs, commerce, and other areas expressly delegated to the federal government by the U.S. Constitution. *Only the issues of local concern, standards of conduct and racial identity would be affected thereby.* [emph. added]

V. ANALYSIS OF PHILOSOPHIES WHICH FOSTER OUR DECLINE
--PART TWO

1. Introduction

In recent years, those whom the world traditionally recognizes as Americans[115*] (those of Western European Stock) have been taught to disregard the richness of their heritage and identity and even be ashamed of it. In certain circles of our society, it is deemed to be misplaced pride to value the achievements of our ancestors and our race. To pride oneself on being descended from the founding Fathers is often considered to be hollow boasting. Yet, our forefathers founded this nation and drafted the Constitution for their posterity and for no one else's [see, for instance, *U.S. Constitution*, preamble], so, in fact, those that can, should rejoice in being of their lineage and heir to that birthright. America must value its past and rejoice in its rich heritage, or forever lose that heritage to other races who *value* theirs. [emph. added]

There is a direct link between our past and our future. If we despise, make light of, or ignore our past, we cannot pass on our identity and culture to our posterity. Our children will abandon our culture and the ideals we hold.[116] They will increasingly marry into other races and allow those races to continue immigrating to America en masse until America is no longer white but thoroughly mixed. At that point, national unity will become impossible to regain until we *are* unified as one dark-skinned race. This darkening of America is rapidly taking place today, and we are so confused by our identity that no one can speak out against it and feel comfortable in society. Unless we remember our heritage and strive to preserve it for our posterity, America will be overrun and ruined.

3. Outline of Incorrect Philosophies on Racial Identity

---

[115] The Japanese, for example, often call Anglo-Saxons the "real Americans."

* [Note: As was stated in ROTW, race-cultures, such as the Japanese, see the West in 'traditional' terms; this includes the rationalization that our Military might comes from 'within', that our *soul* is part and parcel of our 'race-soul', that is, *what we are made of.* Those persons not of the West, whether friend or foe, knows, without a doubt, just *who* are members of the West, and who are not. Ironically, it appears that, for the most part it is, precisely, those very members of the West who have no waking idea of just who they are as it relates to those various and diverse race-cultures which inhabit this world with them. FLS]

[116] [See Text]

The incorrect philosophies regarding our identity will be discussed in this part of the text. Further, this part will deal with the issue of race, how America is being replaced with other peoples and how our incorrect philosophies regarding identity allow this to happen.

Some incorrect notions subscribed to by a large number of Americans and which prevent us from preserving our nation are as follows:

1. Maintaining the racial composition of a society is racist.

2. America is a country for all races. Except for the American Indians from whom we took this land, all Americans are immigrants, so to restrict immigration or citizenship to whites is un-American.

3. History has proved that our past racial discrimination was groundless. Racial diversity enhances our influence in the world community and gives us vitality that racially homogeneous countries do not have.

4. It does not matter if Americans become a nonwhite people.

Following is an analysis of the above mentioned notions.

1. Maintaining the racial composition of a society is racist.

The International Convention on the Eliminations of All forms of Racial Discrimination provides that "racial segregation…[is] condemned by the States' parties, and they pledge to prevent, prohibit and eradicate all such practices in their territories."[117] This UN –sponsored convention is express in its position that maintaining racial identity and communities of one's own people is racist. Further, articles in the UNESCO Courier assert that "integration, both racial and cultural, is certainly an indispensable stop on the road to the eradication of racialism."[118]

    i)   There are pure races

[See Text]

    ii)   These pure races are biologically superior

---

[117] 20 UN Chronicle, Oct. 1983, at 54.
[118] Retamar, Mixed Metamorphosis, UNESCO Courier, Nov. 1983, at 22.

[See Text]

    iii) Superiority explains and justifies their predominance and privileges.

[See Text]

2. America is a country for all races. Except for the Indians, form whom we took the land, all Americans are immigrants. Thus, to restrict immigration or citizenship to whites only is un-American.

[See Text]

    i) We took the land from the Indians.

[See Text]

    ii) America is a country for all races.

[See Text]

3. History has proved that our past racial discrimination was groundless. Racial diversity enhances our influence in the world community and give us vitality that racially homogeneous countries do not have.

We have somehow come to believe that our strength is derived from the literate masses of the third world rather than through a systematic growth of a unified country accepting hardworking additions only from the same source from which America sprang – Europe. This relatively new concept, "the Statue of liberty syndrome," has distorted our view of our country's strengths and weaknesses. Our nation was strong and unified before the word "melting pot" was used at the beginning of this century to describe certain cities in America, and it remained strong throughout the dedicated era of heavy immigration during this period because the waves of immigrants from Europe could easily assimilated themselves into America's European heritage.

Those afflicted with the Statue of Liberty syndrome seem to always use the Irish experience as an example and say: "Look at them; they were discouraged from coming to America and discriminated upon arrival, but they have adjusted. The reasons for discrimination against the Irish were groundless, just as groundless as discrimination is against the nonwhite immigrants of today.

Discrimination against the Irish was relatively mild and was based on two factors. First, territorial fears that a great number of immigrants would divide the nation and cause the Americans to lose their land and possessions. Second, the historical, but intense animosity between the Protestants and the Catholics of the British Isles. The Americans feared that the same problems would erupt here, which has proved not to have occurred. America was able to absorb the large number of Irish immigrants because their differences were minor and would vanish in *one* generation. The same can be said for the immigrants from the other European countries. Such is not the case with the Iranians, Laotians, Samoans or Puerto Ricans. It is more than just silly to say that because the Germans and the Irish adjusted so can the nonwhites; it is fatal tot the future of our country. Nonwhite presence in America will continue to rive the country and prevent progress until we fall apart or are totally overrun.

To make America a white country again is consistent with our history. No nation on earth can point a finger at us or even think ill of us for protecting our borders. They all do it with their own laws and occasionally by force. The world will only wonder why we waited so long.

5. It does not matter if Americans become a nonwhite people.

[See Text]

3. General thoughts in Summation

[See Text]

VI. THE AMENDMENT

1. The Scope of the Amendment

In essence, this section of the text advocates a return to the Dred Scott ruling and submits a proposal for repealing the fourteenth amendment, which would make that event a reality.

This proposal bas been drafted with two objectives in mind. The first one is the practicality in making the proposal law and the second one is achieving a fair and non-burdensome adjustment as the status and situation of the nonwhite population.

The fourteenth amendment is quoted below in full to enable the reader to understand its contents and the rationale for rescission thereof:

Frank L. DeSilva

ARTICLE XIV

Passed By Congress June 16, 1866. Ratified July 23, 1868

Section. 1. All persons born or naturalized in the United States and subject to the jurisdiction thereof, are citizens of the United States and of the State wherein they reside. No State shall make or enforce any law, which shall abridge the privileges or immunities of citizens of the United States; nor shall any State deprive any person of life, liberty, or property, without due process of law; nor deny to any person within its jurisdiction the equal protection of the laws.

Section. 2. Representatives shall be apportioned among the several States according to their respective numbers, counting the whole number of persons in each State, excluding Indians not taxed. But when the right to vote at any election for the choice of electors for President and Vice President of the United States, Representatives in Congress, the Executive and Judicial officers of a State, or the members of the Legislature thereof, is denied to any of the male inhabitants of such State, being twenty-one years of age, and citizens of the United States, or in any way abridged, except for participation in rebellion, or other crime, the basis of representation therein shall be reduced in the proportion which the number of such male citizens shall bear to the whole number of male citizens twenty-one years of age in such State.

Section. 3. No person shall be a Senator or Representative in Congress, or elector of President and Vice President, or hold any office, civil or military, under the United States, or under any State, who, having previously taken an oath, as a member of Congress, or as an officer of the United States, or as a member of any State legislature, or as an executive or judicial officer of any State, to support the Constitution of the United States, shall have engaged in insurrection or rebellion against the same, or given aid or comfort to the enemies thereof. But Congress may by a vote of two-thirds of each House, remove such disability.

Section. 4. The validity of the public debt of the United States, authorized by law, including debts incurred for payment of pensions and bounties for services in suppressing insurrection or rebellion, shall not be questioned. But neither the United States nor any State shall assume or pay any debt or obligation incurred in aid of insurrection or rebellion against the United

States, or any claim for the loss or emancipation of any slave; but all such debts, obligations and claims shall be held illegal and void.

Section. 5. The Congress shall have power to enforce, by appropriate legislation, the provisions of this article.

It should be noted that section 1 is the only important section of the entire amendment. The section 2 language as to apportionment of representatives is found in Article I of the constitution and the rest of Section 2 and the remaining sections contain nothing but punishments directed against the southern states for seceding from the Union.

The fourteenth amendment is an amendment that reflected the zeal of the day and should be repealed. Basically, it grew out of the Northerners' desire to humiliated the South and exact revenge from them for rebellion. It should not be maintained at the expense of the nation as a whole. Of all the laws contemplated by the Congress and the state legislatures, the most important legislation for the preservation of our union would be the proper repeal of this amendment.

There have been many efforts over the years to repeal the fourteenth and fifteenth amendments and to have them declared invalid. Below is a Senate Resolution of the Georgia Assembly, which sought to do just that. It explains in a clear manner the historical argument that the amendments are invalid.[119]

Senate Resolution No. 39 (Res. Act No. 45) of the 1957 regular session of the Georgia General Assembly, passed March 8, 1957, memorializes the United States Congress to declare the fourteenth and Fifteenth Amendments to the United States Constitution invalid. The resolution follows:

RESOLUTION ACT 45

"A memorial to the congress o the United States of America urging them to enact such legislation as they may deem fit to declared that the 14th and 15th Amendments

---

[119] Senate Resolution No. 39 (Res. Act No. 45) of the 1957 regular session of the Georgia General Assembly, passed March 8, 1957. See also *The Maryland Petition Committee, etc., et al. V. Lyndon B. Johnson, etc., et al.* 265 F. Supp. 823 (1967) which was an action in Federal Court against the President of the United States seeking declaratory judgment that the 14th and 15th amendments are null and void.

to the Constitution of the United States were never validly adopted and that they are null and void and of no effect.

"*Whereas*, the State of Georgia together with the ten other southern States declared to have been lately in rebellion against the United States, following the termination of hostilities in 1865, met all the conditions laid down by the President o the United States, in the exercise of his Constitutional to recognize the governments of states, domestic as well s foreign, for the resumption of practical relations with the Government of the United States, and at the direction of the President did elect Senators and Representatives to the 39th Congress of the United States, as a Stated and States in proper Constitutional relations to the United States; and

"*Whereas*, when the duly elected Senators and Representatives appeared in the Capitol of the United States to take their seat at the time for the opening of the 39th congress, and gain at the times for the openings of the 40th and the 41st Congress, hostile majorities in both Houses refused to admit them to their seats in manifest violation of Articles I and V of the United States Constitution; and

"*Whereas*, the said Congresses, not being constituted of Senators and Representatives from each State as required by the Supreme Law of the Land, were not, in Constitutional contemplation, anything more than private assemblages unlawfully attempting to exercise the Legislative Power of the United States; and

"*Whereas*, the so-called 39th Congress, which proposed to the Legislatures of the several States an amendment to the Constitution of the United States, as the 14th Amendment, and the so-called 40th Congress, which proposed and amendment know as the 15th Amendment, were without lawful power to propose any amendment whatsoever to the Constitution; and

"*Whereas*, two-thirds of the Members of the House of Representatives and of the Senate, as they should have been constituted, failed to vote for the submission of these amendments; and

"*Whereas*, all proceedings subsequently flowing from these invalid proposals, purporting to establish the so-called 14th and 15th Amendments as valid parts of the Constitution, were null and void and of no effect from the beginning; and

"*Whereas*, furthermore, when these invalid proposals were rejected by the General Assembly of the Stated o Georgia and twelve other Southern States, as well as of sundry Northern States, the so-called 39th and 40th Congresses, in flagrant disregard of the United States Constitution, by use of military force, dissolved the duly recognized State Governments in Georgia and nine of ht other Southern States and set up military occupation or puppet state governments, which compliantly ratified the invalid proposals, thereby making (at the point of the bayonet) a mockery of Section 4, Article IV of the Constitution, guaranteeing 'to every State in this Union a Republican form of Government,' and guaranteeing protection to 'each of them against invasion;' and

"*Whereas*, further, the pretended ratification of the so-called 14th and 15th Amendments by Georgia and other States whose sovereign powers had been unlawfully seized by force of arms against the peace and dignity of the people of those States, were necessary to give color to the claim of the so-called 40th and 41st Congresses that these so-called amendments had been ratified by three-fourths of the States; and

"*Whereas*, it is a well-established principle of law that the mere lapse of time does not confirm by common acquiescence and invalidly-enacted provision of law just as it does not repeal by general desuetude a provision validly enacted; and

"*Whereas*, the continued recognition of the 14th and 15th Amendments as valid parts of the Constitution of the United States as the World's champion of Constitutional governments resting upon the consent of the people given through their lawful representatives:

"*Now, therefore, be it resolved by the general Assembly of the State of Georgia:*

"The Congress of the United States is hereby memorialized and respectfully urged to declare that the exclusions of the Southern Senators and Representatives from the 39th, 40th, and 41st Congresses were malignant acts of arbitrary power and rendered those Congresses invalidly constituted; that the forms of law with which those invalid Congresses attempted to clothe the submission of the 14th and 15th Amendments and to clothe the subsequent acts to compel unwilling States to ratify these invalidly proposed amendments, imparted no validity to these acts and amendments; and that the so-called 14th and 15th Amendments to the Constitution of the United States are null and void and of no effect.

"*Be it further resolved* that copies of this memorial be transmitted forthwith by the Clerk of the House and Secretary of the Senate of the State of Georgia to the President of the United States, the Chief Justice of the United States, the President of the Senate and the Speaker of the House of Representatives of the United States, and the Senators and Representatives in the Congress from the State of Georgia."

Repeal of the fourteenth amendment and thereby reinstating the Dred Scott v. Stanford ruling that nonwhites cannot be citizens is a proper and necessary action for the preservation of the American people. Absent such legal safeguards for the American people, the course of modern America will continue until we are completely replaced by a new race of people.

The method for achieving this repeal, resulting in the revesting of the states with their rights to cure domestic problems regarding standards of conduct, and the unification of ht American people and retention of our racial identity, would be through the ratification of the following amendment to the Constitution, to be numbered the twenty-seventh amendment.

[Note: Herein lies the proposed Twenty-seventh Amendment to the Constitution of the United States, henceforth known as the 'Pace Amendment', and is the essence of this 'summary'; the analysis to follow is, also, part of the overall Pace Amendment, and it is strongly suggested that the reader should avail himself of the entire work by Mr. Pace, to keep in context his overall construct, and the 'end' to which this amendment would realize. FLS]

ARTICLE OF AMENDMENT XXVII

Section 1.

The fourteenth and fifteenth articles of amendment to the Constitution of the United States are hereby repealed. Further, in order to halt the encroachment into the reserved powers of the states by the United States and its judicial branch, the tenth article of amendment is hereby amended to read as follows:

The powers not expressly delegated to the United States by the Constitution, nor prohibited by it to the States, are reserved to the States respectively, or to the people.

Section 2.

No person shall be a citizen of the United States unless he is a non-Hispanic white of the European race, in whom there is no ascertainable trace of Negro blood, nor more than one-eighth Mongolian, Asian, Asia Minor, Middle Eastern, Semitic, Near Easter, American Indian, Malay or other non-European or nonwhite blood, provided that Hispanic whites, defined as anyone with an Hispanic ancestor, may be citizens if, in addition to meeting the aforesaid ascertainable trace and percentage tests, they are, in appearance, indistinguishable from Americans whose ancestral home is the British Isles or Northwestern Europe. Only citizens shall have the right and privilege to reside permanently in the United States.

Section 3.

The Congress and the several states, except where expressly preempted by the Congress, shall have concurrent power to enforce the provisions of this article by appropriate legislation, in coordination with the President, as such legislation concerns the making of treaties pursuant to Article 2, Section 2 of the Constitution.

Section 4.

This article shall be inoperative unless it shall have been ratified as an amendment to the Constitution by the Legislatures of three-fourths of the several states within seven years of its submission.

2. Analysis of the Sections

The following is a section-by-section discussion of the suggested twenty-seventh amendment.

(a) Section 1.

Section 1 of the amendment would repeal the fourteenth as well as the fifteenth amendments and would amend the tenth amendment by *inserting* the word "expressly" *before* the word "delegated." [emph. added.] The fourteenth amendment has been quoted above. The fifteenth amendment is quoted below.[120]

ARTICLE OF AMENDMENT XV (1870)

Section 1.

---

[120] U. S. Constitution amendment XV

The rights of citizens of the United States to vote shall not be denied or abridged by the United States or by any State on account of race, color, or previous condition of servitude.

Section 2.

The Congress shall have power to enforce this article by appropriate legislation.

A repeal of the fourteenth and fifteenth amendments will have two basic effects. It will eliminate the absorption doctrine whereby the U.S. supreme court has expanded the bill of rights protections to cover state action and, thus, ultimately usurp states' authority.[121] Lest there be any doubt in the minds of the U.S. Supreme court justices, the tenth amendment is amended as well to ensure this result. It will also terminate the right of citizenship by virtue of being born in the United States and could return the law to the state it was in after the *Dred Scott* decision. Since the fourteenth amendment directly reversed that decision, a repeal of the fourteenth amendment could terminate that reversal. The fourteenth and fifteenth amendments are the only references in the entire Constitution, which can be interpreted to bestow the rights of citizenship on nonwhites. In order to ensure this result, Section 2 of the suggested amendment is included. This issue will be discussed in detail in the analysis of Section 2 below.

A repeal of the fourteenth amendment will do much to terminate the illegal encroachment by the central government into the reserved powers of the States and rights of the people. However, a repeal of that amendment alone might not be sufficient in light of the extremely activist nature of the U.S. Supreme Court. The U.S. Supreme Court has impliedly bestowed powers on itself and the other branches of the central government in blatant disregard for the tenth amendment. A mere repeal of the fourteenth amendment may eliminated the due process theory on which the courts have relied to assume ultimate control over the people but might not prevent them from reaching the same ends by different means. The repeal of the fourteenth amendment is but a treatment of the symptoms, not a cure of the diseases. The cure is a reinforcement of the tenth amendment.

The Texas Legislature recognized this fact and by House Concurrent Resolution proposed as follows:

House Concurrent Resolution No. 5 of the second 1957 special session of the Texas Legislature proposes that a national convention be called, as provided by Article V of the United States Constitution, to amend the constitution so as "to clearly and specifically set

---

[121] *See, e.g. Gitlow v. New York* 268 U.S. 652 (1925); *Mapp v. Ohio* 367 U.S. 43 (1961)

out certain limits beyond which the United States government has no authority, as generally provided in the Tenth Amendment..."

HOUSE CONCURRENT RESOLUTION NO. 5

WHEREAS, The Constitution of the United States is bases upon the principle of proper limits being placed on the exercise of all power by all governments and officials, both state and national; and

WHEREAS, The people of the United States have historically believed in a written constitution rather than rule by proclamation; and

WHEREAS, The exercise of power by the United States Government has become so great and centralized as a result of the United States Supreme Court's liberal interpretation of the powers ascribed to the United States Government under the United States Constitution so as to threaten the very existence of all State Governments and states' rights except as political subdivisions of the United States; and

WHEREAS, The United States Supreme Court has virtually repealed the Tenth Amendment by interpretation which has resulted in a central government almost without limit of its powers; and

WHEREAS, The Texas Legislature further feels that individual rights and freedoms are best protected by limiting the powers of government rather than centralizing them; and

WHEREAS, The Legislature of the State of Texas recognizes that the easiest way for a foreign enemy to control the United States is to centralize all power and control in one central government rather than have all powers divided and limited among an "indivisible union of indestructible states"; and

WHEREAS, Article V of the United States Constitution provides a method whereby tow thirds of the States' Legislatures can petition Congress for a National Convention to propose an amendment to the United States Constitution to clearly and specifically set out certain limits beyond which the United States Government has no authority, as generally provided in the Tenth Amendment..."

As set forth above, the Texas legislature petitioned congress and the President to amend the Constitution so as to reinforce the meaning of the tenth amendment. The suggested amendment accomplishes this purpose by inserting the word "expressly" to further limit the powers of the federal government. When the proposed tenth amendment was discussed at the first Congress, the "expressly" was suggested as a clarification of the limitation on the power of the federal government.[122] The Hamiltonians, or Federalists, rejected this proposal while the Madisonians, or states' rights advocates, supported it.[123] The Hamiltonians won, and the word did not become a part of the tenth amendment. However, if the Hamiltonians could have seen how meaningless the tenth amendment would become, surely they would have not opposed the insertion of the word.

(b) Section 2 and 3

The citizenship clause of fourteenth amendment is no longer practical in today's mobile society where foreigners come to live in the United States for a few years with their families. Children are born in the United States and, by virtue of the citizenship clause of ht fourteenth amendment, these children become American citizens, when, in reality, they have no more of a nexus with this country than a birth certificate. Pregnant Mexicans [mestizos], Filipinos and other minority women abuse this clause to gain citizenship for their children by sneaking into this country to have their babies.

Often is the case where a Japanese or Korean company will send a young family to the United States and a baby is born here. When the family returns to it native country, the parents reenter their own country with their Japanese or Korean passports and the baby has a separate U.S. passport. The baby, with no more ties to the United States than a birth certificate, becomes a citizen entitled to live here with the foreign family it brings with it on its next visit. As for the Mexican [mestizo] families who come to America, their companies do not send them, nor do they have proper visas. They come into the country by themselves, illegally, but their children still become citizens. The whole world is taking advantage of these ridiculous laws that allow our country to be turned over to non-Americans. The amendment to the Constitution that this text proposes would plug that one loophole which makes children of Americans and children of illegal aliens equally American under the law.

---

[122] Comment, *An Affirmative Constitutional right: The Tenth amendment and the Resolution of the Federalism Conflicts*, 13 San Diego L. rev. 876, 878 (1976); 3 J. Elliot, *Debates on the Federal Constitution* 608 (1836).
[123] Comment, Ibid., at 878-9.

The sheer force of numbers necessitates this change. There are only 200 million actual Americans, but under current laws, there are 4 billion[124] potential ones.

Further, as mentioned above, we are seeing not just a massive influx of minorities into the country, but are witnessing an epidemic of miscegenation within the native population, which in the space of two generations will darken and alter the racial composition of our entire nation. Opponents of the suggested Amendment question the right of society to take such drastic action against the minorities and the American whites that want to marry them. The answer is simply that the right develops partly out of necessity. If action is not taken, white America is a doomed race. It is the illegal aliens, the pressing mass of minorities and the misceginators who have no right to unalterably destroy the race, heritage, culture and entire makeup of our nation.

The repeal of the fifteenth amendment fits into the overall scheme of the proposal of this text by removing the right to vote regardless of race. It would be incongruous to repeal the fourteenth amendment, which gives citizenship rights to nonwhites, but not repeal the fifteenth amendment, which gives them voting rights. Moreover, as stated above, in the Georgia Senate Resolution, the fifteenth amendment as well as the fourteenth amendment was illegally proposed and ratified by the radicals at the end of the Civil War.*

This step of repealing the fifteenth amendment ultimately is necessary because as the hoards of what we now call minorities increase, they will soon have a more powerful franchise than the so-called American majority. At that juncture, what had been

---

[124] The total world population, as of this writing, is approx. 6 billion. The point, however, remains in effect. FLS.

* Note: A better term would be *'civil war of fratricide'*, a war of racial suicide; based on the assumption that once 'sovereign and independent' states, who voluntarily accepted a form of decentralized 'federalism', were forced, through force of arms, to submit to a stronger and omnipotent federalism which used the onerous practice of slavery to mobilize the emotional content of the Northern States who, in their naiveté, sought to protect those who were unable to protect themselves. Unwittingly, or in spite of it, these same 'easterners' foisted the tyranny of their sanctimonious altruism upon their brethren, not withstanding the tremendous assault with which they, themselves, destroyed the very construct of their forefathers, forever denying themselves and their children's children the right to determine their future, and the right to secure an existence consonant with their needs and desires. No one, now, can honestly submit for intellectual discussion, that those persons, specifically Western in race-culture, have a fairer existence today, rather than that of fifty years ago, or that the introduction of aliens and their compounded alienness, have secured a more harmonious existence for the present generation, or for the future. FLS

mainstream America will not be able to pass one [single] law.$^{\psi}$ We will be at the mercy of a nonwhite majority who will, and are now, no matter how much we try to deny it, act, and are acting, to curtail our freedoms. Soon America could be like the former Rhodesia where power is turned over to the nonwhites and the whites are forced to flee for their protection. Then America could be like a large Haiti, the one white population gone, its once thriving economy collapsed, and its system of democracy having long since passed away.

As mentioned in the previous chapter, much in our society acts to condition us to reject our heritage, and as the nonwhite forces grow stronger, the pressure and conditioning will intensify until remedial action will be no longer possible. At this stage, action is possible if all of us shake off the years of conditioning that have dulled our perception and look at this proposal with a clear, rational mind, weighing the facts, the trends and ultimate justice (justice not construed to be what is easy or nice to each individual who may appear oppressed, but justice that can be disciplined and even harsh when needed). We must look to the future and envision what the results of inaction will be.

(i) Definition of White

In order to enforce t his amendment as it relates to the vast majority of people, there is no real need to define the term "white of the European race". This is because most Americans can be easily defined as either white or nonwhite. Someone of English, German, Swedish, or Polish ancestry would never be confused as being nonwhite. Conversely, a Negro, a Chinese, and Arab, and most Mexicans are, by appearance, obviously nonwhite. The division between whites and nonwhites can easily be drawn in the vast majority of cases. There are, however, arguments and complexities concerning a small percentage of the people, which can be carried to the extreme to bog down the entire process of defining who should and who should not be a citizen of the United States. Moreover, since America is now preoccupied with the concepts of individual rights over the rights of the country as a whole, this issue of unclear lines between white and nonwhite can deter some people from supporting the amendment. With each year, the problem becomes more and more complex.

Such problems concern the classification of part-white/part-nonwhite peoples, or nonwhite Caucasoids such as those from Iran, Armenia, and other parts of Asia, etc. For example, many states had laws providing that a person with one-eight or one-

---

$^{\psi}$ This, of course, is the democracy so sought after by the Modern, as this will usurp the often narrow, and recalcitrant nature of his own people; independent as those of Western stock are, the browning of this nation will, ultimately, make the masses that much more malleable, as opposed to the traditional history and experience of those of the West. FLS

fourth African, American Indian, or Asian blood was classified a nonwhite.[125] Opponents to such classifications have asserted that the same logic should be applied in reverse, that is, someone who is one-eight European should be classified a white. In this manner, much of the black community could claim to be white due to past racial mixing, giving rise to confusion and frustration of progress. The end result of this would be that the Americans will have rationalized away their country. The point to be made here is that this delicate issue of classification can be used to thwart any attempt to solve America's racial problem. Accordingly, we must artfully draw a line and maintain it. We should not let small problems obscure the large picture.

As mentioned above, in the recent past, America had clear standards to determine who was white and who was nonwhite; who would be eligible for citizenship and who would not. We must readopt those measures and classifications or calamity will result. If America would only resort to the citizenship requirements of as recently as the 1940's and 1950's, our heritage would not be in jeopardy. We could, with slight modification, return to those laws to effect a proper solution to our racial problems. Certainly, a reversion to that principle will not be simple, but it is necessary and can be accomplished with minimum amount of difficulty.

The language used to define who will be a citizen is taken from various instances in American law. Until recently, in a number of instances in the United States, classification based on race, color, ancestry or national origin have been utilized for the purpose of drawing distinctions in legal rights and obligations.[126] "Statutory definitions of race [were] generally based on the individuals blood, ancestry, appearance of a combination of these factors. Moreover, the factor of blood is further subdivided into the so-called proportion of percentage test and the ascertainable trace test. The statutes may provide that a person is a member of the racial group either if he has a stated percent of the blood of that group in his veins or if he has any ascertainable basic factor generally provide that a person will be deemed a member of the racial group affected if he has an ancestor who was a member of that group within a specified number of generations removed."[127]

Section 2 adapts a combination of these three tests, ascertainable trace of blood, ancestry and appearance. For the Negro, the test is any ascertainable trace. For the other nonwhites, the test is more than one-eighth or more than one great-grandparent who is nonwhite, and for Hispanics [mestizo], it is appearance and distinguishability from other Americans in addition to the ancestry test.

---

[125] See: *Legal Definition of Race*, 3 Race Rel. L. Rep. 571 (June 1958).
[126] See: *Legal Definition of Race*, 3 Race Rel. L. Rep. 571 (1958).
[127] Ibid. at 573.

Separate tests for Negroes and other nonwhites had been the law in a number of jurisdictions when such laws were commonly on the books. Virginia's code, for example, employed the ascertainable trace test for Negroes and an ancestry test for the American Indians.[128] Mississippi's miscegenation statute, a typical example, proscribed marriage between a white person and a Negro "or person who shall have one-eighth or more Negro or with a Mongolian or a person who shall have one-eighth or more Mongolian blood."[129]

(ii) Repatriation

The last sentence in Section 2 of the draft twenty-seventh amendment, which reads, "only citizens shall have the right and privilege to reside permanently in the United States" will, in effect, provide for the relocation and repatriation of the non-citizens. This sentence mentions both the "right" and "privilege" and only provided that citizens have the "right" to reside in the United States, the result might be a court ruling that even though the non-citizens would not have the right under the Constitution to live in the United States, they would have the privilege to stay by virtue of their presence here and the harshness of repatriation. Such a ruling would defeat the purpose of much of the amendment and would result in the continued growth of nonwhites who would not be citizens and would brood ill-contentedly until their numbers made them powerful enough to force change. The most sensible and prudent way to solve the problem of race would be to institute a comprehensive and fair program of immigration, so that all nonwhites can be repatriated in a manner that is economically beneficial to them. Section 3 of the draft twenty-seventh amendment would provide the foundation for this program.

Section 3 of this amendment reads: "The Congress and the several states, except where expressly preempted by the Congress, shall have concurrent power to enforce the provisions of this article by appropriate legislation in coordination with the President as such legislation concerns the making of treaties pursuant to Article 2, Section 2 of the Constitution."

This places the responsibility and authority to enforce the provisions of the amendment with both the states and the legislative and executive branches of the federal government. This approach provides for the most flexibility and safeguards in enforcing the amendment. Concurrent power vested in the states minimizes the possibility of undue intervention by an activist judiciary on the one hand and systematic injustice by the central government on the other. Unjust action by the states could be checked by express preemption by congress. Moreover, all action for enforcement would be in coordination with the President.

---

[128] Ibid., at 574.
[129] Ibid., at 579.

The entire process of repatriation could be done over a very long period of time if it should be determined that this would be the best approach and would provide for a smoother transition for all peoples concerned. The entire process could take thirty years if such time is necessary.

Once actual repatriation is accomplished other programs related thereto could be performed at leisure, such as guest worker permits for those who have repatriated, continued repatriation compensation, and continued employment opportunities with the United States Government in this country and abroad, such as through military service. These programs could extend for many years into the future until all problems and hardships of repatriation are resolved.

Congress and the states could set a period of time by which all easily repatriatable nonwhites are to leave the country of their own volition. A one-year period of time could be sufficient. A determination could be made according to the facts as to which groups are easily repatriatable can, if they desire, liquidate their belongings, sell their homes, gather their possessions together and relocate. They need not sell their property if they do not desire to do so. They may retain title and rent or operate their businesses *in abstentia*. They would have that choice and a period of time to make all necessary arrangements. Former citizens that voluntarily leave can be paid generous relocation allowances depending upon many factors such a need, length of time in America, economic level of the country they are returning to, etc., and they may be given priority to receive guest worker permits to return to the United States to work for a few years' duration at a time. During this one-year period, the government can assist in all ways possible, such as by the purchase of homes that are not easily marketable, providing subsidized transportation and financing the construction of additional housing in the homelands.

After the expiration of the one-year voluntary repatriation period, stricter yet fair measures could be taken to accomplish repatriation. If the Mexicans [mestizo], for example, have not returned to their country, they could be rounded up and promptly returned across the border and their belongings could be confiscated as a penalty and to help defray the administrative costs. Forced repatriation could begin at this point. The ones who can most easily be repatriated will be, either swiftly and decisively or gradually and methodically, as the situation dictates. Those whose homelands are unwilling to take them may be allowed to stay on a temporary basis in temporary quarters until relocation can be accomplished. With certain adjustments, Hawaii could become a comfortable layover station for them. Below is a general discussion of how each group might be dealt with to effect the fairest and most efficient repatriation possible:

Blacks: Due to the large numbers and deep roots in the United States, it is toward this group that the United States should give the most consideration and allot the largest sums of money in order to ensure a pleasant a repatriation and new life as possible. Moreover, for these reasons, this group will be the most difficult to repatriate effectively and in good faith. The ideal situation would be for Southern African whites to accept U.S. citizenship in return for admitting U.S. blacks into their countries and allowing them to establish their own homelands. In this manner, the racial problems of several nations can be more easily resolved. Tribal problems within the homelands might still remain, and conflicts between blacks repatriated from the United States and local blacks might develop, but those problems can be dealt with in Africa just like national diversity of whites has been dealt with in America. Moreover, an entirely new nation can be established in Africa where the blacks can build their own society. With the current educational level of U.S. blacks and their growing number of professionally trained men and women, this is indeed possible.

Hispanics [mestizo]: Because of the large number of Hispanics [mestizo] in this country and the political instability in their mother countries, repatriation of this group could also be problematic. The vast majority of them can be dealt with simply by returning them to Mexico or elsewhere in Central America or the Caribbean where they or their parents came from illegally. Generally, they should not be greatly compensated for their repatriation unless they were legitimate citizens and then the compensation should be in proportion to their period of stay in the United States. Those who could, but would not, return home voluntarily within the initial one-year period would have their opportunity to take advantage of U.S. government largesse and programs curtailed. In any event, foreign aid to Mexico would be appropriate to help them relocate their citizens.

Hispanic whites who are basically indistinguishable form Americans whose ancestral home is the British Isles or Northwestern Europe, need not be repatriated. They should assimilate into the white society without turning our country into an extension of Latin America.

It should be noted that repatriation has become necessary primarily because of the abuses that the Hispanics [mestizo] have made upon our system. They have come in illegally by the tens of millions and once they become citizens, they use their influence and power to manipulate the system to protect their illegal alien countrymen. This nation is on the brink of becoming a Latin American nation. Strict action must be take to aver this occurrence. Accordingly, stricter standards for citizenship are applied to them than to any other group. They must meet both the percentage tests and the appearance test for citizenship, otherwise they must be returned to Latin America.

Orientals: Orientals, as a whole, have not been in America very long or in large numbers. There are some who have been here several generations but, by and large, the bulk of the Oriental population in America has immigrated after the racial quotas were lifted in the 1960's. Accordingly, the first generation Orientals can be repatriated fairly easily along with their first children for they might still claim citizenship in their mother country. They and their children will not have much culture shock of many adjustment problems. In addition, their English language skills will put them in valuable positions in business when they return. It should be noted that Asia is the future center of world leadership and economic prosperity so repatriation for them should prove to be a blessing. Some Orientals will have a harder time returning than others. A breakdown is as follows:

Chinese: [See Text]

Japanese: [See Text]

Filipinos: [See Text]

Koreans: [See Text]

Indochinese: [See Text]

Native Americans: American Indians, Aleuts, and Hawaiians should be allowed to remain in America and not face relocation. They would not be citizens of the United States and so would have to maintain their residence on their tribal reservations, but they would be permitted to remain within the nation's boundaries. This is how the constitution contemplated the situation concerning them. Orientals and South Pacific Islanders who were born in Hawaii will not be considered Hawaiian just because they were born there.

Peoples of Mixed Parentage: According to the suggested amendment, persons of mixed parentage will not be citizens and will thereby be subject to repatriation to the country of their nonwhite parent. Where this is feasible, it should be done. Where it is not, certain alternative arrangements could be made.

Some flexibility may be necessary when working out the details of repatriation of those of mixed race and those nonwhites who are married to whites. For those of mixed race, it may at times be difficult to determine to which country they are to be repatriated. Factors to be considered are the desires of the individuals, the willingness of the homeland to accept them and the cultures with which they predominantly associate themselves. As for part-whites, it may not be practicable, at times, to return them to the country of their nonwhite origin. Action should be taken to effect repatriation where possible, particularly where the part-white is single. Individuals with a preponderance of white blood, but less than the statutory requirement for citizenship, and no Negro blood, who are nearly white in appearance might possibly be allowed to stay with their spouses in Hawaii, not as citizens, but under some legal fiction, such as granting them renewable guest worker permits, but requiring them to leave the United States every few years for brief durations to comply with the amendment's requirement that only citizens have the right to permanent residency.

In addition, since the repeal of the various state miscegenation statutes in the 1950's and 1960's and the breakdown of social taboos against interracial marriage, this nation has seen a rise in interracial couples. It should not be the policy of the nation to break up marriages, even interracial ones. Whites who are married to nonwhites should be encouraged to accompany their nonwhite spouse to his or her homeland. The fact that a nonwhite is married to a white should not, however, enable the nonwhite to remain in America. Such a ruling might cause a dramatic increase in interracial marriages as a means of nonwhites maintaining residence in the United States. Repatriation of nonwhites married to whites should, in the end, be effected.

The issue of interracial marriage would be indirectly dealt with by the suggested amendment. Since nonwhites would not be allowed to reside in the United States, interracial marriages would be impractical and may proscribed by state law. The white spouse and the offspring of such a union would have to ultimately return to the homeland of the nonwhite spouse. If states allow interracial marriage at all, proof of this intention and the ability to effect that intention should be provided for such a union to occur. If certain accommodations are made for persons of mixed parentage to reside in Hawaii, miscegenation statutes can be drafted as necessity dictates.

Miscellaneous Groups: [See Text]

In spite of the above recommendations for repatriations, America can be flexible in the implementation of its plan. Even so, as a whole we must remain resolute in our decisions. The following are some examples of some areas where flexibility might be available to the Congress or the states.

Questions arise as to what to do about those who cannot be easily repatriated at the initial stages. Such individuals could be granted provisional extensions to stay in America on a temporary basis until the situation changes and arrangements can be made for repatriation. Of course, such an arrangement could be easily subject to abuses. Many individuals might try to use the excuse that their repatriation constitutes hardship in an attempt to remain in the United States. People may be inconvenienced in relocating, but that should not constitute grounds for granting a provisional extension to each of them. This arrangement should be reserved only for the extreme cases with possibly some sort of centralized waiting place like Hawaii where they can work and be productive but not make plans to stay permanently.

Another area of possible flexibility could be concerning nonwhite middle-aged and senior citizens. To repatriate them could be more that a mere inconvenience – it could be extremely burdensome on them in their old age. To require them to start life anew at age 50, 60, or 70 is not a necessary step in the overall scheme of retaining America for the Americans. They are past the age where they will bear children and so would not leave a lasting effect on the racial makeup of the nation. These individuals whose children are grown and who wish to stay in America could be allowed to do so under some special arrangement worked out by the states or by Congress.

Nothing to this effect should be written into the constitutional amendment because of the danger of the judicial branch abusing and defeating the purpose of the amendment through misinterpretation of any written exceptions. Instead, states or Congress could devise some sort of legal fiction to allow the non-citizen elderly to stay in America. For example, the government might issue renewable ten-year residence permits to those individuals over age 60 who would be adversely affected by the draft twenty-seventh amendment.

Each of us probably has several friends and acquaintances who will be seemingly adversely affected by this amendment. Therefore it will be easy for us to become caught up in our concern for our friends to such an extent that we forget about the overall effect massive nonwhite immigration is having on our country. Our love and concern for our friends must not prevent us form doing what is right and best for our country. We must realize that they will get along fine under the new adjustments and be able to succeed in their new situation. Our love and concern for our nonwhite friends and acquaintances should encourage us to act for the ratification of t he amendment and for the institution of fair procedures to protect all our interests.

In the long run, the inevitable inconvenience and hardships the amendment will impose on portions of the nonwhite population is the better alternative. A little inconvenience now to a few people is better than the breakdown and collapse of our system and nation resulting in many deaths and much hardship, which will surely result if no action is taken. We can ensure that justice is served if we control repatriation and our country. We can ensure nothing if we relinquish that control. We will not even be able to secure a place in which our children can raise their families.

(c) Ratification

[See Text]

VII. THE CONVENTION METHOD OF AMENDING THE U.S. CONSTITUTION

1. Overview

[See Text]

VII. CONCLUSION[130]

[See Text]

---

[130] POSTSCRIPT: those of you who favor the concepts embraced by this amendment are urged to support its proposal and ratification by sending (1) a copy of this text to your state legislator with a letter of support and (2) your contributions to: Johnson, Pace, Simmons & Fennell Publishers, POBox 1139, Sunland, Ca. 91040

Appendice III

COMMENTARY ON THE [PACE] AMENDMENT

In the pursuit of wisdom, the various avenues of thought, the rigors of intellectual discipline, the emotive powers of our conscious and unconscious thought, are all brought to bear upon what the human mind decides to challenge; in doing so, he comes to a point where a *conclusion* is made. This conclusion is a matter of orthodoxy to some, to others, it is a simply a milestone, a foothold upon a ledge which ever takes him upward, until he reaches the next level of truth. In either case, the pursuit of knowledge leads inexorably to a greater vision: to *wisdom*.

Wisdom has come, as we know it, through millennia of trial and error, shouldered, as it were, upon the blood and bone of our very familial and real ancestors. The mothers and fathers of yesteryear, through their living and dying, over thousands of generations, each successive turn of the wheel of life has brought new answers to those many thousands of questions which formed on the wisps of thought, moved to the lips and, perchance, was heard by the ears of pupils, children, and those searching for answers themselves. What was learned through this evolution was wisdom in the sense that we know it. This is *experience*.

Experience is the construct of tradition, of those lessons learned by those before us; we, in turn, utilize these lessons, or cast them aside and form new ones. The realm of Law is of the same specie.

Legal tradition is the construct of experience.

James O. Pace has attempted to present an avenue of relief for members of the Western race-culture. His attempt focuses on the traditional application of Western mores and law. The philosophy and practice of a 'system of laws' belongs to the Western experience, and is the legacy and birthright of every member of the West, be they American, European, or any number of the far-flung colonies, which represent the blood and body politic of the West.

The 'democratic' process has been the torch, carried by Western civilization, since Pericles (495-429 b.c.) of Greece; he received this flame from Solon (c. 600 b.c.), a dictator in the benevolent mold, who was preceded by Theseus (c. 1300 b.c.) The process of 'democratization' has traveled from its European antecedents to the modern American expression. An interesting note is that the first, Theseus, was considered an 'Athenian adventurer', and Solon, the 'Law giver', while Pericles, the 'father of democracy', was considered the 'Olympian' because of his eloquence (he was born of high blood) and the 'imperialism' with which he brought riches to Athens. Democracy worked very little, and only for a select few; but it did continue to evolve.

The Pace Amendment follows the legacy of this past. Combining the legacy of this tapestry with the modern application of American experience, including a revolution, a civil war, immigration, and the prospect of losing her direction, sovereignty, and economic power by being seduced into 'international' affairs, which, it was said, would make the world safe for democracy. Not that this was the 'people's choice' but, after all, the 'people' would benefit thereby. Through it all, the machine of government has tirelessly admitted change; the legislative bodies working for ever more and more democratic *change*. The change that this, our nation has seen has, truly, been evolutionary, and documents, mores, and law has adapted thereby.

The amendments to the constitution, as we have generally understood them, were enabled through a democratic process, hard-won, debated endlessly, and 'ratified' through as many 'back door' moves, as public. The government, at that time, was made up of men predominately, and sons of the West, all. The divisions, philosophical, religious, scientific, political differences between them were myriad, and the embryonic 'contest of cultures' was just as dynamic as it is today, but with one difference: The divisions presented at the beginning of this 'great experiment' were but the common differences between family members who, for the most part, saw god, the almighty, or the deity as having bestowed upon these particular persons and nation a just *imperative*, an *obligation* to provide justice and fairness for that body of persons who, rightly or wrongly, looked to them as their servants, as well as leaders. Even then, at the signing of one of the most important documents in the history of man, *authority* raged against *demos*. Law against 'predisposition'.

Authority, as is natural in any government, did not demand a 'bill of rights', demos did. The 'people', concerned with abuse of power demanded, in *writing*, an affirmation of these rights for their *posterity*. The ratification of these 'bills' were duly legislated through a democratic process and passed. The mechanism of government and legislation provided by the Constitution, through its numerous articles, was the template, which they used. This template, however, was based upon the smallest of elements: the individual participant. The Electoral College is but one example. The point is, that the 'decisions' were majority votes, by individuals who, *collectively*, came to the decisions, which affect us now, today. Issues of abortion, inter-racial marriage, homosexuality, were not defined in the 'bill of rights' simply because these issues, and literally hundreds of other modern 'issues' were not contemplated by these restrained, and prudent men; these aforementioned acts were as far removed from these men, as space travel. For over two hundred years, these mores, and individual social traditions, made this nation the envy of the world.

In point of fact, the collaboration between these individuals was nothing short of miraculous, if not predestined. Therefore, we have a homogeneous racial collaboration in a destiny-filled event, all the participants having a knowledge of history, science, economics and a belief in manifest destiny. When it came to campaigning for a system of government, a single leader seemed reasonable; the checks and balances were deemed safer. In any event, even with men of similar backgrounds, religious inclinations, and mental integrity, it was hard-going, this work of building a system of government. It took years to come to *compromise*. Then, after war, discussion, and deliberation, a nation was born.

Mr. Pace, like all men of keen mental discipline, and a vision liken unto his fathers, sees the task of 'change', or reaffirmation possible, through the disciplines of what created this great experiment. And rightly so. In a theoretical discipline, the premise of an amendment is sound, providing the members of government, as well as the demos, were of the same caliber. Add to this, the shared vision of a vibrant present, an acute premonition of the future, and a working knowledge of the past, are all present.

The power of money existed in the time of our forefathers, it is a thousand-fold now, and the human qualities of greed, avarice, envy and the like, have become monstrous. Without the disciplines of old-fashioned morality, and knowledge of who we, as a Western people are, then, to what shall we anchor ourselves? By what ledger do we find accounting? In addition, how, with all this said, are we to convene a new morality, a new convention of political destiny? In fact, split, as we are, into distinct race-cultures inhabiting this continent, just where is *our* majority? Where are we to find, in those deep recesses of the halls of justice, our venue for change, for reaffirmation?

A reaffirmation of our Western values, most certainly.

I think, however, that most of the members of the West are hardly in a position to demand anything; demands come from a sense of knowing what is needed, or what needs to be done. Hardly a viable achievement in a society, which deems racial awareness as akin to 'hate', or worse, as akin to 'self-hate'. If legislation can be passed, in almost every state in this union, to berate, hound, chastise, and legally incarcerate for 'hate crimes' those who stand for the principles of the West, who feel righteous indignation at the thought or the deeds of many who would sterilize the past and make the very blood of this nation of no effect, then to what body politic do we take our pleadings too? In addition, what national convention do we say 'our piece', and by acclimation or dissent, know the value of our claim? I think we all know the answer.

Do we, as men and women of the West, living in these United States, have any way to enforce these desires? Where is *our* army? Who will take up the banner for *our* children? Are the men and women in uniform today fighting for the future of white children, or simply the 'children of the world'? If asked, what do you think these men and women would declare? I think you know the answer. So, once again, *who* do we turn too? If the present system were challenged, just how long, before we are declared traitors, terrorists, seditionists, and persona non grata here, in our own homeland?

How many, indeed, hold offices of power and control, over you and I, who are foreign in thought, and spirit, who demand justice and equality for the 'new' citizen, but none for the old? To whom are they accountable? Moreover, who could ever enforce it?

To the amendment, I say, bravo!! Let us, then, be stalwart and march on the halls of our ancestors and demand a vote. The leaders of our people will welcome us with open arms, and we will be victorious.

Mr. Pace, if you are still of a mind to proceed with this project come, and let us begin, for the wind of resentment is stirring, sacrifices have been made, lives have been given, and what has been given in *return* is sadly lacking. Maybe, like the Great War, there is one who has seen the bloodshed of his comrades, and the betrayal of the mighty, and a resentment will build in the breast of even one as this. But, maybe not.

Frank L. DeSilva

Fallbrook, Ca.

June, 2006

Rise of The West

BIBLIOGRAPHY

1. Agard, Walter R. 'What Democracy meant to the Greeks, U.N.C. Press.

2. Baker, John R. 'Race', Oxford University Press.

3. Benson, Ivor 'Dissecting a Racial Mystique', [Article] "Behind the News," Durban, South Africa.

4. Blumnbach, J.F. 'On the Natural Varieties of Mankind', Bergman Publishers.

5. Brown, Lawrence R. 'Might of the West', Joseph L. Binns.

6. Carrel, Alexis 'Man the Unknown', Harper&Brothers.

7. Glotz, Gustave 'Ancient Greece at Work', Kegan Paul.

8. Glover, T.R. 'Collected Works', Vol. I.

9. Grant, Madison 'Passing of the Great Race', Scribner's 4th revised.

10. Hoffman II, Michael A. 'They were White and they were Slaves', Wisewell Ruffin House.

11. Holmes, S.J. 'The Eugenic Predicament', Harcourt&Brace.

12. --------- "Human Genetics and its Social Import', McGraw.

13. Jung, Carl 'Instinct and the Unconscious', The Viking Press.

14. Keith, Sir Arthur 'A New Theory of Human Evolution', Philological Library.

15. Koman, Victor 'The Real Reason we own Guns', Guns&Ammo, Feb. 1990.

16. Koopman, Roger   'Second Defense', Outdoor Life, Feb. 1990.

17. Lewes, G.H.   'The Life and Works of Goethe'.

18. Maine, Henry Sumner 'Popular Government', Holt.

19. McDougal, William   The Energies of Man', Vol.4.

20. Nietzsche, Fredrich 'Twilight of the Idols', Viking Press.

21. Nott, J.C.   'Types of Mankind', Lippincott, Gambo&Co.

22. DeSilva, F.L.   'One Nation', NPAP Press, 1988.

23. Simpson, W.G.   'Which Way Western Man', Natinal Alliance.

24. Spengler, Oswald   'Decline of the West', Helmet Werner.

25. Sumner, W.G.   'Folkways', 1906.

26. Topinard, Paul   'Anthropology', Chapman&Hall.

27. Hernstein, R.J.& Murray, Charles

    'The Bell Curve', Free Press [Simon&Schuster], 1996.

28. Dublin, Luis I   'Birth Control', reprinted in Social Hygiene, 1920.

29. Ludovici, Anthony   'The Choice of a Mate', London, 1935.

INDEX

A

Achilles vii
Africa ... v, 9, 14, 15, 16, 21, 46, 54, 96, 125, 138, 174, 175, 176, 178, 179, 253, 262, 306, 315
African .... *See* Race
Agamemnon 42
Alexander .... viii, 11, 14, 17, 38, 48, 64, 103, 244
Alexis Carrel 8, 12, 76
Allegory 20
America x, 2, 5, 6, 7, 12, 25, 37, 50, 61, 62, 65, 66, 72, 84, 90, 116, 117, 126, 129, 130, 132, 138, 139, 140, 141, 143, 144, 145, 146, 149, 150, 157, 158, 159, 160, 161, 162, 165, 166, 171, 173, 175, 178, 179, 180, 185, 187, 188, 189, 190, 195, 197, 199, 200, 204, 206, 207, 208, 211, 215, 217, 226, 229, 230, 231, 232, 240, 244, 253, 263, 265, 266, 267, 268, 269, 270, 272, 273, 274, 275, 278, 284, 289, 290, 291, 294, 296, 300, 301, 302, 303, 305, 306, 307, 308
American Imperium viii
apartheid .... 176. See South Africa. See South Africa. *See* South Africa
Apollonius 103
Appolodorus 103
Archimedes 13, 20
Architecture 20
Aristarchus 13
aristocracy 27, 54, 55, 56, 57, 58, 59, 60, 63, 181, 217, 259
Aristotle 11, 13, 49

Art 18, 19, 22, 51, 78, 79, 80, 81, 91, 113, 136, 150
Aryan .... *See* Race
Asia Minor 11, 63, 268, 297
assimilation 61, 166, 188, 196, 202
Augustine 14, 15

B

Baker, John R. 109, 315
Balkanization 188
Beauty 76, 77, 79, 80, 129, 136
biological nation .... See race-culture
Birth. vii, 118, 215, 222, 226, 228, 230, 246, 316
blood iv, vi, vii, 3, 8, 15, 25, 31, 37, 39, 48, 52, 57, 58, 59, 61, 63, 88, 98, 103, 113, 116, 126, 131, 145, 151, 155, 160, 161, 171, 184, 201, 208, 213, 214, 217, 223, 234, 239, 240, 242, 297, 302, 303, 304, 307, 310, 311, 313
Blumenbach, J.F. 127
Boers .... *See* South Africa
Boerstaat Party 178
bone .... iv, 25, 109, 208, 285, 310
Botticelli 18

C

Caesar 11, 38, 103, 219
Cappadocia .... *See* Asia Minor
Caravaggio 18
Carl Jung 39, 50
Carl von Clauswitz 181
Caucasian .... *See* Race
Cause ii
Celtic .... See . See . See . See . See
Charlemagne .... vii, 25, 48
China .... See Chinese. See Chinese

Chinese...21, 43, 91, 96, 167, 170, 221, 302, 307
Christian....... 15, 89, 90, 94, 96, 97, 98, 115, 226, 244, 275
Christianity 90, 95, 96, 115, 216
Cicadas 39
Citizenship .69, 145, 193, 223, 278, 289, 290, 298, 300, 301, 303, 305, 306, 307
Civilization.........v, viii, 49, 74, 168, 213
Constitutional Law 67, 165
Copernican astronomy 13
Corpus Juris Civilis 34, 35
Cottage Industry 230
Crime............................... 122, 185, 270
Cro-Magnon.. iii
cultural-civilizaton .... *See* race-culture
Culture ... ii, iv, v, vii, viii, x, 1, 3, 10, 11, 43, 44, 48, 49, 52, 66, 72, 78, 80, 82, 98, 114, 134, 150, 159, 160, 170, 174, 179, 186, 189, 197, 200, 202, 204, 206, 211, 212, 213, 214, 222, 233, 234, 236, 237, 240, 244, 246, 247
culture-beare.. 130

D

Da Vinci........ See . See . See . See . See
David 18, 20, 121, 151, 250, 260
de jure.................................... 41, 57, 166
decline .. 51, 72, 105, 112, 116, 125, 128, 129, 130, 131, 163, 266
democracy...ix, 11, 28, 45, 46, 47, 49, 50, 51, 54, 55, 57, 60, 61, 62, 63, 64, 66, 68, 70, 71, 139, 147, 151, 152, 161, 165, 171, 175, 176, 181, 188, 192, 200, 201, 207, 209, 215, 216, 234, 248, 256, 257, 263, 265, 302, 311, 315
demos 28, 60, 64, 311, 312
Dictatorship 11, 217, 218

die Bruder Schweigen 250, 251
dual code .... *See* duality
dualist .... *See* duality
duality .. vi, 4, 15, 16, 19, 25, 33, 48, 51, 57, 82, 87, 90, 95, 96, 98, 99, 112, 113, 136, 142, 227, 246, 248

E

Echehart of Hocheim 16
Edda .... See
effect .... *See* Cause
Egyptian 1, 2, 3, 18, 19, 91, 221
Empire 2, 3, 10, 11, 34, 35, 62, 187, 197, 198
England 3, 15, 35, 54, 71, 94, 144, 231
Erastothenes 13
Eros .... *See* Beauty
Ethnic 179, 190, 196, 197
Eugenics 103, 105, 111
euro-folk .See Race-Culture. See Race-Culture. See Race-Culture. See Race-Culture. See Race-Culture
Europe. viii, ix, 1, 2, 3, 6, 9, 34, 35, 61, 65, 74, 84, 90, 92, 106, 113, 128, 132, 138, 140, 143, 171, 175, 187, 188, 206, 207, 217, 231, 232, 244, 253, 269, 291, 297, 306

F

fable 20, 252
Family ...... v, 30, 31, 32, 34, 38, 58, 87, 116, 184, 222, 248, 259, 269, 275
Fatherland .... *See* Homeland
Flesh iv
Folk x, 26, 57, 150, 236, 240, 250, 256
Fouquet, Nicolas.............................. 229
France ..34, 46, 54, 56, 62, 64, 153, 229, 244, 253, 275
Francis Galton 121
Francis Parker Yockey 138, 150
Franz Boas ...See Social-Anthropology

Fratricide .... viii, 66, 156, 161, 163, 181
Frederick Barbarosa 230
Frederick the Great vii
French Revolution 63, 64, 157
Freud 84

G

George Washington 48, 172
Gibbons 34, 151, 213, 282
Goethe 46, 47, 56, 316
Good and Evil .... *See* Religion
Greece vii, x, 11, 31, 32, 37, 58, 60, 62, 75, 128, 221, 274, 310, 315
Greeks 3, 13, 18, 33, 129, 315
gun ownership 183, 184, 185, 187
Gustav Adolphus viii

H

H.F. Verwoerd .... *See*
Hamurabi 3, 38, 48, 174
Hector vii
Hellenes .... *See* Race-culture
Hendrik Strijdom 177
Henry Sumner Maine 63
hereditary diversity .... *See* Heredity
Heredity. 40, 56, 71, 92, 103, 104, 110, 112, 115, 116, 118, 121, 226
Herodotus 103
Heroes 237
higher-culture iii, vii, 2, 3, 4, 5, 13, 14, 18, 19, 25, 30, 31, 34, 36, 37, 38, 43, 52, 66, 75, 82, 91, 188
Hobbs 22, 143
Hoffman II, Michael A 148, 315
Holmes, S.J 104, 121, 315
Home .... *See* Homeland
Homeland .. See . See . See . See . See . See . *See* Territory
Homestead 223, 224
Homogeneity 5
Homosexuality 255, 260
House of Rothschild 229

Humanism, ... 14
hybridity .... *See* Race

I

I.Q 116, 124, 125
India 2, 21, 58, 128, 198
Indian King Lists .... *See* Vedas
individualism 118, 127
Inner-Man 246
Intangible iv
Intelligentsia 156
Iron Chancellor of Germany . *See* Otto von Bismarck
Italy 35, 62, 244

J

Japan 221, 231, 273, 274, 275
Jesse Jackson 203
Jesus 73, 89, 227, 236, 237
Jewish .... See . See . See
Joan de Arc 38
Judiciary Act 70

K

Kalavela .... *See*
keep and bear arms 182, 183
Keith, Sir Arthur 146, 315
King Phillip [the Fair] 229
kith and kin .... *See* Race, Family
Koman, Victor 185, 315
Koopman, Roger 183, 316

L

Lane, David Eden 250
Law 14, 50, 70, 115, 142, 164, 167, 168, 169, 212, 232, 249, 251, 253, 254, 256, 257, 258, 259, 260, 278, 279, 281, 284, 285, 294, 310, 311
leitmotif iii
Levant 21
Levantine .... *See* Levant
Liberalism 54

Life ii, iii, vii, 19, 47, 52, 90, 97, 98, 99, 154, 183, 211, 213, 214, 232, 234, 243, 246, 316

life-force *See* Western man, Rise of the West

Locke 22, 49, 143

Louis XIV 38, 48, 49, 229, 230

M

Mandela .... See

Marriage ... 34, 36, 37, 40, 86, 103, 129, 130, 230, 269, 303, 307, 308, 312

Martyrs 237

mass ..... iv, 3, 10, 12, 23, 28, 29, 33, 38, 39, 40, 42, 44, 45, 46, 52, 55, 60, 61, 66, 69, 70, 79, 90, 93, 101, 102, 114, 131, 134, 136, 139, 144, 146, 147, 150, 151, 152, 153, 154, 155, 159, 160, 161, 165, 170, 171, 173, 182, 185, 195, 197, 215, 216, 217, 218, 219, 220, 225, 228, 229, 237, 247, 248, 262, 301

Mathews, Robert J. 208, 209, 251

Mediocrity 126, 155

mestizo ... 179, 180, 198, 200, 201, 205, 208, 267, 268, 269, 300, 303, 305, 306

metaphor .... *See* Rise of the West

Michael Angelo 3, 22

migrations .... See West

Miscegenation 161, 255

Modern iv, v, vi, vii, viii, ix, x, 5, 9, 12, 18, 21, 23, 25, 30, 31, 34, 36, 37, 38, 41, 42, 45, 46, 47, 49, 51, 52, 54, 55, 56, 57, 62, 64, 68, 99, 100, 101, 102, 103, 105, 106, 110, 113, 114, 115, 120, 121, 122, 123, 124, 125, 127, 132, 135, 136, 143, 144, 146, 147, 148, 149, 150, 151, 152, 153, 154, 155, 156, 157, 159, 160, 161, 162, 163, 165, 166, 167, 168, 169, 170, 171, 172, 173, 174, 175, 176, 177, 178, 179, 180, 181, 182, 183, 184, 185, 186, 187, 188, 189, 191, 198, 201, 202, 203, 204, 205, 206, 207, 209, 212, 214, 215, 216, 217, 219, 220, 222, 223, 225, 226, 228, 230, 231, 232, 233, 234, 236, 237, 238, 240, 243, 246, 247, 248, 249, 263, 281, 302

Mohamed ..... *See* Religion, Race-Culture

Monroe Doctrine viii

Montesquieu 207

motif .... ii, 20, 107

Mount Saint-Michael 78

mystical 8, 15, 19, 20, 21, 25, 58, 59, 74, 80, 81, 90, 91

mysticism 15, 19, 20, 51, 79, 80, 90

Mysticism. 15

Myth 20

N

Napoleon. vii, 34, 38, 55, 64, 174, 230, 232, 244

Nation .. 5, 9, 10, 26, 32, 41, 44, 47, 48, 65, 69, 93, 102, 115, 145, 146, 150, 151, 159, 167, 168, 180, 181, 208, 224, 244, 245, 251, 252, 253, 256, 258, 259, 260, 267, 272, 316

Nationalism 141, 142, 145, 146, 152, 181, 200

Nationalist .... vi, ix, 146, 147, 152, 153, 157, 159, 171, 178, 179, 181, 183, 184, 186, 189, 194, 204, 206, 209, 216, 241

Natural Law 251

Nature ..... iii, 10, 14, 21, 50, 52, 74, 79, 80, 96, 106, 110, 142, 167, 187, 210, 212, 219, 236, 238, 251, 252, 253, 254, 255, 256, 257, 259, 260

Neo-Platonist 15

Nietzsche vi, vii, x, 14, 23, 72, 73, 211, 218, 219, 220, 237, 316
Nobility 31, 45, 59, 72, 76, 136, 152, 157, 248
non-Western.................*See* Race-culture
Nordic See . See . See . See . See . See . See . See . See . See . See
Nott, J.C............................... 108, 316

O

Oligarchy...................................... 70, 217
Order................. 59, 162, 168, 169, 183
organic ii, iv, ix, 1, 3, 11, 12, 13, 26, 27, 29, 30, 33, 34, 36, 37, 38, 40, 42, 43, 45, 57, 62, 75, 82, 105, 135, 139, 150, 152, 159, 160, 166, 168, 170, 172, 187, 206, 211, 212, 213, 217, 246, 248, 256, 258
Oswald Spengler..................24, 72, 146
Otto von Bismarck...........................158

P

P.W. Botha...............................See . See
Pace, James O. 265, 266, 296, 312, 313
Pan Aryanist Party 243
Passions..83
Paterfamilias.......................................33
Pax-Americanum.............................. viii
Pelagianism.............................*See* Pelagius
Pelagius..15
People.. v, vii, 1, 2, 5, 9, 24, 26, 27, 29, 32, 33, 38, 39, 43, 44, 49, 50, 51, 52, 54, 65, 66, 68, 69, 70, 71, 91, 92, 104, 113, 139, 144, 150, 153, 158, 162, 173, 174, 178, 197, 206, 210, 213, 221, 223, 230, 234, 236, 237, 238, 245, 247, 248, 251, 252, 253, 254, 256, 258, 264, 265, 308. *See* race-culture
Pericles.........................28, 62, 63, 66, 310
Persians 2, 62
Physical Anthropology .... See

Plato...13, 103
Pliny.. 103
polygamy... 85
Pompey viii
Pousin........................ 3, 18, 20, 79, 151
primordial 21, 22, 126

R

Race ...ii, iii, iv, vi, vii, viii, ix, x, 1, 3, 4, 5, 6, 8, 9, 10, 11, 12, 13, 17, 18, 19, 20, 23, 25, 26, 27, 28, 29, 30, 31, 33, 37, 38, 39, 40, 41, 42, 43, 44, 48, 49, 50, 51, 52, 54, 57, 59, 60, 61, 62, 70, 72, 73, 75, 78, 79, 81, 82, 84, 87, 88, 89, 91, 92, 93, 95, 96, 97, 98, 99, 100, 103, 105, 106, 107, 108, 109, 111, 113, 114, 119, 120, 122, 123, 124, 125, 127, 128, 129, 130, 135, 136, 138, 139, 140, 141, 142, 145, 146, 148, 149, 150, 151, 152, 154, 155, 156, 158, 159, 160, 161, 162, 163, 164, 166, 167, 168, 170, 171, 172, 173, 174, 176, 178, 179, 180, 181, 182, 183, 184, 186, 187, 188, 189, 190, 192, 195, 196, 197, 198, 199, 200, 201, 202, 205, 206, 208, 209, 211, 213, 214, 215, 217, 218, 219, 220, 221, 224, 228, 231, 232, 233, 236, 238, 245, 246, 247, 248, 249, 251, 252, 253, 254, 255, 256, 258, 259, 260, 262, 263, 266, 267, 287, 288, 289, 296, 297, 298, 301, 302, 303, 304, 307, 310, 312, 315
race-culture...iv, vi, viii, ix, x, 3, 4, 5, 6, 9, 10, 11, 12, 13, 17, 18, 20, 23, 25, 27, 28, 29, 31, 38, 39, 40, 41, 42, 43, 44, 48, 49, 50, 52, 54, 57, 60, 70, 81, 82, 91, 97, 99, 100, 103, 105, 107, 113, 114, 119, 120, 122, 123, 124, 127, 135, 136, 138, 140,

145, 148, 149, 150, 151, 154, 155, 159, 160, 161, 162, 163, 166, 167, 168, 171, 172, 173, 174, 176, 178, 180, 183, 186, 187, 188, 189, 196, 197, 198, 199, 200, 205, 206, 208, 209, 213, 214, 215, 217, 218, 219, 221, 224, 228, 231, 232, 246, 248, 262, 263, 266, 301, 310

Rathenau 61
Rationalism 54
Reason .... iv, 151, 185, 315
Redemption 98, 99
Reims 78
Religion 72, 75, 83, 87, 89, 93, 95, 96, 213, 216, 222, 237, 252, 260, 270
Renaissance . 13, 14, 16, 17, 18, 19, 21, 22
Republic, ... 11, 34, 263, 264
Rise of the West . See
Robert van Tonder 178
Romania 244
Romans 18, 33
Rome .... vii, x, 8, 11, 14, 15, 16, 30, 31, 37, 58, 60, 69, 75, 160, 176, 221
Ronald Regan 242
Rousseau 22, 56, 74, 150, 173
Rubens 3, 18, 20
Rudyard Kipling 7, 149
Russia .... v, 56, 157, 231

S

Samuel Adams 27
Saracen 94
Scandinavia 26, 62, 244
Scipio Africanus 14

second war of fratricide .... *See* Second World War
Second World War 103
Senility .... vii, 246
Separatism 196, 200
Separatists .... *See* Separatism
Shakespeare 103
Social Anthropology..See Freud, et. al.
Socrates 54, 103
Solon 55, 310
soul .... ii, iv, vi, vii, ix, x, 3, 5, 7, 16, 20, 22, 24, 30, 34, 37, 43, 45, 49, 51, 52, 73, 75, 78, 79, 82, 89, 90, 91, 98, 106, 107, 113, 119, 127, 139, 140, 143, 145, 147, 150, 151, 152, 154, 155, 160, 178, 214, 215, 233, 236, 242, 288
South Africa 174, 179
Spartan 33
Spengler, Oswald 81, 146, 316
spiritual . ii, iv, v, 12, 15, 16, 17, 21, 26, 33, 36, 38, 42, 45, 51, 52, 58, 59, 60, 74, 75, 76, 77, 81, 82, 93, 95, 97, 99, 102, 111, 129, 136, 142, 148, 151, 154, 168, 206, 215, 216, 219, 227, 228, 233, 237, 243, 246, 249, 252, 253
Stanford-Binet 125
Statev, 6, 12, 19, 22, 26, 33, 38, 41, 42, 43, 44, 47, 49, 69, 96, 102, 122, 148, 164, 165, 168, 170, 183, 203, 207, 208, 220, 224, 276, 277, 278, 280, 282, 292, 293, 294, 295, 296, 298, 299
Strabo 103
Sumerian 2, 11
Sumner, W.G 93, 149, 166, 316
Supreme Court 67, 70, 163, 270, 277, 278, 280, 282, 284, 285, 286, 287, 288, 298, 299

T

Tangible iv
technic 33, 45, 47, 48, 54, 57, 66, 75, 79, 89, 90, 97, 140, 141, 142, 145, 150, 155, 161, 176, 179, 184, 186, 187, 205, 206, 208, 212, 232, 237, 247, 249, 270
technics ...... vi, viii, 22, 25, 44, 45, 46, 47, 48, 50, 54, 57, 60, 74, 75, 76, 80, 90, 91, 92, 93, 96, 100, 101, 114, 116, 130, 136, 139, 140, 141, 152, 155, 156, 159, 166, 167, 170, 171, 175, 179, 181, 182, 183, 184, 185, 187, 188, 190, 191, 192, 204, 206, 207, 217, 220, 221, 222, 232, 233, 234, 236, 237, 241, 246, 263, 269
territory ... iii, v, vi, 9, 25, 30, 43, 65, 73, 91, 93, 96, 101, 103, 116, 134, 158, 161, 208, 255
Teutonic 59, 91
The Reformation .... *See* Renaissance
Theology 107
Thomas Jefferson 27, 162
Thomas Reid 92
Titian 18, 20
Topinard, Paul 108, 316
Tradition 16, 51, 54, 58, 59, 75, 153, 244
traits .... *See* organic
transvaluation .... ii, 7, 16, 17, 51
tribe .iv, v, vii, 3, 11, 12, 25, 26, 27, 43, 54, 59, 93, 103, 109, 118, 145, 146, 206, 253
Troy .... x, 13, 42

U

Union of Soviets 172
United States . 64, 65, 66, 69, 117, 133, 156, 162, 166, 170, 172, 179, 188, 190, 198, 201, 206, 208, 262, 267, 268, 269, 271, 273, 274, 277, 278, 279, 280, 284, 292, 293, 294, 295, 296, 297, 298, 299, 300, 302, 303, 304, 305, 306, 307, 308, 313
University California Berkley 203

V

Vedas 3
Vereeniging van Oranjewerkers (Union of Orange Workers) 177
Viet Nam War 177
Virgil 103

W

War 139, 205, 232, 256
War Between the States . viii, 149, 171, 177
West vii, viii, x, 1, 2, 3, 6, 9, 10, 12, 13, 15, 16, 18, 20, 21, 22, 23, 24, 26, 29, 30, 31, 32, 36, 37, 38, 40, 43, 44, 47, 49, 50, 51, 52, 54, 56, 58, 59, 60, 61, 62, 65, 66, 67, 72, 75, 76, 78, 79, 81, 83, 85, 87, 88, 90, 92, 96, 97, 99, 100, 101, 102, 104, 105, 107, 111, 113, 114, 115, 116, 117, 122, 124, 125, 126, 128, 129, 130, 131, 134, 135, 137, 138, 139, 140, 141, 142, 146, 147, 148, 149, 151, 154, 155, 156, 157, 158, 161, 162, 163, 164, 165, 166, 167, 170, 174, 177, 178, 179, 180, 186, 187, 188, 195, 197, 200, 201, 202, 204, 205, 206, 209, 211, 214, 215, 216, 217, 218, 219, 220, 221, 222, 223, 224, 225, 226, 227, 228, 230, 231, 232, 233, 234, 236, 238, 240, 242, 243, 244, 245, 248, 249, 250, 262, 263, 265, 266, 271, 275, 288, 302, 310, 311, 313, 315, 316
Western . ii, iii, iv, v, vii, ix, x, 1, 2, 3, 5, 6, 7, 8, 9, 10, 11, 13, 14, 16, 17, 18, 19, 20, 21, 22, 23, 24, 26, 27, 30, 32, 34, 41, 43, 44, 45, 46, 47, 49,

50, 51, 52, 57, 61, 62, 63, 66, 69,
72, 73, 76, 77, 78, 80, 81, 83, 85,
86, 87, 88, 90, 92, 93, 94, 95, 96,
97, 98, 100, 101, 104, 105, 106,
107, 110, 112, 114, 115, 118, 120,
123, 124, 126, 128, 129, 131, 132,
134, 135, 138, 139, 141, 142, 145,
146, 148, 149, 150, 151, 155, 156,
158, 159, 160, 163, 165, 166, 167,
170, 171, 172, 173, 174, 175, 176,
178, 179, 181, 182, 183, 184, 186,
187, 188, 189, 192, 193, 194, 196,
198, 199, 200, 201, 202, 203, 204,
205, 207, 208, 209, 213, 214, 215,
217, 219, 222, 227, 233, 234, 237,
238, 239, 240, 241, 243, 244, 245,
246, 247, 248, 249, 255, 263, 265,
266, 269, 271, 285, 288, 301, 302,
310, 312, 316

Western Civilization ii
Western culture 26, 139, 187, 195
Western man ..... ix, 7, 8, 10, 14, 23, 26,
32, 52, 72, 91, 101, 187, 189, 199,
201, 215, 233
William Galey Simpson 72, 73
will-to-express..iii, v, viii, 9, 13, 22, 23,
24, 30, 38, 39, 43, 50, 88, 100, 186,
187
women ..... ix, 28, 31, 33, 34, 35, 36, 51,
59, 72, 75, 81, 87, 105, 117, 126,
128, 129, 130, 135, 138, 143, 148,
156, 158, 177, 214, 218, 225, 227,
230, 236, 243, 250, 255, 262, 263,
300, 306, 313

Y

Yucca 39, 40
Yucca Moth 39, 40

ABOUT THE AUTHOR

The author of many articles, books, essays, and poems detailing his life-long work to secure the existence of his people, those numerous and diverse individuals belonging to that greater family of Western stock and, without whom, this author would never exist; it is sincerely hoped that this debt will be paid in kind through the works and words of this author, and may be found in numerous forms and venues for consideration.

Other Works

Foundations of The 21st Century

Bruder Schweigen

Song of Albion

Remember Tomorrow

Poems for The Folk

Made in the USA
Middletown, DE
18 July 2018